MW01383362

Ethics and Foreign Policy Series

TABLE OF CONTENTS

INTRODUCTION

Robin W. Lovin

The first question in any discussion of international
ethics is whether ethics is possible in international
relations. In a world divided by superpower confrontations and threatened by terrorist movements and terrorist states, common sense is apt to conclude that
"playing by the rules" is at best a silly pretense and
at worst an acquiescence in the triumph of those who
have long ago cast off any moral restraints. Moral
standards may be important, but if we want to survive
to respect them, we must not be too scrupulous about
observing them in a world arena where they are largely
ignored.

The dominant school of thought among American
foreign policy specialists in this century has shared
the skepticism of the common-sense view. The confident
idealism that marked American thought at the turn of
the century supposed that utopia in foreign and domestic policy was simply a matter of putting well-known
moral and religious principles into practice. After
World War I, this idealism gave way to a realism which
began with the sobering recognition that the moral
ideal is never a "simple historical possibility,"\1 and
developed into the position that where practical matters of foreign policy are concerned, moral principles
need not come into consideration at all. If the question is what we are to do as a nation in the global
arena, attentiveness to the national interest and a
realistic assessment of our own power will tell us all
we need to know.\2

The essays in this volume are written from a
variety of scholarly perspectives, but all the authors
share the common-sense suspicion that moral standards
do not easily translate into principles of foreign
policy. What they reject is the dogmatic realist position that values and moral principles should be excluded from policy discussions, which should then be
conducted solely in terms of what is to be done in "the
national interest."\3 If these authors are aware of the
dangers of moral restraint in a world of unprincipled
action, they also acknowledge, in a way that the thor-

oughgoing realists of an earlier generation did not, the problems of measuring national aims solely in terms of the power required to realize them. They recognize, too, the very real power that recognized moral legitimacy confers on states as they seek their aims in international politics.

There is no precise agreement among these essays about what morality is or how it is to be defined, but there is the broad recognition that however else it may be specified, ethics is an alternative to a decision-making process that frames policies strictly on the basis of national interest conceived in measurable, material terms. Like individual ethics, international ethics judges what we would like to do and what we have the power to do by restraints based on the legitimate interests of others and on the kinds of persons we conceive ourselves to be or that we hope to become. Each of the authors in this volume has his own ideas about the international ethics appropriate for the nuclear age, but they share the conviction that thinking about such moral considerations is not only possible, it is crucial to sound policy choices.

I
Ethics and Interests in Foreign Policy

The essays by Arthur Schlesinger, Jr., Joseph Nye, Jr., and Brian Barry focus on the problems of moving from individual morals to international ethics. Among them, only Nye attempts an extended answer to the moral skeptic, who doubts that ethical arguments are meaningful in any context. Their concern is with the specific problems posed by the dogmatic realist, who acknowledges the importance of moral thinking in personal choices and in relations between individuals within a society, but who doubts that these moral values, concepts, and principles have any meaning when they are applied to relationships that cut across societies, and especially to relationships between states.

Arthur Schlesinger does not reject the realist's probing questions, but he finds the traditional realist answer dangerously shortsighted. He suggests that instead of substituting national interest for moral absolutes, we must recognize that moral principles are a part of our national interest. Part of the reason why we make willing sacrifices to the wider community is

2

because we believe it embodies those values, and we demand a measure of consideration for them from our leaders, even when it seems unlikely that these concerns will be reciprocated by others in the international arena.

Joseph Nye undertakes a similar demonstration of the importance of our society's shared moral norms to international relations. Public officials in a democracy are not centers of arbitrary power. They are trustees of the values and interests of the whole society, and they owe some moral restraint in the conduct of foreign affairs as an obligation to their fellow citizens. Beyond that, moreover, there are values and obligations within our national ethic that do not neatly stop at national boundaries. Accepting responsibility for the consequences of our actions and offering "readily available assistance to another who is in dire need,"\4 for example, are principles that seem to define a minimal obligation to foreigners implicit in our own national morality and incumbent upon those who this society entrusts with pursuit of the national interest.

Brian Barry develops a somewhat different approach to the problem of international ethics, asking not whether recognized values in American society can be meaningfully applied to international relations, but whether the patterns of interdependence and cooperation which are specific to relations between states create in themselves the basis for a minimal international ethic. Conventional political wisdom since Hobbes has held that in the absence of a sovereign to enforce compliance, moral expectations cannot be controlling in international politics.\5 Barry rejects this idea, not on the basis of moral standards that have a transnational application, but by appeal to a logic of cooperative action that is inherent in the prevailing relationships between states and that also provides the basis for the constraints that common-sense morality imposes on action, even when the compliance of others is not assured or cannot be enforced.

The authors of these first three essays thus agree that a transition can be made from the requirements of morality as these are ordinarily understood to moral constraints that apply in international relations. Barry, Nye, and Schlesinger share no common moral theory, and they differ on exactly how moral considerations should be balanced with the requirements of national interest, political prudence, and international order in the formulation of specific policy decisions. Never-

3

theless, their basic agreement on the possibility of moral considerations that apply to international relations is significant, and it marks for all of them an important departure from the realist treatments of ethics that have dominated many policy discussions since World War II.

For Schlesinger, Nye, and Barry, a discussion of foreign policy choices that excludes attention to values and moral principles is incomplete. It inevitably results in an inadequate account of the reasons for or against a particular policy choice, and it may lead to a dangerous overestimate of what can be accomplished by the simple exercise of power in pursuit of limited national interests. This initial consensus between historian, political scientist, and political philosopher that the dogmatic realist approach to international ethics needs rethinking is an important point to keep in mind as we approach the complexities of the policy choices which are analyzed in the subsequent essays in the collection.

II
Moral and Strategic Problems of Nuclear Weapons

Questions about the application of ethics to relations between states are sharpened by a thinking about diplomacy and strategy in the nuclear age. On the one hand, as religious leaders, scientists, and moralists repeatedly point out, the predictable social and ecological consequences of a massive nuclear exchange impose an especially stringent obligation on military and political leaders to see that that exchange does not occur and perhaps renders preparations for the use of nuclear weapons immoral in itself.\6 On the other hand, the national interest in security, in conditions under which an enemy's nuclear weapons should threaten national survival, seems to render all other considerations, including moral considerations, secondary.

What links the essays in this section to the broader theoretical discussions by Schlesinger, Nye, and Barry is the idea that moral considerations at least belong in the policy discussion. Robert Jervis, Earl Ravenal, Sidney Drell, and Henry Rowen do not always agree on how these moral considerations are to be framed or what they imply for policy, and the commentators, Ernst Haas and Dennis Ross, add new perspec-

4

tives to the already-rich mix of moral theory, policy, and political analysis. All agree, however, that the problems of nuclear weapons raise moral questions that cannot be resolved by attention to issues of strategy alone.

Robert Jervis reminds us, however, that if we expect moral questions to be taken seriously as independent issues in policy discussions, we must face the possibility that moral and strategic judgments will not always neatly coincide. Too often parties in the nuclear debate begin with a moral conviction and then insist that it also makes good strategic sense, or start with a strategy and then go in search of moral arguments to back it up. Bishops, of course, tend to argue in one direction, while generals argue in the other, but the coincidences of morality and strategy that result seem a little forced.

Jervis's conclusion is that we must view moral principles that forbid harm to the innocent or require us not to inflict disproportionate damage on an enemy as restraints or limits on strategic choices, not as moral absolutes that dictate policy conclusions by themselves. Ernst Haas regards this position as a kind of limit-case formulation of realism, far more receptive to moral concerns than the dogmatic exclusion of values, but far less than the evolutionary development of an international moral consensus that Haas himself thinks is possible.

The remaining essays in this section largely share Jervis's method of treating moral principles as restraints, as reference points that set the outer limits of acceptable policy, rather than as absolutes that require specific policy choices. Earl Ravenal calls morality "a limiting rather than an enabling principle,"\7 and contrasts it to "moralism," which seeks immediately to define a moral good and enforce it on the world situation. Sidney Drell says little about morality directly, but he speaks as a scientist to caution against a purely scientific or technical approach to strategic choices. His affirmation of diplomacy and political process surely includes the sort of moral discussions that Jervis and others contemplate.

Henry Rowen, similarly, deplores the "inward-looking and moralistic character"\8 of much public debate about arms limitation, and he proposes an approach to nuclear strategy that moves away from the current MAD (mutually assured destruction) deterrent.

Rowen acknowledges the moral objections to MAD, but his
solution is shaped by strategic and technical considerations. Commentator Dennis Ross observes that Rowen's
dissatisfaction with what diplomacy has achieved in
arms control may lead him to neglect the political
expectations that the arms control process has created
-- expectations which are important, even though they
may be tinged with an unrealistic "moralism."

Among these authors, then, Henry Rowen comes closest to the dogmatic realist position that dismisses
moral issues from the discussion or suggests that they
can be covered by strategic and technical considerations. Jervis goes the farthest toward establishing
moral issues as distinct and unavoidable questions.
Taken together, the essays present a spectrum of positions within a revised realism, positions that reflect
more agreement on the method of analysis than on the
resulting policy.

Ravenal, for example, favors massive "countervalue" nuclear targeting to deter a nuclear attack on
the United States and an end to attempts to provide a
limited nuclear defense of our European allies. Rowen
favors the development of more limited "counterforce"
weapons that would pose a credible threat of nuclear
response to any serious Soviet expansion. Each author
would argue that his proposal is morally superior to
the present extended MAD deterrent, but neither would
regard the moral case alone as a decisive argument for
the policy. A moral principle is a restraint, a consideration that comes into play when setting limits rather
than when establishing positive goals. In the present
situation of global conflict, morality cannot by itself
determine what our policy ought to be.

III
Ethical Perspectives on Policy Choices

The study of ethics in relation to specific policy
problems continues in the essays by Dwight Perkins and
Aristide Zolberg. Dwight Perkins suggests that a full
understanding of the variations between countries in
patterns of economic development may require a closer
examination of traditional value systems. The striking
economic successes of Japan, China, and Korea depend on
many historical and political factors that distinguish
East Asia from other developing regions, but Perkins

suggests that traditional values concerning work, trade, organization, and order may help us understand differences between East Asia and South Asia or East Asia and Africa that cannot be fully explained by more obvious economic factors. Perkins's essay calls to mind Max Weber's classic studies of the economic attitudes of the world religions.\9 But what Perkins wants are more specific studies of particular countries at particular times, studies that would draw on the field skills of the anthropologist, as well as the expertise of the historian and the economist.

Aristide Zolberg's study of immigration shows the greater importance that moral issues may have when we shift from problems of nuclear strategy and national survival to policy problems in which the range of possible goals is wider. To be sure, the national interest dictates that we must not adopt an immigration policy so broad or uncontrolled as to destroy the nation and its policy. While some might argue that this concern for national survival is the only goal we need to set defense policy, Zolberg points out that the survival requirement is so minimal as to tell us almost nothing about appropriate immigration policies. He goes on to develop an argument from the basic values of a liberal society to an immigration policy that would be far more open to refugees from political violence and economic exploitation than our present policies are.

The exploration of specific values that shape life in Asian societies or in liberal democracies leads us back, in the two final essays, to more general reflections on values and their role in historical social transformations. As if to answer Perkins's request for specific anthropological studies, Marshall Sahlins develops a detailed study of the rise of Thakombau, a nineteenth-century warrior king in the Fiji Islands, and his violent subjugation of surrounding peoples and kingdoms. "One is tempted to suggest," Sahlins remarks apropos of this Fijian example, "that the state originates in the projects of terrific kings, rather than as commonly thought, the other way round."\10 Nevertheless, terrific kings do not draw their ideas of terror out of the air. Sahlins locates an important source for Thakombau's triumph in a Fijian myth system that identifies divine power not with the everyday order of social life, but with a force of nature that opposes and masters culture.

Barry Karl's concluding essay on nationalism and international order recapitulates, in a study of Ameri-

7

can history, a theme that runs through many of these studies: the very way we see the facts of our national history is laden with the values that define our aims as a nation and our role as citizens in it. Karl brings us back to the point that marked Arthur Schlesinger's initial essay, that our values are a part of the national interest. Karl wants, however, to see this truth in a complex, dialectical context. It is not only true that we must in some way acknowledge our values and attempt to live up to them in order to secure the national interest; we must also see the ways in which the values are a product of the national interest, shifting and changing as those interests have changed. American historians may be uncomfortable with this link between their professional tasks and the formation of public opinion about contemporary public choices, but the connections between history, value, and policy make that formative power of historical scholarship an unavoidable responsibility.

IV
A Revisionist Realism

The authors of the essays and comments in this volume speak from a variety of academic disciplines. They do not share a common political perspective, nor do they agree on a single moral theory, or even a single, unambiguous definition of what will count as a value or a moral principle. Nevertheless, their works agree in suggesting important revisions in the habit of "realistic" thinking about international relations that has largely excluded ethics from deliberations about foreign policy. Where earlier realists saw dangers of a self-righteous moralism that would embark on interventionist crusades and ignore the limits of genuine national interest, these writers see a danger that follows when leaders ignore the limits that moral opinion, both at home and abroad, imposes on power and the pursuit of interest. Dogmatic realism, or "pseudo-realism," as Robert Jervis prefers to call it, shares in the problems of any other ideology that limits the ability of its adherents to respond to their own situation. "The egoism of pseudo-realism blinds statesmen to the complexities and uncertainties of international politics. It leads them to consider others as instruments, if not puppets, and to overestimate their own ability to control events.\11

8

At the same time, it is important to see that these authors, who largely reject the realist label for themselves, employ a distinctly realist form of argument to correct the excesses of earlier expressions of realism. If the first generation of foreign policy realists were particularly taken with Reinhold Neibuhr's dictum that a moral ideal is not "a simple historical possibility," this revisionist realism gives more attention to the ways in which moral ideals remain, nonetheless, indispensable reference points in the discussions in which policies are actually formulated. Another Niebuhr dictum, that the pursuit of goals without reference to these ideal possibilities degenerated into "a mere calculation of mutual advantages,"\12 suits today's realism as a necessary corrective to its own tendency to moral skepticism.

It is clear that if this revisionist realism were adopted, the discussions in which foreign policy is made would move in different terms than they do now. Repeatedly, these authors, who often have practical experience in policymaking along with their academic credentials, report that in today's climate, explicit reference to moral principles or values in policy discussions would have no effect on the choices, and might well cast doubt on the speaker's ability to face the harsh realities of international diplomacy. The authors do not always agree on how the outcomes would be different if the participants made their moral commitments explicit, but they are clear that a discussion in which this could happen would be very different from those in which they have participated.

The point, of course, is not to encourage opinionated moralizing in the State Department, but to encourage studies that will make the inevitable influence of religious traditions, moral principles, and national character more explicit and intelligent elements in the policymaking process. Arthur Schlesinger and Aristide Zolberg, especially, stress the importance of understanding our own liberal, democratic values in formulating policy, while Dwight Perkins and Marshall Sahlins suggest the need for studies which would improve our understanding of the relationship between values, politics, and social change in a variety of cultural contexts. Brian Barry calls attention to the imperatives of cooperation which are part of the structure of international relations and which help to insure compliance, even when coercion is not possible.

What would still connect such new policy discus-

sions and the relevant background studies to the realist tradition which our authors want to revise is that
the moral principles which would be considered more
explicitly would nonetheless remain one factor among
others in the formulation of policy. For many philosophers, it is characteristic of moral claims that they
override other kinds of claims. Moral principles have
an autonomy and superiority that render them independent of interests and preferences and require that
morality be observed whenever morality and interest
come into conflict.\13 None of the authors of these
essays would propose such a role for ethics in international relations, and several of them explicitly warn
against it. Moral principles provide restraints on
interest-based conduct; moral ideals suggest new patterns of international cooperation which may evolve.
But a policy based on moral considerations alone is apt
to produce a moralistic crusade quite out of keeping
with the requirements of a prudent pursuit of the
national interest and a judicious assessment of the national resources.

Some rigorists would say that what we have in
these essays is not ethics at all, but merely another
way of evading moral requirements, this time instead of
by refusing to admit them at all, by considering them
and then subordinating them to other considerations.
For our authors, however, the point is not that there
is something about moral principles in particular that
renders them unfit for policy formation, but that no
single consideration or set of rules is adequate to the
complexities of international relations. The revisionist realists of this volume share with the dogmatic
realists of an earlier generation the idea that policy
decisions are pragmatic attempts to find a workable
combination for the present of factors that, taken
singly, might lead policymakers in quite different
directions. Realists in international affairs have
always stressed that all factors that may influence
outcomes in significant ways must be explicitly considered in policy formation. For an earlier generation of
realists, this meant a disciplined exclusion of moral
ideas that dictated in advance goals of limited action.
What revisionist realists insist, without abandoning
the pragmatic approach to policy, is that moral beliefs
and values are among those factors that must be considered if the policy that results is to be acceptable to
a democratic public, to world opinion, and finally, to
the policymakers themselves.

That may seem a slight revision, but its ramifica-

10

tions across the range of issues in foreign policy would be widespread. It would imply, in all discussions, a more careful attention to the values that motivate actions, rather than to the reductionist interpretation of all action as a response to an opposing force. It would lead to more careful studies of religious and political traditions alongside the studies of economics and military strategy as background for policy choices. Policymakers trained to think in these terms would be less likely to underestimate the political power of nationalism or to be surprised by the rise of fundamentalist Islam, or, for that matter, the growing international activity of American Protestant evangelicals. They would be more attentive to the forms of cooperation which sustain such international order as we now have and more alert to changes and convergences in value systems which would open the way for agreements that once seemed improbable or impossible. In all of these ways, foreign policy informed by the ideas developed in these essays would be more "realistic" than many of the policies we have had, even if the realism results from putting behind us the more dogmatic forms of realism that once obscured the place of ethics in international relations.

Notes

1. Reinhold Niebuhr, _Faith and Politics_, Ronald Stone, ed. (New York: George Braziller, 1968), pp. 33-45.

2. For a recent formulation of this position, see George Kennan, "Morality and Foreign Policy," _Foreign Affairs_ 64, Winter 1985/86, pp. 205-18.

3. Cf. Hans J. Morgenthau, _In Defense of the National Interest: A Critical Evaluation of American Foreign Policy_ (New York: Alfred A. Knopf, 1954).

4. Chap. 2, p. 67.

5. Thomas Hobbes, _Leviathan_, C.B. Macpherson, ed. (Harmondsworth: Penguin Books, 1968), pp. 187-88.

6. See, for example, The National Conference of Catholic Bishops, _The Challenge of Peace: God's Promise and Our Response_ (Washington, D.C.: United States Catholic Conference, 1983); and The United Methodist

Council of Bishops, <u>In Defense of Creation: The Nuclear Crisis and a Just Peace</u> (Nashville: Graded Press, 1986).

7. Chap. 5, p. 178.

8. Chap. 7, p. 211.

9. Max Weber, <u>The Protestant Ethic and the Spirit of Capitalism</u> (New York: Scribner's, 1958); and his <u>The Sociology of Religion</u> (Boston: Beacon Press, 1963), pp. 262-74.

10. Chap. 10, p. 322.

11. Chap. 4, p. 132.

12. Reinhold Niebuhr, <u>Faith and History</u> (New York: Scribner's, 1949), p. 185.

13. For a discussion of the autonomy and superiority of Moral "action-guides," see <u>David Little</u>, and Sumner B. Twiss, <u>Comparative Religious Ethics: A New Method</u> (San Francisco: Harper and Row, 1978), pp. 28-32.

PART I:

ETHICS AND INTERESTS

IN FOREIGN POLICY

Chapter 1

NATIONAL INTERESTS AND MORAL ABSOLUTES\1

Arthur M. Schlesinger, Jr.

For centuries theologians have distinguished between just and unjust wars, jurists have propounded rules for international conduct, and moralists have pondered whether a state's course in foreign affairs was right or wrong. Yet the problem of the relationship between ethics and international politics remains perennially unsettled. It has been a particularly vexing problem in the United States, at least since the Mexican and Spanish-American wars and more than ever during the Vietnam War; for an Anglo-Saxon ancestry and a Calvinist heritage have endowed Americans with a mighty need for seeing their exercise of power as morally virtuous.

In recent years, Americans have debated with renewed urgency the ethics of power and the dilemmas that confront moral man in an immoral world. Above all, in this nuclear age, we are compelled to wonder, as Robert Kennedy did after the missile crisis of 1962, "What, if any, circumstances or justification gives...any government the moral right to bring its people and possibly all people under the shadow of nuclear destruction?"\2 Historians cannot hope to resolve questions that have stumped philosophers through the ages. Still, some historical notes on this hopelessly amorphous subject may have their uses.

I

William James said that temperaments determine philosophies. People who respond to international affairs divide temperamentally into two schools: those who first ask of a policy, "Is it morally right?" and those who first ask, "Will it work?"; those who see policies as good or evil, and those who see them as wise or foolish. One cannot presume an ultimate metaphysical antagonism between the moralist and the realist. No realist can wholly escape perceptions of good and evil, and no policy can wholly divorce ethical from geopolitical considerations. Nor in the impenetrability of human motives can we easily know when moral reasons are realistic concerns in disguise (more frequent than one might think; Israel is an obvious example). Still the very choice of disguise reveals something about temperaments -- and about philosophies.

Let us begin with those who hold that moral values should control foreign policy. This was not the view of the Founding Fathers, who saw international affairs as a function of the balance of power. But in the century after 1815, as Americans turned their backs on the power struggles of Europe, they stopped thinking about power as the essence of international politics. The moralization of foreign policy became a national penchant, nor did the subsequent return of the republic to the world power game much enfeeble that cherished habit. Woodrow Wilson's mission was precisely to move the world beyond power politics. In our own day moralists on both right and left, while quarreling about everything else, concur in thinking that moral principles should dominate foreign policy. The key question, as Ronald Reagan said in his first 1984 debate and as many of his radical critics would agree, is: "Is it morally right? And on that basis, and that basis alone, we make a decision on every issue."\3

Yet many foreign policy decisions remain questions of prudence and adjustment, not of good and evil. Even moralizers would probably go along with their searching critic George Kennan in doubting that "it matters greatly to God whether the free trade area or the Common Market prevails in Europe, whether the British fish or do not fish in Icelandic territorial waters, or even whether Indians or Pakistanis run Kashmir. It might matter, but it is hard for us, with our limited vision, to know."\4 The raw material of foreign affairs is, a good deal of time, morally neutral or ambiguous. In consequence, for the great majority of foreign policy transactions, moral principles cannot be decisive.

But these, it may be said, are technical transactions. On the great issues, surely moral principles should be controlling. Yet how are right and wrong to be defined in dealings among sovereign states? Here the moralist of foreign affairs has recourse to the moral code most familiar to him -- the code that governs dealings among individuals. His contention is that states should be judged by principles of individual

16

morality. As Wilson put it in his address to Congress on the declaration of war in 1917, "We are at the beginning of an age in which it will be insisted that the same standards of conduct and of responsibility for wrong done shall be observed among nations and their governments that are observed among the individual citizens of civilized states."\5 John Foster Dulles said it even more directly during the Second World War: "The broad principles that should govern our international conduct are not obscure. They grow out of the practice by the nations of the simple things Christ taught."\6

The argument for the application of simple Christlike principles to questions of foreign policy is thus that there is, or should be, an identity between the morality of individuals and the morality of states. The issues involved here are not easy. One cannot doubt, as I shall contend later, that there are cases in foreign affairs where moral judgment is not only possible but necessary. One may also suggest that these are extreme cases and do not warrant the routine use of moral criteria in making foreign policy judgments.

"The rule of morality," Alexander Hamilton pointed out in the early years of the American republic, "...is not precisely the same between nations as between individuals. The duty of making its own welfare the guide of its actions, is much stronger upon the former than upon the latter. Existing millions, and for the most part future generations, are concerned in the present measures of a government; while the consequences of the private action of an individual ordinarily terminate with himself, or are circumscribed with a narrow compass."\7

Reinhold Niebuhr renewed the argument against the confusion of moral categories half a century ago in Moral Man and Immoral Society. The obligation of the individual, Niebuhr wrote, is to obey the law of love and sacrifice; "from the viewpoint of the author of an action, unselfishness must remain the criterion of the highest morality." But states cannot be sacrificial. Governments are not individuals. They are not principals but agents. They are trustees for the happiness and interest of others. Niebuhr quoted Hugh Cecil's argument that unselfishness "is inappropriate to the action of a state. No one has a right to be unselfish with other people's interests."\8

In short the individual's duty of self-sacrifice

17

and the state's duty of self-preservation are in conflict. This makes it impossible to measure the action
of states by a purely individualistic morality. "The
Sermon on the Mount," said Winston Churchill, "is the
last word in Christian ethics....Still, it is not on
those terms that Ministers assume their responsibilities of guiding states."\9

This is not to say that might makes right. It is
to say that the morality of states is inherently different from the morality of individuals. Max Weber
noted the contrast between the "ethic of ultimate ends
-- that is, in religious terms, 'The Christian does
rightly and leaves the results with the Lord'" and the
"ethic of responsibility," which takes into account the
foreseeable results of one's action.\10 Saints can be
pure, but statesmen must be responsible. As trustees
for others, they must defend interests and compromise
principles. In consequence, politics is a field where
practical and prudential judgment must have priority
over simple moral verdicts.

II

Now it may be urged against this view that the tension
between individual morality and political necessity has
been, to a considerable degree, bridged within national
societies. This takes place when the moral sense of a
community finds embodiment in positive law. But the
shift of the argument from morality to law only
strengthens the case against the facile intrusion of
moral judgment into foreign affairs.

A nation's legal code can set down relatively
clear standards of right and wrong in individual behavior because statutory law is the product of an imperfect but nonetheless authentic moral consensus. International life has no such broad or deep areas of moral
consensus. It was once hoped that modern technology
would create a common fund of moral imperatives transcending the concerns of particular nations -- common
concepts of interest, justice, and comity -- either
because the revolution in communications would increase
mutual understanding or because the revolution in weaponry would increase mutual fear. Such expectations have
been disappointed. Until nations come to such a common
morality, there can be no world law to regulate the
behavior of states as there is law within nations to

regulate the behavior of individuals. Nor can international institutions -- the League of Nations or the
United Nations -- produce by sleight of hand a moral
consensus where none exists. World law must express
world community; it cannot create it.

This is not to ignore the growth of an international consensus. Humanity has begun to develop standards for conduct among nations -- defined, for example, in the Hague Conventions of 1899 and 1907, in the
Geneva Protocol of 1925 and the Geneva Conventions of
1949, in the Charter and Covenants of the United Nations, in the Charter, Judgment, and Principles of the
Nuremburg Tribunal, and so on. Such standards outlaw
actions that the civilized world has placed beyond the
limits of permissible behavior. Within this restricted
area a code emerges that makes moral judgment in international affairs possible up to a point. And within its
scope this rudimentary code deserves, and must have,
the most unflinching enforcement.

But these international rules deal with the limits
rather than with the substance of policy. They seek to
prevent abnormalities and excesses in the behavior of
states, but they do not offer grounds for moral judgment on normal international transactions (including,
it must be sorrowfully said, war itself, so long as war
does not constitute aggression and so long as the
rules of warfare are faithfully observed). These international accords may eventually lead to a planetary
consensus. But, for the present, national, ideological,
ethical, and religious divisions remain as bitterly
intractable as ever.

To summarize the argument to this point, I am
constrained to doubt the easy relevance of personal
moral criteria to most decisions in foreign policy,
first, because few issues in foreign affairs lend themselves to categorical moral verdicts; second, because
governments in their nature must make decisions on
different principles from those of personal morality;
and third, because no international moral consensus
exists in sufficient depth and strength to sustain a
comprehensive and binding international morality.

III

The problem is not only that simplistic moral princi-

19

ples are of limited use in the making of foreign policy
decisions. It is that moralistic foreign policy may
well add troubles of its own creation.

For many Americans, morality in foreign policy
consists in the application to the world of a body of
general precepts, a process accompanied by lectures to
others and congratulations to ourselves. The assumption is that we are the anointed custodians of international behavior, and that the function of United States
policy is to mark others states up and down according
to their obedience to the rules as we see them. Laying
down the moral law to sinning brethren from our seat of
judgment no doubt pleases our own sense of rectitude.
But it fosters dangerous misconceptions about the nature of foreign policy.

Moralizers prefer symbolic to serious politics.
They tend to see foreign policy as a means of register-
ing ideological attitudes, not of producing hard results in a hard world. Moralistic rhetoric, moreover,
often masks the pursuit of national advantage -- a
situation we Americans recognize at once when foreign
states pursue their selfish objectives under a cloak of
moral universalism. Should we be surprised that foreigners are just as cynical about American claims to
moral disinterestedness? In practice, moralistic declarations serve less as a restraint on self-serving action than as a pretext, generally transparent, for such
action. The one law that rules all others, said Henry
Adams, is that "masses of men invariably follow interests in deciding morals."\11

The moralization of foreign policy creates still
graver problems. Indeed, moral reasons cynically exploited may do the world less harm than moral reasons
fervently believed. The compulsion to convert conflicts
of interest into conflicts of good and evil undermines
diplomacy. For diplomacy is above all the adjustment of
conflicting interests. Moralization shifts international relations from the political mode, which is
conditional, to the ideological mode, which is unconditional. And moralization often ends by combining the
most lofty intentions with the most ghastly consequences. "I do not like to hit a village," an American
pilot in Vietnam told a newspaperman. "You know you
are hitting women and children. But you've got to
decide that your cause is noble and that the work has
to be done."\12 The more passionately people decide
the cause is noble, the more likely they are to reject
accommodation and seek the final victory of their prin-

20

ciples. Little has been more pernicious in international politics than excessive righteousness.

The moralizing fever may, as noted, strike at any
point along the political spectrum. From one standpoint, there is little difference between moralists on
the right who see the Soviet Union as the focus of all
evil and moralists on the left who ascribe all sin to
the United States. They are equal victims of the same
malady. Both regard foreign policy as a branch of
theology. Both rush to judgment on erring humanity.
They end as mirror images of each other. "Moral indig-
nation," the Christian historian Sir Herbert Butterfield observed, "corrupts the agent who possesses it
and is not calculated to reform the man who is the
object of it."

Butterfield added: "The passing of what purports
to be a moral judgment -- particularly a judgment which
amounts to the assertion that they are worse men than I
am -- is...really a demand for an illegitimate form of
power. The attachment to it is based on its efficacy as
a tactical weapon, its ability to rouse irrational
fervour and extraordinary malevolence against some
enemy."\13 "The English are indeed a great and noble
people," said Gladstone, a Christian statesman if there
ever was one; "but it adds nothing to their greatness
or their nobleness that...we should trumpet forth our
virtues in elaborate panegyrics and designate those who
may not be wholly of our mind as a knot of foreign
conspirators."\14

In the conduct of foreign policy, moral absolutism
leads on to crusades and the extermination of the
infidel. Failure is blamed not on intractable obstacles or on mistaken judgment but on traitors (or war
criminals) in high places. We hear much about the
great need of the modern world for religious faith.
But religion, far from serving as a check on international ferocity, is in the 1980s the prime cause of
most of the killing taking place in the world: in the
Middle East, in the Persian Gulf, in Ireland, in India,
in Cyprus, in the Philippines, in Sri Lanka, throughout
Africa -- not to mention the havoc wrought by the
totalitarian religions of the twentieth century. A
fanatic, Mr. Dooley reminds us, "does what he thinks
th' Lord wud do if He only knew th' facts in th'
case."\15

21

If moral principles have only limited application in foreign affairs, and if moral absolutism breeds fanaticism, must we abandon the effort to bring about restraint in international relations? Is the world therefore condemned to jungle anarchy? Not necessarily; the argument moves rather to the conclusion that foreign policy decisions must generally be taken on other than moralistic grounds. It is necessary now to consider what these other grounds are.

Those "who act upon the Principles of disinterestedness," wrote George Washington during the American Revolution, "are, comparatively speaking, no more than a drop in the Ocean." Washington acknowledged the power of patriotism. "But I will venture to assert that a great and lasting War can never be supported on this principle alone. It must be aided by a prospect of Interest....We must take the passions of Men as Nature has given them."\16 What was true for men, Washington believed, was even more true for nations: no nation was to be trusted farther than it is bound by its interest. In short, where the embryonic international community cannot regulate dealings among nations, the safer basis for decision in foreign policy lies not in attempts to determine right or wrong but in attempts to determine the national interest.

The idea of national interest faded from the national consciousness after the United States receded from the European power equation. When America made its return in 1917, Wilson, the international moralist par excellence, rejected national interest as an explanation for American entry into the First World War. Thirty years later, when the Cold War undermined the Wilsonian dream of a world beyond power politics, the revival of the national-interest perspective came almost as revelation. National interest seemed for a season the key to the foreign policy riddle. Its apostles styled themselves realists. They took the passions of nations as history had given them. They saw international politics as a struggle for power. They rejected cant and sentimentality. And George Washington had plainly been right in saying that every nation _must_ respond to some conception of its interest. No nation that abandons self-preservation as the mainspring of its policy can survive; nor, indeed, can any nation be relied upon in international dealings that acts against its national interest. Without the magnetic compass of national interest there would be no order or predictability in international affairs.

Moreover, every nation has a set of fairly definite strategic interests. One has only to recall the continuities of Russian foreign policy, whether directed by czars or by commissars. When one moves on to politics, economics, and culture, identification of national interest becomes more debatable. Still, even here nations often retain, through changes of government and ideology, an impressive amount of continuity: consider France from de Gaulle to Mitterrand.

National interest is obviously not a figment of the imagination. But, as critics began in time to point out, neither is it a self-executing formula. In practice, we quarrel endlessly over what national interest prescribes in particular situations. Hans Morgenthau, the great theoretician of national interest, argued that German leaders had twice in one generation betrayed Germany's national interest; but that is hardly what the Kaiser and Hitler thought they were doing. In the United States in the 1960s, the prominent realists -- Morgenthau, Kennan, Niebuhr, Walter Lippmann -- condemned American participation in the Vietnam War as unwarranted by national interest. But Lyndon Johnson decided to Americanize the war because, he explained, "we felt our national interest required it."\17 History, it is true, has vindicated the realists; but who could _prove_ at the time where the national interest truly lay? When indeed have statesmen ever believed that they were acting against the national interest of their countries? Not only government departments but corporations, trade unions, lobbies domestic and foreign, always present their parochial concerns as the national interest. The idea of national interest, critics concluded, is dangerously elastic. Far from providing clear answers to every international perplexity, national interest turns out to be subjective, ambiguous, and susceptible to great abuse.

Moralizers have still deeper objections. They consider national interest a wicked idea on which to found national policy. It nourishes, they say, a nation's baser self. It becomes a license for international aggrandizement. The pursuit of exclusively national goals leads ineluctably to aggression, imperialism, war. As many follies have been committed in the name of national interest as in the name of national righteousness. National interest, in short, is a mandate for international amorality.

23

In practice, this is often so. In principle, however, national interest prescribes its own morality.
After all, the order and predictability valued by
George Washington in international affairs constitute
the precondition for international moral standards.
More important, national interest, consistently construed, is a self-limiting motive. Any rigorous defend-
er of the idea must accept that other nations have
their legitimate interests too. The recognition of
equal claims sets bounds on aggression. Unless transformed by an injection of moral righteousness, the idea
of national interest cannot produce ideological crusades for unlimited objectives.

This self-limiting factor does not rest only on
recognition of other nations' interests. It is reinforced by self-correcting tendencies in the power equilibrium -- tendencies that prevent national interest,
at least when the disparity of power is not too great,
from billowing up into unbridled national egoism. For
national interest is linked with the idea of an international balance of power. History has shown how often
the overweening behavior of an aggressive state leads
to counteraction on the part of other states determined
to restore a balance of power. National egomania turns
out to be contrary to long-term national interest.
States that throw their weight around are generally
forced to revise their notions as to where their national interest truly lies. This has happened in this
century to Germany and Japan. In time it may even
happen to the Soviet Union and the United States.

For these reasons, it may be suggested that national interest, realistically construed, will promote
enlightened rather than aggressive policy. So a realist
like Hamilton said that his aim was not "to recommend a
policy absolutely selfish or interested in nations; but
to show, that a policy regulated by their own interest,
as far as justice and good faith permit, is, and ought
to be, their prevailing one" (emphasis added).\18

                                V

The idea of national interest appears neither altogether subjective nor altogether amoral. But a further
objection arises: may it not be obsolescent, an idea
overtaken by the onward rush of history? Is not the
realist view in fact a romantic extrapolation from the

pattern of interstate relations prevailing in Europe in the eighteenth and nineteenth centuries? Realism's operative ideas -- national interest, the balance of power, _raisons d'etat_, limited objectives, foreign policy conducted by professional elites and protected from the vagrant emotions of domestic politics -- all may have been no more than the functions of a specific historical epoch, an era of absolute monarchies when states agreed on the rules of the game, and citizens made no claim to democratic control of foreign policy. Realism may well be inadequate in a new age character-ized by the democratization of foreign policy, by total war, by absolute weapons, by ideological crusades, by the crashing into the international equilibrium of new states that do not accept the rules of the game and by the rise of transnational forces, from international agencies to multinational corporations to terrorist gangs, all draining power from national states.

Of these changes, the democratization of foreign policy bears most fatefully on the idea of national interest. The classical balance of power was a mechan-ism operated by professional diplomats. In the nine-teenth century, diplomacy was, in G.M. Young's phrase, "what one clerk said to another clerk."\19 "Govern-ments were made to deal with Governments," observed young Henry Adams when he served as a secretary in the American legation in London during the Civil War, "not with private individuals or with the opinions of for-eign society."\20 But when Adams returned to Washing-ton a decade later, he found not one but three State Departments -- the official one, nominally presided over by the Secretary of State (who in this case "seemed to have vanished"); a second on Capitol Hill in the Senate Foreign Relations Committee, which Charles Sumner ruled with a high hand; and a third in the War Department, with President Grant himself for chief.\21 Two decades later, Adams bemoaned the added influence of the foreign lobbies -- the German and Russian lega-tions and the Clan-na-Gael.\22

By the twentieth century the professional monopoly was shattered beyond recall. The era of government as a unified entity in foreign affairs, rationally calculat-ing costs and benefits, came to an end (to the extent that the 'rational-actor' model ever had much reality). Policymakers in a democracy now had to take account of bureaucratic rivals within the executive branch; of skeptics in the legislative branch; of the press; of pressure groups, idealistic and crooked; of national and of foreign opinion. The increase in economic in-

terdependence among nations and the spread of the idea
that government was responsible for the economy multiplied the number of groups claiming the right to define
the national interest in foreign affairs. A new scholarly literature examining 'bureaucratic politics' and
'domestic constraints' grew up to deal with the transformation of diplomacy.

The democratization of foreign policy no doubt
complicates the management of foreign affairs. Professional diplomats echo more poignantly than ever Tocqueville's lament that foreign policy calls for exactly
those qualities in which democracy is most deficient.
"A democracy can only with great difficulty regulate
the details of an important undertaking, persevere in a
fixed design, and work out its execution in spite of
serious obstacles. It cannot combine its measures with
secrecy or await their consequences with patience."\23

Yet democratization was, as Tocqueville well understood, inevitable. Is it really after all such a
calamity? Is it a bad thing that those who will be
ordered to kill and to die should have a voice in
forming the policies that decide their fate? Nor for
that matter does history demonstrate that the professionals are always right and the people always wrong.
The requirement of consent may even make it easier for
governments to sustain policies, to demand sacrifice,
to persevere in a fixed design, and to await consequences with patience.

Nor does the democratization of foreign policy
necessarily mean the rejection of the realist emphasis
on interest and power. Democratization no doubt exposes
the conduct of foreign affairs to those gusts of moralizing demagoguery that turn expedients into crusades.
Still the concept of national interest can provide the
focus and framework within which the debate over the
idea's application takes place. It is the debate itself
that gives the idea its content and, in a democracy,
its legitimacy. And the play of democratic pressures on
foreign policy often strengthens the latent moral content in the idea of national interest. "Let the people
get it into their heads that a policy is selfish and
they will not follow it," A.J.P. Taylor has written.
"...A democratic foreign policy has got to be idealistic; or at the very least it has to be justified in
terms of great general principles."\24

So a realist like Theodore Roosevelt could say,
"It is neither wise nor right for a nation to disregard

26

its own needs, and it is foolish -- and may be wicked -- to think that other nations will disregard theirs. But it is wicked for a nation only to regard its own interest, and foolish to believe that such is the sole motive that actuates any other nation. It should be our steady aim to raise the ethical standard of national action just as we strive to raise the ethical standard of individual action."\25

All human actions are subject to moral judgment. And it may well be that the compulsion of nations to justify their actions by abstract moral principles is an involuntary tribute to the vision of a world public opinion, a potential international consensus, that we must all hope will one day be crystallized in law and institutions. This is what Jefferson had in mind when the Declaration of Independence enjoined "a decent respect to the opinions of mankind."

VI

Despite the perils of absolutism, the moral critique of national policy has its value. Wise statesmen understand the importance of preserving the distinction between what morality prescribes and what circumstances are held to compel -- and thereby preserving the integrity of ideals in a world of distasteful necessity. In 1962 a delegation from the World Council of Churches presented President Kennedy with a resolution calling for the cessation of nuclear tests. Kennedy responded by discussing the problem he faced now that the Soviet Union had resumed testing. Impressed by his analysis, a member of the delegation said, "Mr. President, if you do resume tests, how can we help you?" Kennedy replied, "Perhaps you shouldn't." "This was a very different reaction," the theologian John C. Bennett has commented, "from the common one of seeking more church support the more one feels uneasy about one's decision. Kennedy...did not want the church to be a mere moral echo of the state even though, as a representative of the state, he may have felt shut up to a course of action that gave him moral distress."\26

It is precisely through the idea of national interest that moral principles enter most effectively into the formation of foreign policy. The function of morality is not to supply directives for policy. It is to supply perspectives that clarify and civilize con-

27

ceptions of national interest. Morality primarily resides in the content a nation puts into its idea of national interest.

The moral content of national interest is determined by three things: by national traditions, by political leadership, and by public opinion. The meaning of moral values in foreign policy lies not in what a nation says but in what it does. Morality is basically a matter of keeping faith with a nation's own best ideals. If a course in foreign affairs involves behavior incompatible with the standards of the national community, either the nation will refuse after a time to follow the policy, or else it must foresake its standards. A democracy is in bad trouble when it keeps two sets of books -- when it uses one scale of values for its internal polity and uses another in foreign affairs. The consequent moral schizophrenia is bound to convulse the homeland. This happened to France during the Algerian War. It happened to the United States during the Vietnam War.

Nor was this the first time the moral critique caused Americans to think harder about the meaning of national interest. "The United States will conquer Mexico," Emerson wrote in 1846, "but it will be as the man swallows the arsenic, which brings him down in turn. Mexico will poison us."\27 "My patriotism," William Graham Sumner wrote during the Spanish-American War, "is of the kind which is outraged by the notion that the United States was never a great nation until in a petty three months' campaign it knocked to pieces a poor, decrepit, bankrupt old state like Spain. To hold such an opinion as that is to abandon all American standards...and to go over to the standards of which Spain is a representative." He called his essay "The Conquest of the United States by Spain."\28 Watching the American subjugation of the Philippines, Mark Twain explained sardonically to the person sitting in darkness, "We have been treacherous; but that was only in order that real good might come out of apparent evil. ...We have debauched America's honor and blackened her face before the world; but each detail was for the best." Let us wave the flag, Mark Twain said, but "with the white stripes painted black and the stars replaced by the skull and crossbones."\29

Morality in foreign policy, in short, consists not in preaching one's values to lesser breeds but in living up to them oneself. The moral force of any foreign policy derives from the moral vitality of the national community, and the test of that vitality lies in the character of policies at home. The American leaders who had the greatest impact on the world in the twentieth century -- Wilson, Franklin Roosevelt, Kennedy -- exerted their influence because, in the world's view, their record at home had earned them the right to speak of justice and freedom abroad. Their professions before mankind, the abstractions to which they harnessed American policy, expressed visible realities of their domestic performance. Wilson's New Freedom validated his Fourteen Points, as FDR's New Deal validated his Four Freedoms. So ideals themselves, when verified by performance, become instruments of national power and therefore an essential component of national interest.

Moral language is nevertheless something the prudent statesman uses warily. And the statesman who talks in moral terms had better be sure that national performance does not refute his words. Policy that invokes abroad principles the government ignores in its dealings with its own people is the diplomacy of Pecksniff. Foreign policy has its moral meaning as a projection of what a nation is at home.

VII

There are certain international questions with so clear-cut a moral character that moral judgment must guide political judgment -- slavery, genocide, torture, atrocities, racial justice, human rights. Some of these questions are already defined in international documents. Others define themselves when the consequences of decision transcend the interests of individual nations and threaten the very future of humanity.

The supreme case is nuclear war. This essay began with Robert Kennedy's terrifying question. The question has never been answered. Perhaps it is unanswerable. Unilateral renunciation of nuclear weapons is an escape from the question, raising moral and practical questions fully as awful as those it purports to solve. Deterrence through the matching of nuclear arsenals is a practical answer so long as it preserves the nuclear peace. But it is a perilous answer. When the guardians of the arsenals foster the delusion that nuclear weapons are usable and nuclear wars winnable, deterrence heads straight toward Armageddon. Should 'existential deterrence' break down, we are in a darkness, analytically as well as literally; for no one can foresee the character of nuclear war. Perhaps the vision of Nuclear Winter, falling impartially on aggressor and victim alike, will be the ultimate deterrent.

On lesser issues, two standards serve to mediate the tension between moral and political judgment. The first standard is prudence, the quality implied by Weber's ethic of responsibility. When is a nation justified in using force beyond its frontiers or in providing armed support of or opposition to revolutions in other countries? Plainly such questions cannot be answered by a priori moral principle, only by case-by-case assessment of the consequences of alternative courses. Burke long ago pointed out the difference between the statesman and the moralist: "The latter has only a general view of society; the former, the statesman, has a number of circumstances to combine with those general ideas, and to take into his consideration. Circumstances are infinite, are infinitely combined, are variable and transient....A statesman, never losing sight of principles, is to be guided by circumstances."\30

So Daniel Webster, considering the Greek War of Independence in the 1820s, condemned intervention by the Holy Alliance, which had moved in to crush the rebellion, but did not propose to act against it. The danger to America, Webster explained, was remote, and remoteness, while it could not change principle, could affect policy. Intervention by the Holy Alliance in Greece was one question; intervention in South America would be quite another question. The principle remains the same, but "our duty to ourselves, our policy, and wisdom might indicate very different courses as fit to be pursued by us in the two cases."\31

Prudence implies the old theological principle of proportionality -- the principle that means must have a rational relationship to ends. American intervention in Vietnam lost its last claim to legitimacy when the means employed and the destruction wrought grew out of any rational relationship to the interests threatened and the objectives sought. In fact, the interventionist policy lacked legitimacy from the start. No administration asked in any searching way what danger to national security, what involvement of national interest, could justify the commitment of American troops to what became the longest war in American history, the systemat-

30

ic deception by American leaders of the American people and of themselves, the death of thousands of Americans and of hundreds of thousands of Vietnamese, Laotians, and Cambodians. Prudence vanished in Vietnam before strategic misconceptions and illusions of moral obligation.

VIII

The second standard mediating between moral and political judgment is law. International law, as noted earlier, is patchy and limited. There is no world legislature to enact it, no world court of universal jurisdiction to interpret it, no world police to enforce it. Yet international law is not negligible; and the steady extension of its reach is a necessary condition of lasting peace. For most of their history, Americans regarded the establishment of neutral standards of international behavior -- freedom of the seas or whatever -- as a good thing for the United States. In the old days realists used to deride American statesmen for investing excessive faith in legal formulas.

In recent years American commitment to a world of law has been in decline. One factor sapping the old faith has been the increasing weight placed on the Central Intelligence Agency as an instrument of foreign policy. All powers of course have espionage services. Spies routinely break the law and, when caught, accept the consequences. Rival services may even develop a reciprocal ethic of their own, as intricately imagined by John Le Carre in his tales of MI-6 and the KGB. But, except in wartime, most intelligence services concentrate on the collection and analysis of intelligence. The CIA's great innovation has been to concentrate in peacetime on 'covert action' -- that is, the use of clandestine means to change policies and regimes in other countries. Instead of contenting itself with finding out what is happening, the CIA surpasses other intelligence services in trying to make things happen.\32

Espionage is in a sense 'normal', with an accepted if illegal status in interstate relations. Covert action carries a far more drastic threat to treaty obligations and to interstate comity. But successive American administrations have ignored the implications of CIA covert action for a world of law. The vice

31

chairman of the Senate Select Committee on Intelligence, Senator Daniel Patrick Moynihan of New York, observed in 1983 that, although covert operations are almost in their nature violative of treaty law, "in six and more years of seemingly interminable closed hearings and briefings, I do not ever recall hearing a discussion of legal obligations of any kind."\33

The erosion of American concern about a world of law intensified after 1980. A renascent CIA launched a secret (or not so secret) war against Nicaragua, doing so in defiance of the Neutrality Act of 1794, which makes it a crime to subsidize or prepare an armed expedition against a country at peace with the United States; in defiance too of congressional prohibitions of attempts to overthrow the Nicaraguan regime; in defiance of nonintervention pledges repeatedly made to the Organization of American States ever since the Montevideo conference of 1933, when the United States first subscribed to the declaration that "no state has the right to intervene in the internal or external affairs of another"; in defiance of the United Nations Charter. After Nicaragua appealed to the World Court, the Reagan administration rejected the Court's jurisdiction in Central America for the next two years, doing so in defiance of the 1946 agreement in which the United States pledged six months' notice of any such termination. Subsequently the administration, repudiating the policy of forty years, withdrew from the compulsory jurisdiction of the World Court.

In 1983 Reagan dispatched an expeditionary force against the island of Grenada, an action undertaken without warning, without congressional authorization, and in violation of the charters of the United Nations and the Organization of American States. The pretext -- the rescue of American citizens -- had ample standing under international law; but the real and unconcealed purpose was to destroy an obnoxious regime. The legal fig leaves failed to impress the British Prime Minister or the U.N. General Assembly. The fact that the people of Grenada and of neighboring islands applauded the invasion affected the politics of the action but did not alter the principle.

It is ironic that Americans remember December 7, 1941 as the date that will live in infamy. But Japan, in carrying out its surprise attack on Pearl Harbor, was at least picking on someone of its own size. In October 1962, when the Joint Chiefs of Staff advocated a surprise attack to take out the nuclear missiles in

Cuba, Robert Kennedy successfully opposed the idea as a "Pearl Harbor in reverse." "For 175 years," he told the group advising the President, "we had not been that kind of a nation. A sneak attack was not in our traditions....We were fighting for something more than just survival...all our heritage and our ideals would be repugnant to such a sneak military attack."\34 The popularity of Reagan's sneak attacks on Grenada and Libya showed how far we have progressed since 1962.

Unquestionably there are occasions when nations, their security mortally endangered, are justified in acting beyond the law: salus populi suprema lex est. But such occasions are rare. Grenada was not one of them. To override international law casually, on the basis of ideological obsessions and hypothetical fears, would appear to abandon American standards and to go over to the standards of which the Soviet Union is the representative. "If you are going to pronounce a new law that, wherever communism reigns against the will of the people, even though it has happened internally there, the United States shall enter," said Mrs. Thatcher, "then we are going to have really terrible wars in the world." Most Americans, I judge, dismissed such thoughts as tiresome legal quibbles. A Wall Street Journal editorial approvingly quoted a dinner party remark: "We are only going to be able to talk sensibly about Grenada if anyone here who is an international lawyer agrees to keep his mouth shut." "What is missing from this," Senator Moynihan commented, "is the sense we once had that it is in our interest to advance the cause of law in world affairs."\35

In 1983 Reagan explicitly affirmed "the right of a country when it believes its interests are best served to practice covert activity." In 1985 he added a novel principle: "Support for freedom fighters is self-defense, and totally consistent with the OAS and U.N. Charters." "Freedom fighters" is Reagan's term for guerrillas on our side, and he applied his principle to "every continent, from Afghanistan to Nicaragua."\36 The Soviet Union operates on the same principle, only its preferred term is "wars of national liberation." Each superpower in effect thus proclaims its right to act as a law unto itself in world affairs. But is the United States wise to abandon neutral standards of international behavior? Does our interest lie in imitating the Soviet model, or does it lie in opposing the Soviet model with the idea of a world of law?

To deny that the United States has a fundamental

interest in the operation of law in international affairs is to embark on a course that, in harder cases
than Grenada (i.e., more American casualties), Congress
and public opinion will likely not sustain. "A policy
is bound to fail which deliberately violates our
pledges and our principles, our treaties and our laws,"
Walter Lippmann wrote after the Bay of Pigs. "...The
American conscience is a reality. It will make hesitant
and ineffectual -- even if it does not prevent -- an
un-American policy."\37

IX

Moral values do have a fundamental role in the conduct
of foreign affairs. But, save in extreme cases, that
role is surely not to provide abstract and universal
principles for foreign policy decisions. It is rather
to illuminate and control conceptions of national interest. The righteousness of those who freely apply
their personal moral criteria to the complexities of
international politics degenerates all too easily into
absolutism and fanaticism. The assumption that other
nations have legitimate traditions, interests, values,
and rights of their own is the beginning of a true
morality of states. The quest for values common to all
states and the embodiment of these values in international covenants and institutions is the way to establish a moral basis for international politics.

This will not happen for a long, long time. The
issues sundering our world are too deep for quick
resolution. But national interest, informed by prudence, by law, by scrupulous respect for the equal
interests of other nations, and above all by rigorous
fidelity to one's own national sense of honor and
decency, seems more likely than the trumpeting of moral
absolutes to bring about restraint, justice, and peace
among nations.

Notes

1. This chapter was originally given as a lecture
by Professor Arthur M. Schlesinger, Jr. at Hunter College, New York City, as part of the Carnegie Council's
"Ethics and International Affairs" ongoing lecture

series. It was later revised and incorporated into his book, <u>The</u> <u>Cycles</u> <u>of</u> <u>American</u> <u>History</u>. Copyright 1986 by Arthur M. Schlesinger, Jr. Reprinted by permission of Houghton Mifflin Company.

2. Robert F. Kennedy, <u>Thirteen</u> <u>Days: A</u> <u>Memoir</u> <u>of</u> <u>the</u> <u>Cuban</u> <u>Missile</u> <u>Crisis</u> (New York, 1971 ed.), p. 106.

3. <u>New</u> <u>York</u> <u>Times</u>, October 8, 1984.

4. George Kennan, "Foreign Policy and Christian Conscience," <u>Atlantic</u> <u>Monthly</u>, May 1959. See also Kennan's more recent discussion, "Morality and Foreign Policy," <u>Foreign</u> <u>Affairs</u>, Winter 1985/86.

5. Address to Congress, April 3, 1917.

6. John Foster Dulles, <u>A</u> <u>Righteous</u> <u>Faith</u> <u>for</u> <u>a</u> <u>Just</u> <u>and</u> <u>Durable</u> <u>Peace</u> (New York: Federal Council of Churches, 1942), p. 10.

7. Alexander Hamilton, <u>Pacificus</u>, No. 4, July 10, 1793.

8. Reinhold Niebuhr, <u>Moral</u> <u>Man</u> <u>and</u> <u>Immoral</u> <u>Society</u> (New York, 1932), pp. xi, 258, 267.

9. Winston Churchill, <u>The</u> <u>Gathering</u> <u>Storm</u> (Boston, 1948), p. 320. The Sermon was the "last word" in a sense Churchill may not have intended; for it defined the moral life in the context, not of day-to-day living, but of an imminent Day of Judgment.

10. Max Weber, "Politics as a Vocation" in <u>From</u> <u>Max</u> <u>Weber: Essays</u> <u>in</u> <u>Sociology</u>, H.H. Gerth and C. Wright Mills, eds. (New York, 1958), p. 120.

11. Henry Adams, <u>The</u> <u>Education</u> <u>of</u> <u>Henry</u> <u>Adams</u> (Boston, 1918), chap. xxii.

12. <u>New</u> <u>York</u> <u>Times</u>, July 7, 1965.

13. Herbert Butterfield, <u>History</u> <u>and</u> <u>Human</u> <u>Rela</u><u>tions</u> (London, 1951), pp. 109-10.

14. Quoted in Gordon A. Craig and Alexander L. George, <u>Force</u> <u>and</u> <u>Statecraft</u> (New York, 1983), p. 264.

15. [Finley Peter Dunne], <u>Mr.</u> <u>Dooley's</u> <u>Philosophy</u> (New York, 1900), p. 258.

16. Washington to John Bannister, 21 April 1778, in E.S. Morgan, The Genius of George Washington (New York, 1980), pp. 50-54.

17. Speech of July 27, 1965.

18. Hamilton, Pacificus, No. 4.

19. G.M. Young, Victorian England: Portrait of an Age (Oxford, 1953 ed.), p. 103.

20. Adams, Education, chap. x.

21. Adams, Education, chap. xviii.

22. Adams, Education, chap. xxiv.

23. Alexis de Tocqueville, Democracy in America, I, chap. xiii.

24. A.J.P. Taylor, Europe: Grandeur and Decline (London, Penguin, 1967), p. 357.

25. Theodore Roosevelt, sixth annual message, December 3, 1906.

26. John C. Bennett, "Moral Tensions in International Affairs," in Moral Dimensions in American Foreign Policy, K.W. Thompson, ed. (New Brunswick, N.J., 1984), p. 184.

27. Joel Porte, ed., Emerson in His Journals (Cambridge, Mass., 1982), p. 358.

28. William Graham Sumner, The Conquest of the United States by Spain and Other Essays, Murray Polner, ed. (Chicago, n.d.), p. 173.

29. Mark Twain, "To the Person Sitting in Darkness," North American Review, February 1901.

30. Quoted in Colin Bingham, ed., Men and Affairs (Sidney, 1967), p. 69.

31. Daniel Webster, "The Revolution in Greece," in the House of Representatives, January 19, 1824.

32. On this point, see R.W. Johnson, "Making Things Happen," London Review of Books, September 6-19, 1984, and H.S. Ferns, "This Spy Business," Encounter, May 1985.

33. Daniel Patrick Moynihan, "The Role of Law in World Affairs," _Bulletin of the American Academy of Arts and Sciences_, November 1983.

34. Arthur M. Schlesinger, Jr., _Robert Kennedy and His Times_ (Boston, 1978), pp. 508-09.

35. Daniel Patrick Moynihan, _Loyalties_ (New York, 1984), p. 94.

36. Ronald Reagan, press conference, October 19, 1983; State of the Union address, February 6, 1985.

37. Walter Lippmann, "Today and Tomorrow," _New York Herald Tribune_, May 9, 1961.

Chapter 2

ETHICS AND AMERICAN FOREIGN POLICY

Joseph S. Nye, Jr.\1

Americans are a moralistic people, and their concern about morality carries over into foreign policy. Indeed, many see moralism as one of the characteristic features of American foreign policy.\2 Some applaud this fact, others deplore it. Serious students of international politics often fall in the latter category. George Kennan, for example, saw "the most serious fault of our past policy formulation to lie in something I might call the legalistic-moralistic approach to international problems."\3 The horrors of Hitler's war made a postwar generation of scholars worry about idealism in foreign policy, and the conventional wisdom in the professional study of international relations since 1945 has awarded the "realists" a clear victory over the "idealists."

To some extent, the applause and condemnation in the realist-idealist debates over American foreign policy are beside the point. Given the nature of American political culture, there will always be a demand for moral expression in foreign policy. To ignore it in one period is likely to lay grounds for exaggerating it in the next. By trying to banish moral arguments, professional students of foreign policy abdicate their responsibility to discipline moral arguments to standards of clarity, consistency, and good causal analysis. For example, moral arguments were used by both supporters and opponents of our role in Vietnam and by both defenders and critics of our intervention in Grenada. The appropriate question is not how to avoid, but how to handle morality in foreign policy.

A common problem in moral reasoning about foreign policy is the overly simple or one-dimensional approach. Extolling high principles can be such a form of one-dimensional moral reasoning. For example, Irving Kristol asks,

> What is the moral dimension of American foreign policy? Well it can be summed up in one

39

Not true of course

proposition: the only governments whose moral
legitimacy we recognize are those that are (a)
based on popular consent, and (b) are respectful of the rights of the citizenry to life,
liberty and property.\4

That we should be motivated by our national ideals is
unexceptionable, but moral actions in foreign policy
require equal attention to means and probable consequences.

It is not all that difficult to get broad agreement on the substance of the values that Americans
should express in foreign policy. The United States is
a Lockean democracy committed to government by popular
consent and to individual rights to life, liberty, and
property. The difficult problem is how to bring such
values to bear on foreign policy in a reasonable manner. As Robert Osgood wrote three decades ago, "The
real moral task facing the American people is to fix
their eyes upon ultimate ideals without losing their
footing on the solid ground of reality."\5

This essay will address four key questions surrounding moral reasoning about foreign policy. First,
is foreign policy a fit domain for ethical reasoning?
Part I rejects the arguments of the total skeptics, but
spells out the particular difficulties of moral reasoning in a domain where order and balance of power often
take priority over justice. Second, if foreign policy
is a proper domain for some type of moral reasoning,
how should we judge such moral arguments? Part II
argues for a three-dimensional approach which weighs
motives, means, and consequences rather than the frequently encountered one-dimensional judgments based on
motives or consequences alone. Third, should citizens
and statesmen be held to the same ethical standards in
their foreign policy behavior? Part III argues that
statesmen and citizens should be judged by somewhat but
not totally different standards. Fourth, what is the
international scope of our ethical obligations? What
duties do we owe to foreigners? Part IV argues for a
merger of the realist and cosmopolitan approaches that
admits obligations to foreigners but within realist
constraints of a world currently organized into sovereign nation-states. The central thesis of the essay is
that one cannot avoid moral reasoning about foreign
policy, but that no simple moral theory is adequate.
The nature of the subject requires one to give balanced
consideration to the various kinds of moral claims
discussed here.

I
The Difficult Domain of International Politics

The task of moral reasoning about international politics is not a simple one. The realists deserved to win
the debate with the shallow, moralizing idealism of
the interwar years. There are good reasons why ethical
behavior is more difficult to define and carry out in
international than in domestic politics, and why the
simple use of personal moral maxims in the international domain can have immoral consequences. The structure
of moral language stresses universality and impartiality among individuals -- "do unto others as you would
have them do unto you." But international politics
occurs among individuals organized into states. We
practice our daily moral habits in a sheltered space.
Sovereign states provide enough domestic order to allow
us to follow moral intentions, but many of our normal
moral intuitions are "off balance" in international
politics. A simple-minded transposition of individual
moral maxims to relations among states can lead to
immoral consequences. A statesman who chooses to turn
the other cheek may put his people's lives in peril.
When there are such gaps between our moral intuitions
and the consequences of following them, it is easier to
moralize than to act morally. The Oxford students who
in 1933 vowed never to fight may well have encouraged
Hitler in his belief that Britain would not resist his
aggression.

A second problem arising from the existence of
states is the prospect of ethical egoism. Many moral
philosophers admit the logical possibility of a totally
amoral, egoistic life, but believe it is extremely
difficult for individuals to practice.\6 On the other
hand, amoral behavior may be more feasible for sovereign states. This is a point that Thomas Hobbes recognized three centuries ago when he argued that the
roughly equal insecurity of individuals draws them out
of the state of nature into government, but that once
people are organized into states, they feel safe enough
in their daily lives that they would rather tolerate
the state of nature than submit to the leviathan of a
world government.

Another problem growing out of the existence of
states is the relationship between order and justice.
Both values are important. As Paul Ramsey points out,
"Order is a means to justice, but also justice is a
means of serving order." A well-ordered domestic poli-

41

ty can concentrate its political debate and efforts on improving justice. But if efforts to promote justice internationally ignore the power of states, they may promote disorder, which makes justice unachievable. As an instrumental value, some degree of order is necessary though not sufficient for justice. In Ramsey's words, "There is an asymmetry between these values... [W]e must attend to the preservation of an ordered polity and an orderly interstate system so that there can be the conditions for improving the justice actualized among men and between states."\7

The absence of international institutions means there are only weak legislative or adjudicative means of balancing conflicting claims of order and justice. At best, there are prudence, custom, and the weak institutions of international law and organization. A lack of substantive consensus on values among widely disparate cultures exacerbates the problem. (Simply consider the different premises of American moralizing about the rights of individuals, Soviet moralizing about advancing the right class through history, and Khomeini's moralizing about the revealed truths of Shiite Islam.) It is not surprising that the reciprocity and trust which help to sustain impartiality are difficult to develop internationally. Finally, there is the additional difficulty of assessing the consequences of actions when one must consider a third level of effects on the system of states as well as on individual states and persons. International politics is just that much more complicated. Considering the nature of the international milieu, it is not surprising that serious students of international politics have tended to be cautious about the role of ethics in foreign policy and have warned about the possibly disastrous consequences of well-intentioned moral crusades in a domain as difficult as that of international politics.

At the same time there is a difference between healthy realism and total skepticism. It does not follow from the difficulty of applying ethical considerations that they have no role at all. The cynic or total skeptic who argues that there is no role for ethics in international politics tends to smuggle his preferred values into foreign policy, often in the form of narrow nationalism. When faced with moral choices, to pretend not to choose is merely a disguised form of choice.

Philosophers say that "ought" implies "can." When something is impossible, we have no moral obligation to do it. But situations of absolute necessity where im-

42

possibility precludes obligation are relatively rare. "Do or die" situations are the exception. For example, the acute security dilemma that Israel faced in June 1967 may have allowed few choices other than pre-emptive attack, but there were many choices before and after June 1967.\8 And most day-to-day relations among states do not involve acute security situations. Obviously, there is less leeway for moral consideration in wartime conditions or when survival is at stake. But one cannot legitimately banish ethics by arguing that international politics is a "state of war" or that we are engaged in a "cold war" with an amoral adversary. As Arnold Wolfers has pointed out, much of international politics allows choices about the definition of indefinite concepts like "national interest," "survival," and "prudence."\9 The statesman who says, "I had no choice," usually did have choices, albeit unpleasant ones!

The fact that international politics is a difficult domain for ethics means that one must be cautious about too simple a transposition of moral maxims from the domain of individuals to the domain of states. But this does not mean the statesman is released from the duty of moral reasoning; it merely complicates the task. One must examine the arguments given for why there is "no choice" or why normal moral rules are alleged to be inapplicable in particular cases. The burden of proof rests on those who wish to depart from normal morality. While that burden may often be met, the quality of the arguments and conclusions deserves close examination. Some arguments for disregarding normal moral rules may be fallacious. For example, it does not follow from the fact that idealists often made foolish decisions in the past that skeptics are justified in banning all moral reasoning from the domain of international politics.

There are at least three arguments used by total skeptics to exclude ethics from international politics that simply do not carry the weight attributed to them. For example, it is sometimes argued that ethical behavior requires self-sacrifice, and that nations cannot sacrifice themselves.\10 This argument is based on the false juxtaposition of sacrificial love versus egoism, whereas the proper comparison is impartial justice versus egoism. Love may be a higher virtue in personal relations, but in ethical language, it is a supererogatory virtue. Justice does not require sacrifice of one's interest; it only requires impartial treatment of competing interests. To act with justice may be diffi-

43

cult in international politics, but it is not impossible.

Similarly, the fact that states must act to defend
their interests if they wish to survive in international politics does not mean that only selfish acts are
possible. It does mean that most international acts
will involve mixed motives. However, some degree of
altruism or consideration of others can often safely be
included in the motives for foreign policy. The existence of different national moral standards does not
make our own moral choices impossible. The sociological fact of normative relativism alerts us to the
danger of conflicting moral views and may engender
caution about the potentially immoral consequences of
blindly trying to impose our moral standards on other
cultures, but it does not excuse us from making moral
choices about our own actions. Just because others may
execute prisoners of war or assassinate opponents does
not make it right for us to do so. Two wrongs don't
make us right.

It is sometimes questioned whether the United
States can afford to act ethically when it is locked in
a bipolar rivalry with an adversary whose doctrine
rejects "bourgeois morality" and sees the goal of pro-
letarian victory as justifying the means. (The difference in moral views should alert us not to expect the
Soviet Union necessarily to behave as we do, but it
does not justify our behaving as they do.) We may choose
to act morally because of our desire to preserve our
integrity as a society. To ignore Soviet behavior would
be foolish, but to imitate it would be a particularly
insidious way of losing the political competition.

Some skeptics question the application of moral
concepts to individuals who live beyond our borders
because of the absence of a common community that
defines rights and obligations. Where political processes and communities are separate, why should we be
concerned about justice beyond our borders? One answer
is that we are concerned to the extent that our interactions and interdependence (economic, political, security) affect the conditions for justice in other countries. Another answer is the fact that many of our
citizens do feel at least some sense of community
beyond our borders -- whether it be ethnic, religious,
or cosmopolitan. They define their welfare to include a
sense of virtue in relation to such transnational communities.

44

In short, no domain of human activity can be categorized a priori as amoral when choices exist. But the particular characteristics of international politics make it much more difficult to apply ethics in this domain than in that of a well-ordered domestic polity. The fact that shallow or superficial moral reasoning often neglects this distinction is grounds for cautionary warnings. It is not grounds for maintaining that ethics should play no role in international politics and foreign policy. The danger of shallow moral reasoning must be met by better moral reasoning that takes into account the difficulty of the domain, not by futilely pretending to ban moral reasoning from foreign policy. The dangers of shallow moral reasoning -- whether in the form of the soft moralizing of the idealists or the spurious a priori exclusion of ethics by the total skeptics -- can only be cured by more rigorous moral reasoning.

II
Judging Moral Arguments

How should one judge moral reasoning? Obviously I must start with certain normative assumptions. Since I am writing about American foreign policy, I assume the traditions of Western moral and political philosophy and the values and procedures of American liberal democracy. This still leaves wide room for moral disagreements over how to express our values in foreign policy. Moreover, some people merely state their moral views and refuse to reason about them. My interest is with arguments about morality and foreign policy that go beyond primitive assertion.

Relativists and "emotivists" sometimes deny the prospect of judging moral arguments and assert that moral statements are mere expressions of taste. Ultimate ends are not susceptible to proof, but it is not senseless to discuss them. People do it every day, even if they sometimes fail to convince each other. Much of moral reasoning occurs in the area of argument that is beyond mere assertion but short of proving ultimate values. Moreover, much of ethical reasoning is not about ultimate ends, but about means, consequences, and the balancing of competing moral claims. Sometimes one encounters a primitive intuitionist or a believer in revealed truth who refuses to provide any reasons, but this is rare and their case is rarely compelling to those who do not already share their assumptions. In practice, we find ourselves constantly examining the clarity, logic, and consistency of moral reasoning in many domains, including international politics. And the formal structure of ethical language -- prescription, overriding, and "universalizability" -- differentiate it from mere expressions of taste.\11

Nonetheless, even within Western ethical tradi-tions, significant differences still exist, particular-ly over the role of rules and personal virtue versus the weighing of consequences. The consequentialist tradition -- which includes but is broader than utili-tarianism -- places its emphasis on outcomes. The deon-tological or Kantian tradition stresses following rules and having the right motives as sufficient for judging the morality of actions. The aretaic or Aristotelian approach stresses an ethics of virtue rather than an ethics of consequences, and it can be described as the difference between an emphasis on the integrity of "who am I?" and an emphasis on the consequences of my choices -- an ethics of being versus an ethics of doing.\12

The significance of these differences can be cap-tured by an adaptation of a hypothetical case used by Bernard Williams in his attack upon utilitarianism.\13 Imagine that you are visiting El Salvador and you happen upon a village square where an army captain is about to order his men to shoot two peasants held against a wall. When asked the reason, you are told that someone in this village shot at his men last night. When you object to the killing of possibly innocent people, you are told that civil wars do not permit moral niceties. Just to prove the point that we all have dirty hands in such situations, the captain hands you a rifle and tells you that if you will shoot one peasant, he will free the other. Otherwise both die. He warns you not to try any tricks because his men have their guns trained on you. Will you shoot one person with the consequence of saving one, or will you allow both to die but preserve your moral integrity by refusing to play his dirty game?

Integrity is clearly an important value. But at what point does the principle of not taking an innocent life collapse before the consequentialist burden? Would it matter if there were twenty or a thousand peasants to be saved? What if killing or torturing one innocent person could save a city of ten million persons from a terrorist's nuclear device? At some point, does integ-

46

rity not become the ultimate egoism of fastidious self-righteousness in which the purity of the self is more important than the lives of countless others? Is it not better to follow a consequentialist approach, admit remorse or regret over the immoral means, but justify the action by the ends?\14 And in the domain of international politics, where issues of survival sometimes arise, will not an absolute ethics of _being_ rather than _doing_ run the additional risk that you will not survive to be?

On the other hand, the dangers of too simple an application of consequentialism are well known. Once the ends justify the means, the dangers of slipping into a morality of convenience greatly increase. The "act-utilitarian" who tries to judge each case without the benefit of rules may find the task impossible to accomplish, except with a shallowness which makes a travesty of moral judgment. And given human proclivities to weigh choices in one's own favor and the difficulties of being sure of the consequences of complex activities, impartiality may be easily lost in the absence of rules. Moreover, when it becomes known that integrity plays no role and one will always choose the lesser of evils in terms of immediate consequences, one opens oneself up to blackmail by those who play dirty games. When it becomes known that one will always choose the lesser evil in any situation, there may develop a Gresham's law of bad moral choices driving out the prospect of good ones. Once a departure from rules and integrity is allowed, is it not a "slippery slope" to rationalizing anything? Particularly in complex organizations like governments, a widespread permission to waive rules and think only of consequences can lead to a rapid erosion of moral standards.

It is clear that we need both rules and the weighing of consequences in moral reasoning, and the sophisticated consequentialist will consider the broader and longer-term consequences of valuing both integrity of motives and rules that constrain means. S/he will also realize the critical role of rules in maintaining moral standards in complex institutions. In short, a sophisticated consequentialist analysis must take the view of an "institutional utilitarian," asking the question, "If I override normal moral rules because it will lead to better consequences in this case, will I be damaging the institution by eroding moral rules in a manner which will lead to worse consequences in future cases?"\15

But if we need both rules and the consideration of consequences, how do we reconcile them in practice? One way 'is to treat rules as prima facie moral duties and appeal to a critical, consequentialist level of moral reasoning to judge competing moral claims. But if every rule has its exception, how do we protect against too easy a collapse into consequentialism? How does one introduce handholds or stopping points on the slippery slope? Two devices help. The first is always to start with a strong presumption in favor of rules and place a substantial burden of proof upon those who wish to turn to consequentialist arguments. This burden must include a test of proportionality which weighs the consequences of departure from normal rules not only in the immediate case but also in terms of the probable long-run effects on the system of rules. For particularly heinous practices such as torture, the presumption may be near absolute and the burden of proof may be "beyond reasonable doubt."

The second device is to develop procedures that protect the impartiality which is at the core of moral reasoning and is so vulnerable in the transition from the deontological to the consequentialist approach. For example, structuring justification from the perspective of the victim or the deceived and developing ways to consult or inform third parties in order to protect against selfish assumptions are useful approaches. In the case of lying, Sissela Bok argues that such procedures may involve publicity.\16 The practice of consulting courts, congressional committees, allies, and other countries can serve as a means to protect impartiality. In other words, while there is no perfect procedure for incorporating rules in a sophisticated consequentialist approach, the presumptivist and procedural approach is less self-serving and more impartial than others.

One of the most common pitfalls in moral reasoning might be called "one-dimensional ethics." An action is said to be justified because it has good motives or because it has good consequences. In common practice, however, people tend to make ethical judgments along the three dimensions of motives, means, and consequences, and this introduces additional complexity and degree into ethical judgments.

It is easy to agree on the moral quality of actions that are good or bad on all three scores -- bad motives, bad means, and bad consequences. And we might agree to rank low those acts that have good conse-

48

quences but inadvertently grew out of bad motives. But there is less agreement about the ranking of two acts that both rest on good motives, but differ in that one uses good means and produces bad consequences while the other uses bad means but produces good consequences. In practice, we judge particular means in terms of auxiliary principles such as double effect (having unintended but foreseeable consequences); omissions being (sometimes) less culpable than acts; and a general sense of proportionality. None of these principles is without pitfalls (which are spelled out in the literature of moral philosophy), but if used carefully, they allow us to introduce some order into our moral dilemmas.\17 No formula can solve moral problems, but some formulas can aid us in the unavoidable task of weighing competing moral claims.

A good example of one-dimensional moral reasoning is the case of those who equated the American intervention in Grenada with the Soviet intervention of Afghanistan. Along the dimension of motives -- to maintain a sphere of influence -- the two actions were similar, but the bloodiness of the means and the probable consequences (in terms of restoring local autonomy) were quite different. Or, again on a one-dimensional approach, likening the American intervention in the Dominican Republic in 1965 to the Soviet intervention in Czechoslovakia in 1968 was similarly flawed, for the American action was partially redeemed by the eventual consequences of creating a more autonomous and democratic Dominican society. But good consequences alone are not sufficient to make an action good. If a murderer is trying to kill me and I am saved because a second murderer kills my would-be assailant first, the consequences are good, but the action is not. An invasion that has fortuitous consequences is better than one with disastrous consequences, but a three-dimensional judgment might still judge it as a morally flawed action.

This was part of the problem with the American intervention in Vietnam. Norman Podhoretz has argued that our involvement was moral because we were trying to save the South Vietnamese from totalitarianism.\18 The people who led us into Vietnam were those who had learned from the Munich experience that totalitarian aggression must be resisted even if it is costly. But if American idealism was part of the cause of our role in the Vietnam War, that same idealism tended to blind leaders to the facts of polycentric communism and local nationalism as alternative means to America's less

49

idealist end of preserving a balance of power in Asia. It also blinded them to the inappropriateness of involvement in a guerrilla war in an alien culture and to the immoral consequences that would follow from the disproportion between our goals and our means.

In a sense, American policy in the Vietnam War might be compared to a well-intentioned friend trying to bring your child home on time on an icy evening. He speeds, the car skids off the road, and your child is killed. His motives were good, but the consequences were horrible because of his inattention to the facts and means. It is not murder, but it may be negligent homicide -- his good intent reduces the charge, but it does not exonerate him. Our moral judgment is one of degree; it is not a binary choice of completely wrong or completely right.

Ends, means, and consequences are all important. A careful appraisal of the facts and a weighing of the uncertainties along all three dimensions are critical to good moral reasoning. Right versus wrong is often less difficult to handle than right versus right and degrees of wrong. And this is particularly complicated in international politics, where there is less agreement about what is right, and where the consequences of actions are often more difficult to estimate than in well-ordered domestic polities. But once again, the difficulty of moral reasoning in foreign policy does not justify our avoiding it; rather it necessitates that we work harder to do it better.

III
Citizens and Statesmen\19

Another complication in thinking about ethics and foreign policy is being clear about the different levels of analysis and relationships involved. We often speak of a state acting morally or immorally when we refer to its behavior toward the citizens of other states, which assumes that states have moral obligations to other states and their citizens -- a question that is examined in the next section. But what do we mean when we speak of a state acting: all the citizens or just the top leaders? Do the citizens and the statesmen have the same moral duties to foreigners? And what are the obligations that citizens and statesmen owe to each other?

When we speak of states, we are referring to
collectivities, and collective responsibility is a
difficult concept. Different people have different
degrees of responsibility for state actions and deserve
different degrees of blame or approbation. Moreover,
institutions such as governments develop standard operating procedures which take on a life of their own. For
example, in assigning moral responsibility for the
Soviet Union's shooting down of a Korean civil aircraft
with the loss of 269 lives, was the interceptor pilot
to blame for firing, or were his immediate supervisors
to blame for giving orders, or were the leaders to
blame for permitting procedures to exist that failed to
allow adequately for uncertainty and mistakes? Whatever
one's views about the allocation of blame, we are not
prevented from making the moral judgment that the Soviet action was wrong.

It is perfectly appropriate to make moral judgments about the consequences of actions by institutions.\20 Our awareness of the complexities of collective responsibility draws our attention to questions of
structural factors that constrain moral choices in
particular cases, and it may allow us to partly exonerate a person who is acting in a state role in a manner
that we would not accept if he were acting simply as an
individual. For example, if the director of the CIA
went to Managua as a tourist and shot three civilians
on the street, we would judge him guilty of murder. If
he followed presidential orders and consulted with
Congress before approving a covert action in which
three Nicaraguan civilians were killed, we would face a
more complex moral judgment in which he would share
only a portion of any blame (if we decided the action
to be blameworthy at all). In short, we judge people
acting in institutional roles somewhat differently than
those who are acting as individuals.

On the other hand, while the standards of judgment
for statesmen are more complex, they are not completely different from those for individuals. Filling an
institutional role does not exonerate a person from all
observance of normal moral standards. The burden of
proof still rests on the individual who claims exemp-
tion, and the quality of the arguments he uses must be
carefully judged in terms of motives, alternative
means, and probable long-run consequences. Just as we
found it was not enough for a statesman to say that
anything is acceptable "because international politics
is an amoral realm," so also is it unacceptable to
justify any action simply on the grounds that one is

acting as a political leader rather than as an individual. In fact, some role-based defenses ("I was only following orders, only carrying out policy") have been judged inadmissible for individuals since Hitler's atrocities and the Nuremberg trials focused new attention on issues of collective responsibility. The statesman, bureaucrat, or soldier may claim to be judged by a different standard at the critical consequentialist level rather than by the rules that apply to an individual, but he is not excused from asking moral questions about whether the action, the procedure, the policy, the role, and the institution are justifiable before he acts in a manner that deviates from normal moral rules. Institutional roles complicate our moral choices. Careful moral reasoning about foreign policy must pay particular attention to arguments given for any transition from the normal moral rules that govern individual behavior to a different behavior allegedly (and possibly) justified by institutional and collective reasons.

The Perspective of the Citizen

What levels of moral behavior should citizens expect of their leaders? Some citizens may demand a higher- or lower-than-normal moral standard. Sometimes a leader must act in one or the other manner for important long-run consequentialist reasons. What citizens can expect of their leaders are good reasons and procedures when they make the case for going from normal rules to consequentialism.

What then are the obligations that citizens owe each other when they introduce their ethical concerns into foreign policy preferences? One can argue that there should be few restrictions except the obligation to think through the consequences and weigh the effects on their fellow citizens. These might be called rules of reason.

To have a constructive influence on foreign policy, an individual's moral views should be well thought out. Too often, actions based on normal moral rules and good intentions have morally offensive consequences in the complex arena of world politics. The full consequences of actions usually cannot be predicted with certainty, but neither are we totally ignorant about the future results of a given course of action. Citizens can ask each other to consider the full range of likely consequences. The responsible citizen in a de-

mocracy should be aware of the costly and sometimes
dangerous effects of a situation in which all citizens
press for their personal moral solutions to all issues.

What norms and procedures can protect against such
problems? Democratic theory is a start, but alone is
not sufficient. If citizens wish to express a moral
preference in foreign policy, there should be a presumption in favor of expression. But given the danger
of mass hysteria (or indifference), long-run interests
may be neglected. And the practice of building major-
ities by logrolling may undercut the common interest.
Simple pursuit of the interests of pressure groups can
lead to lowest-common-denominator solutions, which may
risk long-run prudential interests as well as lead to
immoral consequences. For example, legislated curtail-
ment of aid to Turkey as punishment for genocide
against Armenians in World War I could greatly reduce
our defense and deterrence capabilities vis-a-vis the
Persian Gulf.

Arthur Schlesinger, Jr. has suggested a rule that
as many issues as possible be disposed of on prudential
grounds.\21 Such a rule would help to reduce the amount
of heated moral debate in a democracy. But Schlesinger's rule still begs the question of how to deal with
strong moral preferences and how to define prudence. We
need to go further and qualify moral debate and pressure by a Rawlsian-type rule of reason: A citizen
should press a moral concern upon his government's
foreign policy so long as he would agree to incorporate
that concern even if he did not know his own position
in society. Under such an approach, the obligations
that citizens owe each other when introducing their
moral preferences into foreign policy are prudential
attention to the realities of international life and a
restraint of universalizability when they urge actions
that might jeopardize common interests.

The Perspective of the Statesman

If individuals should and will apply their moral views
to foreign policy, qualified only by democratic practice and a Rawlsian rule of reason, what of the statesman? How are officials limited in what they may do for
moral reasons by their obligations to their constituents? The obligation of a statesman is to maintain and
improve the well-being of the people he represents, in
all of the dimensions that are relevant to them. His
objectives would thus normally encompass their physical

security and economic well-being; but they also should include their psychological security and well-being. He must, so far as possible, consider all the consequences of the action he directs, now and in the future. He should act as a trustee for the interests of those he represents.

As Reinhold Niebuhr and others have pointed out, a trustee is not entitled to sacrifice the interests of others.\22 He must act prudentially on their behalf. But a prudent statesman approaching his task with utter realism must take into account the moral views of citizens in weighing his actions. There are three major reasons why this is so.

First, the realistic statesman must consider the influence of his current actions on the ability of his successors to exercise a degree of discretion appropriate to the management of foreign policy. To systematically ignore the moral sentiments of his citizenry will undermine trust not only in him, but in his office. It will lead to loss of the public support for foreign policy which is so necessary especially in a democracy, but also in other forms of government. Second, since the psychological well-being of his citizenry is part of the statesman's responsibility, he must take the self-respect of his citizens as citizens directly into account, quite apart from the possible ultimate loss of their support.

Third, an important element in the ability of any country to carry out its foreign policy objectives is its reputation abroad. This reputation rests in part on consistency and reliability in behavior. Underlying this is the confidence of other nations that a nation will carry out its commitments. The ability to make credible commitments can aid the statesman enormously in pursuit of his current and future objectives. Confidence and credibility depend upon a number of factors, by no means only on morality, but the establishment of trust among nations is immeasurably easier if they share common moral values and if those moral values are seen to inform foreign policy actions. With trust based on shared moral sentiment, certain commitments become credible that would not otherwise be possible (e.g., placement of tactical nuclear weapons in densely populated friendly nations).

Does this prudential approach exhaust the statesman's use of morality in foreign policy? Is there room for the statesman to interject his own moral standards, higher or lower, into his decisions and actions in foreign policy? If two courses of action are assessed to be completely equivalent in their net benefit to the nation, taking into account all expected future as well as present consequences, the choice between them from the trustee's role is a matter of indifference, and he might as well decide between them on the basis of his personal moral code as on any other criterion. On the other hand, once the trustee is allowed to interject his personal moral code into his decisions, when his personal code differs from the public's, the trustee could become involved in sacrificing the well-being of his citizenry.

Statesmen as trustees must sometimes violate their individual moral code for long-range consequentialist reasons such as protecting the very public order that makes it possible for citizens to adhere to normal moral rules.\23 A statesman who was perfectly consistent by individual moral standards might often find himself in conflict with his consequentialist responsibilities as a trustee. For example, Henry Stimson held the noble personal moral view that "gentlemen do not read one another's mail." Simplistic moral consistency might have required Stimson to oppose the creation of the National Security Agency and its predecessors. Yet breaking diplomatic and naval codes in the 1930s probably altered the outcome of the Second World War, and in any case greatly shortened it.

It does not follow from this discussion of the trustee's role that the statesman's personal moral views have no role in foreign policy. For one thing, the statesman is a moral educator as well as a trustee. Part of his role is to help the community shape its moral preferences and to understand issues. The educator helps the citizenry to define and evaluate particular situations.

In the simple terms used by Theodore Roosevelt, the presidency is a "bully" pulpit. Public views of morality are not indelibly fixed. The statesman can seize opportunities to raise the moral level as well as to warn against the dangers of moralism. By "educating his electorate," the statesman may reduce the tension between his personal moral views and his obligations as a trustee. For example, a leader may view institutionalized racial injustice in South Africa as morally repugnant. He may also see prudential reasons (e.g., Soviet influence, security of sea routes, nonproliferation) for not breaking relations with the white South

African government. But he may believe it right to expend some of his country's political influence on the racial issue rather than to husband it all for use on the security issues. And he may use a combination of moral and prudential arguments to persuade the public to see the trade-offs in the same manner that he does. Should he fail, however, his trustee role limits the extent of his personal moral intervention.

Just how constraining the trustee's role should be is a debatable point. On an overly simple plebiscitary model of direct democracy, if the statesman finds a situation morally repugnant (and assuming that his efforts at public education have failed), he can only resign as trustee and have full freedom to press for his individual moral preferences in the definition of the national interest. But as Edmund Burke pointed out two centuries ago, the trustee in representative government must consider the long-term interests of his people, not merely their current preferences, even if he thus risks electoral defeat. Such long-term interest may include the prospect that a decade hence the public may regret a failure to have taken a moral stance on South Africa. In retrospect, many Americans wish their trustees in the 1930s had taken greater electoral risks to rescue more Jews from Hitler's genocide. Nonetheless, while there is some flexibility in the Burkean conception, the notion of trusteeship constrains the statesman. If his educational efforts fail despite ample time and information, the democratic presumption in favor of the public's considered views must ultimately limit the statesman.

Second, the exception allowed above -- where two courses of action are equivalent in benefit -- is defined narrowly, but in practice it encompasses a relatively wide range of situations because of the uncertainty of calculating consequences in the complex international system. Many situations arise where prudential considerations could go either way. For example, in deciding whether to give asylum to a prominent refugee from China, the statesman must consider the effects on relations with China and the balance of power in East Asia. But he must also consider the effects on America's reputation as a country that defends the rights of individuals and the long-run effects of opening one's country to blackmail once it departs from a standard of integrity. Since the uncertainty about consequences and net benefit is likely to be great, the actual leeway to decide the issue on a personal moral proclivity toward the rights of individ-

56

uals may be quite large in practice.

Finally, the statesman's moral roles are not fully exhausted by the obligations to those for whom he acts as trustee. His primary obligations are to his own people, but as I shall argue in the next section, he has a residual cosmopolitan obligation to respect the rights of other peoples in situations where there are choices among means to promote his own people's interests. This residual obligation may shrink to almost zero in the realm of survival and necessity -- for example in a situation of impending enemy attack. (Even in such a situation there are moral questions about the future of humanity if the statesman chooses to respond with a preemptive nuclear strike.) But as Arnold Wolfers has pointed out, much of international politics is not in the realm of necessity, and even in the definition of security interests the statesman can make moral choices among means.\24 In just war theory, his obligation to respect the rights of those beyond his borders includes just cause, reasonable chance of success, proportionality, and discrimination between combatants and civilians. He may follow such an approach for prudential reasons or as a reflection of the moral preferences of his citizenry. But even faced with an indifferent citizenry, he might accept a moral obligation to choose means that reduce the loss of the rights or life imposed on other human beings.

There are certain risks to admitting exceptions to the trustee theory. Insofar as public opinion in the statesman's country admits some obligation to foreigners (such as just war theory), there is no problem. But if the trustee role is weakened to allow the statesman to follow his personal moral code, whether higher or lower, how can we be sure that his actions will have good consequences? Suppose the statesman is a cosmopolitan religious fundamentalist who places no value on the souls or lives of atheists. Would we still wish to weaken the trustee theory to admit idiosyncratic moral preferences? One view would restrict the statesman to the role of trustee, albeit with a Burkean degree of flexibility. Another would rely upon the protections of constitutional checks and balances. There may be no way to use procedural principles to tie the hands of the reckless fundamentalist that would not also have tied the hands of a statesman trying to rescue Jews in the 1930s. Thus some flexibility and open moral debate is bound to remain.

Even taking these qualifications into account, the

statesman's exercise of personal moral choice, whether by a higher or lower standard in terms of normal rules, will be more constrained in foreign policy than that of the citizen because of his institutional role. This is not to say that morality plays no role for the statesman. As we have seen, his transition from normal rules to consequentialism requires careful moral reasoning. Nor does it mean that morality plays no role in foreign policy. The citizen is not so constrained, and citizens may demand that their trustees express widely held moral values in national policy. But the statesman must temper this popular preference by introducing prudential considerations.

IV
Obligations to Foreigners

Thus far, although I have alluded to cosmopolitan values, I have concentrated on the obligations that citizens owe each other and that statesmen owe citizens when introducing ethical considerations into the difficult domain of international politics.

There are four basic views about the moral obligations we owe to people who are not our fellow citizens. I have already argued that one view, that of the total skeptic who denies any duties beyond borders, rests on premises that do not stand up to careful scrutiny. When we turn to those who admit obligations owed to foreigners, we encounter three quite different schools of thought: the realist, the state-moralist, and the cosmopolitan approaches.\25 The realist and the state-moralist tend to stress the value of order; the cosmopolitan values individual justice more highly.

In contrast with the total skeptic, the realist accepts some moral obligations to foreigners, but only of a minimal sort related to the immoral consequences of disorder. More extensive obligations exist only where there is a community that defines and recognizes rights and duties. Such communities exist only in weak forms at the international level, and this sets strict bounds on international morality. Moreover, the world of sovereign states is a world of self-help without the moderating effects of a common executive, legislature, or judiciary. In such a domain, chaos is the greatest danger. The range of moral choices is severely constricted because the government which attempts to indulge a broad range of moral preferences may fail in its primary duty of preserving order. As Hans Morgenthau has written, "The state has no right to let its moral disapprobation...get in the way of successful political action, itself inspired by the moral principle of national survival....Realism, then, considers prudence...to be the supreme virtue in politics."\26

This form of realism can be distinguished from the position of the radical skeptic or cynic discussed earlier. The realist places the greatest stress on national survival and on the instrumental value of order. The most significant means of preserving international order is the balance of power. International politics is characterized by so much inequality and so little structure that, on consequentialist grounds, maintaining the balance of power deserves a strong priority over both interstate and individual justice. Prudent pursuit of self-interest will at least produce order and avert the disastrously immoral consequences which the unbridled pursuit of justice might produce in a world of unequal states. This is accentuated by the existence of nuclear weapons. We owe foreigners the minimal obligation of order that avoids the chaos that can lead to nuclear war. As Henry Kissinger replied to critics who accused him of an amoral policy because of his lack of zeal in pursuit of human rights, "peace is a moral priority." There are no rights among the incinerated!

The realist has a strong argument in reminding us that justice depends upon a degree of order and that international moral crusades can lead to disorder, injustice, and immoral consequences. But while it is true that the problem of order makes international politics less hospitable ground than domestic politics for moral arguments about justice, it does not follow that justice is totally excluded in the international realm. Order may deserve priority, but it need not be treated as an absolute value in a lexicographic ranking. One can assign a high value to order and still admit degrees of trade-off between order and justice. Both statesmen and citizens constantly weigh such trade-offs in international affairs. As we saw earlier, survival may come first, but much of international politics is not about survival. Choices among alternative courses of action must be (and are) informed by many moral values. Moreover, while the balance of power is the primary means of preserving order in international politics, it is not the only means or a totally unambiguous means. There are not strong institutions to enforce norms, but weak international institutions of law and diplomacy do supplement the balance of power in preserving some degree of order.

The second approach, that of the state-moralists, stresses morality among states and the significance of state sovereignty and self-determination. One variant of the state-moralist viewpoint stresses a just order among a society of states. For example, John Rawls asks what rules the states would choose or would have chosen for just relations among themselves if they did not know in advance how strong or wealthy each would be.\27 The principles that Rawls derives -- self-determination, nonintervention, and an obligation to keep treaties -- are analogous to existing principles of international law. The realist would object that in addition to the ambiguities in the concepts, justice among states does not always contribute to order in a world of radical inequality. On the contrary, some degree of hierarchy and balance of power based on force may be necessary to keep order in a world lacking effective institutions to enforce the principles of international law. The cosmopolitan, on the other hand, would object that justice among states would not necessarily produce justice for individuals.

Michael Walzer seeks to alleviate this moral problem by portraying the rights of states as a collective form of their citizens' individual rights to life and liberty. The nation-state may be seen as a pooled expression of individual rights, representing "the rights of contemporary men and women to live as members of a historic community and to express their inherited culture through political forms worked out among themselves...."\28 Thus, there is a strong presumption against outside intervention. However, this presumption is not absolute. Foreigners have an obligation to refrain from intervention unless the lack of fit between a government and the community that it represents is radically apparent. Thus, for example, Walzer would allow intervention to prevent massacre and enslavement, to balance a prior intervention in a civil war, or to assist secession movements that have demonstrated their representative character. In such circumstances, it would be contradictory to regard the state as representing the pooled rights of its individual citizens. This presumption and its exceptions are again analogous to many of the existing rules of international law. But again, international law does not guarantee either realist order or cosmopolitan individual rights.

The virtues of Walzer's refined state-moralist approach is that it bases the rights of states on the rights of individuals while taking account of the reality of the way that international politics is structured and while conforming quite closely to existing principles of international law. A weakness in the approach is the ambiguity of the concept of self-determination.\29 Who is the self that determines? How do we know when there is a radical lack of fit between government and people? Must an oppressed group fight and prevail to demonstrate its claim to speak as a people worthy of international recognition? If so, is not might making right? Or as a critic asks,

> In Walzer's world, are there not self-identified political, economic, ethnic, or religious groups (for example, capitalists, democrats, communists, Moslems, the desperately poor) who would favor foreign intervention over Walzer's brand of national autonomy (and individual rights) if it would advance the set of rights, or interests, at the core of their understanding of justice?...Why should Walzer's individual right to national autonomy be more basic than other human rights, such as freedom from terror, torture, material deprivation, illiteracy, and suppressed speech...? Walzer's ideal is but one normative, philosophical conception among others, no more grounded and often less grounded in people's actual moral attitudes (and social identities) than other conceptions.\30

In short, the state-moralist approach is particularly weak when it treats self-determination and national sovereignty as absolute principles which must come first in a lexical ordering. In practice, peoples do want self-determination and autonomy, but they want other values as well. There is a constant problem of trade-offs and of balancing competing moral claims.

The third, cosmopolitan, approach stresses the common nature of humanity. States and boundaries exist, but this does not endow them with moral significance. "Ought" does not follow from "is." As David Luban has written,

> The rights of security and subsistence...are necessary for the enjoyment of any other rights at all. No one can do without them. Basic rights, therefore, are universal. They

are not respecters of political boundaries and
require a universalist politics to implement
them; even when this means breaching the wall
of state sovereignty.\31

Many citizens hold multiple loyalties to several communities at the same time. They may wish their governments to follow policies which give expression to the
rights and duties engendered by other communities in
addition to those structured at the national level.

While the cosmopolitan approach has the virtue of
accepting transnational realities and avoids the sanc-
tification of the nation-state, an unsophisticated
cosmopolitanism also has serious drawbacks. First, if
morality is about choice, then to underestimate the
significance of states and boundaries is to fail to
take into account the main features of the milieu in
which choices must be made. To pursue individual justice at the cost of survival, or to launch human rights
crusades that cannot hope to be fulfilled yet which
interfere with prudential concerns about order, may
lead to immoral consequences. Applying ethics to foreign policy is more than merely constructing philosophical arguments; it must be relevant to the domain in
which moral choices are to be exercised.

The other problem with an unsophisticated cosmopolitan approach is ethical: it discards the moral
dimension of national politics. As Stanley Hoffmann has
written, "States may be no more than collections of
individuals and borders may be mere facts. But a moral
significance is attached to them...."\32 There are
rights of people to live in historic communities and
autonomously to express their own political choices. A
pure cosmopolitan view which ignores these rights of
self-determination fails to do justice to the difficult
job of balancing rights in the international realm.

The difference between realists, cosmopolitans,
and state-moralists is a difference over how to balance
transnational and national values. Different people may
approach the balancing of such values in different
ways, but the statesman's trusteeship role requires
that he give priority (though not exclusive attention)
to interstate order and national interests. Since sophisticated realists admit that justice affects the
legitimacy of order, since sophisticated cosmopolitans
admit the political significance of boundaries, and
since sophisticated state-moralists admit the possibility of duties beyond borders, the three positions often

tend to converge in practice. Each has a part of the wisdom that must be considered in balancing competing moral claims in hard cases. But they start with different presumptions and thus specify different conditions for qualifying or overriding their presumptions as they are applied to particular cases.

For example, the three approaches could lead to quite different conclusions regarding the obligations to foreign citizens involved in any U.S. intervention against the Sandinista government of Nicaragua, other (prudential) things being equal. The realist might try to justify intervention on the grounds of the hierarchical order of spheres of influence, which he sees as critical to maintaining nuclear peace. The state-moralist would prohibit intervention unless conditions in Nicaragua approached genocide. The left-wing cosmopolitan might justify intervention by forces in Costa Rica that had a reasonable prospect of producing better human rights conditions than exist now, but might oppose intervention by forces in Honduras that would restore a repressive Somoza-style regime. (The right-wing cosmopolitan might argue that the consequences of totalitarianism justify either intervention.) In practice, of course, prudential and national interest considerations might lead all three to a common policy position, but to the extent that the argument involves ethics, the three approaches are still distinctive. Each must be subjected to the standards of good moral reasoning described earlier, and no one seems fully adequate. It may be possible, however, to construct a composite position.

If one wishes to avoid metaphysical arguments about natural law, it is safer to ground arguments about rights and obligations in the existence of a sense of community: where a sense of community exists, it is possible to define rights and obligations. There are multiple senses of community in world politics today, but those which transcend national boundaries in universal form are relatively weak. Nonetheless, many people, including realists, acknowledge a weak form of community symbolized by the notion of "common humanity." Defining another being as part of the human community entails restraints on how we treat him or her. For example, we do not kill other persons for food or pleasure (as is done with animals by those who do not define community in terms of all sentient beings).\33 Nor do we allow them to starve if we are in a position to help.

It is still debatable what rights and obligations follow from such a weak form of community as the notion of "common humanity." Rights and their correlative obligations can involve modest claims (being left free from interference) or strong claims (being provided something one does not have). A weak sense of community may give rise to more than weak forms of rights and obligations. Walzer argues, for example, that

> the idea of distributive justice presupposes a bounded world, a community within which distribution takes place, a group of people committed to dividing, exchanging, and sharing, first of all among themselves. It is possible to imagine such a group extended to include the entire human race, but no such extension has yet been achieved. For the present, we live in smaller distributive communities.\34

Some cosmopolitans would reply that the fact that the current sense of community is bounded does not mean that it is right to draw conclusions about limited obligations.\35 Again, "ought" does not follow from "is." The sense of community in world politics was more limited at times in the past and may be more expansive at times in the future. Rather than derive norms from current facts, one should derive them from an ideal sense of human community. This would be more consistent with the criteria of impartiality and universalizability that are essential characteristics of moral reasoning. If one were to engage in Rawls's mental experiment of imagining what principles of justice all people might agree to if they were behind a "veil of ignorance" regarding their actual advantages, one would not allow enormous inequalities of wealth based on nationality. From this point of view, the burden of proof rests with those who depart from the cosmopolitan ideal; they must justify any preference to compatriots.

Although "ought" does not follow from "is," the facts about what exists severely shape and constrain normative judgments. If "ought" implies "can" then "is" and "ought" are logically distinct but empirically intertwined. To apply Rawls's concepts of justice without regard to boundaries (which Rawls himself eschews) is a debatable procedure. If communal identity is one of the essential attributes of a person, assuming the disembodied "selves" implied in Rawls's veil-of-ignorance thought experiment may be a poor way of approaching the issue of impartiality and universalizability.\36

Impartiality is not the same as egalitarianism -- it does not mean "each one equals one." Universaliza-bility means similar actions in similar situations. It prohibits moral justification based simply on the ego-ism of the actor, but it does not exclude considera-tions of the interests of the actor if similar inter-ests would be allowed weight for similar actors. It is not moral to justify an action "because it is me." It may sometimes be moral to justify an action "because the object is mine." For example, if you could save only one of two drowning children, one of which is your own, you may be morally justified in saving your own. Your child has a right to expect such a duty from you on the basis of the roles of parent and child in the family community relationship. Of course, one would have to admit the same justification for any parent similarly placed, even if one were the absent parent of the child not saved.

Social roles create and carry rights and duties -- regardless of whether they are voluntarily assumed -- whether the roles are those of family or citizenship. But given the existence of multiple levels of community and multiple roles, the preference for one's own child or compatriot cannot morally be admitted as absolute. If one assumed the role of lifeguard and then noticed the drowning children, one would have an additional obligation to save the child where there was a higher probability of success. And at some point, a consequen-tialist would object to a preference for saving one's own child that did not consider the relative probabili-ties or the numbers of other children involved. In short, some preference for family or compatriots may be justified on grounds of impartiality and universaliz-ability, but it would not be possible to reconcile an absolute preference with these criteria.

What obligations do we owe to foreigners in the world as it now exists? Imagine a thought experiment in which rational people were trying to answer that ques-tion before the deck of national cards was dealt and one did not know if one would be dealt a high (rich-nation) or low (poor-nation) card. Assume we, one, accept a sense of common humanity, but, two, have a preference for autonomous national community (or assume that it is the only feasible form of organization at this time), and, three, realize the dangers and diffi-culties of preserving order in a world organized into states. Moreover, four, we lack a common, ideal vision of the good, and our concern for order must often have priority over justice. But even in this imperfect world, we would wish to set some limits on national exclusivity and preference for compatriots. If we knew that we all had this dangerous preference for (or accepted the existence of) national communal identity at this point in history, but did not know whether we would belong to a rich, strong nation or to a poor, weak one, what limitations would we want all nations to follow regarding preference for compatriots? What obligations would we wish all nations to accept toward foreigners? The result might produce at least four clusters of obligations.

First, because we recognize each other as part of common humanity despite national differences, one would admit negative duties not to kill, enslave, or destroy the autonomy of other peoples. While community generally implies reciprocal awareness of obligation, reciprocity may not be necessary to justify adherence to these duties. Even if another people lacks a sense of common humanity at this time, our definition of them as human and a thought experiment about universalizability would produce such restraints. We do unto others as we would have them do unto us. Thus, even in wartime a cosmopolitan realist could accept the morality of limits on killing of innocent civilians (and other restraints of just war theory), despite the failure of the enemy to observe such restraints. Whether he would live up to this moral standard or succumb to psychological pressures to respond in kind is another question, but the moral standard is clear.

These negative duties include a prima facie obligation not to intervene in other states on Walzer's grounds that such intervention destroys the autonomy of the common life of another community. We could disregard these prohibitions on intervention in situations where genocide, enslavement, or egregious deprivation of human rights made a mockery of the prima facie assumption that the autonomous political process in that state represented the pooled rights of the individual citizens. Deciding whether such conditions exist will be debated in the light of the facts of particular instances. But while such conditions would release us from the negative duty of nonintervention, they would not necessarily create a positive duty of intervention, particularly if such intervention would be costly or dangerous in a world of states. Positive duties exist, but they are limited.

A second obligation to foreigners (and limit on our preference for compatriots) is the generally accepted consequentialist principle of taking responsibility for the consequences of our actions. It may be that "the great majority of actions that occur within the boundaries of a nation-state are not either the direct or indirect results of the actions of those who are outside its national borders."\37 But as the literature on interdependence shows, many actions and conditions that affect the prospects for justice within a nation are affected by actions of others outside the nation.\38 Such interdependence is a matter of degree, and the effects are often difficult to ascertain. Moreover, there are thorny questions about time and a moral "statute of limitations."\39 Nonetheless, according to the principle of responsibility for the consequences of our actions, we have obligations to foreigners in some proportion to the strength of the effects that we can ascertain as ours.

A third obligation to foreigners is Samaritanism -- the obligation to provide readily available assistance to another who is in dire need.

> It is commonly said of such cases that positive assistance is required if (1) it is needed or urgently needed by one of the parties, and (2) if the risks and costs of giving it are relatively low for the other party.... But the limit on risks and costs is sharply drawn.\40

The Samaritan need not comb "the bushes along the roadsides to insure that there are no needy sufferers" lurking there.\41 The Samaritan obligation differs from the first category in being a positive rather than a negative duty, but its rationale is similarly related to the definitions involved in a weak sense of common humanity: it refers to situations where the distinction between acting to take life and omitting to save a life are so fine that the distinction between acts and omissions seems wholly arbitrary.

Samaritanism creates an obligation to help other foreigners achieve their basic rights of subsistence and autonomy where we are able to do so at relatively low cost and risk. But it does not require us to give our wealth to the poor up to some point of imagined common utility. And while there are ambiguities in defining the extent of the principle in particular cases, it will not sustain obligations to promote extended definitions of basic human rights, nor will it justify interventions to advance justice that simul-

67

taneously run great risks in terms of disorder. It would lead to obligations to respond to particularly horrendous behavior such as genocide, but the nature of the response would be limited where costs and risks were very high. In short, Samaritanism establishes minimal positive obligation -- the extent of which will be debated in light of the facts of particular cases; but it still leaves a large area of foreign need which individuals and groups may wish to fill but which would not be a national obligation derived from the assumptions above.

A fourth obligation to foreigners is to practice beneficence or charity in situations where the foreigners can be made better off without making compatriots significantly worse off. This obligation extends more broadly than Samaritanism but remains a modest limit on preference to compatriots since it does not make them significantly worse off. Situations do arise where we can make foreigners better off at virtually no cost to ourselves -- for example, by maintaining fair trade or by proffering food aid at a time of large domestic surpluses. It would seem morally arbitrary to fail to act simply because the beneficiaries were foreigners. Again the difference between an omission and an action would be too close to sustain scrutiny. A thought experiment about impartiality in an imperfect world of nations would quickly include such a rule among the obligations that all would wish to observe even if they did not know their eventual nationality or social advantages.

Finding pure Pareto-optimal situations is often difficult in practice. Some costs exist -- if not to the nation, then to some groups of compatriots -- but if the obligation of beneficence is to have any meaning, minimal costs to the nation must be ignored and particular groups which do incur costs should be compensated. This is the argument, if not always the practice, for providing adjustment assistance to small groups that suffer from expanded trade while larger groups (at home and abroad) benefit. In short, the beneficence principle creates a modest (but nontrivial) positive obligation to foreigners.

Cosmopolitans would go further and adduce a fifth cluster of obligations to assist others in achieving basic rights, even at high costs. Given the assumptions in our thought experiment, would our rational people want an obligation to assist others in the achievement of their rights at any cost? If others were suffering severe deprivations such as genocide, enslavement, or invasion, would not a sense of common humanity make us accept an obligation to help them even at costs not admitted by the Samaritan or beneficence principles? Not necessarily. Such an obligation would be severely constrained both by the realist and state-moralist assumptions about order, which we allowed in our original thought experiment. Given the widespread practice of minor deprivations of human rights and the power of some states (such as the USSR) involved in major deprivations, the costs of becoming a global moral policeman would be unacceptably high. To prevent an Idi Amin from massacring Ugandans, a South Africa from practicing apartheid, a Lebanon from practicing religious fratricide, and a Soviet Union from incarcerating dissidents -- all at the same time -- would involve an extremely high, if not impossible, level of costs for American foreign policy. It seems unlikely that the participants in our thought experiment would demand such actions as obligations. On the other hand, they might hope that states would stretch the Samaritan and beneficence principles and occasionally incur certain costs on a voluntary or charitable, if not obligatory, basis.

The realist and state-moralist concerns about order imply limits on the fifth sort of obligation, but they do not prohibit supererogatory actions where they can be prudently reconciled with interstate order. And they do not prevent individuals from taking supererogatory personal charitable actions which their state might have to eschew for reasons of interstate order. Nor do they prevent citizens from encouraging the evolution of a stronger sense of community beyond the nation-state for the future. In short, a realistic thought experiment about the limited obligations beyond borders in the imperfect world of today does not preclude more idealistic thought experiments about worlds that might evolve in the future.

V
Problems of Intervention and Autonomy

I will exemplify these approaches by considering problems of intervention, but first it is important to clarify the concept of intervention. An important aspect of competing moral claims in a world of nation-states is national autonomy and self-determination. For example, if the government of a country needing land

69

reform were so weak that the only way to effect reform would be for an outside government to administer it through a colonial administration, most people today would argue that such outside involvement would not be justified.

Part of what we owe to others in recognition of their special status as humans is respect for their autonomy. Autonomy cannot be absolute, but as Jonathan Glover has written, a concern for basic human rights includes a presumption in favor of autonomy.\42 Even if one argues that moral obligation is owed only among individuals, nation-states can be seen as communities of pooled individual rights. At the same time, national autonomy may sometimes conflict with the autonomy of individuals and groups within a nation. Moreover, unlike the legal concept of sovereignty, national autonomy is often highly qualified in practice. Thus moral proscriptions against outside involvement cannot be absolute.

Walzer argues that the state is the arena where self-determination is worked out and from which foreign armies have to be excluded. He says there should be a presumption of legitimacy of internal processes unless there is a radical lack of fit between government and community. But the rules allowing foreigners to disregard the presumption against outside involvement are as important as the presumption itself. These rules are rightly restrictive when one focuses, as Walzer does, on extreme forms of intervention associated with large-scale use of lethal force, but they do not give much guidance when one is dealing with an issue like human rights or economic assistance.

When we consider outside involvement in the socio-economic realm, it is important to remember that national autonomy is not absolute. Sovereign nations do not fully control their destinies. First, the workings of the international economy typically have important effects across national boundaries even in the absence of any overt governmental intervention. And in some cases, these transnational economic effects may have life and death consequences for impoverished people in poor countries that are just as significant and even more likely than military action.

Second, nation-states are not like billiard balls, hard and closed unto themselves and merely ricocheting off each other. As argued earlier, many citizens in many states have multiple loyalties both below and above the national level, which give rise to various senses of community. Citizens may welcome outside involvement in their national affairs -- up to a certain point.

Third, few countries are fully self-sufficient, and outside assistance and involvement can help to turn a theoretical autonomy in the current period into a greater real autonomy in the future. Some outside involvement may strengthen a national capacity to influence its own destiny. If this strengthens a state, it may reduce the chances of outside intervention in the future.

Finally, self-determination is not a precise concept. To say that every group has the right to choose its own sovereignty begs the question of how such a choice is to be made. A democratic principle is not enough because the decision of where (within what boundaries), when (now or later), and on what agenda (what is excluded) one votes will often lead to radically different outcomes. In other words, there is always a certain degree of moral arbitrariness in the decisions about which rights of national self-determination are observed and which are not. We can think of degrees of self-determination in proportion to the extent to which sectors of a society are able to participate in determining national views. Self-determination can be seen as an attribute of societies, while sovereignty is an attribute of states. When a small and unrepresentative elite sets national policies that are against the interests of large parts of the population, national autonomy may conflict with self-determination. Thus the respect for autonomy of the state cannot be absolute.

Not only is there a porousness and relativism about the concept of national autonomy, but the concept of outside involvement must also be seen as complex. One can imagine a variety of dimensions with respect to method, scope, purpose, and duration; one can envision a variety of actors inside and outside a country having intended and unintended effects; and one can imagine a variety of degrees of outside involvement.

From a moral point of view, the degree of coercion involved in outside involvement is very important. Governments have coercive powers. One can imagine a range of actions by outsiders extending from, at one end of the spectrum, declarations or speeches aimed at the citizenry in the other country to, at the other end, full-scale military invasion. In between, one

71

would find such actions as economic assistance, military assistance, support for opposition groups (usually covert), and small-scale military intervention.

Intervention: Foreign Coercion, National Autonomy

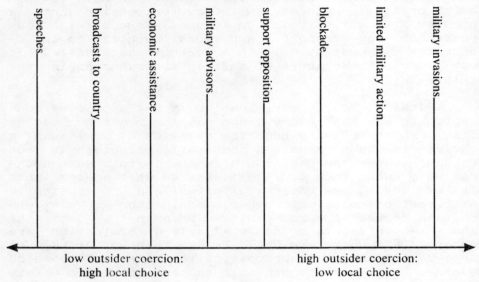

The term "intervention" is sometimes used broadly to refer to the entire spectrum of deliberate outside involvements in another country's domestic affairs. More commonly in international law and diplomacy, it is used more narrowly to refer to the right half of the scale -- where an outsider "interferes coercively in the domestic affairs of another state."\43

We might judge some outside involvement to be immoral, regardless of the degree of coercion, if the intentions were malevolent -- for example, if the purpose were to exercise domination or if the consequences were bad. But if we judged the intentions and consequences to be good, then we would focus on the means of outside involvement, particularly the degree of coercion, because of its costs in terms of autonomy and its inconsistency with the established rules of international law. Whether one is looking at a broad or narrow definition of intervention, one would look at questions of "proportionality" -- the costs of outside involvement in relation to the danger being averted or the

severity of the wrong being righted. In assessing proportionality, one must look both at the direct consequences and at the unintended ones. An assessment of
proportionality in highly coercive cases (i.e., in
relation to the narrow definition of intervention), are
doubly complex because they must include the long-run
consequences for an existing system of international
rules if one violates them in a particular case.

Military Intervention

Consequentialist arguments about proportionality are
easily abused, and once there is a departure from an
absolute prohibition against military intervention, it
is essential that good moral reasoning protect against
such abuse. It is not adequate moral reasoning for a
statesman to justify violation of international laws
against intervention by invoking a low-probability,
hypothetical future ("they might have gone Communist
and that might have tipped the balance of power"). Nor
is it adequate to justify intervention on the moral
imperative of preventing an abstraction like "totalitarian rule," if the conditions for totalitarianism are
unlikely. Even if there is some danger, consistent
moral reasoning requires an explanation of why one does
not intervene in other equally egregious cases of present or potential injustice.

In terms of the arguments developed earlier, one
can protect against spurious consequentialist reasoning
by starting with a strong presumption in favor of
rules, by requiring broad and careful causal analysis
in the calculation of consequences, by preferring to
observe rules where the calculation of consequences
involves large uncertainties, and by developing procedures to ensure impartiality when one concludes that
a departure from normal rules is justified.

Among the negative duties we owe to foreigners is
not to kill them or take away their autonomy. The
prohibitions against military intervention in international law help to reinforce these negative duties.
Thus it makes sense to start with a state-moralist
position with its presumption in favor of nonintervention unless Walzer's rules of disregard apply (e.g.,
genocide, counterintervention, etc.). The cosmopolitan
who contemplates military intervention because of the
severity of the injustices being suffered must consider
both the competing moral claims of autonomy and of the
interstate legal order. Similarly, the realist contem-

73

plating military intervention must weigh the degree of the threat presented to our interests by a potential change in the balance of power against the same competing moral claims. The consequences considered must include the long-term effect on the institutional framework of international law, which not only contributes to interstate order but reinforces important negative moral duties to foreigners.

Even if the severity of the security threat is real or the deprivation of rights is egregious, careful causal analysis is needed to calculate consequences. The prospects of success at reasonable costs in terms of lives and local autonomy must be weighed. Unintended consequences must be estimated. Will it be possible to withdraw quickly? Is it reasonable to believe that proportionality can be maintained once intervention has begun? If the purpose is to replace a government, what is the probability that the successor government will be better? And if the only way to ensure that the government is an improvement is to maintain a presence that approaches imperial rule, will not the costs to local autonomy be disproportionate to the ends sought? Such considerations are analogous to those required by traditional just war theory.\44

Another consideration is the assessment of the probable consequences of not intervening. Are there alternatives? What are their risks and costs? What about responsibility for our past actions? Should we intervene to counter the effects of past intervention, particularly if the net effect is to increase local autonomy over the long run? Similarly, in some instances where a high degree of outside intervention by others exists, to refuse to counterintervene means, in Talleyrand's phrase, that intervention and nonintervention may amount to the same thing. The distinction between acts and omissions may vanish in such instances.

The probability of success is another important consideration derived from just war theory. This is not because success makes everything all right. Quite the contrary. Had Hitler won, he would still have been wrong, but a reasonable prospect of success protects against a disproportion between goals and means leading to immoral, unintended consequences. Vietnam is a case in point. Ironically, in the area of military intervention, too limited a use of force may contribute to immoral consequences. On the other hand, the converse is not true unless one can be sure that an overwhelming

74

force is able to discriminate between civilian and military targets.

All such assessments of consequences are highly problematic. We can never know the full consequences of our actions. The more tenuous or uncertain the causal reasoning about consequences, the more cautious one should be about departing from the rules against intervention. The costs to the system of rules, to local autonomy, and in human lives of a military intervention is likely to be more immediate and certain than the hypothesized benefits and dangers averted. There should be a "clear and present danger" test. When the uncertainties are large and the dangers lie at the end of a long hypothetical causal chain, the presumption in favor of the rules is reinforced.

If, despite such careful analysis, it seems that military intervention is still justified, it is essential to take steps to assure the preservation of impartiality. The higher one goes on the scale of coercion, the greater the presumption should be in favor of multilateral efforts in order to limit the tearing of the fabric of international legal order and to ensure against the dangers of national hubris and egoism when calculations of proportionality are invoked. Multilateral actions, consultation with allies, and public diplomacy in international organizations are all cumbersome, but they help to protect the quality of moral reasoning about competing moral claims once there is a departure from the rules.

Nonmilitary Intervention

The same considerations are true of less coercive degrees of outside involvement in the domestic affairs of other countries. Even when they are not so clearly proscribed by legal rules, there are still difficult tasks to be undertaken in weighing competing moral claims. The presumption in favor of local autonomy still stands, but we may choose to override it when our relatively noncoercive actions are commanded by obligations of Samaritanism, beneficence, responsibility for the effects of our past actions, or by a supererogatory desire to promote justice. We still must consider proportionality and the severity of the situation. For example, in terms of the subsistence rights, are people starving? If so, higher degrees of involvement would be justified than if conditions were not so severe. Similar arguments can be made in relation to arguments based upon political liberty and order. Are the prospects for enhancing political liberty particularly promising? In the absence of outside intervention, is violent disorder highly likely? If so, a higher degree of international involvement may be justified.

A second factor to be considered is the degree of existing transnational interdependence. When there is a high degree of interdependence, we may need to be involved in order to be responsible for the effects of our actions. A new involvement may counter other forms of involvement. In addition, where there is a high degree of interdependence, there is also likely to be a higher degree of leverage and capability to affect a situation. In short, where it is not possible to be uninvolved, as for example in the historical U.S. relationship to Central America, some deliberate outside involvement may be justified to redress the negative effects of other forms of involvement. Indeed, some deliberate involvement can lead to a net increase in overall autonomy.

One can also assess the justifiable degree of relatively noncoercive international involvement in terms of the effects on individual and local autonomy within another country. Some communities may be structured in such a way that large portions of the population that are strongly affected by these decisions are not able to participate in the decision-making process or even significantly affect it. In such instances, a degree of outside involvement that tends to strengthen the weaker parties by promoting devolution, decentralization, or otherwise providing them with resources may actually increase the capability of an indigenous political process to make autonomous trade-offs in a fashion that reflects the wishes of a large portion of the population. Conversely, however, the outside involvement cannot extend to the point that it is the outsider rather than the indigenous people who have the strongest effect on these decisions.

Finally, one must consider procedures to ensure impartiality in balancing competing moral claims even in relatively noncoercive outside involvement. It is all too easy for humans unconsciously to weigh their own interests more heavily when balancing competing moral claims. This is particularly true for outside governments where power politics and idealism often create a complex mix of motives. Thus, it is important that a procedure for making such judgments includes the perspective of the country in which the intervention occurs. This argues for both a high degree of local involvement in decision making and for an explanation of policy judgments that is accessible and acceptable to local audiences. It also suggests the value of involvement of international agencies as a means of protecting against cultural imperialism, conscious or unconscious, in processes of implementation. As with military intervention, while the rules are not absolute, the presumption should be in favor of the negative obligation to respect the autonomy of others, and special care must be taken to preserve impartiality in the consequentialist moral reasoning used to justify outside involvement.

VI
Conclusions

Ethics and foreign policy are inextricably intertwined for Americans. To deplore this fact, as did the mainstream conventional wisdom of post-World War II realism, is to abdicate responsibility for disciplining moral reasoning in this domain. We do not need a new debate between realism and idealism. Quite the contrary, we need to marry realist insights about the dangerous consequences of too simple an application of the rules of individual moral behavior in the complex domain of international politics with insights about the limited but real moral obligations to foreigners that arise from the effects of interdependence and the admission of a (weak) sense of common humanity.

I have argued that one must give balanced consideration to various kinds of moral claims about obligations to foreigners and the duties of citizens and statesmen, because no simple moral theory is adequate in the domain of international politics. Politics among nations without a common sovereign is different from life in a well-ordered domestic polity. In the absence of strong institutions and in the absence of a common culture upon which such institutions could be built at this point in history, international politics remains a domain of self-help in which force is the ultimate arbiter. In a world where force plays a significant role, balancing power to maintain order must often take priority over questions of individual justice. Failure to preserve order can lead to disastrously immoral consequences.

But I have shown that the fact that international politics is a difficult domain for moral reasoning does not preclude all considerations of justice. Even in our morally imperfect world, a primitive sense of common humanity and the concern for universalizability built into the structure of ethical language give rise to some obligations to foreigners. What we need are not thought experiments based on assumptions about our obligations in an imaginary world of disembodied individuals, but efforts to specify our obligations in our imperfect world of states, and to think about how to develop attitudes and institutions that may permit the evolution of a broader scope for justice in some future international politics. In short, the best answer to the question of what obligation we owe to foreigners must combine the insights of the realist and cosmopolitan approaches.

Similarly, in answering the question about the moral duties of statesmen, we need to avoid the complete double standard of behavior that implies that a statesman can totally avoid normal standards of morality because of the allegedly amoral nature of international politics or the license implied by too simplistic a view of the trustee's role. Quite the contrary, we have seen that total skepticism about ethics in international politics is not justified and that the statesman's role does not provide full exoneration from normal moral standards. While the statesman must be considered as a trustee whose ultimate appeal is to a critical level of institutional utilitarian reasoning, the grounds on which he justifies his transition from normal rules to consequences must be held up to careful scrutiny. Simple consequentialist arguments are not enough.

Finally, in answering the question of how we judge moral arguments in foreign policy, one-dimensional moral reasoning makes it too easy to rationalize what is convenient. And grand appeals to national ideals or ideological motives (democracy, human rights, stopping totalitarianism) can blind one to relevant facts and the two other dimensions of moral choice. All three dimensions -- motives, means, and consequences -- are important, and the task of weighing competing moral claims cannot be solved by application of a simple formula, but must be reasoned in the light of the facts in particular cases. The importance to good moral reasoning of facts and careful causal analysis does not mean that morality is merely the same as prudence. While there is a good deal of overlap between sound prudential and moral reasoning about foreign policy, a moral position includes basic assumptions about impartiality which establish certain minimal obligations to foreigners (e.g., negative duties, responsibility for consequences, Samaritanism) which must be weighed in any moral calculations.

Dealing with multidimensional moral judgments is not easy. The presumptivist approach helps us to avoid sliding too quickly down a convenient and slippery consequentialist slope by requiring a strong burden of proof which places the benefit of doubt in favor of the rules when the facts are highly uncertain. Procedures for protecting impartiality and structures which encourage serious moral reasoning are equally important -- though often inconvenient for statesmen. Approaches, such as just war theory, which combine rules and consequentialism provide a device which can force attention to facts that are relevant to all three moral dimensions. We would have been better served before intervening in Vietnam had we turned to just war theory rather than to the amoral theories of counterinsurgency and limited war popular at the time. In retrospect, those in government who feared to appear soft by raising moral issues might have appeared realistic -- ethical choice is part of American foreign policy; the unrealism is to ignore it. One of the critical tasks for statesmen is to structure situations in advance so that there is occasion for serious moral reasoning. Left until too late, there may often be no choice.

International politics is not like domestic politics, and ethical considerations in foreign policy are more complex than in domestic policy. But they arise. The role of ethics in foreign policy is modest, but it is also inescapable. Neither politics nor morality stops at the water's edge. They just become more complicated. The dangers of simplistic moralism do not justify equally simplistic cynicism. What is required are further efforts to refine the scope and methods of our moral reasoning in this particularly difficult domain.

Notes

1. I am indebted to Sissela Bok, Richard Cooper, Tom Donaldson, Stanley Hoffmann, Stephen Holmes, Carey Joynt, Robert Keohane, John Langan, William Maynes,

Michael Novak, M.J. Peterson, Michael Sandel, and Judith Shklar for their written comments, as well as to many others for oral arguments at meetings convened by the Aspen Institute with the financial support of the Ford Foundation. These views are applied to nuclear issues in my <u>Nuclear Ethics</u> (New York: The Free Press, 1986).

2. Dexter Perkins, "What Is Distinctly American About the Foreign Policy of the United States?" in Glyndon Van Dusen and Richard Wade, eds., <u>Foreign Policy and the American Spirit</u> (Ithaca: Cornell University Press, 1957), pp. 3-15.

3. George Kennan, <u>American Diplomacy</u> (New York: Mentor Books, 1952), p. 82.

4. Irving Kristol, "Toward A Moral Foreign Policy," <u>Wall Street Journal</u>, November 15, 1983.

5. Robert Osgood, <u>Ideals and Self-Interest in America's Foreign Relations</u> (Chicago: University of Press, 1953), p. 21.

6. R.M. Hare, <u>Moral Thinking</u> (Oxford: Clarendon Press, 1981), chap. 10. See also J.L. Mackie, <u>Ethics</u> (Harmondsworth: Penguin, 1977), p. 192.

7. Paul Ramsey, "Force and Political Responsibility," in Ernest W. Lefever, ed., <u>Ethics and World Politics</u> (Baltimore: Johns Hopkins University Press, 1972), p. 72.

8. Michael Walzer, <u>Just and Unjust Wars</u> (New York: Basic Books, 1977), pp. 82-85.

9. Arnold Wolfers, <u>Discord and Collaboration</u> (Baltimore: Johns Hopkins University Press, 1962), chap. 4.

10. See Reinhold Niebuhr, <u>Moral Man and Immoral Society</u> (New York: Scribner, 1932); and the criticism in J.E. Hare and Carey B. Joynt, <u>Ethics and International Affairs</u> (New York: Saint Martins Press, 1982), pp. 27-33.

11. W.D. Hudson, <u>A Century of Moral Philosophy</u> (Guilford: Lutterworth Press, 1980); Bernard Williams, <u>Morality</u> (New York: Harper & Row, 1972); and R.M. Hare, <u>Moral Thinking</u>, op. cit., chap. 10.

12. William Frankena, <u>Ethics</u> (Englewood Cliffs:

Prentice Hall, 1973), pp. 63ff.

13. J.J.C. Smart and Bernard Williams, _Utilitarianism: For and Against_ (Cambridge: Cambridge University Press, 1973), pp. 98ff.

14. On remorse versus regret, see R.M. Hare, _Moral Thinking_, op. cit., pp. 28-29.

15. I am indebted to Russell Hardin for the term "institutional utilitarianism," which avoids some of the reductio ad absurdim objections that can be levelled against "rule utilitarianism."

16. Sissela Bok, _Lying: Moral Choice in Public and Private Life_ (New York: Random House, 1978), chap. 7.

17. See Jonathan Glover, _Causing Death and Saving Lives_ (Harmondsworth: Penguin, 1977), chaps. 6, 7.

18. Norman Podhoretz, _Why We Were in Vietnam_ (New York: Simon and Schuster, 1982).

19. This section draws on work done jointly with Richard N. Cooper for the 25th Anniversary Conference of the Harvard Center for International Affairs.

20. Peter A. French, "Morally Blaming Whole Populations," in Virginia Held et al., eds., _Philosophy, Morality and International Affairs_ (New York: Oxford University Press, 1974), pp. 266-86. See also Dennis Thompson, "Moral Responsibility of Public Officials," _American Political Science Review_ 74, December 1980, pp. 905-15.

21. Arthur Schlesinger, Jr., "National Interests and Moral Absolutes," in Ernest W. Lefever, ed., _Ethics and World Politics_ (Baltimore: Johns Hopkins University Press, 1972), p. 22.

22. Reinhold Niebuhr, _Moral Man and Immoral Society_, op. cit. See also Robert Osgood and Robert Tucker, _Force, Order, and Justice_ (Baltimore: Johns Hopkins University Press, 1967), p. 281.

23. Stanley Hoffmann, _Duties Beyond Borders_ (Syracuse: Syracuse University Press, 1981), pp. 17ff.

24. Arnold Wolfers, _Discord and Collaboration_, op. cit., chap. 4. See also Stanley Hoffmann, _Duties Beyond Borders_, op. cit., pp. 14-17.

25. Charles Beitz, "Bounded Morality," _International Organization_ 33, Summer 1979, pp. 405-24.

26. Hans J. Morgenthau, _Politics Among Nations_ (New York: Alfred A. Knopf, 1955), p. 9.

27. John Rawls, _A Theory of Justice_ (Cambridge: Harvard University Press, 1971), p. 378.

28. Michael Walzer, "The Moral Standing of States," _Philosophy and Public Affairs_ 9:3, Spring 1980, p. 211.

29. Stanley French and Andres Gutman, "The Principle of National Self-Determination," in Virginia Held et al., eds., _Philosophy, Morality and International Affairs_ (New York: Oxford University Press, 1974), pp. 138-54.

30. Gerald Doppelt, "Statism Without Foundations," _Philosophy and Public Affairs_ 9:4, Summer 1980, pp. 401-3.

31. David Luban, "The Romance of the Nation State," _Philosophy and Public Affairs_ 9:4, Summer 1980, p. 392. See also Robert Amdur, "Rawls' Theory of Justice: Domestic and International Perspectives," _World Politics_, April 1977, pp. 438-61.

32. Stanley Hoffmann, _Duties Beyond Borders_, op. cit., p. 155.

33. For a challenge of this distinction, see Peter Singer, _Practical Ethics_ (Cambridge: Cambridge University Press, 1979).

34. Michael Walzer, "The Distribution of Membership," in Peter G. Brown and Henry Shue, eds., _Boundaries_ (Totowa, NJ: Rowman and Littlefield, 1981), p. 1.

35. See, for example, Charles Beitz, "Cosmopolitan Ideals and National Sentiment," _The Journal of Philosophy_ LXXX:10, October 1983, pp. 591-600; and Henry Shue, "The Burdens of Justice," _The Journal of Philosophy_ LXXX:10, October 1983, pp. 600-8.

36. See the critique of Rawls in Michael J. Sandel, _Liberalism and the Limits of Justice_ (Cambridge: Cambridge University Press, 1982).

37. Gerard Elfstrom, "On Dilemmas of Interven-

tion," _Ethics_ 93:4., July 1983, p. 711.

38. For examples, see Robert O. Keohane and Joseph S. Nye, "Transgovernmental Relations and International Organizations," _World_ _Politics_ XXVII:1, October 1974, pp. 39-63.

39. Richard Cooper, "A New International Economic Order for Mutual Gain," _Foreign_ _Policy_ 26, Spring 1977, pp. 81ff.

40. Michael Walzer, "The Distribution of Membership," op. cit., p. 3.

41. Gerard Elfstrom, "On Dilemmas of Intervention," op. cit., p. 719.

42. Jonathan Glover, _Causing_ _Death_ _and_ _Saving_ _Lives_, op. cit., p. 74.

43. R.J. Vincent, _Nonintervention_ _and_ _International_ _Order_ (Princeton: Princeton University Press, 1974), p. 13.

44. See the discussion of just war and intervention in J.E. Hare and Carey B. Joynt, _Ethics_ _and_ _International_ _Affairs_, op. cit., chaps. 3, 7.

Chapter 3

CAN STATES BE MORAL?
INTERNATIONAL MORALITY AND THE COMPLIANCE PROBLEM\1

Brian Barry

It is quite a mistake to suppose that real
dishonesty is at all common. The number of
rogues is about equal to the number of men who
act honestly; and it is very small. The great
majority would sooner behave honestly than
not. The reason why they do not give way to
this natural preference for humanity is that
they are afraid that others will not; and the
others do not because they are afraid that
they will not. Thus it comes about that, while
behaviour which looks dishonest is fairly
common, sincere dishonesty is about as rare as
the courage to evoke good faith in your neigh-
bours by showing that you trust them.\2

I
Common Sense, Utilitarianism,
and International Morality:
The Domestic Analogy

In the last few years I have presented a number of
papers to various audiences on issues of international
morality and have also conducted several courses for
college students and professionals. From experience, I
can safely make the generalization that in any such
context sooner or later (and usually sooner) the objection will come up that this is merely flailing the air.
For, it is said, the conduct of states is not an appropriate subject for moral evaluation or censure. Of
course, some people will suggest that there is no point
in moral discourse in any sphere of life. This kind of
universal moral skepticism raises deep philosophical
issues which would be well worth discussing on some
other occasion. But for the present purpose I wish to
direct my attention to those who do not deny the appropriateness of moral appraisal in ordinary life but who

do nevertheless hold that it is inappropriate in the international arena.

Why might someone make a distinction along these lines? Two reasons seem to be most commonly put forward for skepticism specifically about international morality. The first is that governments almost invariably pursue the national interest whenever it conflicts with the interests of other countries, and in any case, they have a duty to their citizens to do so. The second reason has been expressed as follows by Terry Nardin (although this is not his own view):

> The international system is not to any appreciable extent a society united by common rules, but simply an aggregate of separate societies each pursuing its own purposes, and linked with one another in ways that are essentially ad hoc, unstable, and transitory. The conduct of each state may in fact be rule-governed, in the sense that each observes rules of its own choosing. But because the decisions of each are governed by different rules, the separate states cannot be said to be members of a single society of states united by common rules of conduct -- rules whose authority is acknowledged by all states.\3

The reasoning that connects the two is, roughly speaking, that if each state pursues its own national interest, a given state will comply with common rules only to the extent that it can be made to be in that state's interest to comply. But in the absence of "a common Power to keep them all in awe," as Hobbes put it,\4 there is no way of ensuring that most states will comply most of the time with any set of rules. So there are not, in any real sense, any rules governing international conduct.

Before going any further, it is worth observing that both of these points have analogues in common-sense morality as it operates within societies. This would cut no ice if we were dealing with a universal moral skeptic. But since we are not, this is a potentially significant finding. Thus, in common-sense morality it is generally held to be acceptable (and indeed under some conditions praiseworthy) for different people to have different "moral aims."\5 That is, we do not believe there is a single good that all have an equal moral obligation to pursue. Instead we be-

lieve, for example, that it is right for a given individual to pay more attention (or, give more weight) to
the interests of persons to whom he or she is related
by ties of family or other association and commitment
than to the interests of others. (This includes giving
more weight to one's own interests than to those of
randomly selected others.)

In common-sense morality it is generally thought
that there is a class of social norms to which adherence is morally obligatory only if enough other people
adhere to them. With a practice that is collectively
beneficial, provided that it is generally observed (the
standard philosophical example is refraining from wearing a path by taking a short cut across a lawn), the
presumption is that fairness requires each person to
observe it on the condition that enough others do to
achieve the object served by the norm. On the other
hand, if the norm is not efficacious in providing
people with a reason that they accept (and act on) for
eschewing their private, antisocial interests then the
moral obligation on each one to observe the norm tends
to evaporate.

I am being deliberately vague about the form of
the relation between compliance by others and the obligation to conform to a rule oneself because I believe
that relation will vary according to the details of the
case. In some instances, just one bit of noncompliance
releases everyone else from an obligation to refrain
from doing what the norm prohibits. If one neighbor
shatters the peace of the neighborhood by using a power
mower early on a Sunday morning, it does not make much
difference if others do so too. But in other instances,
much of the collective benefit may be achieved even
with a substantial amount of noncompliance.\6 If only
three-quarters of householders in a city center comply
with a rule against burning garden refuse, the air may
be much less dirty than if there were no restraint, and
this might plausibly be thought to generate an obligation of fairness to comply, albeit a weaker one than if
compliance were closer to being universal.

I should emphasize that the structure of common-
sense morality is not utilitarian, since this may not
be apparent from these examples. The question is not
simply which act -- compliance or noncompliance --
would have the most net beneficial consequences, given
what all the others are doing. In some cases, however,
the dictates of common sense will coincide with those
of utilitarianism. If, for example, so many people have

already walked across the grass that a path of completely bare earth has been created, utilitarianism and
common sense would agree that there is no moral obligation on anyone to refrain from taking the short cut.
This can be called the "threshold effect." Here utilitarianism and common sense unite in dissenting from the
view held by some philosophers that, when some threshold has been passed, the right thing to do is unaffect-
ed by the absence of beneficial consequences.

Such a view is characteristically arrived at by
taking a framework for moral decision making that is
not unreasonable in itself, but then applying it too
immediately and simplistically, without recognizing the
need for institutional mediation between the ultimate
criterion and the demands of morality in concrete situations. One way this happens is that Kant's formulation
of the categorical imperative -- that one must be able
to will the maxim of one's action as a universal law --
is misapplied. (One can with perfect consistency will
universal adoption of the maxim that one walks across
the grass whenever, because of the actions of others,
there is no point in not doing so.) Another route which
can lead to the same conclusion is to take ideal rule
utilitarianism -- the doctrine that the best set of
rules is that which would have the best consequences if
it enjoyed general adherence -- and then to say that
the right thing to do in any actual situation is to act
on the rules of ideal morality so understood, whether
or not others either recognize or act on these rules.

According to common sense it is mere quixotry to
feel obliged to do something that is in fact pointless
simply because it would have a point in some counter-
factual state of the world. And I think the common-
sense position will withstand any amount of philosophical scrutiny. There are some who claim to find an
argument against utilitarianism (that is, act utilitarianism, not the curious form of ideal rule utilitarianism mentioned above) in that it gets what they regard
as the "wrong answer" in threshold cases. They are, in
my view, kicking the ball through their own goal; what
they regard as an argument is actually a <u>reductio</u> <u>ad</u>
<u>absurdum</u>.

Common-sense morality is thus not unconcerned with
beneficial overall consequences in evaluating actions.
But it differs from utilitarianism in that it is not
concerned solely with the production of beneficial
overall consequences. The prescriptions of the two will
normally coincide in threshold cases, but even then the

way in which they reach their shared conclusions is not quite the same. For utilitarianism the decisive point -- and the only one that could possibly matter -- is simply that, given that others have already worn a path in the grass, there is no collective benefit gained from walking around the edge that can be set against the benefit the agent himself gains from cutting across. There is obviously a net overall benefit from cutting across. The line taken by common-sense morality includes all of the above considerations, but it does not stop there. It goes on to say that there is no collective benefit that others can help provide: if other people go to the trouble of walking around, they are merely taking gratuitous exercise. Since there is no collective benefit from which one gains as a result of the forbearances of others, there can be no unfairness in not contributing to it oneself, and this is the real reason why it is morally permissible to walk across the grass. To introduce a new metaphor, one cannot properly be accused of being a free rider if the train never leaves the station.

In a threshold case, this extra loop is trivial because there is no way in which one can help provide any collective benefit by one's own action, even if one wishes to. This is precisely the reason that the conclusion of common-sense morality coincides with that of utilitarianism. Fairness does not enter in because the issue of fairness is preempted by the recognition that the "cooperative" move does not in fact do anybody any good. We might say that whereas the utilitarian conclusion is determined by its own single criterion, the more complex common-sense conclusion is overdetermined.

To see that there really is a difference between the practical implications of common sense and those of utilitarianism, we need only look at a non-threshold case. It does not have to be one in which the net benefit from an agent's contributing to a public good is invariant with respect to the number of others who contribute. That is the simplest case. But the general form of the relation we require is simply that, even when few other people are contributing, there is still a net benefit to be gained from any given agent's contribution (after subtracting the cost to the agent of producing the increment of collective benefit enjoyed by all). Such cases are quite common in real life, though it will often be hard to establish the amount of collective gain from a single contribution in order to compare it to the cost of that contribution to the actor. But Parfit is correct in calling it a "mistake in moral mathematics" to suppose that a small effect diffused over a large number of people is not a real effect; it may be significant in determining the moral quality of the act that brings it about.\7

Returning to the example of air pollution, it is possible that there is no upper threshold in many cases. Even if everyone living in the city center except me is burning soft coal, it is quite possible that there is still a net benefit from my refraining from doing so; the overall reduction in air pollution outweighs the cost to me of using some alternative means of heating. On the utilitarian criterion, this is enough to generate the conclusion that I have a moral obligation to refrain from adding my smoke to the pall already created by the others. But, according to the dictates of common-sense morality, I have no such obligation. The failure of the others to contribute to the collective good -- clean air -- releases me from the moral obligation to do so myself. I cannot reasonably be accused of behaving unfairly if I fail to act on a norm that so many others who are similarly situated are failing to act on.

Returning to the "free rider" metaphor, the point is not (as it was before) that there is nothing I can do by myself to make the train go, but simply that I am not riding at the expense of others. In this case, my fare would suffice to move the train a minute fraction of an inch, but then the others would be free riding at my expense. I have no obligation to give them a free -- even if extremely short -- ride.

Common-sense morality is capable of discriminating between different kinds of moral judgment. Thus, although in the situation described it would not be morally obligatory to refrain from burning soft coal, it would certainly be admirable. Anyone who did so would be exhibiting the virtue of beneficence. Common-sense morality differs from utilitarianism in that it denies that what does the most good is in general obligatory and that it recognizes other virtues besides beneficence, such as that of behaving justly toward others.

For utilitarianism, then, the relevance of what other people are doing is purely contingent: we need to know what they are doing simply because it may make a difference to the net benefit that a single act of contribution would bring. But once the presence of a net benefit has been established, there is an obliga-

90

tion to contribute, regardless of how few others are contributing. Indeed, we can imagine a case, such as traffic congestion, in which the fewer who contribute by refraining from driving, the larger the net benefit from a single act of contribution. Then, by the utilitarian criterion, the obligation to contribute becomes more stringent the smaller the proportion of others who contribute. By common-sense morality, however, the obligation of fair play would always diminish as the number of contributors diminished. Nonetheless, if a single contribution would do a lot of good, and particularly if it would alleviate suffering or destitution, then it might be required by common-sense morality as an obligation of humanity. Normally, however, benefits that fit this description are not collective in character.

II
National Interest and Moral Norms:
The Compliance Problem

So far I have suggested that the two grounds most often advanced for denying that international affairs can be subjected to moral appraisal have clear analogues in what common-sense morality holds about morality within societies. Corresponding to the claim that political leaders have a right, perhaps even a duty, to pursue the national interest is the notion that people have their own legitimately differing "moral ends," which will permit or possibly even require them to give more weight to their own interests and to those of people connected to them than they give to the interests of others. And, corresponding to the claim that the lack of assurance that other states will comply with international norms releases states from any obligation to observe them, there is in common-sense morality a complex connection between the degree of compliance by others and the obligation to conform to a norm oneself.

My purpose in pointing out these connections is simply to examine the following question: If these two features of common-sense morality are not usually thought to cause it to self-destruct as a source of moral obligations and other moral phenomena (and I believe that in fact they do not), why should it be supposed that their international analogues must have such devastating implications for the possibility of moral appraisal in international affairs?

Let us take up in turn the two alleged grounds for the amorality of the international order. The relevant implication for states of the notion of different "moral ends" is that governments have some duties -- possibly quite extensive -- toward their own citizens that they do not owe to citizens of other countries. (Those who prefer to formulate issues of political obligation in lateral rather than hierarchical terms could express this by saying that citizens of a single country owe one another things that they do not owe citizens of other countries.) But this does not mean that anything goes. Generally speaking, my special obligation to my family does not legitimate lying, stealing, cheating, or killing on their behalf. The special obligation is set in a context of constraints on the morally acceptable means of advancing my moral ends.

It would seem that countries are in a position exactly analogous to this. We can easily allow that a government has duties to its own citizens that it does not owe to people in other countries. But again, this does not mean that the government has moral license to do anything to advance the national interest without regard to possible violation of the legitimate interests of others. (Is there anything magical, after all, about one particular grouping -- a nation-state -- that can dissolve all wider moral considerations? Why should this one level of association be exempted from moral constraints that apply to all others?)

To the extent that we can talk about a common international morality, it takes the form of a belief that there are morally binding constraints on how governments can pursue their national interest. This raises the second alleged ground for the amorality of the international order: How can there be morally binding constraints without a centralized agency of enforcement? In the Hobbesian "condition of mere Nature" which characterizes the relations of states with one another, would not anyone adhering to moral constraints "but betray himself to his enemy"? "For he that would be modest, and tractable, and perform all he promises, in such time, and place, where no man else should do so, should but make himself a prey to others, and secure his own certain ruine."\8

The simple answer, which is not complete but is still worth giving, is that moral norms that govern everyday life in a society are generally not backed by legal sanctions either but are nonetheless quite broadly effective in restraining conduct. The response will inevitably come that this evades the issue because the security provided by legal enforcement provides the essential underpinnings of a whole system of mutual constraints within a society. This argument undeniably has an element of truth. International relations, on the other hand, are fundamentally conditioned by the absence of an agency capable of enforcing compliance. A state normally commands a monopoly on the use of violence within its territory, whereas international law and morality permit the waging of war under certain conditions. However, the notion that in the absence of a core of centrally enforced norms there can be no others that are effective is simply erroneous. Huge numbers of international transactions take place every day on the basis of norms that the parties rely on and, in fact, adhere to -- some codified into international law and others developed through custom.

It is true that much of the compliance with these norms can be accounted for by the rational pursuit of interest. It is to a state's advantage to not be excluded from the system of diplomatic relations, to have a reputation as a reliable trading partner, and so on. Hobbes, who is often regarded as an authority by the realists, deduced from the postulate of survival that one should "seek peace" in the state of nature. He drew up a long list of prescriptions -- "laws of nature" -- that should be acted upon as long as doing so is compatible with safety. "He that having sufficient Security, that others shall observe the same Lawes towards him, observes them not himself, seeketh not Peace, but War; & consequently the destruction of his Nature by Violence."\9

In practice, states can often follow the (admittedly quite undemanding) prescriptions of positive international morality without putting their security at risk in the slightest. It is equally true that much of the time there are self-interested motives for sticking to the prescriptions of common-sense morality in everyday life. And ordinary experience shows that to the extent that others observe the norms, we feel an obligation to do so too. Perhaps the truth is that most of the time we do not inquire too minutely into the reasons for doing what is required. We recognize the general advantageousness of the system and accept its authority in guiding our actions. States are, I would suggest, not very different in this respect. Their standard operating procedures are to adhere to the appropriate international norms; it would actually be unworkable to have to determine on every occasion where the exact balance of long-term and overall interests lies before taking action.

I have conceded, however, that because common international morality does not ask a lot, the question of reasons for adhering to it is not a very pressing one. Nardin has summed it up as follows:

> The moral element in international law is to be found in those general principles of inter- national association that constitute customary international law, and above all in the most fundamental of those principles, such as the ones specifying the rights of independence, legal equality, and self-defense, and the duties to observe treaties, to respect the immunity of ambassadors, to refrain from ag- gression, to conduct hostilities in war in accordance with the laws of war, to respect human rights, and to cooperate in the peaceful settlement of disputes.\10

When we look at economic affairs, what is striking is the absence of any international system comparable to that within nations to tax those who can afford it to provide assistance to those who would otherwise be destitute. This does not mean that there is no mecha- nism for international redistribution; the World Bank does after all make loans on favorable terms to poor countries. But these are discretionary and, in any case, do not represent a sizable transfer. The domestic analogue would be closer to a system of soft loans from the government to small businesses than to a welfare system. Here, no doubt, the absence of coercion makes itself strongly felt. If contributions to government coffers were raised by voluntary subscription, even tax rates of ten percent would be regarded as visionary and utopian, as they are in the international context. We would hear that it asks far too much of human nature for the wealthy to tithe themselves to benefit the poor. The affluent countries are committed in principle to give 0.7 percent of gross national product as offi- cial aid, but even that rate greatly exceeds the amount almost any country actually provides.

III
A "Full Compliance" Theory of Morality

Is this an inevitable consequence of the lack of an international sovereign? The best way to approach this question is indirectly. Let us first ask what the ideal would be if we were to ignore the problem of compliance and then see what adaptations would be required. We must know our aim before we can tell how far short of the target we are bound to fall.

What exactly do we mean by "ideal morality"? Derek Parfit, who makes heavy use of the notion, defines an "ideal act theory" as one that "says what we should all try to do, simply on the assumptions that we all try, and all succeed." This is not quite right, because ideal morality should not include prescriptions to attempt things that we have good reason to believe people, or collectivities such as states, could not succeed in doing if they tried. We are interested here in utopian thinking not science fiction. In constructing a "full compliance" theory of morality,\12 we should look for one that abstracts from what I have called the "compliance problem." This is the problem that people may not act on the prescriptions embodied in a normative system that covers them, even though they could do so perfectly well if they chose. We normally focus on the prospect that people will fail to comply because prescriptions of morality ask them to act in some way that runs contrary to (what they perceive as) their self-interest. But we must also allow for the prospect that people may simply not accept as valid the particular set of prescriptions with which we are concerned.

Since many people are familiar with the concept of "ideal theory" as introduced by John Rawls in <u>A Theory of Justice</u>, it may avoid confusion if I discuss the ways in which my notion of ideal theory agrees with or departs from his. The point of similarity is that Rawls equates ideal theory with what he calls "strict compliance theory,"\13 by which he means a theory of justice constructed on the assumption that "the parties can depend on one another to conform to them."\14 But my conception of ideal theory diverges sharply from that of Rawls in an important way.

In constructing an ideal theory we must address what Rawls calls "the strains of commitment." By this he means that people may find it difficult or impossi-

ble to adhere to some sets of principles.\15 This might
be interpreted as being equivalent to my demand for
utopia rather than science fiction: we do not want
principles that require people to do what is impossible
or even difficult if this implies that people are
liable to fail if they try. But this is not what Rawls
has in mind.

Rawls says that even when designing an ideal theory, we should throw out "principles which may have
consequences so extreme that [people] could not accept
them in practice." And his example of an "extreme"
principle is the utilitarian principle that people
should act to maximize overall well-being. For this
requires some people "to accept lower prospects of life
for the sake of others." (By lower prospects Rawls
presumably means lower than the prospects under some
alternative principle.) Thus, the utilitarian principle
as a basis for a social ethic "is threatened with
instability unless sympathy and benevolence can be
widely and intensively cultivated." Without a word of
discussion, Rawls assumes that this cannot be done, and
immediately concludes that we should "reject the principle of utility."\16

This cavalier disposition of an important and
difficult psychological question illustrates precisely
what is wrong with Rawls's conception of ideal theory.
By incorporating the problem of compliance (as I have
defined it) under the description of "the strains of
commitment," Rawls moves too fast in the direction of
practicality, while at the same time stopping short of
it. His "ideal theory" is an unsatisfactory hybrid of
ideal and practical considerations -- and is neither
really ideal nor really practical.

The theory makes large concessions (perhaps too
large) to the fact that people may not be willing to do
things that are perfectly within their power but which
would require them to make sacrifices. At the same
time, the theory assumes that, provided some threshold
of "non-demandingness" is passed -- Rawls supposes that
his own theory passes this threshold -- we can assume
absolute and invariable compliance with the dictates of
the theory. It is hard to know what to do with such a
theory. It seems better to start from an ideal uncon-
taminated by the compliance problem and then, moving
away from that point, to introduce all the problems of
compliance in their awful variety and complexity.

In thinking about the dimensions of the compliance

96

problem, there are two ways in which an ideal theory
may run into difficulties with compliance. These two
ways do not invariably go together and there is some
reason to believe that they tend to be inversely related.\17 First, an ideal theory of morality may run
into practical difficulties because it is excessively
liable to noncompliance. Second, it may run into difficulties if it is excessively vulnerable to noncompliance.

Other things being equal, a rule will be less
liable to noncompliance the less conformity with it
entails a conflict with some strong desire, the more
readily noncompliance can be monitored by others, and
the more incentive others have to react to noncompliance in a way that reduces or eliminates the advantage
gained. Other things being equal, a rule will be less
vulnerable to noncompliance the less any level of noncompliance affects the value of the rule. In particular, it is important that the point of the rule -- the
ends that justify it -- not be frustrated by a small
number of cases of noncompliance.

IV
Ideal Morality
and International Economic Distribution

I shall return to noncompliance later. For now let me
relax the constraint imposed by problems of compliance
and ask what an ideal set of international norms would
look like, focusing particularly on the question of
international economic distribution.

There is an influential view, put forward by John
Rawls in A Theory of Justice, among others, that distributive justice can be predicated only on relations
within a society, where a society is understood as a
scheme for mutual advantage through joint participation
in cooperative undertakings. The idea is that distributive justice concerns the distribution of gains from
social cooperation. This seems mistaken if it is seen
as setting the limits of distributive justice.

If one country builds tall smokestacks and pumps
sulphur into the atmosphere which descends on another
country downwind in the form of acid rain, then it has
injured the other and, as a matter of justice, should
either clean up its industry or compensate the other

97

country. There need be no reciprocal advantage or even
any other form of relationship between the two. Not all
economic value is created by the cooperative effort
that goes into it; production requires a production
site, capital, and usually raw materials. The notion
that claims of justice can arise only among those
engaging in a cooperative enterprise puts things back-
wards. Before cooperation can occur, distributive questions must have already been answered -- for good or
bad -- about rights over land, resources, and other advantages that would-be cooperators did not themselves
create. As a matter of ideal morality, the answer
currently accepted in the international community --
that each state has an absolute right to everything
within, under, over, and extending two hundred miles
beyond its national boundary -- is a rotten one. But
the present point is simply that an answer must be
given to these distributive questions, and that that
answer will establish a global distribution of some
kind among countries that need have no cooperative
relations at all.

     The insistence on cooperation as a condition of
morality stems from a conception of morality as a
scheme of mutual advantage from mutual restraint. This,
however, introduces the compliance issue too soon and
too strongly. It provides a self-interested motive for
compliance with moral norms by making the content of
moral norms entirely coincident with what a sophisticated calculation of self-interest would require.

     There is an alternative conception of morality
that can be found in Rawls, sitting uneasily alongside
the one discussed above -- one which has been put
forward most clearly by Thomas Scanlon,\18 although it
was anticipated by, for example, David Hume and Adam
Smith. According to this tradition of thought, there is
a strong connection between morality and impartiality.
A moral position is one that can be accepted from any
viewpoint. It is not enough for me to say, "This arrangement suits me." The arrangement must be capable of
being defended to all those affected; if any other
person affected could not reasonably be expected to
accept it in the absence of coercion, then the arrangement cannot be morally justified. I have already pointed out that much of the time there are good reasons of
self-interest for doing what the moral norms of one's
society require. According to this alternative conception of morality, the primary motive for behaving morally for its own sake is simply "the desire to be able
to justify one's actions to others on grounds they

could not reasonably reject," where the basis for others' reasonable rejection of one's actions is given by _their_ "desire to find principles which others similarly motivated could not reasonably reject."\19

This may appear to be a circular definition of morality and the moral motive because the notion of "reasonableness" already presupposes that people have some moral ideas. I am not sure how Scanlon would reply to this charge, but I believe it ought to be admitted. There are two ways we can avoid giving reasonableness a moral tinge, but both of them mask the central idea of the theory in the process of tidying it up.

One possibility is to impute to the parties purely self-interested motivations, so that each will agree only to whatever will best serve his or her interests. Reasonableness is thus construed as if it corresponded to the "rationality" of game theorists and decision theorists, and indeed, this interpretation of reasonableness would make morality theory a subject for one or the other of those disciplines.

If we set things up so that the parties have conflicting ends (as they usually do in real life) -- i.e., what is optimal for me is rarely optimal for everybody else -- we get a problem for game theory. It seems plausible that there must be some arrangement that is better for everybody than a free-for-all. The problem is to identify the payoffs offered by a free-for-all and then to devise some rule for distributing the gains that can be achieved by moving away from a free-for-all toward this other arrangement. We thus arrive at a theory like that of David Gauthier,\20 behind whom stands the sardonic figure of Hobbes.

If, on the other hand, we eliminate conflicting interests by introducing constraints on the information available to the parties about their respective positions -- a "veil of ignorance," as Rawls calls it -- we get a decision-theoretic problem. Since the veil of ignorance, whatever the precise details of its construction (thick or thin, etc.), gives each party identical information to work with -- information laundered of any clues that would enable them to differentiate among themselves -- they are all faced with the same set of calculations. Hence, we can represent the problem as one presented to a single decision maker. This produces theories such as Harsanyi's derivation of utilitarianism from the maximizing of expected utility\21 or one strand of Rawls's theory of justice, where

99

a conservative, risk-aversive (maximin) rule for making choices under uncertainty is seen as leading to the difference principle, which prescribes that the position of those who are worst off should be raised to as high a level as possible.\22

The other method we could use to purge the notion of reasonableness of any moral content would be to take Scanlon's formula literally and suppose that the parties are solely motivated by the desire to reach agreement. Under this version we would not impute to them any substantive views at all about the acceptability of one outcome over any other. This line of thought would bring the problem of the terms of agreement under yet a third branch of formal theory. It would not be part of game theory because there are no conflicting interests, nor would it come under individual decision theory because it requires the parties to make estimates about each others' decisions. Instead we would look to the work on pure coordination problems pioneered by Thomas Schelling in The Strategy of Conflict\23 -- the sort of problem that arises when two people want to meet in a town without having made prior arrangements, and therefore each tries to decide where he will have the best chance of meeting the other, given the knowledge that the other is trying to make the same decision.\24 The moral theory that arises from this is conventionalism: The content of morality is arbitrary, but it is still binding because it matters that we all act on the same rules, whatever they may be. Morality, in this view, becomes the search for "prominent solutions" (or "Schelling points," as they have come to be known) in situations where some rule is needed.\25

The youthful David Hume, ever on the lookout for paradoxes with which to jolt the world of polite learning into paying him some attention, came close in the Treatise to maintaining that rules governing property are conventional in this way. The operations of the "fancy" -- the disposition of the human mind to make associations between different ideas where there is no connection in reality -- were invoked to explain why the details of the rules about property took the form they did.\26 But by the time he wrote the Enquiry,\27 Hume had modified his position and maintained only that fanciful analogies or associations of ideas might come into play in order to settle the issue between two or more alternative rules that were equally beneficial. This is surely much more plausible. The rule, for example, which assigns the lambs to the owner of the ewe stems not merely from a tendency for the "fancy" to run from the one to the other but also from the rule's convenience and its avoiding the creation of perverse incentives.\28 The rule of the road -- to drive on the right or to drive on the left -- is scarcely the paradigm of a moral rule. Usually it does make a difference what the content of the rule is.

I have spoken of two ways to construe the notion of reasonableness so as to purge it of distinctly moral content. If we assimilate reasonableness to the rational pursuit of self-interest, we get a problem in game theory or in decision theory, depending upon what we do about information conditions. If we press to the limit the idea of seeking an agreement with others who are also seeking one, we get a problem of coordinating expectations. I have mentioned in passing the great implausibility of the second approach. Regarding the first, I shall only say that seeking to transform what was intended as a guide for thinking about morality into a calculus capable of deriving moral conclusions from premises devoid of any moral content seems to me to miss the original point.

The notion of reasonableness is admittedly indefinite, but it is not devoid of content. What we need to do to build up the theory is to specify it further, not substitute some simpler and more tractable notion. Thus, if we say that somebody has made a reasonable offer, we generally mean that it is an offer that the other party would be reasonable in accepting. A reasonable person is one who has a tendency to make -- and accept -- reasonable offers. We will have to tighten this definition if we want to further characterize the range of reasonable offers in some specific situation (and it is likely to be a range rather than a unique position). But even without going further, we can be quite sure that a reasonable offer will not be identified with a rationally maximizing offer, either with full information or behind some kind of veil of ignorance. Nor can we be sure that a reasonable person will not turn out to be a rational maximizer.

I do not now have the fully developed theory in hand, though I hope to in a few years' time. For now I must press on with the problem of this paper. So far I have only pointed at the way in which morality might be understood as that which would be reasonable for all to accept. Let me suggest, without filling in all the steps, how evidence from the real world can be brought to bear in order to establish what this conception of morality dictates for international distribution.

101

As the theory stands, it sets up an ideal decision-making context of uncoerced agreement that is
found only rarely and, it seems safe to say, never in
large groups such as states.\29 Nevertheless, societies approach the ideal to varying degrees, and it is
not mere sentimentalism or unreflective submission to
the local ideology to suggest that the modern, Western
liberal-democratic states are, by comparative and historical standards, relatively high on the criterion of
unforced agreement. With obvious exceptions such as
Northern Ireland, the jails do not contain many political prisoners, and no sizable section of the population
is thoroughly alienated from the society's major institutions. Suppose, then, that we look for invariant
features of these societies. If we find them, can we
not at least say that we have a presumption in favor of
assuming that these features are ones that arise in
conditions of uncoerced agreement? There are two features that are common to all liberal-democratic societies. They may not be equally well-developed in all of
these societies, but there is a positive correlation
between the degree to which these features are present
and the extent of universal, uncoerced consent.

The first feature is this: These countries are all
to some extent market societies, and wherever the operations of the market cause people's incomes to vary
widely from year to year, due to factors outside their
control, the state will suppress or heavily intervene
in the market to mitigate or eliminate these effects.
An obvious and striking example is responses to the
income levels of the agricultural sector. The U.S. --
that bastion of the free market -- no less than the
countries of the European Economic Community (EEC), has
an elaborate system of quotas, subsidies, and price
supports to cushion farmers from the rigors of the
market.

The second invariant feature of these countries is
that they have some kind of system for the relief of
indigence caused by illness or injury, unemployment,
age, or youth. The well-being of those who, for some
reason beyond their control, are unable to maintain
themselves at a certain minimum standard is regarded as
the responsibility of society, with the state collect-
ing the taxes necessary to make the required payments.
That a mechanism of this kind is crucial for the uncoerced acceptance of basic social institutions is evi-
denced by the way such schemes have typically expanded
as suffrage has been extended to new groups further
down the social hierarchy. It is particularly signifi-

cant that in some cases welfare legislation was introduced by a conservative government as a concomitant of
the extension of the franchise precisely in order to
forestall destabilizing demands on the system (Bis-
marck's Germany is the famous example).

When we turn from this domestic intervention and
redistribution to the world economy, we are immediately
struck by the absence of anything remotely comparable
to either feature. Countries with one-crop or one-
mineral economies are at the mercy of the ups and downs
of the international market, with only very spotty
exceptions (e.g., the STABEX scheme for certain primary
commodities operated by the EEC countries and their
former colonial dependencies). There is no scheme for
the systematic transfer of funds from affluent countries to poor ones, although there have been proposals:
the demands of Third World countries for a New International Economic Order center around the attempt to
bring commodity markets under some kind of international control, and proposals for the continuous creation
under the International Monetary Fund of Special Drawing Rights for poor countries might be seen as an
imperfect way of easing the constraints on their economies.

Both lines of initiative have foundered on the
unwillingness of rich countries, led by the U.S., with
Japan, Germany, and lately, Britain in support, to
countenance any steps toward a new deal for the poor
countries. It seems clear that this refusal sticks only
because the rich countries have the power to make it
stick. The poor countries do not accept the reasonableness of the status quo, and neither would we if we were
in their position. I have argued that it is a basic
presupposition of the domestic politics of all countries in which the basic institutions achieve a fair
level of popular consent that people should not face
ruin and destitution as a result of circumstances beyond their control. This presupposition should also
apply in international situations, where people's life
chances are set primarily by their having been born
into a particular social position in a certain country,
and where no plausible amount of personal exertion can
raise the majority of people in a desperately poor
country above poverty.

It is not necessary to argue here the precise
implications of these ideas for the amount and nature
of international redistribution that is called for as a
matter of ideal morality. I shall assume, however, that

it is very much larger than the current level of transfers, including the maximum of one percent of GNP currently given by any of the relatively wealthy countries. There must be practical limits on what the poorer countries can absorb, and these might well limit transfers. But the point is that there is no need to settle these questions in order to see the direction in which things ought to go.

V
Conclusions:
International Distributive Justice
and the Compliance Problem

Let us now return to the problem of compliance. The immediate question is: Wherein does the compliance problem actually reside? It would be easy to assume that we need to come up with a scheme that all actors -- in this case states -- find to be in their interest to comply with. But this was not how we approached it in discussing compliance in everyday life. There it was argued that the system of obligations should not be too prone to subversion by noncompliance. The analysis had two components. First, I suggested that liability to noncompliance is a function of the sacrifice demanded and the degree to which noncompliance could be monitored and sanctioned by others. Second, I treated vulnerability to noncompliance as a matter of how serious a threat was posed to the achievement of one's "moral ends" by the noncompliance of others.

If we relate this approach to international affairs, we can conclude, perhaps surprisingly, that the problem of compliance is not a serious impediment to moving toward a much greater degree of international cooperation on economic matters and a greater international redistribution of income. Looking first at vulnerability, it seems clear that no government's moral ends would be gravely jeopardized if it cooperated in an international scheme (say, that proposed in the Law of the Sea Convention) with which there was some noncompliance. The state can cease to comply or pull out if enough others do so, and in the meantime, the relative disadvantage from complying where others do not is unlikely to be of disastrous proportions. Similarly, for countries that pay their share in some redistributive arrangement (say, a percentage of GNP into some international fund), it is irritating but not a major setback to their interests if some countries pay less than their share. We might say that the self-sufficiency of states, in comparison with individuals, has the implication that norms for states are generally less vulnerable to noncompliance than norms for individuals.

Of course, it might be thought that international norms would thereby be particularly liable to noncompliance: Because states are less dependent on the cooperation of others to achieve their moral ends, they have less of a self-interested motive to observe any set of international norms. I have already noted the obvious point that legal sanctions of the centralized kind available within countries do not exist internationally. But that should not blind us to the ways in which states already feel constrained, not by fear of military force directed against them, but simply by the anticipated consequences of violating international norms. The standard case is the reluctance of governments to repudiate loans, even when the regime has changed and the previous regime's loans were misappropriated (as in Nicaragua). A more complex example is that of the EEC, which has a system of taxation and a body of economic regulations but has no sanctions except the disadvantages to a member state of withdrawing or being expelled. In other words, to the extent interdependence exists, it tends to make compliance with the norms defining that interdependence more reliable.

The number of states in the world is small enough that there is some real chance of monitoring compliance with a set of norms, which have been defined as states' obligations, and of making continuation of the arrangement dependent on the achievement of a certain level of compliance. There is nothing in the problem of compliance to prevent governments from looking for ways of implementing the requirements of ideal justice by setting up international schemes. What makes such moves so difficult is not compliance but motivation, and one of my major aims in this paper has been to try to avoid confounding the two. The problem of compliance, as I have presented it, presupposes some willingness to act morally simply for the sake of acting morally, but allows for a legitimate concern about the performance of others. The structure is, in terms of game theory, an assurance game rather than a prisoner's dilemma: so long as others cooperate, cooperation is preferred to noncooperation.

F.M. Cornford, in his classic analysis of academic politics, _Microcosmographia Academica_, remarked that there is only one argument for doing something -- that it is the right thing to do -- and all the rest are arguments for doing nothing.\30 It sounds much more portentious to say that a desirable change is unfeasible because it depends on too many other people doing the right thing than to confess simply that you choose not to make the change because, although it's the right thing to do, by doing it you would incur some cost.

The current celebration of selfishness at home and chauvinism abroad that is apparently electorally popular in both Britain and the U.S. may mean that hypocrisy -- the tribute paid by vice to virtue -- is no longer in fashion. The pure assertion of naked national self-interest may not raise a blush. Unfortunately, in the account of morality I have relied on here there is no way to make logically coercive arguments to get people to behave morally. I cannot, for example, maintain that those who violate the requirements of morality are engaged in some kind of self-contradiction. In the view I have advanced, people must want to behave in a way that can be defended impartially -- in a way that has a chance of being accepted by others without coercion -- for moral motivation to take hold. This is a psychological phenomenon rather than a logical one. Once people have moral motivation, rational argument has a place in helping determine what the concrete requirements of morality are. But people cannot be persuaded into having moral motivation if they lack it. Psychopaths are not necessarily lacking in ratiocinative capacity.

If this is correct, it is natural to ask what conditions predispose people to acquire moral motivation, or, in other words, what conditions arouse the moral motive. I speculate that part of the answer is that the experience of dependence on others is an important predisposing factor. Those who are in a position to control the lives of others commonly become tyrannical. They behave in ways that they would not voluntarily accept if they were on the receiving end. It is in situations where one must gain the cooperation of others in order to achieve one's own ends that one cultivates the habit of looking at things from the other person's point of view and considering what type of conduct the other person might reasonably find acceptable.

As a proposition of speculative moral psychology, the suggestion is that equality of power -- or at least not too extreme an inequality of power -- is

conducive to formation and elicitation of moral motivation. But I do not mean to reinstate the Hobbes/Gauth-
ier conception of morality through a back door; I am
not saying that the reason for acting morally is that,
under conditions of approximately equal power, it is
necessary for the pursuit of one's own advantage to
cooperate with others on terms that can be mutually
accepted as reasonable. The motive for acting morally
remains what I have said: the desire to be able to
justify our conduct. And that desire is more likely to
come to the fore in conditions of approximately equal
power than in conditions of serious inequality.

If there is anything to all of this, the application at the international level is fairly apparent. The
world is a place in which states are unequal in power.
The question is whether to follow Robert Tucker in
rejoicing in this fact, as he did as an adviser to
President Reagan in the 1980 election campaign, and as
he did in his book The Inequality of Nations,\31 or
whether to regard it as regrettable. Clearly, for
anyone who would like to see more moral motivation in
the conduct of international relations, the current
degree of inequality must be seen as a great misfor-
tune. The problem is not only one of global inequalities of power, but one of extreme regional imbalances
of power as well. The Soviet invasion of Afghanistan
and the U.S. invasion of Grenada are paralleled by the
Israeli invasion of Lebanon and the South African invasion of Angola -- all were carried out in the face of
virtually unanimous disapproval from the rest of the
world. There could be no better illustration of Lord
Acton's dictum that all power tends to corrupt than the
arrogant reactions of all four of those governments to
international criticism, as typified by Reagan's reaction to the U.N. vote (108 to 9) condemning the invasion of Grenada: "It didn't upset my breakfast at
all."\32

The best prospect for the future is the hope that
the present extreme inequalities of power among nations
will be reduced. And there is some hope for the long
run. The period since World War II has seen massive
decolonization and the creation of new states that,
though individually weak, are certainly better placed
to defend their interests than they were before independence. The American postwar hegemony has also ended;
it was inevitable in the aftermath of World War II but
was bound to disappear once recovery set in. There
seems to be a long-term trend toward a more interdepen-
dent world.

Unfortunately, however, it looks as if this evolution will be opposed by the superpowers with all the forces at their command: covert destabilization operations, military aid to regional surrogates, and if all else fails, direct intervention. It seems doubtful that this will prevent the equalization of power in the long run. But in a world brimming with nuclear weapons, there is the danger that, adapting Keynes, in the medium run we shall all be dead. Ultimately, if we are to be saved, it will be by political action rather than by political philosophy.

Notes

1. I gratefully acknowledge the contributions made to this paper by my commentators at two meetings at which earlier drafts were read: Robin Lovin at the University of Chicago, and Robert Fullinwider at the University of St. Andrews.

On the first occasion (April 1984), the paper was delivered under the auspices of the Committee on Public Policy under a grant from the Carnegie Council on Ethics and International Affairs (formerly the Council on Religion and International Affairs). On the second occasion (September 1984), it was presented as a part of a Fulbright Anglo-American Colloquium on Ethics and International Affairs held at the University of St. Andrews to mark the opening of the Centre for Philosophy and Public Affairs. I am also grateful for the points made by both audiences and for comments from colleagues at Caltech.

2. F.M. Cornford, Microcosmographia Academica, 6th ed. (London: Bowes and Bowes, 1964).

3. Terry Nardin, Law, Morality, and the Relations of States (Princeton: Princeton University Press, 1983), p. 36.

4. Thomas Hobbes, Leviathan, C.B. Macpherson, ed. (Harmondsworth: Penguin Books, 1981 [1651]), chap. 13, p. 185.

5. Derek Parfit, Reasons and Persons (Oxford: Clarendon Press, 1984). For an earlier, simpler, and clearer exposition, see "Prudence, Morality, and the Prisoner's Dilemma." 1979. Proceedings of the British

Academy 65:539-64, especially 559.

6. Brian Barry and Russell Hardin, eds., Rational Man and Irrational Society? (Beverly Hills: Sage Publications, Inc., 1982), p. 108.

7. Derek Parfit, Reasons and Persons, op. cit., pp. 78-82.

8. Thomas Hobbes, Leviathan, op. cit., chap. 14, p. 196, and chap. 15, p. 215.

9. Ibid., chap. 15., p. 215.

10. Terry Nardin, Law, Morality, and the Relations of States, op. cit., p. 23.

11. Derek Parfit, Reasons and Persons, op. cit., p. 99.

12. Ibid.

13. John Rawls, A Theory of Justice (Cambridge: Harvard University Press, 1971), pp. 8, 9.

14. Ibid., p. 145.

15. Ibid.

16. All quotes in this paragraph are from John Rawls, A Theory of Justice, op. cit., p. 178.

17. I am indebted to Robert Goodin for pointing this out to me.

18. Thomas M. Scanlon, "Contractualism and Utilitarianism," in Amartya Sen and Bernard Williams, eds., Utilitarianism and Beyond (Cambridge: Cambridge University Press, 1982), pp. 103-28.

19. Ibid., pp. 116 and 116 n.12.

20. David Gauthier, Morals by Agreement (New York: Oxford University Press, 1986).

21. John C. Harsanyi, "Cardinal Welfare, Individualistic Ethics, and Interpersonal Comparisons of Utility," Journal of Political Economy 63, 1955, pp. 309-21.

22. See Brian Barry, The Liberal Theory of Justice (Oxford: Clarendon Press, 1973), chap. 9, pp. 87-107;

and Rolf E. Sartorius, Individual Conduct and Social Norms (Encino, CA: Dickenson Publishing Co.), pp. 122-29.

23. Thomas C. Schelling, The Strategy of Conflict (Cambridge: Harvard University Press, 1960), chap. 4, pp. 83-118.

24. See also David Lewis, Convention (Cambridge: Harvard University Press, 1969).

25. Karol Soltan, Causal Theory of Justice (Berkeley: University of California Press, 1987).

26. David Hume, A Treatise of Human Nature, L.A. Selby-Bigge, ed., 2d ed. by P.H. Niddich (Oxford: Clarendon Press, 1978 [1740]), vol. 3, sec. 3, pp. 501-13.

27. David Hume, "An Enquiry Concerning the Principles of Morals," in Enquiries, L.A. Selby-Bigge, ed. 3d ed. by P.H. Niddich (Oxford: Clarendon Press, 1975 [1779]).

28. Ibid., pp. 195-6.

29. It is commonplace in the literature that Rawls's "original position" has some similarities to Habermas's "ideal speech situation." More interesting are their dissimilarities. The spirit of the present enterprise is, I believe, closer to Habermas, who writes: "it is a question of finding arrangements which can ground the presumption that the basic institutions of the society and the basic political decisions would meet with the unforced agreement of all those involved, if they could participate, as free and equal, in discursive will-formation." See Jürgen Habermas, "Legitimation Problems in the Modern State," in Communication and the Evolution of Society, Thomas McCarthy, trans. (Boston: Beacon Press, 1979), p. 186; see also Joshua Cohen and Joel Rogers, On Democracy (Harmondsworth: Penguin Books, 1983), chap. 6, 146-83.

30. F.M. Cornford, Microcosmographia Academia, op. cit., p. 22.

31. See Jeff McMahan, Reagan and the World (London: Pluto Press, 1984), p. 11; Robert Tucker, The Inequality of Nations (New York: Basic Books, 1977).

32. Jeff McMahan, Reagan and the World, op. cit., p. 166.

PART II:

MORAL AND STRATEGIC PROBLEMS

OF NUCLEAR WEAPONS

Chapter 4

MORALITY AND NUCLEAR STRATEGY

Robert Jervis

I
Introduction

In the realist tradition of international politics, questions of morality do not arise. The spirit of this approach was well put by the Athenian response to the Melian plea for justice: "They that have odds of power exact as much as they can, and the weak yield to such conditions as they can get."\1 In the same vein, when some of the nastier activities of the CIA were challenged, Henry Kissinger replied: "Covert action is not to be confused with missionary work." To the realist, morality applies to individuals within domestic society. It neither has nor should have a role in the relations among nations (a normative statement which presumably is based on moral values).

This conclusion is based on the central tenet of realism: because of the lack of a sovereign, international politics is the realm of compulsion not choice, and morality has no role (and perhaps no meaning) where there is no choice. Statesmen must act as they do because the external environment is such a harsh one. Since there is no international government to make or enforce laws, national leaders must think only of the good of their nation. Because others will be behaving in this way, any attempt to take nonnational or supranational interests into account will only weaken the state, if not endanger its security. Under these circumstances, the statesman who eases his conscience by acting morally does so at the cost of crucial national values. Personal morality is thus actually evil, or at least selfish. (Realism's view of the good statesman shows an interesting tension here. Such a person must commit all manner of crimes for his country, but must place his country's well-being above his own and must not be tempted by the desire for personal power, wealth, or salvation. One wonders whether such creatures exist.)

113

Three central questions should be kept in mind, although only the last will be discussed here at much length. First, Is the international environment really so harsh and dominated by compulsion that morally based choice usually threatens national security? Second, To what extent does realism as an ideology not describe the world, but serve other functions and blind both the general public and statesmen themselves to alternative patterns of behavior? The very fact that denying a possible role for morality enables statesmen to shield themselves from a painful kind of criticism should make us suspicious of the validity of the approach. Third, Are decision makers in fact guided by moral principles? They often claim to be. Even such a realist as Henry Kissinger employed terms like obligation and right, which make sense only if morality carries some weight. Today those who normally avoid discussion of ethics defend their favored nuclear strategy in unusual language: according to Secretary of Defense Caspar Weinberger, seeking missile defense "is perhaps the most morally right, and indeed I might say the most noble, of the enterprises in which we are engaged."\2 Of course, statements like these may be public rationalizations. But if so, they imply that ethical considerations are important to some significant audiences.

Indeed, it seems clear that morality, in the broadest sense of the term, does play a major role in setting states' general goals. What societies and decision makers see as desirable -- the worlds they seek to create -- is strongly influenced by the values they hold. In most cases, the security of the state itself, taken by realists as a given, is undertaken because the individuals in power see this as the means to reach other objectives. States have given up at least some degree of sovereignty to bring unifications with co-nationals, greater wealth, or an increased ability to influence world politics.

The "national interest" is such a vague concept that in making it the basis for action, people must be guided by more specific values. Sometimes the role of morality is clear here, as it was in President Carter's concern for human rights. In other cases, morality may be a crucial part of the attempt to build a world based on principles foreign to realism. This was one motivation for the British policy of appeasement of the Nazis, and while the policy was misguided, we should neither fail to appreciate the significance of the attempt nor scorn the considerations involved. Nevile Henderson, the British ambassador to Berlin, argued for basing one's policy toward [Germany] on moral grounds and not allowing oneself to be influenced by consideration about the balance of power or even the Versailles Treaty. We cannot win the battle for the rule of right versus might until our moral position is unassailable. I feel this very strongly about the Sudeten question.\3

But because a concern with anything other than power and security is generally seen as soft-headed if not illegitimate, and because security itself is often incorrectly seen as purely objective,\4 statesmen often try to disguise the motivations of their own conduct. By justifying all that they do in terms of national security, not only can they try to smuggle in base personal or partisan objectives, as President Nixon did, but they can also render obscure to others -- and perhaps to themselves -- some goals and motives more noble than those they profess. Thus I think it is more than hindsight that enables us to say that America fought in Vietnam not because of its security but because of the desire to see Vietnamese society develop with at least a modicum of freedom and decency. Even at the time, it was hard to believe that the fate of South Vietnam would determine the fate of the rest of Asia, let alone that of West Berlin. It was, however, easy to believe -- as indeed turned out to be true -- that a North Vietnamese victory would be disastrous for many of the people of South Vietnam.

II
Morality, Restraint, and Self-Interest

In the rest of this paper I will be concerned about the role morality plays not in setting national goals but in influencing the means that states employ in pursuit of those goals. Of course means and ends often blur into each other, but the distinction still has some utility. Furthermore, I will largely be concerned with morality as a restraint -- that is, with cases of and arguments for doing less harm to others than we could do, even if such restraint is not to our narrow and short-run advantage. This formulation fails to encompass cases in which states act to help others, seek to reduce conflict, or otherwise take positive actions, but it is a standard usage which will serve us adequately here. Furthermore, it should be noted that there can be nonmoral reasons for inflicting less harm on others than would be called for if considerations of power dominated. For example, John Nef argues that during the Middle Ages the construction of more effective firearms was restrained by the dominant sense of esthetics.\5 In addition, the conduct of warfare was influenced by the code of chivalry, and many kinds of weapons and tactics were resisted by soldiers themselves (or, more often, by officers) because they were seen as incompatible with proper, "manly," or soldierly conduct. Indeed, violating these norms may have been seen as endangering the broader structures of the military profession or even the society as a whole. If this was the case, these restraints are rooted in fundamental values and perhaps could be called morally based. But, the derivation of these restraints is very different from those that flow from general principles concerning the way people should act that prohibit injuring certain kinds of people or injuring them in a certain way.

Although morality is not easy to define, we usually take it to mean following values which are not strictly based on self-interest -- for example, doing things to benefit others, suffering so that others will gain (or will not have to suffer), and not taking advantage of others' weaknesses. In international politics the most obvious example would be spending the lives of your own people, and perhaps increasing the chance of losing a war, in order to save the lives of people on the other side, usually civilians. The simplest prescription would be to choose the policy that would minimize the loss of life, irrespective of whether the lives were those of your countrymen or your adversaries. This is not pacifism: killing people on the other side might save the lives of an even larger number of your own nationals. Of course, values other than life can be stressed. To the extent that Secretary of War Henry Stimson decided to spare Kyoto from atomic attack because he valued the Japanese cultural heritage, he was acting on the basis of morality.

Is morality an effective restraint? Perhaps because of the hold of realism, scholars have not carried out sufficient research to venture an answer. Possible cases come to mind, but they would have to be explored in detail before a judgment could be rendered. During the Cuban missile crisis, Robert Kennedy resisted an air strike on the grounds that his brother would not be another Tojo, but whether the operative motive was morality or prudence is not clear. Two general points

116

seem likely to be true. First, the most effective restraints are those which make certain actions literally unthinkable. Obviously, we cannot identify these restraints by the normal method of looking at controversies and contested decisions. Instead, we would have to think of what horrid policies were possible but never contemplated. Because even realist scholars are rarely motivated to follow through with this unpleasant exercise, we do not know if there are many such cases. Some current restraints do, however, seem to be of this kind, including, for example, the civilized treatment of prisoners in most modern wars. It follows that even though questions of morality are rarely raised explicitly in decision-making circles (indeed, to speak of morality is to mark one as "soft" and naive), this does not mean that moral principles are without influence.

Second, moral standards will not be obeyed, or perhaps will not even be seen as moral, if they conflict too much and too clearly with self-interest. For example, as technology has come to favor surprise attack, declarations of war have ceased. We may have regarded December 7, 1941, as a "day of infamy," but states just do not endanger their vital interests for the sake of upholding general principles. The view that Geoffrey Best attributes to the Royal Navy applies more widely: "International law was...not to be observed beyond the point of serious strategic disadvantage."\6 The real question, both normative and empirical, is whether states make sacrifices of lesser significance for the sake of moral principle.

In the same way, high conflict, especially war, tends to erode moral restraints. Available capabilities tend to be used, breaking through limits which seemed well-established during peacetime. In 1914 none of the combatants thought they would soon be bombing civilians and sinking ships without warning. In 1911 Corbett said: "No power will incur the odium of sinking a prize with all hands," and no one disagreed.\7 While revulsion against unrestricted submarine warfare was a major cause of American entry into World War I, the U.S. adopted this policy without a second thought upon its entry in World War II.\8 Similarly, once the British found that they could not hit specific targets, they quickly shifted to area bombing. That the U.S. resisted this owed more to better capabilities than to a stronger morality, as was shown by American adoption of the British approach in the Far East when precision bombardment proved impractical. By 1945 only lip service remained of the old restraint. President Truman noted

in his diary that he had instructed Stimson to make
sure "that military objectives and soldiers and sailors
are the targets [of the atom bombs] and not women and
children."\9 If what now seems like relatively primitive technology could so cripple traditional moral
standards, what can nuclear weapons do?

III
The Nuclear Revolution

Technology changes what is possible; it changes what is
seen as moral by the participants; it may even change
what is moral.\10 Like many other students of the
subject, I have argued that the mutual vulnerability
created by nuclear weapons has brought about a revolution in statecraft.\11 The superpowers can no longer
gain what is called "deterrence by denial," denying
others the ability to harm them by maintaining military
superiority. Instead, they deter by being able to harm
the other side, what is called "deterrence by punishment."\12 Such a radical change affects not only strategy but morality. Just as the use of a prenuclear
conceptual framework -- what Hans Morgenthau called
"conventionalization"\13 -- is misleading in empirical
and policy analysis, so it is also misleading in questions of ethics. But even a better understanding of the
situation will not alter the fact that unless only
those who are guilty are being hurt (an alluring possibility discussed below), punishment always involves
immorality. It is therefore hard to reconcile the basic
facts of the nuclear age with our moral impulses.

Noncombatant Immunity in the Nuclear Age

Because deterrence by punishment is central to nuclear
strategy, and because deterrence by denial cannot work,
noncombatant immunity -- one of the basic principles in
all conceptions of a just war -- is undermined. In what
the American Catholic bishops refer to as a "universally binding principle,"\14 it is argued that it is
acceptable to attack only those engaged in fighting or,
more broadly (and more debatably) those directly engaged in supporting the war effort, for instance, muni-
tions workers.\15 Of course, as more and more civilian
sectors have become involved in the war effort, this
distinction has tended to erode, although various lines
can still be drawn. Indeed, since a nuclear war would

118

be fought with the stock of weapons on hand, it might be possible to return to a fairly strict separation between combatants and noncombatants,\16 although attacking the former without killing many of the latter might be impractical. But the more important point is that the relevance of the distinction between combatants and noncombatants is now questionable. Although some of the rationale for not attacking civilians was that this restraint contributed to proportionality (another basic principle of just war doctrine, discussed below), it also remained as a principle in its own right. Presumably, the reason for this is not that civilians are not involved in the war -- of course they can be -- but that attacking them cannot be reasonably related to the legitimate goals of the war. Killing civilians inflicts pain on them and the state as a whole, but in most of the prenuclear era, it could not determine the outcome of the conflict. The only path to victory was through defeating the other side's army. The principle was thus rooted in the nature of the warfare.

But the nature of warfare, or rather potential warfare, between the superpowers is very different from what it was in the past. The existence of mutual second-strike capability means that gaining a military advantage does not provide the kind of leverage it previously did. Because military advantage cannot release cities from being held hostage to the threat of a second strike, it cannot change the essential vulnerability that characterizes the nuclear era. Military advantage can neither bring victory nor force termination of the war on acceptable terms. Why, then, is it moral to kill soldiers? If they are volunteers, we can say that they have agreed to make themselves targets. But this is not true for the bulk of the Red Army and, given the inequality of income and opportunity in this country, is of only doubtful validity for American armed forces. Why, then, is it moral to kill a nineteen-year-old who is wearing a uniform, but not one who is a civilian? The answer was clear when weakening the other's army protected the state and its values, but this reply is no longer valid. Being able to deny the other side a military advantage -- the cornerstone of the current American doctrine, called the "countervailing strategy" -- no longer protects the state or its values because the society remains hostage to second-strike capabilities.

The principle of civilian immunity is often the basis of the argument that morality requires us to

119

avoid indiscriminate targeting of a population -- the basis of mutual assured destruction (MAD) -- and to return to the older ideas of limiting our fire to the enemy's military. William Stanmeyer has outlined the argument:

> First, the mutual assured destruction strategy is probably immoral, if we grant the usual distinction between "innocent" civilians and "non-innocent" military....Second, the counterforce strategy is moral, since one wills the destruction only of combatants and only permits collateral harm to civilians. A corollary is that limited nuclear is, morally, permissible if one respects the injunction not to will directly the destruction of innocent civilians. Third, an ABM defensive strategy... is undoubtedly moral. Indeed, it is to be preferred.\17

Later in this paper I will discuss two features of this argument: the assumptions about what is practical, and the interesting consistency between people's moral and strategic judgments. Here, I want to argue that this view, while attractive at first glance, fails because it is conventionalized. That is, it assumes that nuclear weapons help reach political goals in the same manner as conventional weapons in the prenuclear era -- through the defeat of the other side's forces. Since this is not true, the morality, like the logic, no longer works. As long as escalation is possible, crises and even the use of force between the superpowers function as generators of risk. A nuclear confrontation is like a game of chicken, in which at least one side must retreat if both are to survive. This means that the outcome is heavily driven by each side's willingness to risk destruction and its perception of the other's willingness to do the same. The threatened targets may well be military, as they were in the past, but pressure is being brought to bear on the other side not through the weakening of its military capability but through the increased destruction and fear of all-out war.\18 This does not make killing civilians moral; it only makes killing them no less moral than killing soldiers. Once a major military clash between the superpowers starts, their soldiers are harmless, like POWs, and civilians cannot claim a privileged position.

A Counter-Argument:
Threatening What the Soviets Value

Perhaps we are being ethnocentric. Many analysts have
argued that while Americans value cities and civilians,
Soviet leaders do not and so the threat to destroy
those targets is pointless. What Soviet rulers value,
this argument goes, are the sinews of Soviet power --
the Red Army, KGB headquarters, party cadres, internal
security forces, and the top leadership itself. Handily
enough, none of these people are "innocent," and so
morality and effectiveness are joined, as they often
were in earlier eras. There is something to be said for
this argument, but it is not without its problems.
First, while it is plausible to believe that the Soviet
leaders value Communist power and not civilian lives,
there is little evidence. It fits with our image of an
evil adversary and so is psychologically satisfying,
but it may not be correct. Would the Russians consider
a war victorious if the party survived but, say, 80
million civilians did not? I find this unlikely, if for
no other reason than because widespread civilian devastation could not but eviscerate Soviet power.

Even if killing civilians is sufficient for deterrence, it may not be required. On what strategic or
moral grounds could one object to threatening to destroy the sources of Soviet power while killing as few
civilians as possible? Indeed, this argument seems very
reasonable, and this is a clue that something is wrong
with it; the existence of mutual second-strike capability has altered so many things about force and foreign
policy that what makes sense within earlier patterns of
thought often is wildly inappropriate now.

There are several problems with such an attempt to
return to a more familiar and comfortable stance. The
most obvious is one of practicality. Even with the
latest technology -- or that expected in the near future -- can we destroy the Soviet power base without
killing enormous numbers of civilians? Of course no one
can be sure until we have tried, but I am doubtful.
First, we cannot destroy most of the Soviet strategic
forces because they are simply too numerous, hardened,
or hard to find. We cannot, in other words, return to a
world of deterrence by denial. Even if we concentrate
on other forms of Soviet power, the practicality of the
strategy is questionable. Many important targets lie
within cities. Small warheads attached to missiles with
terminal guidance <u>might</u> be able to destroy the KGB
headquarters without touching the surrounding build-

ings, but we do not yet have the required weapons. Furthermore, while buildings cannot move, people can. The party cadres and members of the KGB are not likely to be sitting there waiting to be killed, especially after we have told them they are targets. Top leadership can do more than move, they can go to protected shelters whose locations we probably cannot know and which we would have trouble destroying in any event. Internal security forces and the Red Army are harder to camouflage or protect, but even they are not easy to find. Even limited mobility is quite effective unless the U.S. has real-time (i.e. immediate and current) intelligence during a war, which is extremely unlikely. Thus, to destroy Soviet power, large parts of the country will have to be hit. The distinction between a pure city-busting strategy and one which seeks to spare civilians while destroying Soviet power would be much less apparent in practice than in theory.

Even if much greater discrimination were possible, this strategy would be more moral than MAD only if there were good reasons to expect the war to remain limited. The pressures for and dangers of escalation are very great; neither side has the command, control, and communications capability (known as C-3) to fight a prolonged limited nuclear war. Indeed, it would be very hard to keep the forces under control even if both sides tried.\19

Furthermore, there is no reason to think that the Russians would cooperate with our strategy even if they could. While there is a great deal of controversy about exactly what their strategy is, there is a consensus that it mirrors neither MAD nor the countervailing strategy. The Russians do not seem to target American cities for the purposes of revenge, but they do not seem to be willing to spare them either. As far as we can tell, their strategy most closely resembles that held by the U.S. Strategic Air Command (SAC) in the late 1950s. (I say SAC rather than the U.S. government because at this time war planning was done by SAC with little control by the Pentagon, let alone the White House.\20) In the event of a nuclear war, the Soviets would probably seek to destroy U.S. military, economic, and political power. Many targets would be in or near cities, so the U.S. could not hope to limit damage to itself by limiting the damage done to the Soviet Union. As the Soviets see it, American ideas of intrawar deterrence are impractical and dangerous. Two implications follow: while trying to spare Soviet cities might save Soviet lives, it would not protect the U.S., and unless American leaders blind themselves to this reality, the credibility of the threat to implement such a strategy will be undermined by the fear that the resulting war would destroy the U.S.

A final objection to a strategy that threatens Soviet power while killing as few civilians as possible is that if the strategy were to succeed, it would fail. If the U.S. was able to destroy Soviet power and political control, the Russians would have no reason -- other than morality -- not to destroy the U.S. If the Soviets value their power, then we must spare this power if we want the war to remain limited. The basic logic underlying criticism of MAD applies here: the threat to destroy what the Soviets value is not credible because if it is implemented, we must expect an unrestrained Soviet response.

Proportionality

I have argued that the nuclear revolution has undermined the rationale for noncombatant immunity, and I have tried to refute the claim that this principle can be restored by targeting Soviet power. What about the rule of proportionality? Has mutual vulnerability altered the rule that, in the words of the American Catholic bishops, "the damage to be inflicted and the costs incurred by war must be proportionate to the good expected by taking up arms"?\21 An all-out war could now lead to incredible devastation. Even if it did not produce a "nuclear winter," the level of destruction would constitute a human loss of incomprehensible magnitude and would set civilization back for generations, if not centuries. This raises three questions. The first, treated mainly by philosophers, is whether it can be rational or moral to intend to retaliate when doing so would be immoral and pointless. I think David Lewis is correct to respond that this is largely a nonproblem, the modern equivalent of asking how many angels can fit on the head of a pin.\22 No statesman can know how he or she would behave in the awful moment of decision. More central are problems of credibility and their links to the proportionality of the response.

This leads to the second question: Could anything be worth the price of all-out war? No matter how much we value liberty, would it not be better -- both more expedient and more moral -- to submit and then struggle to overthrow the tyranny than to fight World War III? There is much to be said for this, but the familiar reply also has great merit. The policy of deterrence allows us to have the best of both worlds -- to be neither "red" nor dead. Furthermore, to deny the possibility of resort to nuclear weapons, to put a severe bound on the violence which might be employed, would be to undercut a great deal of American policy.\23 I think this view is correct, and elsewhere have argued that mutual second-strike capability creates an unusually secure world.\24 Nevertheless, the obvious challenge lies in the fact that deterrence is not certain. Here the objection branches in two directions. The dovish branch argues that because deterrence can fail with catastrophic results we must look for radical alernatives, such as drastic and perhaps unilateral disarmament. The hawkish branch argues that the credibility of deterrent threats must be enhanced, preferably by a posture which would also maximize our chances of surviving a nuclear war if one were forced on us. At best this would be done by returning to deterrence by denial by means of an ABM system. Lacking or supplementing this, we must develop the capacity to respond to less-than-total attacks with a spectrum of less-than-total measures -- a strategy of flexible response, which is a part of the countervailing strategy.

This raises the third question, which is one of morality as well as credibility: Even if an all-out response were credible -- and even if the Russians could not retaliate in turn -- to destroy the Soviet Union in reaction to a minor transgression would be disproportionate and therefore immoral. Flexible response thus seeks to reinstate both credibility and morality through the mechanism of proportionality -- we would adjust our military means to the magnitude of the issue at stake. However, this line of argument is fundamentally misleading because it is conventionalized and so fails to deal with the fact (discussed earlier) that meeting a limited threat on its own terms does not take American cities out of hostage. Because escalation can occur, either in a calculated manner or through events getting out of control, superpower confrontations are like a game of chicken. Each side knows that the worst outcome for both will come about if neither of them makes concessions, and the knowledge of this shared interest provides the basis for competitive bargaining as each tries to shift the costs of avoiding war onto the other. It is then the willingness to run risks which is both dangerous and crucial. If proportionality is to be maintained, each side must limit itself to only running risks that are roughly proportional to the stakes. The military requirements for such a policy are quite different from those called for by the policy of flexible response; what one needs is the ability to take actions that increase the chance of total war but do not make escalation certain.

What is less clear, however, is whether proportionality is meaningfully reestablished when statesmen seek to adjust the chance of total destruction. While any policy, especially in a crisis, must be chosen in part because of estimates as to how dangerous it (and the alternatives) will be, congratulating ourselves that this way of behaving is moral may be an attempt to rationalize an unpleasant reality. Proportionality was easier to maintain in the past because a state had to defeat the other's armies before it could do great damage to civilians, and once it had defeated the armies, there was no point in doing this damage. Now either superpower can do harm from the start, and military success cannot prevent the other from doing harm.

The leverage that comes from this ability is central; I do not see how morality can tame it any more than it could tame unrestricted submarine warfare in World War I or area bombing in World War II. It is, if not the trump card, then at least the weapon of last resort. For this reason the nuclear revolution has created insoluble moral dilemmas. The possibility of total destruction is inherent in a world with nuclear weapons, and therefore no policy can meet all our moral standards.

Nuclear Weapons, Freedom of Action, and Morality

Mutual second-strike capability has implications for morality in foreign policy as well as in defense. In the past, great powers generally had surprisingly little freedom of action. We often think of power and the ability to choose as almost synonymous -- the powerful should, almost by definition, have more leeway than the weak to choose what challenges they will accept and adventures they will undertake. In fact, it is often for the major states that the environment is most compelling. If they are to maintain their position, they will have to enter many undesired conflicts and sometimes will have to side with allies who, if deserted, would in turn desert them, leaving them isolated. To the extent that the nuclear revolution has led to bipolarity, it has altered this situation. As Kenneth Waltz has persuasively argued, because the superpowers are so strong, the relative weight of their allies counts for much less. The U.S. and USSR therefore have unprecedented freedom to engage in or abstain from conflicts.\25 The basic argument made by realists as to why leading states are not bound by morality may therefore apply less today than it did in the past.

The superpowers' freedom is perhaps most limited in the military arena. It may be no accident that both superpowers have followed quite similar patterns of doctrine and weapons procurement: both have sought to be in the best possible position to fight if war should be forced upon them; on the other hand, while neither has welcomed MAD, both have realized that it exists. In broader questions of foreign policy, however, the situation may be different. There is more freedom for the U.S. to decide to support human rights or stand aside, to provide humanitarian aid or withhold it, and to get involved in Third World conflicts or stay out. Obviously, people will make diverse and conflicting arguments in every case and the dictates of neither morality nor narrow self-interest are likely to be clear. Nevertheless, the realists' reasons for dismissing moral considerations are not as persuasive as they used to be. The frequent reiteration of the claim that the U.S. has no choice but to act in ways which violate or ignore moral principles again uses an intellectual framework which was appropriate to earlier eras but which serves less well under current conditions.

IV
The Hesitancy to Perceive Trade-Offs

When we look at people's views on the ethical aspects of important issues, we notice a suspicious consistency: people who see a policy as immoral also tend to see it as ineffective. This is an aspect of the general tendency of people to avoid value trade-offs, which I have discussed elsewhere. To summarize this argument, when people think that a policy is better than the alternatives on one value dimension, they are also likely to see it as superior on other, logically unrelated, dimensions. Yet, unless we believe in a benign God, there is no reason to believe nature would be so conveniently arranged. For example, in the late 1950s and early 1960s, those people who favored a nuclear test ban believed that such an agreement was verifiable, that it would contribute to U.S. foreign and military policy, and that atmospheric testing was a significant hazard to public health. Those who opposed an agreement disagreed on all three points. Logically, all that should have been expected was for people on different sides of the issue to reach different conclusions as to the total gains and costs of a test ban. There was no reason for them to disagree on each specific -- and logically independent -- issue, but in fact they did. Almost no one said that although testing was medically harmless it was bad for our foreign policy; few argued that testing was a military necessity even though it killed thousands of innocent civilians.

The reasons for this configuration of beliefs are psychological, not logical. Not all of the mental processes are entirely clear, but two kinds of factors appear to be at work. First, trade-offs are avoided because they are difficult. It would take a great deal of thought to judge a policy on separate dimensions and reduce all the values at stake to a common yardstick. People's cognitive capacities are limited, and so they need to simplify the problems they face. They may reach a decision based on the consideration of only one value and then bring other perceptions into line with this judgment. Second, and particularly important in the context of morality, trade-offs are avoided because they are painful. This is clearly true in the previous example. To say that testing must be continued even though it kills people is to admit a willingness to sacrifice innocent lives for foreign policy goals. Much more comfortable is the belief that testing is not only necessary but harmless.

The same pattern holds with questions of war and morality -- for example, with the views about strategic bombing during World War II mentioned earlier. The RAF, which throughout much of the war could only engage in area bombing, not only thought that destroying German cities was making a major contribution to the war effort, but also had no doubts as to its morality. The U.S. Air Force had both more faith in its ability to hit specific targets and more questions about the moral justification for indiscriminate bombardment.

Many disputes about Cold War strategy display a similar suspicious consistency. Thus those who opposed the development of the H-bomb were largely moved by moral and political considerations, but bolstered their view with arguments that building the Super, as it was called, might be beyond our capabilities, that it could

127

have little military role, and that the scarce fissionable materials and scientific talent would be better employed on various forms of atomic weapons. Those who wanted to proceed not only were preoccupied with the fear that the Soviets might develop the H-bomb first and saw real military utility in the new weapon, but also denied any moral difference between the large atomic bombs which were being developed and the Super.

In the current period, it is more than a coincidence that most people who favor the countervailing strategy on grounds of foreign policy also see it as more moral than MAD. In a parallel fashion, those who attack the morality of doctrines which seek deterrence through the ability to fight nuclear wars also question their strategic value. So it is not surprising that those who, like Pope John Paul II, say that deterrence may be morally acceptable, "certainly not as an end in itself but as a step on the way toward a progressive disarmament,"\27 also believe that disarmament would make peace more and not less likely. Logic plays a role here: MAD is seen as immoral in part because of the belief that it is not capable of preventing war or Soviet aggression. Doctrines that seek deterrence through the ability to fight limited wars are seen as immoral in part because they are thought to increase the chance of a war -- a war which could not be kept limited to military targets. Presumably, the pope sees disarmament as more moral than continued deterrence because he thinks that weapons contribute to international tensions and that war cannot be indefinitely avoided as long as we rely on nuclear threats.

It would be odd if moral judgments were entirely divorced from estimates of the consequences of alternative actions. Indeed, for the utilitarians, the former must follow the latter. (I might add that this makes their writings of little interest to strategists. Since they try to do the same sort of thing strategists do, they do not provide new perspectives.) Even deontologists, who search for different moral standards than "the greatest good for the greatest number," must estimate the effects of alternative strategies when making moral judgments.

But the result is that it is hard to separate arguments about morality from arguments about empirical questions, if one can so classify questions such as, What deters the USSR? or, Can nuclear war be kept limited? This leads to three related difficulties. First, it may not be clear when we disagree on morality and

128

when we disagree on empirical judgments. Are the disputes between those who say that MAD is moral and those who deny this proposition really based on different conceptions of morality? If people could agree on their estimates of the consequences of adopting various policies, would any disagreements remain? To put this another way, is there any point in discussing morality? The moral dialogue cannot lead anyone to change her mind or even to see the issues more clearly if it is really the strategic judgments which are in dispute.

A second and related question is, How much are moral verdicts based on hidden empirical assumptions? Much of the moral objection to various counterforce doctrines rests on the belief that nuclear war cannot be kept limited. Bruce Russett joins the American Catholic bishops in arguing that "limitation of nuclear war fails a third principle of the just war tradition: reasonable chance of success."\28 Here the assumption is explicit, which aids analysis, but it still raises the question of whether there is anything particularly moral about the judgment being made. Even more troublesome are the numerous occasions when the assumptions lie beneath the surface. Those who accept the need for nuclear deterrence but reject the morality of the countervailing strategy assume that Soviet goals and beliefs do not require American threats to be supported by the perceived ability to fight a range of limited wars. The bishops argue: "If deterrence is our goal, 'sufficiency' to deter is an adequate strategy; the quest for nuclear superiority must be rejected."\29 But if the proponents of the countervailing strategy are correct, then something like superiority _is_ needed to deter limited nuclear wars. On this point the question of whether war could actually be kept limited is irrelevant, as administration spokesmen keep reminding us. If the Soviets can only be deterred by the belief that the U.S. is ready to fight a certain kind of war, then the U.S. is compelled to convince the Soviets that the U.S. can and will fight such a war. Similarly, the argument for the moral superiority of a disarmed world makes some convenient assumptions about the USSR and about the connections between arms and the chance of wars. Unpacking these beliefs can point to questionable strategic judgments and possible clashes among values.

The close connection between empirical and moral judgments raises a third difficulty: Do views on one of these subjects lead to conclusions on the other in a way which is psychologically comfortable but logically -- and morally -- illegitimate? For some people, moral

129

judgments are a handy stick with which to beat their adversaries over the head. Few of the proponents of counterforce targeting were originally preoccupied with considerations of morality. Rather, they were seeking the best way to deter war and protect American interests. These are not minor values, and to say that they were the driving motivations is not to slander the people involved. It is only recently, as concern about morality has grown, that this position has been strongly defended on moral grounds. It seems clear that the moral evaluation is not really independent, but merely ratifies the strategic judgment previously made. No one who favored counterforce on strategic grounds reacted to the new concern with morality by saying, "Why yes, now that I think of it, my policy is immoral." Similarly, the new interest in morality has not led those who had come to favor MAD on the grounds that it was most likely to prevent war to say, "MAD may be effective; but it is also immoral."

Cynical readers might note that my argument that the nuclear revolution undermines the rationale for civilian immunity nicely reinforces my opposition to the countervailing strategy, a view I had arrived at on other grounds. In still other cases it is a moral judgment which comes first and leads conveniently to support of certain strategic views. This is probably true for most of the clerics and philosophers who have joined the strategic debate. When the pope calls for disarmament he has not reached this preference by a thorough examination of the military and political arguments. More likely the moral imperative for this position led to the belief that disarmament is also justified on grounds of strategy. But no matter which value is driving, no one on either side of the debate sees the need for a trade-off between national interest and morality.

In part this happy consistency in people's views is an aspect of the unwillingness to face the possibility that there may be a conflict between decreasing the chance of any superpower war and minimizing casualties if such a war should occur. Some proponents of MAD escape the dilemma by arguing that a limited war would automatically escalate; proponents of the countervailing strategy deny the trade-off by arguing that their approach would not only save lives during a war, but would also deter war because the Russians will find the threats particularly credible. Thus our beliefs are psychologically and morally reassuring, but it is hard to believe that an independent judgment has been reached on each point. Perhaps the first step toward taking morality seriously would be to see that doing so will often complicate our lives, making us less rather than more comfortable. Morality should make us face difficult choices and often alter, not reinforce, our behavior.

V

Morality and Prudence

Although morality and prudent self-interest cannot always call for the same course of action if the latter is to have any independent meaning, there are links between them. Most conceptions of morality enjoin a concern with others' welfare, arguing that people and nations should be willing to sacrifice at least some of what directly benefits them in order to benefit others. In a parallel manner, most scholars argue that being too selfish and greedy is likely to harm the state, although it may yield advantages in the short run. (I will return to the question of long- versus short-run considerations in the next section.) To act only on the basis of what puts your country ahead -- to interpret the precepts of realism crudely -- is to court great dangers, at least for a major power. Most dramatically, it can lead to isolation and ruin. David Calleo's interesting treatment of the failure of German expansionism points out that the German conception of Europe -- either under the kaiser or under Hitler -- left little role for the ideas and interests of the other powers.\30 Balance-of-power theory predicts and prescribes that states band together to prevent anyone from dominating, but the speed, cohesiveness, and vehemence of these efforts can be influenced by the character of the would-be hegemon. Germany brought on her own doom not only by seeking dominance, but by paying so little heed to others' interests that few nations could see a legitimate place for themselves in Germany's world. Symptomatic was the fact that many of the Russians who welcomed Hitler's troops as liberators were soon supporting the resistance movement against them.

The obsession with power and self-interest -- what might be called pseudo-realism -- leads to the dissipation of power and eventually undermines self-interest. Statesmen become not only contemptuous of others' values, but also insensitive to others' reactions. The others' power, skill, and willingness to suffer are then underestimated. It is all too easy for the strong to see only their own concerns and thus to endanger first others and then themselves. Michael Walzer argues that it is no accident that the Athenians' refusal to heed the Melians' pleas for considering the dictates of justice as well as power was followed a year later by their dispatch of the fatal expedition to Sicily.\31 Interestingly enough, the conduct of this adventure may reveal the same flaw in microcosm. Donald Kagan argues that the expedition might have succeeded had it been smaller, which was the original plan, but when the Athenians enlarged the force, their potential allies on the island feared that they would be the next targets if Syracuse were conquered and so stayed neutral or aided their old rival.\32 That the Athenians failed to anticipate this reaction was due, at least in part, to what we now call the arrogance of power. The egoism of pseudo-realism blinds statesmen to the complexities and uncertainties of international politics. It leads them to consider others as instruments, if not as puppets, and to overestimate their own ability to control events.

A lack of consideration of the adversary's perspective often leads statesmen to fail to utilize an important tool for deterrence. The preoccupation with the perceived evil of the other side, the resulting emphasis on issuing warnings, and the failure to realize that the adversary may fear unprovoked attack, combine to render the statesman insensitive to the importance of giving the adversary reassurances as well as threats. The other's decision to start a war (or to undertake actions which could lead to war) depends not only on the gains and costs it expects from aggression but also on what it thinks the future will bring if it is restrained. A state should try to convince the adversary that it will not strike if the adversary does not and that a future without war is not unacceptably bleak. If the other side believes the alternative to an attack or expansion to be the loss of its influence and values, it may rationally decide to strike, even in the face of credible threats of retaliation. For example, Janice Stein has shown how the Egyptian decisions for peace or war in the early 1970s were strongly influenced by their evaluations of what would happen to them if they did not use force; Richard Ned Lebow has shown the operation of similar calculations in Argentina before the invasion of the Falklands; and McGeorge Bundy and I have argued that American statesmen often neglect this factor in dealing with the Soviet Union.\33 Failure to consider the other side's alternatives is shortsighted because it often leads the state into unnecessary conflicts. It also is immoral in that it treats them as though they had no legitimate interests, as though they had no hopes and fears, and as though there were no way to build common interests.

Pseudo-realism also violates the standards of both morality and prudence by leading statesmen to ignore "the decent respect to the opinions of mankind." All good realists are supposed to know that world public opinion is a myth, as E.H. Carr so vividly argued.\34 "How many divisions has the pope?" Stalin is supposed to have asked, and even those who abhor the questioner agree with his position. In fact, while it is hard to tell how many divisions the pope has, the answer surely is not zero. Grossly offending moral standards incurs a cost -- often a high one. The state sacrifices international sympathy and creates fear which, while perhaps cowing opposition in the short run, is likely to turn to resistance before too long. Others will wonder if a state that acts immorally in one situation can be trusted in others and will ask whether it is a menace which needs to be contained or eliminated. Thus President Reagan is not alone in believing that the Soviet destruction of the Korean airliner and the shooting of Major Nicholson in East Germany show that the USSR has antihumanitarian values which must be thwarted for reasons of both morality and national interest. As Reagan put it after the shooting down of the airliner: "What can be the scope of legitimate mutual discourse with a state whose values permit such atrocities?"\35 The Soviets reasoned similarly after the American invasion of Grenada, when they questioned the utility of arms control negotiations: "If one is a bandit, liar, and murderer, one could not be different on the shores of Lake Geneva."\36 The same kinds of considerations explain why oppressive domestic practices usually harm the state internationally. Even though pseudo-realists argue that what a regime does within its borders is its own business, in fact the whole world does watch and judge. It is hard to believe that none of the opposition to Hitler or to the USSR is based on moral revulsion against their internal affairs. Even though international moral standards are not enforceable by a central authority, a state cannot disregard them without paying a price.

Another set of links between morality and prudence is of quite a different kind. A democratic regime will suffer if it tries to emulate the nastier foreign policy practices of its adversaries. First, such actions usually will erode the domestic support on which a foreign policy must rest. This seems a clear lesson of the American "overt covert" support for the Nicaraguan contras and, to take one minor example, of the CIA's pamphlet which instructed the rebels in assassination. (Of course such efforts caused fewer problems at the height of the Cold War; the erosion I am describing is not automatic.) Second, and through a quite different mechanism, prudence and morality join together in that threats to take actions that are widely discrepant with the state's values are not likely to be credible. A vicious tyranny can make some effective threats that are barred to a democracy. The Russians can behave much more brutally in Afghanistan than the U.S. could in Vietnam; an American threat to act as the Russians do would be incredible as well as immoral.

Morality, Prudence, and the Prisoner's Dilemma

"War is cruelty and you cannot refine it," said General William Tecumseh Sherman.\37 The major reason for this is the competitive nature of the fighting -- if you refrain from using a nasty tactic but your opponent does not, you have lost, and perhaps have lost a great deal. Furthermore, if you use the tactic and your opponent does not, you have gained a unilateral advantage. This kind of situation can be analyzed in terms of the Prisoner's Dilemma (PD) and the problem of how to avoid mutual defection (DD), a task in which morality and prudence may be joined.

When situations resemble the Prisoners' Dilemma (and it is often hard to determine whether they do), each state's first choice is to exploit the other and gain unilateral advantage. For example, a state could choose not to cooperate with the other (to defect) while the other is unilaterally cooperating with it (DC). The second choice is mutual cooperation (CC); the third choice is mutual competition or defection (DD); and the worst outcome is to cooperate while the other defects, or to be exploited (CD). There are, then, both offensive and defensive motives for disregarding restraints, and the result can be that adversaries are unrestrained (mutual defection, DD) when they both would have preferred mutual cooperation (CC). (I am putting aside cases in which the state would prefer to be restrained no matter what the other does, as may be the case, for example, with the humane treatment of POWs.) This configuration of preferences characterizes not only many wartime situations, but peacetime inter-

134

national interactions as well. It is a basic characteristic of collective action in the context of anarchy.

There are a number of ways of increasing the
chance of cooperation under these conditions. One mechanism is the development of habits and rules of reciprocal restraint. Each side may restrain itself in the
expectation that the other will behave similarly. Under
some circumstances, such mutual cooperation, based only
on self-interest, can thrive,\38 but high conflict and
misperception tend to erode this happy pattern. As we
noted earlier, violence tends to expand during wars.
Part of the reason for this is that states tend to
overestimate the degree to which they are cooperating
with others and to underestimate the extent to which
they are defecting and their adversaries are cooperating.\39 Each sees itself as being exploited and believes that its own defections are justified -- and
will be seen as justified -- by the need to respond to
the other's previous defections. Thus bombing in World
War II lost all its restrictions, although at the start
Hitler wanted to keep it limited and Britain's top
military officer felt that "it is entirely to our
advantage to keep within the accepted codes for the
conduct of war."\40 If restraints are to be maintained,
then, self-interest may need to be reinforced by norms
rooted in morality.

Before elaborating this argument, I want to note
the perverse possibility that moral restraints may
decrease rather than increase the likelihood of arriv-
ing at mutual cooperation. Two forces can be at work
here. First, morality can operate on the ends as well
as the means. To the extent that the conflict is imbued
with moral fervor, either or both sides may believe
that what is at stake is nothing less than supreme
values. The war will then be total -- it will be a
zero-sum game, no interests will be seen as common, and
cooperation will be impossible. Second, even if it
remains a Prisoners' Dilemma, cooperation will be less
likely if either or both sides believe that the other
has no choice but to continue cooperating. For mutual
cooperation (CC) is sustained not only by the desire to
avoid mutual defection (DD), but also by the realization that unilateral defection (DC) is not a possibility for more than a short time. If one state thinks that
the other's morality is so constraining that it will
not retaliate no matter what the first does, then only
morality, and not self-interest, will keep the first
restrained. Given the fact, however, that high conflict
usually leads each state to see its adversary as immor-

al, this danger is not likely to be more than a theoretical possibility.

More often, morality can play an important role in maintaining restraints.\41 When only self-interest is operating, the combination of fear, temptation, and misperception is often enough to prevent cooperation. Morality can supply additional reasons for restraint which will inhibit defection and thus lead to a cooperative solution. Morality and prudence are joined because the former can lead to an outcome which is in the state's long-run interest. Doing good can lead to doing well. Furthermore, if the state believes that its adversary lives by the same morality, it will have reason to expect it to obey the restraint also. This will usually increase the incentives for restraint because a state will not defect out of fear that the other is about to defect. The system of cooperation will be even more stable if the particular restraint is not only supported by moral judgments, but is also embedded in a whole framework of ethics. In this case, restraint is especially likely because breaking it will be seen as not only evil in itself, but as a breach of a wider system of ethics.\42

One can only wish that morality played a greater role in this regard. Although it cannot be assumed that any particular situation is a Prisoner's Dilemma -- and the Cold War is an obvious case in point -- it is striking that statesmen often overlook the possibility of mutually cooperative solutions.\43 That is not to say that they ponder them and reject them, although that is common enough, but that sometimes they do not even think of them. At many crucial points since 1945, American leaders failed to even think seriously about the possibility of reaching mutual cooperation (CC), or to contemplate the long-run implications of their lack of restraint.\44 For example, although the U.S. thought about alternatives to dropping the atomic bomb on a Japanese city in 1945, all choices were evaluated in terms of whether they would bring the war to a quick end. Some people thought of the moral questions (although they had not been raised in connection with the even more destructive fire raids), but no one in a position of responsibility asked whether dropping the bomb would increase or decrease the chances of postwar control of nuclear weapons. Although this question was raised in one official report, it was not taken up by the panel of senior scientists involved, let alone by the political decision makers.\45

Similarly, when the American leaders were deciding whether to proceed with the development of the H-bomb, little thought was given to the possibility of long-run cooperation with the USSR, especially by means of a test ban. Those who called for development of the bomb argued that the Russians would move ahead no matter what we did -- a familiar (and perhaps accurate) conclusion. And those who urged holding back, although (or perhaps because) they were strongly influenced by morality, did not stress the possibility of mutual restraint.\46 The development of MIRVs provides another dreary but instructive example. It should have been clear from the start that the only choices were CC and DD; although we could gain DC in the immediate future, it was hard to imagine that the Russians would fail to develop MIRVs unless they were banned. If we preferred CC to DD, the only way out was by formal agreement or tactic bargaining. (In fact, we may have preferred DD, in part because of domestic considerations.) But in the SALT process the subject came up only in a half-hearted manner, the choice of CC versus DD was never explicitly faced, and the resulting question of how to maintain cooperation was never seriously addressed. (It is ironic that Henry Kissinger should have said that "the age of MIRVs has doomed the SALT appproach,"\47 when he deserves much of the credit for the latter and blame for the former.) Indeed, the greatest moral failing of statesmen may be their lack of attention to mutually cooperative solutions -- the repeated pattern of not considering alternatives to unrestrained, competitive policies.

Anthropologists have argued that widely shared taboos can provide important social restraints by helping to protect society against the temptations of short-run self-interest.\48 If in the past Hindus had been guided only by immediate, individual calculations, they would have killed their cattle during severe droughts. But the effect would have been devastating over the longer run since when the rains returned they would have been unable to reestablish a flourishing agriculture, which depended on the use of these animals. To tell people to ignore their immediate hunger in order to protect their future would not be effective; indeed a rational, self-interested person would not heed the plea, but would kill his oxen and hope to buy, borrow, or steal someone else's after the drought. The result of this individual and short-run rationality, however, would be disaster for everyone. This outcome is avoided because killing cattle is not seen as a matter for such calculations. Instead, it is flatly prohibited by religion. Some people starve as a result, but the society continues. The world as a whole and most of the people and states in it might be better off if morality could play the same role today. Perhaps a kind of irrationality -- or at least nonrationality -- is necessary if nations are not to act on the fears and temptations which are so strong and which can be so self-defeating.

VI
Conclusions

If an analysis of morality and international politics is difficult, firm conclusions are even harder. Thus I will be both brief and tentative. I agree with Bruce Russett that

> There is no perfect practical solution to the problem of nuclear deterrence. Moral consider-
> ations further complicate the problem....Every possibility contains practical and moral dan-
> gers.\49

Any way of gaining security may involve the chance of killing hundreds of millions of innocents. As the pre-
vious discussion indicates, in some situations morality can help ameliorate problems of security by helping reach a solution acceptable to both sides, but to imagine that morality could solve our most pressing international conflicts is unrealistic. It assumes that Soviet and American aims are compatible over the long run and does not explain how the greater role for morality is going to be put in place.

I would suggest several more modest functions for morality. As Stanley Hoffmann notes, "it is good to remind statesmen that the ends do not justify all means, that humanity must somehow be preserved."\50 The temptation to believe that the environment is so extreme as to compel the most awful actions and the hubris of thinking that the statesman's acts are beyond judgment are strong and must be constantly resisted. This does not tell us how to act and may not even alter our behavior, but it at least serves to remind us of what we must strive for as human beings.

Perhaps even more disturbing than the calculated violations of moral standards are the many cases in which statesmen do not even think of the cost of their actions in terms of innocent lives, deplorable precedents, and values sullied. In extreme circumstances -- and such occcasions are not uncommon in international politics -- states may have to break moral standards in order that other values they hold may survive. At least decision makers should be aware of the crimes that they are committing. Michael Walzer argues that Britain was right to engage in area bombing in the most desperate hours of World War II, but was also right not to honor the airmen involved after the war.\51 Much as it was cruel to the men of Bomber Command, the snub they received constituted a national admission that the country had, under grave duress, acted immorally, an admission which paid homage to moral standards and the values for which the British fought the war.

A consideration of morality can also help statesmen avoid pseudo-realism -- the preoccupation with power and interest narrowly conceived, which is so often not only evil but also self-defeating. It is too easy for decision makers to overestimate the efficacy of brutal actions. Uncertainty, which is so important in nuclear strategy, is present in most other international situations as well. Only rarely can statesmen predict with certainty the consequences of their acts, but they must act nevertheless. Since they cannot be sure what will be effective, they should perhaps care more often about acting morally.

The clash between morality and self-interest will remain, however, especially in issues involving the use of force. Clausewitz was, unfortunately, correct:

Kind-hearted people might...think there was some ingenious way to disarm or defeat an enemy without too much bloodshed, and might imagine this is the true goal of the art of war. Pleasant as it sounds, it is a fallacy that must be exposed.\52

The difficulties are even greater in the nuclear era. Unless only those who are guilty are being hurt (an alluring but impractical idea), punishment always involves at least an element of immorality. It is thus hard to fit our best impulses to the basic facts of nuclear weapons. Morality seeks to limit harm; international coercion seeks to threaten if not inflict it. The two can never be entirely reconciled.

Notes

1. Thucydides, The Peloponnesian War, Thomas Hobbes, trans., David Green, ed. (Ann Arbor: University of Michigan Press, 1950), p. 365.

2. Department of Defense News Release No. 564-84, October 30, 1984.

3. Williamson Murray, The Change in the European Balance of Power, 1938-39 (Princeton: Princeton University Press, 1984), p. 167.

4. The classic corrective is Arnold Wolfers, Discord and Collaboration (Baltimore: Johns Hopkins University Press, 1962), chap. 10.

5. John Nef, War and Human Progress (Cambridge: Harvard University Press, 1950).

6. Geoffrey Best, Humanity in Warfare (London: Weidenfeld and Nicolson, 1980), p. 250.

7. Corbett is quoted in Geoffrey Best, Humanity in Warfare, op. cit., p. 255.

One British scientist recorded his thoughts on his own involvement in the process of the expansion of the bombing during World War II:

> ...in [the] final weeks [of the war] I began to look backward and to ask myself how it happened that I let myself become involved in this crazy game of murder. Since the beginning of the war I had been retreating step by step from one moral position to another, until at the end I had no moral position at all. At the beginning of the war I believed fiercely in the brotherhood of man, called myself a follower of Gandhi, and was morally opposed to all violence. After a year of war I retreated and said, "Unfortunately nonviolent resistance against Hitler is impracticable, but I am still morally opposed to bombing." A few years later I said, "Unfortunately it seems that bombing is necessary in order to win the war, and so I am willing to go to work for Bomber Command, but I am still morally opposed to bombing cities indiscriminately." After I arrived at Bomber Command I said, "Unfortu-

140

nately it turns out that we are after all bombing cities indiscriminately, but this is morally justified as it is helping to win the war." Freeman Dyson, _Disturbing the Universe_ (New York: Harper & Row, 1979), pp. 30-31.

8. Ronald Spector, _Eagle Against the Sun_ (New York: Free Press, 1985), pp. 179-80.

9. Robert Ferrell, ed., _Off the Record: The Private Journals of Harry S. Truman_ (New York: W.W. Norton and Co., 1980), p. 55.

10. For a somewhat parallel discussion of the impact of technology on morality in earlier eras, see James Turner Johnson, _Just War Tradition and the Restraint of War_ (Princeton: Princeton University Press, 1981), chap. 6.

11. Robert Jervis, _The Illogic of American Nuclear Strategy_ (Ithaca: Cornell University Press, 1984), chap. 1.

12. Glenn Snyder, _Deterrence and Defense_ (Princeton: Princeton University Press, 1961), pp. 12-16.

13. Hans Morgenthau, "The Fallacy of Thinking Conventionally About Nuclear Weapons," in David Carlton and Carlo Schaerf, eds., _Arms Control and Technological Innovation_ (New York: John Wiley and Sons, 1976), pp. 256-64.

14. National Conference of Catholic Bishops, _The Challenge of Peace: God's Promise and Our Response_ (Washington, DC: United States Catholic Conference, 1983), p. 4.

15. This general rule obviously leaves open important questions, which are hotly debated, such as the moral status of the bombing of cities in World War II, whether civilian casualties are proscribed if they are the adjunct to operations aimed at the other side's armed forces, and whether operations which will kill civilians are only justified under certain conditions -- e.g., precautions are taken to minimize such casualties and the military necessity for undertaking the operation is great.

16. Robert E. Osgood and Robert W. Tucker "The Rationale of Force," in _Force, Order, and Justice_ (Baltimore: Johns Hopkins University Press, 1967), p. 209.

17. William Stanmeyer, "Toward a Moral Nuclear Strategy," Policy Review 21, Summer 1982, pp. 65-66.

It should be noted that while American decision makers had often talked as though American policy was based on retaliation against cities, in fact this has never formed the basis of American targeting policy. See, for example, David Rosenberg, "The Origins of Overkill: Nuclear Weapons and American Strategy, 1945-1960," International Security 7, Spring 1983, pp. 4-71; and Desmond Ball, Can Nuclear War Be Controlled? Adelphi Papers No. 169 (London: International Institute For Strategic Studies, 1981).

18. For an elaboration of the argument for the central role of risk, see Robert Jervis, The Illogic of American Nuclear Strategy, op. cit., chap. 5.

19. For a good discussion of C-3, see Desmond Ball, Can Nuclear War Be Controlled? op. cit., and Bruce Blair, Strategic Command and Control (Washington, D.C.: The Brookings Institution, 1985).

20. David Rosenberg, "The Origins of Overkill: Nuclear Weapons and American Strategy, 1945-1960," op. cit.

21. National Conference of Catholic Bishops, The Challenge of Peace, op. cit., p. 31.

22. David Lewis, "Devil's Bargains and the Real World," in Douglas MacLean, ed., The Security Gamble: Deterrence Dilemmas in the Nuclear Age (Totowa, NJ: Rowan & Allanheld, 1984), pp. 141-54.

23. For a further discussion of this point, see Robert E. Osgood and Robert W. Tucker, "The Rationale of Force," op. cit., pp. 233-34, 301.

24. Robert Jervis, The Illogic of American Nuclear Strategy, op. cit., pp. 153-62.

25. Kenneth Waltz, Theory of International Politics (Reading, MA: Addison-Wesley, 1979), chap. 8. See also Glenn Snyder and Paul Diesing, Conflict Among Nations (Princeton: Princeton University Press, 1977), chap. 6.

26. Robert Jervis, Perception and Misperception in International Politics (Princeton: Princeton University Press, 1976), pp. 128-42.

27. Quoted in Bruce Russett, "Ethical Dilemmas of Nuclear Deterrence," *International Security* 8, Spring 1984, pp. 36-54.

28. Bruce Russett, "Ethical Dilemmas of Nuclear Strategy," op. cit., p. 46.

29. National Conference of Catholic Bishops, *The Challenge of Peace*, op. cit., p. 59.

30. David Calleo, *The German Problem Reconsidered* (Cambridge: Cambridge University Press, 1978).

31. Michael Walzer, *Just and Unjust Wars* (New York: Basic Books, 1977), p. 7.

32. Donald Kagan, *The Peace of Nicias and the Sicilian Expedition* (Ithaca: Cornell University Press, 1981), p. 214.

33. Robert Jervis, Richard Ned Lebow, and Janice Stein, *Psychology and Deterrence* (Baltimore: Johns Hopkins University Press, 1985); McGeorge Bundy, "The Bishops and the Bomb," *New York Review of Books*, January 16, 1983; and Robert Jervis, *The Illogic of American Nuclear Strategy*, op. cit., pp. 165-67.

34. E.H. Carr, *The Twenty Years' Crisis, 1919-1939* (New York: Harper & Row, 1964).

35. *New York Times*, September 3, 1983.

36. *New York Times*, October 29, 1983.

37. Quoted in Michael Walzer, *Just and Unjust Wars*, op. cit., p. 32.

38. See the special issue of *International Organization* on regimes, edited by Stephen Krasner (vol. 36, Spring 1982), and the special issue of *World Politics* on cooperation under anarchy, edited by Kenneth Oye (vol. 38, October 1985).

39. Robert Jervis, *Perception and Misperception in International Politics*, op. cit., pp. 67-76, 319-27, 338-42, 349-55.

40. Quoted in George Quester, *Deterrence Before Hiroshima* (New York: John Wiley and Sons, 1966), p. 64. For a discussion of how the restraints eroded, see chap. 7 in Quester's book; see also Frederick Sallager,

The Road to Total War (New York: Van Nostrand Reinhold, 1969).

41. For a related argument, see Robert E. Osgood and Robert W. Tucker, "The Rationale of Force," op. cit., pp. 205-6.

42. The importance of embedding specific norms and rules in a wider supporting framework is stressed by Vinod Aggarwal, "Textiles: International Negotiations," International Organization 37, Autumn 1983, pp. 617-45.

43. Douglas Lackey, "Missiles and Morals: A Utilitarian Look at Nuclear Deterrence," Philosophy and Public Affairs 11, Summer 1982, p. 199.

44. My thoughts on this point owe much to reading McGeorge Bundy's unpublished manuscript on decisions about nuclear weapons, to be published by Random House (New York) in 1988.

45. McGeorge Bundy, untitled manuscript (New York: Random House, forthcoming 1988), chap. 2.

46. McGeorge Bundy, untitled manuscript, op. cit., chap. 5, and Herbert York, The Advisors: Oppenheimer, Teller, and the Superbomb (San Francisco: Freeman, 1976).

47. Time, March 21, 1983, p. 2.

48. Marvin Harris, Cows, Pigs, Wars, and Witches: The Riddles of Cultural Materialism (New York: Random House, 1974), and Marvin Harris, Cultural Materialism (New York: Random House, 1979).

49. Bruce Russett, "Ethical Dilemmas of Nuclear Deterrence," op. cit., pp. 51, 54.

50. Stanley Hoffmann, Duties Beyond Borders: On the Limits and Possibilities of Ethical International Politics (Syracuse: Syracuse University Press, 1981), p. 81.

51. Michael Walzer, Just and Unjust Wars, op. cit., pp. 323-25.

52. Clausewitz, On War, Michael Howard and Peter Paret, eds. and trans. (Princeton: Princeton University Press, 1976), p. 75.

Comments by Ernst B. Haas

The major conclusions of Robert Jervis's paper are so acceptable to me, the subtlety of argument and the aptness of the distinctions are so striking, that I am at a loss in making meaningful comments. Professor Jervis makes clear that whatever notions of international morality may have prevailed before the advent of the nuclear era, nuclear weapons have changed them all. The old standards, even when widely accepted, are obsolete in the face of the technological temptations offered by the new weaponry. He shows us that just because the argument for a given strategy can be justified morally, that is not usually the reason why that strategy is chosen in the first place. He demonstrates that just because a strategy is condemned on moral grounds, that need not mean that it also fails on logical grounds. And he reminds us that moral disagreements among protagonists of strategic doctrines are sometimes actually disagreements on empirics, and that differences argued in terms of empirics may really hide a deep moral "dissensus." We are therefore entitled to doubt whether much is really gained by singling out the moral dimension in the first place. Why not confine ourselves to clearing up the empirical disagreements about weapons and war? Why not concentrate our skills on pointing out the logical flaws and the mistaken historical analogies in the arguments of our opponents? Why muck it up further with considerations of morality?

I can think of several reasons for not dismissing the moral dimension. As citizens and individuals we want policy to conform with our values. We therefore need criteria for judging the acceptability of policies on nonempirical grounds and for reasons that go beyond logic. As scholars we wonder whether things in international life are getting better or worse. We speculate about progress, about evolution or regression, even about the evolution of moral sensibilities or their deterioration. We would like to fix the world's trajectory, and hope that it happens to conform to our preferences. Such exercises entail judgments about what we mean by improvement and regression, and these are moral judgments. Finally, like Professor Jervis, we are curious about the limits of the theories we profess. He tests the limits of realism, and he does it very well. I, however, not being a realist, am indifferent to that aspect of his demonstration. I am far more concerned with the evolutionary aspect of morality as applied to nuclear weapons and war. And I, too, want to make judgments of my betters.

On Making Judgments

Is there even a problem with morality and nuclear war?
One might say that we can talk either about nuclear war
or about morality, but since nuclear war entails the
most horrible catastrophes relating to welfare and
happiness short of the sun's going nova, the answer is
considered by many to be too obvious to require further
discussion. Nuclear war is obviously immoral; nothing
further needs to be said. However, Professor Jervis
shows us that the problem may be more complicated even
within the confines of realist thought. I want to make
a different argument. I wish to show that a good deal
depends on which rule of moral conduct we take to be
paramount. The immorality of nuclear war is more self-
evident under some rules than under others. Since we do
not agree on a single set of moral rules we ought to
remind ourselves that a judgment depends on what we
take morality to be. I will now explore three possible
meanings, clearly not an exhaustive list.

Suppose we say that moral conduct means that we
adopt Kant's categorical imperative or the golden rule,
a close variant. If we enjoin ourselves to behave only
so as to be able to feel capable of elevating our rule
of conduct into a universal rule of behavior, then
clearly we should not use the rules of engagement
propounded for either the counterforce or countercity
kinds of nuclear warfare. If we wish to have our antagonist behave toward us as we think we ought to behave
toward him, we cannot very well threaten him with
nuclear annihilation. Nuclear warfare, according to
this test of judgment, is clearly immoral.

The same conclusion follows if we say that morality consists of not taking a certain course of action
if the risk of general suffering is great and if the
outcome is totally in doubt. The rule then would be:
under conditions of great risk and uncertainty, do not
act at all. True, in all past wars the earth and mankind recovered remarkably rapidly. Bellicose behavior,
no matter how destructive, did not permanently damage
us. In many cases, it even produced unanticipated benefits in industry and medicine. But all our scenarios
tell us that this will not occur after a massive nuclear exchange. This rule condemns nuclear war as irre-
vocably immoral.

146

The same conclusion cannot be drawn about the third rule. Suppose we say that morality consists of not using nuclear weapons if we are certain that the cost in loss of life and suffering is greater than the gain of remaining an independent nation; in short, that it is "better to be red than dead," if that choice has to be made. The "good end" of national survival does not justify the "bad means" of nuclear warfare. I am not at all sure that the choice to surrender is a moral choice under such circumstances. But I am not sure that the choice to fight is the more moral one either. Everything depends on a number of unresolved empirical judgments. How long will it take the country to recover after a nuclear exchange, ten years or a hundred? Can the opponent recover, and how long will that take? If I surrender and the country becomes a totalitarian tyranny, how long is that regime likely to last? Can passive resistance, distance, or the incompetence of the new rulers be counted on to limit the period of tyranny? Or are we stuck forever? Since a judgment entails a guess as to whether being involuntarily "red" is a matter of a few years or an eternity, the process of choice becomes an exercise in balancing possibilities, an exercise in relativism. No clear judgment seems possible. It is perfectly legitimate for equally moral and equally reasonable people to disagree.

On Observing the Evolution of Morality

Because we cannot say that any one of the three rules explored above is presently paramount in politics, we are entitled to wonder whether the world may nevertheless be moving toward one or another of them. Are things getting better or worse? Is there an evolutionary thrust to moral concerns? In discussing this question, I part company from Professor Jervis's mode of demonstration.

He, like most realists, juxtaposes morality and self-interest. Morality means altruistic behavior, conduct that cannot be explained in terms of serving one's own interests. Self-interest means assuring the military security of one's country. Values and interest are opposing concepts. One acts _either_ in the service of one's values (i.e. altruistic aspirations) _or_ one seeks one's interests, but not both. (The sharpness of the juxtaposition is relaxed only in the realist's treatment of the notion of prudence and restraint.) Self-interest is the enemy of altruism, in this view, because altruistic behavior is dangerous to one's sur-

vival in the short run. Unless one remains alive in the
short run, there will be no chance to behave differently in the future. A moral world demands that short-run
behavior contain a lot of shortcuts around morality,
say the realists.

I do not accept this formulation. It is impossible
to conceive of a perception of national self-interest
that does not also contain a core of values. National
survival is central, of course. But it never merely
means the physical survival of the state; survival also
implies a set of values associated with the state, the
way of life considered good by its citizens and worthy
of being defended. Self-interest is also the moral
interest of the nation. This is as true of Hitler's
Germany, Stalin's Russia, and Castro's Cuba as it is of
Woodrow Wilson's, Franklin Roosevelt's, and Ronald
Reagan's America. When antagonistic nations confront
one another each thinks itself moral, and each nation's
confrontation probably is in terms of its own scheme of
morality. German Nazis and Russian Communists certainly
thought so at the time of their duel, despite the
radical difference in the particular values each defended. In short, each state justifies itself in terms
of a particularistic -- a national -- set of moral
standards. There is no supreme arbiter who rules on the
relative merits of these claims.

A judgment of whether moral evolution is taking
place cannot let matters rest at this point. We must
still ask whether these particularistic moralities have
come to resemble each other over time, whether certain
rules of behavior are accepted in all moralities. We
must look for universals; we must determine whether
cosmopolitan moral standards are growing from the sub-
soil of particularistic ones.

But this poses a problem. If there is no agreed
moral rule and no supreme arbiter, what are the criteria of a cosmopolitan morality? How do we recognize one
when we see it? Believers in natural law have no difficulty here: the principles of natural law are the
guideposts for judging the convergence or divergence of
particularistic moralities. I believe that natural law
is just another particularistic morality, the morality
associated with the Western Christian tradition, and is
in no sense universal. Hence, in a cosmopolitan perspective, natural law is entitled to no more respect
than any number of other competing moralities.

As individuals and small groups we assert the

values we happen to accept for ourselves as the preferred candidates for a cosmopolitan morality. But
nuclear war is planned by the collectivities we call
states, not by individuals or small groups. Moral standards that characterize the behavior of collectivities
are amalgams of, and compromises among, the standards
accepted by the groups that inhabit the state. Standards of behavior we impose on ourselves, our colleagues, and even our enemies -- as individuals --
cannot be simply transposed to impersonal collectivities, even though these are also made up of individuals. States continue to disappoint us because they do
not act like individuals writ large. We have no warrant
to present our individual moral codes as the models for
a cosmopolitan morality.

What we can do, however, is investigate whether
conflicting moralities contain common elements. We can
study congruencies and divergencies. We can ascertain
whether, since the beginning of the nuclear era, conceptions of proper international conduct have converged
or diverged. Professor Jervis suggests that they have
diverged as contrasted with the rules of war in earlier
periods. The fact that the superpowers and the large
states in Europe and Latin America have not fought any
direct battles with each other since 1945, nuclear or
conventional, suggests that the whole story has not yet
been told.

We can do more. We can seek to influence our
governments in such a way as to induce behavior that
will gradually widen the area of overlap among particularistic moralities so as to produce a cosmopolitan
morality. That does not mean that we must mount human
rights campaigns, preach the universal virtues of democracy, denounce communism, or prepare for strategic
surrender. It means conducting foreign and defense
policy in such a way as to create expectations of
mutual restraint. It means deliberately fostering perceptions of reciprocity and reciprocal caution. It
means not ever being the first to refuse a collabora-
tive step if by so doing the evolution of reciprocity
is foreclosed. Instead of abandoning the rule of proportionality in the planning of military measures, we
should actively seek to practice proportionality. Instead of refusing to consider the trade-offs among
policy options, we ought to sensitize ourselves to see
such trade-offs more clearly, to differentiate among
arguments and options more sensitvely than the practices of our strategic planners do now. These are self-
interested steps, practical measures that can advance

congruence among values. Not altruism but self-adjust-
ing self-interest becomes the engine of a cosmopolitan
morality. In such a perspective even MAD-type nuclear
deterrence is moral, <u>provided</u> it is used as a short-run
policy designed to transform perceptions of hostility
in the longer run.

     And so, by a different route, I arrive at the same
conclusions as Professor Jervis, and I am delighted to
do so.

Chapter 5

THE MORAL IMPLICATIONS OF NUCLEAR WEAPONS

Earl C. Ravenal

I
Introduction:
The Scope of the Problem

The overarching task is to establish, and reconcile, the requisites of strategy and morality. These requisites must be both confronted and met. But, though strategy and morality are related, we cannot substitute judgments of moral propriety for judgments of strategic prudence, or vice versa. Moral and strategic arguments must be compatible, but they must be independent. That is, each argument must be sufficient to make a case for a certain nuclear strategy -- level and type of arms acquisition, deployment, and prescription for use.

Now we must also cope with "environmental" factors. Of course, no set of effects of nuclear attack could ever qualify as benign; and it would be, in a way, foolish to give the impression that such concerns exhaust our intention or design. But, as the effects of nuclear detonation, such as "nuclear winter," are revealed, we must build into our strategy, in addition to moral restraints, environmental restraints, even at considerable cost to military and deterrent efficacy. We must impose these restraints with regard for the strategic consequences of such a choice, but in the realization that the choice must be made, and made in favor of the continuance of life, nature, and human structures.

In the end, I will conclude that a correct strategic and moral stance toward nuclear weapons must reconcile, as well as it can, stability -- that is, minimizing the possibility of nuclear war -- and the limitation of damage -- that is, minimizing "expected losses," particularly casualties. These two desiderata are, as we shall see, already somewhat antithetical. When we overlay a quasi-absolute moral principle, avoidance of the intentional targeting of innocent civilians, on the probable reduction of noncombatant casualties, we have a complex strategic and moral structure indeed.

Finally, it will emerge that the inevitable context for moral choice, at the national level -- just as it is for strategic choice -- is the structure and character of the international system, which in turn provides opportunities for and sets limits on the conduct of any nation. Thus, to take a position on ethical theory or strategic policy is also to venture some predictions and prescriptions about the world of nations and the appropriate role of a power such as the United States.

II
The Strategic Case

Nuclear Stability

In an age that threatens intense and widespread nuclear devastation, and yet an age in which nations feel they must keep the arsenals that could inflict this devastation, a premium must be placed on preventing escalation to nuclear war. In other words, nations must aim at stability -- more precisely, "crisis stability" -- in the design of their nuclear postures and doctrines, and even in their larger national strategies and their foreign policies. (Another approach -- sometimes proposed as a substitute for either nuclear stability or nuclear war-winning capability -- strategic defense, is seen here not as a radical substitute for retaliatory deterrence or preemptive nuclear attack, but rather as a possible adjunct to either of these and as a condition for preserving our extended deterrence over allies. Indeed, strategic defense, even if it can be technically devised, economically developed, and practically installed, will not obviate the desideratum of stability. One of the criteria for judging strategic defense is whether it conduces to or derogates from stability, particularly crisis stability.)

Strategic stability presumes, but also transcends, the correct design of nuclear forces and doctrines. Insofar as it involves the broader objective of war-avoidance and the possibility of compartmentalizing conflicts among nations, it invokes the structure of

152

the international system, in two directions: The kind
of international system affects the prospects for arms
control and a stable nuclear balance; and the degree of
strategic stability and the distribution of nuclear
arms affect -- and in a sense define -- the kind of
international system.

Strategic stability can be defined in terms of the
pattern of incentives, for both sides, to initiate or
not to initiate nuclear war under a variety of circumstances. And the circumstances that are of most interest are not the placid moments in international relations, but the crisis situations -- those rare and
rather improbable confrontations that are, nonetheless,
as anticipated by the powers of the world, at the
foundation of the arms race. Simply put: To have a
nuclear war, someone must start it. Thus, the key
question is: Why would either side want to strike
first? What would have to be the scenario, the anteced-
ent moves, the impending situation? We can dispose of
the notion that a nuclear war would start "out of the
blue" because one of the contestants, the moment it
reached some critical ratio of "superiority," either
initially or after projecting the result of a hypothetical nuclear exchange, would have an incentive to attack. A future nuclear war might grow out of some
festering, escalating crisis -- say, a confrontation in
the Middle East or the Persian Gulf, or a series of
political and social upheavals and ambiguous moves in
Central Europe -- where conflict had already been
joined and each side had developed reasons to be ner-
vous about the other's resort to nuclear weapons. Then,
in this game theorist's nightmare, an edgy or desperate
enemy might be inspired to unleash a nuclear strike, if
it had the ability to destroy a large portion of its
adversary's nuclear forces while reserving enough weapons to hold the adversary's society hostage.

Thus, the capability of each side's nuclear forces
in a counterforce mode, and the vulnerability of each
side's forces to a counterforce strike, are critical
elements in the logic of incentives. Capability and
vulnerability are interrelated. A simple way of summa-
rizing the relationship is this: If they can't disarm
us, they aren't going to hit us.

Counterforce and Extended Deterrence

The competition in counterforce weaponry is driving the
current stage of the arms race. Counterforce represents

the dedication of some portion of one's nuclear arsenal
to attacking enemy military installations, logistical
complexes and nets, military-related industries, command facilities, nuclear storage sites, nuclear forces
in general, and -- specifically -- "time-urgent" nuclear weapons such as missiles in silos. To the extent
that one believes that the United States is not simply
addicted to aggressive force expansion or gratuitous
coercive pressure, one must explain its current incli-
nation to a counterforce nuclear strategy.

I reckon that America's drift to counterforce is
neither perverse nor accidental. To grasp the rationale
of counterforce, it is necessary to understand the
logic of extended deterrence. For ultimately it is
adherence to alliance commitments that skews our strategy toward counterforce weapons and targeting and warps
our doctrines of response toward the first use of
nuclear weapons, prejudicing crisis stability and increasing the likelihood of escalation of nuclear war.
Few realize how intertwined our weapons and strategies
are with our commitments. And few understand how inte-
gral to our entire foreign policy stance has been the
strategic paradigm of deterrence and alliance that we
have maintained for almost four decades -- and therefore how much would have to change, if we set about to
achieve an alternative, more stable, nuclear stance,
that might provide greater safety for Americans in an
age of pervasive danger.

Counterforce, since it involves hard-target kill
capability, is an extremely demanding requirement for
our nuclear force. To cover some 2,000 silos and nuclear weapons storage sites in the Soviet Union, and some
700 leadership centers, requires at least two independent nuclear weapons each, 5,400 out of the 9,400
needed for the entire target system. And since our
hard-target kill weapons would themselves be the prime
targets of a Soviet preemptive strike, more than the
usual redundancy is needed in these categories. Thus,
hard-target kill is responsible for the major part of
the current "ideal" deployment of 15,000 to 20,000
reentry vehicles in our strategic nuclear force. (These
are in addition to the cruise missiles, short-range
attack missiles, and bombs carried by bombers).\1

Why would the United States have opted for this
demanding strategy? We can bypass the stated rationales
of merely "neutralizing" the Soviets' hard-target kill
capability or symmetrically matching their nuclear
force. There must be more to counterforce than that. A

more interesting rationale is to induce crisis stability. In this explanation, our counterforce deployment would threaten Soviet fixed land-based missiles and thus force the Soviets to redeploy those missiles to sea or, second best, to land-mobile basing, thus eventually leading to the mutual invulnerability of both sides' nuclear forces and so ensuring crisis stability. But even this more attractive rationale for counterforce is tenuous, for this more stable state of affairs would exist only at the end of a long process that must pass through a phase of acute _instability_. Since no basing mode for our land-based counterforce missiles would credibly confer invulnerability, our attainment of hard-target kill capability would be correctly construed as a first-strike posture. The Soviets might initially react by planning to launch their threatened missiles on warning, or even preemptively.

In fact, there is a more compelling motive for counterforce: damage limitation -- that is, limiting the damage to the United States in a nuclear war. Part of that intent would be to destroy Soviet missiles in their silos. Such a damage-limiting attack, to have its intended effect, must be preemptive.

By exploring the logic of the preemptive strike, I do not accuse anyone of plotting a preventive war -- the definition of which is a war, _ex nihilo_, to destroy an adversary before he reaches the point, allegedly, of waging a war to destroy one's own country. In distinction, a preemptive strike is contingent and occurs only in an already developing confrontation. But the logic remains: Counterforce and first nuclear strike are mutually dependent. A first strike implies counterforce targeting, since the only initial attack that makes sense is a damage-limiting strike, the destruction of as much of the enemy's nuclear force as possible. And counterforce targeting, in return, implies a first strike, a preemptive attack, because a second strike against the enemy's missiles is useless to the extent that one's missiles would hit empty holes.

Thus we come to the matter of extended deterrence. American alliances, particularly NATO, have always depended on the threat of American first use of nuclear weapons, and our promise of continuous escalation from battlefield nuclear weapons to more potent theater types, to the final use of our intercontinental strategic force. Any American strategic policy will try to protect certain values that are at the core of our national identity and sovereignty. These values include our political integrity and autonomy and the safety and domestic property of our people. These are the proper -- and largely feasible -- objects of our defense or deterrence. It is when we attempt to protect more than these objects with our strategic nuclear force that we court the peculiar problems of extended deterrence. Then the calculus of credibility that we make with regard to strict central deterrence does not hold. The assumptions of deterrence apply to peripheral areas and less-than-vital interests with much less strength and validity. American protection of Western Europe, in particular, requires both initial conventional defense and credible extended deterrence. One cannot be substituted for the other. Extended deterrence, in turn, requires the practical invulnerability of our society to Soviet attack. (This is not to be confused with the invulnerability of our nuclear weapons.) I say practical invulnerability since absolute invulnerability is beyond America's, or anyone's, reach. Rather, what is necessary is the ability to limit damage to "tolerable" levels of casualties and destruction. This is so an American President can persuade others that he would risk an attack on our homeland, or that he could face down a threat to attack our homeland, in spreading our protective mantle over Western Europe and other parts of the world.

The United States would have to achieve societal invulnerability through both its defensive and its offensive strategic systems. But could this be done? First, we would have to achieve a strategic defense. This would require measures such as area antiballistic missiles (ABM) and laser or particle beam weapons in space, air defense against Soviet bombers and cruise missiles, and antisubmarine warfare against Soviet submarines, and a vast program of shelters and evacuation. These measures are very expensive; they might cost, conservatively, hundreds of billions of dollars to even a trillion dollars, over a decade. And we could not assume that they would work well enough to engage in nuclear escalation and entrust our further safety to strategic defense.

As a second condition of societal invulnerability, America would have to hold in reserve, after any of the earlier stages of a protracted nuclear exchange, enough destructive power to threaten counter-city strikes, so the enemy would never with relative impunity threaten to attack our cities and exact a political price that might include our surrender.

Finally, an indirect but most significant requisite of societal invulnerability is the acquisition of nuclear counterforce capability, specifically hard-target kill capability. Counterforce contributes to damage limitation in several related and mutually reinforcing ways, both indirect and direct. High accuracy in our missiles, great destructive power in our warheads, and large numbers of independently targeted reentry vehicles (MIRVs) would enable us to execute a damage-limiting strike against the Soviets' time-urgent nuclear forces, primarily their missiles in silos. Thus -- indirectly damage-limiting -- our counterforce capability would erode the enemy's ability to attack our nuclear forces; in turn, our nuclear forces would survive in larger numbers, the better to deter the enemy's eventual attack on our cities by holding his own cities hostage. And -- directly damage-limiting -- our counterforce capability would erode the enemy's ability to attack our cities in his earliest nuclear strike.

We see that counterforce "makes sense," as an attempt to fulfill some of the necessary conditions of extended deterrence -- but, it is fair to say, only as such. Our willingness to protect our allies rises or falls with the prospective viability of counterforce and, more generally, with our ability to protect our own society from nuclear attack. If there is any explicit doubt -- technical, economic, political -- that we will achieve that invulnerability, then there is implicit doubt that our extensive commitments, especially to Western Europe, can survive.

The Possible Role of Strategic Defense

Strategic defense is the only novel strategic thrust of the Reagan administration (that is, innovation beyond the designs of the late Carter administration). It comprises two related, but conceptually distinct, subjects: the Strategic Defense Initiative (SDI) as such -- that is, the defense of American society or American intercontinental strategic nuclear forces (or both) against ballistic missiles launched by the Soviet Union; and antisatellite weapons, to destroy or blind Soviet space satellites that might support, in various functional ways, a Soviet nuclear attack on the United States.

Both strategic defense and counterforce, insofar as they are adjuncts to societal invulnerability, are designed to enhance the ability of the United States to deter threats to objects beyond our normal sphere of credibility -- that is, to give the United States more freedom of strategic action, a wider scope of foreign policy. Of course, strategic defense also has the more limited intermediate mission of directly shielding our deterrent itself. But this mission, too, does not differ much, in function, from a preemptive counterforce attack. Thus, strategic defense competes with deterrence in the usual conception, but enhances it in another important way.

Three sets of questions arise with respect to strategic defense. The most obvious relates to our arms control stance: the impact, and use, of strategic defense and antisatellite weapons in the current strategic arms bargaining. Are strategic weapons to be bargaining chips or "crown jewels"? The latter means technology that is so unique, unchallengeable, and unmatchable by the Soviet Union, so inherently useful and cost-effective, and so technically feasible -- in a word, so "sweet" -- that the United States must hold onto it and continue to develop it, no matter what the Soviets might offer in exchange; in other words, technology that is not negotiable at all.

The second question is how the American tilt toward strategic defense might affect the integrity of deterrence. Does the prospect of even a relatively impermeable societal defense against incoming nuclear weapons, or of the effective defense of our offensive weapons against a Soviet first strike, make deterrence of nuclear war more certain, by denying entirely or just lowering the confidence of a Soviet countervalue retaliation, in one case, or a preemptive counterforce strike, in the other? Or, on the contrary, does it make the strategic balance more precarious -- does it derogate from crisis stability -- by creating the presumption of a now unanswerable American first strike and forcing our adversary to consider, and offset in various ways, our own preemptive counterforce strike?

And third, is strategic defense even feasible, technologically and fiscally? There is a wide divergence of assessments of the feasibility of this proposed system in meeting various levels and weights of stress. And estimates of the overall cost of putting in place some sort of strategic ballistic missile defense have ranged from about $50 or 60 billion to $1 trillion over a decade or two.\2

My own view is as follows: First, strategic de-

fense, insofar as it may be reasonably hoped, eventually, to substitute partially for strategic offense and
may serve as an adjunct, not a barrier, to some form of
arms control, is a morally worthy and strategically
interesting concept. Second, it is not absolutely foreclosed that strategic defense, including some form of
boost-phase interception, is technically inaccessible,
or beyond the fiscal capability or the political will
of our society, but the odds, in those two categories,
are against it. Third, American programs for research
and development in strategic defense were responsible,
in significant measure, for bringing the Soviet Union
back to the negotiating table, and seem to have eli-
cited more substantive and satisfactory Soviet proposals to constrain their heavy, counterforce, potentially first-strike missiles (SS-18s and SS-19s and
successors). Finally, a sensible American bargaining
strategy must attempt the precise and difficult (because apparently contradictory) feat of keeping strategic defense alive, in order that it <u>remain</u> a bargaining
chip, and seeming to be forthcoming, at some point and
at some responsible price, in trading it away for the
proper Soviet concessions, in order that it <u>be</u> a bargaining chip and not become a fixed feature in the
American strategic firmament.

An Alternative Strategy

Our present nuclear strategy is costly and demanding,
because of the target system it addresses, the types
and numbers of weapons needed, the protection those
weapons require, and the urge to acquire societal defense. Moreover, it is crisis-unstable and makes nuclear war more likely.

But it cannot be easily and directly fixed. A real
alternative prescription for our nuclear strategy would
diverge more radically from the present strategy than
most critics of that strategy realize. A nuclear policy
cannot be a string of self-contained prescriptions for
quantities or qualities of forces. It must implement
some national strategy and in turn express some foreign
policy design. That is why relevant nuclear strategies
will come in wide step-functions, not an infinite gra-
dation of nuanced options. In this case, there can be
no middle positions, certainly none that merely borrow
and cobble together the attractive features of several
other proposals. We must either satisfy the requisites
of extended deterrence or move to a nuclear stance
compatible with a disengaged position.

Thus, an alternative nuclear policy will serve a different national strategy: Instead of the paradigm of deterrence and alliance, which is synthesized in extended deterrence, it will support and implement a policy of nonintervention, consisting of war-avoidance and self-reliance. War-avoidance and self-reliance indicate the compartmentalization of conflict. Our security would depend on abstention from regional quarrels. This strategy implies the delegation of defensive tasks to our regional allies and the acceptance of the consequences, win or lose. We would, over time, accommodate the dissolution of defensive commitments that oblige us to overseas intervention. In doing so, we would be concerned to decouple conflict in another region of the world from our ultimate resort to strategic nuclear weapons.

In the strategic nuclear dimension, a policy of war-avoidance and self-reliance would be implemented by what I would call "finite essential deterrence." In a nuclear age, crisis stability is the key to central peace and relative safety. To achieve safety for ourselves (though not necessarily for others), our strategy should enhance crisis stability.

A nuclear strategy consists of posture and doctrine. We can strengthen crisis stability by designing our posture and our doctrines of targeting and precedence of use -- or, more generally, occasion or context of response -- to discourage either side's first use of nuclear weapons. First, we can dissuade the other side from starting a nuclear war, by eliminating the vulnerability of our nuclear weapons. Since an enemy's first strike must logically be a damage-limiting attack on our nuclear forces, we can change our posture to eliminate our fixed land-based systems. These systems are inevitably vulnerable, despite the efforts of a succession of administrations to put them in multiple or closely-spaced shelters (as with the MX), or to acquire a redundant and dispersed force (as with the prospective "Midgetman" single-warhead missiles).

The abandonment of land-based missiles would move our nuclear posture from the present triad of forces to a diad consisting of submarine-launched missiles and bombers armed with medium-range cruise missiles. We would make this move only as we developed the technology to insure sufficiently reliable coverage of the required targets with undersea weapons systems. Among other things, we would need to solve the command-and-control problem, sending orders and receiving timely

160

information from submarines on station. The 1981 decision by President Reagan to accelerate the development
and deployment of the longer-range Trident II (or D-5)
missile and the Trident (Ohio-class) submarines was not
unconstructive, though it will be expensive and premature. And we have been installing medium-range cruise
missiles in our existing B-52 bombers. There is no need
to have revived the penetrating bomber (the B-1B --
and, for that matter, the "Stealth"), although it is,
at worst, expensive, not provocative or destabilizing.

With respect to the doctrine of targeting, we
would not aim at enemy missiles in their silos. To do
so might provoke the Soviets, in a crisis, to launch
preemptively. Rather, we would develop a list of some
3,000 military targets -- such as naval and air bases,
concentrations of conventional forces, and military
industrial complexes and arms industry -- that are
relatively far from large civilian population centers.\3 We would also not deliberately target Soviet
cities. This doctrine is derived from both moral and
strategic reasons: If we avoid the enemy's cities, we
give him no incentive to strike our cities. Of course,
if our cities came under an enemy's nuclear attack, it
would be excruciatingly difficult, politically and
psychologically, for a president to restrict our counterattack to military targets. Yet even in that extrem-
ity, striking enemy populations would make no more
strategic sense than it ever did, and no moral sense at
all.

With respect to the doctrine of precedence and
occasion of use, we should also seal off the temptation
to start a nuclear war. (That is why we should not
design our forces to execute a preemptive strike.) Such
a first use of nuclear weapons could hardly occur
unless we were to escalate in the midst of a conventional war. Thus, war-avoidance would be most comprehensively implemented by dissolving our defense commitments. To reinforce that, or even short of that, we can
express our overriding interest in avoiding the spread
of nuclear war to our homeland by imposing upon ourselves a stringent doctrine of no first use. Such a
policy, joined with the targeting restrictions on our
retaliatory strike, creates a triply restrained doctrine: We would not use nuclear weapons except 1) in
response to a nuclear attack 2) on our homeland; and
our riposte would be 3) confined to military objectives
of a non-silo nature.

161

No First Use

The doctrine of no first use requires further explanation, particularly in its appropriate context of extended deterrence over Western Europe.

Nuclear war can occur only if someone starts it. Therefore, the most important move toward a stable nuclear balance is for nations to adopt, and to build into their defensive plans and postures, an intention -- amounting to a propensity -- not to use nuclear weapons first.

But some recent arguments for no first use (such as that made by McGeorge Bundy, George F. Kennan, Robert S. McNamara, and Gerard Smith in Foreign Affairs\4) fall short of logical closure in that they insist on maintaining the integrity of our extended deterrence for Europe. If one is committed both to defend Europe and to avoid the extension of conflict to our own homeland, one must try to reconcile these awkward objectives. What conditions would be necessary to effect this reconciliation?

Important in the Bundy-Kennan-McNamara-Smith proposal is that the apparent renunciation of the first use of nuclear weapons is conditional on the attainment of adequate conventional defense. But those who opt reflexively for conventional defense cannot mean just any conventional effort. They must mean the high-confidence defense of Europe with conventional arms. And they have the further burden of not just prescribing or exhorting that the United States and its allies must do more to guarantee the integrity of Western Europe, but predicting that this will happen.

In order to determine the feasibility -- and so the predictive probability -- of conventional defense, we must have a bill of costs. But nowhere in the Foreign Affairs article is that bill set forth. In fact, our present share of the conventional defense of Europe -- and this is not even designed to be a self-contained conventional defense -- is about $133 billion for 1987. This is 42.5 percent of the $312 billion requested for defense by the Reagan administration. Given a reasonable projection of current cost growth, over the next ten years Europe will cost us $1.8 trillion. Will even those resources be forthcoming, let alone the greater ones required for self-sufficient conventional defense?

Moreover, it is the very fear of inevitable exten-

162

sion of a nuclear conflict to American territory that constitutes the essential element in the coupling of our strategic nuclear arsenal to the local defense of our allies. For extended deterrence to work, the escalatory chain -- from conventional war to theater nuclear weapons to the use of America's ultimate strategic weapon -- must seem to be unbroken. Yet Bundy et al. propose to introduce a "firebreak" at the earliest point of nuclear war. Since firebreaks and coupling are antithetical, we cannot have both.

A consistent stance of no first use of nuclear weapons by the United States implies the dissolution of the Atlantic alliance. Those who opt for no first use without considering its impact on NATO are implicitly opting for the disengagement of the United States from the defense of Europe.\5

There are problems with my war-avoiding nuclear strategy. By limiting the occasion of our response, we would terminate extended deterrence, and so increase the odds of a war in some region that is under pressure. Even by limiting just the weight of our response, we would perhaps also weaken deterrence of direct threats to the United States. Thus we encounter the ultimate contradiction between crisis stability and deterrent stability.

There is no way to escape this contradiction. There is an essential tension, not an easy complementarity, between achieving safety for ourselves through crisis stability and achieving safety for the objects of our protection in the world through deterrent stability. But we can lessen the incidence of this tension by diminishing our obligations to extend nuclear protection. Crisis stability more closely coincides with deterrent stability as we shed external commitments and concentrate on our own defense.\6

A Different International System

With the purpose of enhancing strategic stability, and also, if possible, achieving reductions in the burden of arms and the contingent destruction of war, we have reviewed a panoply of measures. Independent national actions, in the design of forces and in the implementation of selected measures of restraint and reduction, supplement initiatives in more formal arms limitation. Such measures are intended to minimize the chance of nuclear conflict, as consistently as we can with other

163

objectives, such as strategies that are as moral as possible.

The attainment -- even the consistent pursuit -- of these objectives by a nation entails a fundamental change in its foreign policy and national strategy, to disengagement from defensive commitments and to a much lower propensity to intervene in conflict. A nation that adopted such a strategy would tend not to pursue "milieu goals" -- the shape and character of the international system; balance, in general or with a particular antagonist; and even the more abstract notion of order in the system. These generic milieu goals would be distinguished from more palpable security interests. The term "vital" would be reserved for those truly supreme interests that derive so strictly from the identity of the nation that they could not be credibly alienated.

In turn, such a fundamental change in the foreign policy of the United States, an essential participant in the international system, would entail a concomitant change in the structure of the system. Lacking a large portion of the extended deterrence it had enjoyed, the system would be marked by the further disintegration of alliances and the advent of general unalignment. A dozen or two of the nations that are now coopted or subordinated by the superpowers could exercise, or even flaunt, a good deal of autonomous political and military initiative, particularly in their own regions, and would have greater (though not always sufficient) incentives to acquire more potent arms.

Thus, it is not to be imagined that the achievement of strategic nuclear stability by a pair of superpowers in their own global relationship would necessarily dampen regional conflict, either in its incidence or its scale. In some cases (perhaps even in Europe), a policy of war-avoidance and self-reliance by the United States could lead to cooperative regional initiatives across the present East-West political boundary. But, conversely, it could lead (especially in other regions) to a competitive and in some cases uneven scramble by individual nations to compensate for the loss of immediate defensive resources and assurances. Ironically, the restraint of nuclear weapons by some nations (particularly the principal guarantor nations) might encourage the proliferation of nuclear arms throughout the international system.

This is not to say that widespread and rapid

proliferation would be inevitable. Each nation, in contemplating its concrete moves, would be faced with a host of practical impediments and inhibitions: the cost, the exposure to other nations' countermeasures, the alienation of regional friends, some sanctions by the larger nuclear powers. And some moves could be taken in international agencies and cooperative circles to slow or impede the process of nuclear diffusion. But it should be realized that, in theory and in aggregate reality, extended deterrence and proliferation run in opposite directions.

The discussion so far has been on the strategic side -- prudential military policies, national strategies, and to some extent foreign policies and the politics of the international system. It remains to expound and elaborate a moral treatment of the creation, acquisition, deployment, and possible use of nuclear weapons.

III
The Moral Argument

Morality and Strategy

Any serious discussion of nuclear strategy must lead to the consideration of the larger, underlying moral questions, principles, and theories.

In modern times, war means mass, deliberate killing, organized by states and foisted on individuals, and usually employing the most advanced, lethal, and destructive devices, and the most indiscriminate means, including instruments of general destruction such as nuclear weapons. Virtually anyone would want to minimize, or eliminate, war. But here the trouble starts. For this is a world of states -- not all, in fact, quite sovereign, but practically independent enough. Moreover, there will not be any overarching world government in our time; and I am not even sure that there ought to be, given the importunities of even existing partial concentrations of political power. Thus, it becomes the proper strategic stance, as well as the necessary moral stance, for states, in their own several policies, to minimize the occasion for armed conflict.

Even the most ambitious statesmen normally attempt

to diminish the costs or even the necessity of war, in their pursuit of other objectives. But, particularly in the matter of nuclear war, there are convolutions of reason that link, in all sorts of elusive ways, questions of strategy and morality. That being so, we must not succumb to the easy pseudo-explanation that those who prefer paths that seem to make war more probable are motivated by a desire for war. The trouble is that the nuclear age confronts us with a number of possible paths to war -- and therefore also with a number of comparative paths to peace.

Also, it will not do to express one's horror of war by being squeamish about discussing the strategic proprieties of using nuclear weapons. Not only do strategic dispositions set the stage for moral choices, but, vice versa, moral pre-choices limit and dispose strategic moves. There has to be some correspondence between what we plan to do and what we would contingently do -- if for no other reason than what we plan to do becomes woven into our actual systems and their deployment and control. Thus, an earlier distinction between what we do and what we threaten to do is invalid -- as if we could condemn the act but condone the threat (a saving grace for those who would preserve deterrence without taking responsibility for war).\7

What would a moral case for acquiring, deploying, and using nuclear weapons consist of? The discussion of morality in the use of nuclear weapons has been virtually monopolized, over the past several years, by the successive drafts of the American Catholic bishops.\8 But we should not confine the discussion of nuclear morality to the boundaries of the contemporary Catholic debate, useful and welcome though it is. If I could encapsulate all of my dissatisfactions with the bishops' pastoral letter in one phrase, it would be to say that it suffers from its dependence on, and derivation from, the church's tradition of the "just war." True, the letter has been criticized by more militant Catholics for ignoring the just war strictures and proclaiming more stringent reasons for prohibiting the use or threat of nuclear weapons -- reasons or grounds that have more to do with the nature of these weapons.\9 As Michael Novak admonishes the bishops: "For more than thirty years, a primary moral imperative placed upon governments and peoples has been to assure that these weapons shall not be _unjustly_ used" (emphasis added).\10 I would have said "not used," period. My naive reaction to Novak's qualification "unjustly," is that, when the nukes are "justly" used, I do not want to be

166

around.

On second thought, this is not such a naive reaction, from the standpoint of moral theory in the nuclear age. In fact, it is the point. Even such a strict,
self-abnegating, and guarded a document as the pastoral
letter yet recognizes extensive values, such as the
American guarantee of the political integrity of the
free nations of Western Europe, that could be "honored"
by military moves that lead to nuclear war. Whether,
and how, such larger values can be safely, feasibly
preserved is the essential question. We must face the
consequences and entailments of what we propose -- an
injunction to which Catholic moral philosophers are
usually responsive. Instead of extending deterrence --
initially of whatever kind, conventional or nuclear --
to protect other values that are less than vital or
less than ultimate, or that belong to others, I would
confine it to the minimal, irreducible elements and
objects that define the integrity of our own life,
lawful property, and freedom of choice, including the
choice of our governance. In an age of nuclear weapons
and long-range delivery vehicles, and in a world of
quasi-anarchy, we must pursue war-avoidance and indeed,
because of linkages and the specter of escalation,
conflict-avoidance. In a nuclear age, there are no good
wars, and few, if any, just ones.

The Moral Design of Strategy

A strategy for the use of nuclear weapons that would
meet the requisites of morality would have two main
characteristics. First, it would, as far as possible,
avoid the destruction of the lives and property of
innocents on all sides. This stricture would suggest
restrictions on the targeting of missiles, and the
insurance of sufficient accuracy and tailoring of yield
and burst to avoid collateral damage from intended
strikes.

The case for targeting restrictions was made by
Nixon's secretary of defense, James R. Schlesinger, and
by Fred Charles Ikle before he became director of the
U.S. Arms Control and Disarmament Agency under Nixon.
Struck by the incredibility and inhumanity of the previous nominal strategy of "assured destruction" of
enemy civilian targets, Ikle called for a policy of
assured destruction "first" of "the conventional military might of the aggressor nation -- its navy, army,
and air force with their logistic support."\11

167

Bruce M. Russett expounded the concept of a second strike against military, paramilitary, and "political" targets, including "those basic enemy nuclear striking forces and immediate support facilities that are subject to attack under current strategy," but not including "any effort to _extend_ anti-submarine warfare to effective attack on missile-launching submarines at sea, nor any _incremental_ effort to attack land-based missiles" (emphasis added). Russett recognized that this posture might be misinterpreted by the adversary, as the accuracy of our missiles inevitably improved through technological creep; and this suggested posture _is_ counterforce, though that is not its centerpiece. While Ikle and Russett were influenced strongly by moral considerations, Schlesinger was almost exclusively interested in strategic considerations: perfecting deterrence and enhancing crisis bargaining.

Second, a moral nuclear strategy would also minimize the possibility of ever using nuclear weapons. This would suggest two co The first is reducing the chance that an adversary would attack our missiles and precipitate our second strike. The second, which is implied by the first, is reducing the incentive for such a strike against us by removing those forces of ours that combined vulnerability and a potentially disarming, or first-strike, capability. In the present state of the art, these objectives would translate, tangibly, into the elimination of fixed land-based missiles. An early proposal to this effect was made by the American Federation of Scientists and, surprisingly, echoed by Fred Ikle (then director of the U.S. Arms Control and Disarmament Agency), with the suggestion that this should be done unilaterally "in our own force planning" if it could not be accomplished "through negotiations."\12

Ikle argued for achieving a counter-military capability, but not necessarily with weapons accurate enough to destroy hard targets -- it could be by selective targeting with submarine-launched or air-delivered weapons of no more than the present degree of accuracy. But both the Schlesinger and the Ikle version allow first use, and thus are still compatible with our manipulation of the threat of initiating nuclear war. In this respect, selective targeting and increased accuracy enhance the credibility of our use of nuclear weapons in responding to less than all-out attack, or to less than nuclear attack; if these moves enhance deterrence of nuclear war, or of any war (as they are intended to do), it is by enhancing war-fighting first.

The second component in minimizing the possibilities of nuclear war is no first use. Up to recently, selective targeting with submarine-launched or air-delivered weapons of no more than the present degree of accuracy would have assured, or at least suggested, a second-strike posture. But now, with emerging technology in accuracy, simply confining our delivery means to submarines and bombers will not even, in itself, constitute a second-strike posture. Because of the development of accurate navigational guidance for submarine-launched missiles, such as the D-5 (or Trident II), at this point, only adopting a comprehensive no-first-use doctrine, in conjunction with retargeting and with eliminating land-based vulnerability, will lead to a sufficiently restrictive formula.

The two characteristics of a moral strategy are, then, that it avoids harming innocents and that it minimizes the possibility of using nuclear weapons. The moves presented above might mitigate both the destruction and the moral burden of nuclear weapons. By what criterion do we sort out and judge those moves? What are we comparing when we make moral comparisons of alternative nuclear strategies?

Countervalue strategies -- the second-strike "assured destruction" of cities, population, and industry -- might reduce the likelihood of war because they increase the horror of retaliation. The weapons are more destructive and the targets are deliberately chosen to maximize casualties and civilian damage. Also the weapons systems that are most suitable for civilian targets (submarines, and to some extent bombers) are relatively invulnerable and create less incentive for a preemptive attack against them.

Counterforce strategies, on the other hand, imply the use of some fraction of the U.S. strategic nuclear force to attack a portion of the enemy's target system consisting of military installations, logistical complexes, command bunkers, and time-urgent nuclear weapons such as missiles in their silos. Their purpose is, broadly, war-fighting, and more specifically, damage-limiting, by taking out the enemy's capability to destroy first our forces and ultimately our value targets, that is, population and industry. Counterforce might reduce damage to our own, as well as the adversary's, population, but it implies weapons systems that destabilize the nuclear balance and so increase the likelihood of their use in war. That is because counterforce weapons systems are not as useful in a second strike as they are in a first, preemptive strike, and because they must also be seen by the adversary as potent and dangerous first-strike weapons, because of their yield and accuracy, and therefore either become the objects of the adversary's own preemptive strike, or at least cause the adversary to put his vulnerable missiles on a launch-on-warning basis, destabilizing the nuclear balance.

Although countervalue and counterforce strategies have contrary purposes, there should be some common standard by which we might evaluate them, and some common, ulterior, purpose for which they are designed. What we are comparing, implicitly, is "expected losses" -- more specifically, the probable death and destruction to innocent parties on all sides, but more reckonably our own. Expected losses are the magnitude of the losses multiplied by a fraction that expresses the probability of their occurrence. The moral aspect consists, first, of this question: Which strategy -- that is, which combination of weapons posture and associated doctrines of targeting and precedence of use -- produces, or contributes to, the lowest expected losses?

We have here an antithesis of two strategies within a common criterion. Those who stress counterforce and the avoidance of civilian targets would reduce expected losses by reducing the number of contingent casualties while accepting some increase in the probability of nuclear war. Those who stress countervalue and the stability of deterrence would reduce expected losses by reducing the probability of nuclear war while accepting some increase in the number of contingent casualties.

Within the common criterion of expected losses, the question is whether there will be less expected losses with countervalue -- which, if we grant its rationale, poses more destructive potential, yet thereby offers greater crisis stability in the sense of deterring escalation to the nuclear level of war -- or with counterforce, which purports to limit collateral destruction, but imparts more instability in crisis situations and may specifically provoke preemptive nuclear attack because of its combination of threatening characteristics.

Beyond that, we must delve into another level of moral discourse. We find that we have an antithesis between absolute and contingent criteria -- that is, between an absolute prohibition of a certain intent and

170

design, and a comparison of consequential results. Some
of the proponents of counterforce affirm it because it
deliberately avoids the absolute evil of counter-city
targeting, and yet they admit that it may create crisis-unstable conditions that lead more readily to the
failure of deterrence and the escalation to nuclear
war, so creating in the end a larger number of expected
casualties. These proponents might thus be compelled to
admit that the aggregate result, in terms of expected
losses, might be greater with counterforce than with
countervalue; yet they hold fast to the absolute principle of not targeting civilians. The proponents of
counterforce are adhering to, or at least conforming
to, an absolute moral principle (sparing innocents or
noncombatants), while the proponents of countervalue
can only be adhering to a utilitarian standard based on
a relative calculation of probability times destructive
effect. It is precisely this comparative, or utilitarian, calculus that the Catholic bishops rule out, when
they say: "Under no circumstances may nuclear weapons
or other instruments of mass slaughter be used for the
purpose of destroying population centers or other predominantly civilian targets....Our condemnation applies
especially to the retaliatory use of weapons striking
enemy cities after our own have already been struck."
Their statement could not be more categorical.

This is a higher level of argument, about, not
within, the criterion of expected losses, questioning
whether it is even a licit criterion. The "right"
metaethical choice may be the more absolute, more profound, more unalterable stricture -- the deontological
moral premise. An expected-loss criterion, applied to
targeting, may be entirely too circumstantial and consequential, because it rests on a calculus of two
aggregates -- both the products of probability times
magnitude. In the deontological view, the superordinate
horror of countervalue targeting -- city-busting
strikes -- is ruled out on grounds of absolute principle, even though it might make escalation to nuclear
war less probable and thus conduce to lesser expected
losses.

At the bottom of this contrariety, we have a
choice between moralities, a metaethical choice between
schemes of ethics. But is this the end of the discussion? We might ask, What is the source, after all, of
the validity of an ethical principle? Are so-called
absolute prohibitions really as unconditional, conse-
quence-free, or purpose-free, as they might seem? Here
is perhaps the ultimate paradox, for the deontological

ethic, which purports to be founded on unalterable principle and to carry the insistence on unconditional application, may yet be derived from something else -- may yet be a comparison of evil consequences. It would go something like this: In the fullness of time, since all things (or at least all logically and generally possible things) could happen, including several failures of deterrence and several outbreaks of nuclear war, the principle of action that promises the best result for humanity, or for the cosmic order, is that which not just should be chosen now, but, in a kind of retroactive reasoning, yields the best <u>principle</u> of action. Indeed, that may be what we mean by the best principle of action.

So, ironically, the principle of targeting seems to have the best absolute claim which promises the best result.\13 And the only reason, really, that we call a principle "absolute" is that we cannot now foresee, in fact, all the consequences of an act. It may be only in the ignorance of the cumulation of its consequences that we adhere to a principle as if it were absolute.

The paradox involved here stretches further: A deontological principle may fail, in its long-term consequences, to yield the beneficial results that support its ethical force. For the test of a principle, even though it purports to be unconditional, is: If you knew all the consequences of the principle, and they were, on balance, bad, would you change the principle (in which case the principle would not be absolute)? Or would you continue, nevertheless, to adhere to the principle (in which case the principle would not be moral)? The paradox consists in this: Under the hypothesized circumstances of omniscience and bad consequences, if the principle is moral, then it is not absolute (that is, unexceptionable); if it is absolute, then it is not moral.

Perhaps, in the end, we are always, inevitably, comparing expected losses. But perhaps, even so, we should try to keep away from immediate, short-term utilitarian criteria. We should, I think, gravitate toward absolute principles in important matters and have some faith that in the longer run those principles will be vindicated.

For the present, we can consider the principle of sparing innocents as an absolute constraint -- and one that has intuitive clarity -- that cuts across our somewhat dimmer judgment of the comparative contingent

172

merits of counterforce and countervalue. And perhaps we
can reconcile, to some extent, the absolute moral principle with the concern for predictable consequences by
observing a double (or, in a sense, triple) limitation:
Rather than either the unfolding evolution of counterforce and first strike, or reversion to the previous
doctrine of countervalue in a second strike, our moral
considerations urge: (1) no use of nuclear weapons
except after an adversary's first nuclear strike (2) on
our own territory, and (3) even then, only against
military targets (excluding missile silos), even if the
adversary has attacked our cities. Of course, on the
one hand it might be nearly impossible, politically and
psychologically, to restrict our counterattack (and
this alone argues for the tightest and most explicit
command and control), and, on the other hand, nothing
would seem "worth" doing. In short, it is as hard to
believe that a President, or his survivor, would not
push the button as that he would.

At least this "last ditch" countermilitary strategy, in addition to being consistent from a moral standpoint, would provide a certain strategic baseline: some
damage-limiting, some deterrence, even some war-fighting capability (though none of these is the main point
here), and a total "system" that would be no less stable, since an enemy would have no more incentive than
ever to attack our civilian population, and less incentive to attack our nuclear forces.\14 Thus, the principle that reconciles, to the extent possible, the requisites of strategy and the requisites of morality is the
most restrictive principle.

The Ethics of Statecraft

The advent of nuclear weapons, because they enable
national leaders credibly to threaten wholesale and
terminal destruction, seems to have posed a new order
of moral problems. But perhaps, rather, nuclear weapons
have only raised the old moral problems to a new order.
They have accentuated some of the older antinomies and,
moreover, have endowed them with an urgency and a
poignant reality, where they might have seemed remote
or abstract. Some of the crucial antinomies have been
broached earlier in this essay. They include the morality of principle or consequence; the ethic of individual responsibility or collective governance; and sometimes, even more starkly, and unfortunately, the competing claims of the good and the necessary. The compelling aspects of nuclear weapons cause us to pursue

questions of the source of ethical strictures, the force and scope of their obligation, and their application to statecraft. Particularly prescriptions, as I have put forward here, of unilateral no first use of nuclear weapons and some selective unreciprocated disarmament -- prescriptions which, in the first instance, seem to imply strategic disadvantage -- evoke the question of a higher principle, or a ground, on which the pursuit of ethics and the practice of statecraft can be reconciled.

I will argue that the direct, extensive, and aggressive pursuit of morally sanctioned objectives by the state, as if it were an individual operating in an authoritatively governed environment, constitutes "moralism" and leads perversely to harmful conduct and a warped international environment. In that sense, the assimilation of the morality of the state to the morality of the individual is false and potentially destructive.\15 But in an entirely other sense, international morality does depend on the creation of conditions that allow the state to pursue conduct that is comprehensible to the individual -- that is, measured on the same scale, judged by the same rule, and described in the same, whole, simple, intuitive terms.

This necessitates dispelling two fallacies that are associated with the judgment of statecraft. One is the utilitarian fallacy, an extension of the attempt by Bentham, Mill, and Sidgwick to construct a universally commensurate moral calculus. This position would condone, even commend, any conduct that produced the aggregate greatest good. In the case of the security of society, the uncritical application of the utilitarian principle could, internationally, advise the appeasement of large and urgent national appetites at the expense of the lesser, poorly articulated needs of other states and societies. It could also, within nations, lead to the sacrifice, or averaging, of the desires of certain groups, which would be pressed into collective enterprises for the sake of majority preferences. Utilitarianism also encourages an unprincipled and opportunistic treatment of occasions for intervention, by supplying a calculus by which a nation's policymakers can override discrete principles to realize immediate prospects for gain. Moreover, it allows a nation, in its own aggregate and abstract "interests," to take actions that bring damage or extinction to actual, affective units within itself and in other nations.

174

All these utilitarian tendencies -- trading off, averaging, aggregating values -- are vices to which liberal democracy is especially prone. At base, the fallacy of the utilitarian position derives from its placing all pains and evils on a single scale: from the most trivial and routine effects of ordinary behavior or organizational practice to the most severe and egregious actions, such as torture or murder to advance the cause of state.\16

A second, related, fallacy in the judgment of statecraft is the two-tier moral system elaborated by the "realists" and the "Christian pessimists." This system has achieved the sanction of a wide spectrum of political scientists, ethical philosophers, and theologians. It posits two domains, more or less autonomous: roughly, that of the statesman operating as statesman and that of the individual. It asserts the license of the amoral statesman to balance good and evil and to choose policies that would be considered immoral -- even criminal -- if perpetrated by individuals, in order to bring about a superior result for the collective. Paradoxically, the homogeneous and aggregate calculus of the utilitarians -- a common measure of good and evil -- supports the two-tier moral system -- a segmented judgment of the acts of individuals and the "reason of state." It accomplishes this by providing the rationale that underlies the second tier of this bifurcated ethic, the moral neutrality of the statesman. In this way, ironically, the "optimistic," secular ethic of utilitarianism is compatible with the strain of historical pessimism in Christianity.

The modern scripture for the two-tier moral system is the writing of Reinhold Niebuhr. In a passage attacking pacifism, he says: "It is because men are sinners that justice can be achieved only by a certain degree of coercion on one hand, and by resistance to coercion and tyranny on the other hand." (Thus, Niebuhr's moral policy implies repression internally and intervention externally.) "The refusal to recognize that sin introduces an element of conflict into the world invariably means that a morally perverse preference is given to tyranny over anarchy (war)." (But preference for tyranny represents simply passive acquiescence, while preference for war represents active intervention.) Niebuhr's bifurcated ethic proceeds from the fear, on the one hand, of the inapplicability of Jesus's standards if kept absolute and pure, and, on the other hand, of the dilution of Jesus's standards if applied indiscriminately: "Those of us who regard the

175

ethic of Jesus as finally and ultimately normative, but
as not immediately applicable to the task of securing
justice in a sinful world, are very foolish if we try
to reduce the ethic so that it will cover and justify
our prudential and relative standards and strategies."
Thus, in order to reconcile the ethic with the situation, Niebuhr is led to posit two tiers of action, with
a separate, but not equal, morality for each: "The
collective life of man undoubtedly stands on a lower
moral plane than the life of individuals."\17

A more earthly chorus of exegesis of this scripture is conducted by political scientists and diplomatic and constitutional historians, particularly of the
realist school. A single article of Arthur Schlesinger,
Jr. epitomizes the realist position and provides a
catalog of illustrations of the two-tier approach to
morality and international politics:

> Should...overt moral principles decide issues
> of foreign policy? Required to give a succinct
> answer, I am obliged to say: as little as
> possible....It was to expose such indiscrimi-
> nate moralism that Reinhold Niebuhr wrote
> Moral Man and Immoral Society forty years ago.
> Though the lesson of the penetrating book
> appears to have been forgotten in this moral-
> istic age, I cannot see that the passage of
> time has weakened the force of Niebuhr's anal-
> ysis...[T]he individual's duty of self-sacri-
> fice and the state's duty of self-preservation
> are in conflict; and this makes it impossible
> to measure the action of states by a purely
> individualistic morality...[T]he morality of
> states is inherently different from the moral-
> ity of individuals....[G]overnments in their
> nature must make decisions on different prin-
> ciples from those of personal morality."\18

The two-tier moral system legitimizes not only war
itself, but potentially all kinds of immorality to
insure the success of war. It licenses, in the sphere
of public action, the balancing of sacred and reserved
values against ordinary and tradable values. It can
lead to preemptive defense, anticipatory attacks, "efficient" means of conducting hostilities (on a scale
from political assassination to nuclear attack), and
the regimentation and repression of citizens. Encased
in authoritative governmental structures, leaders may
commit grave crimes; they may readily substitute
threats of mass murder for the more elusive and less

tangible conditions of international stability.

The realists labor a rather obvious point: that morality is difficult to pursue, let alone attain, in the "real world" of responsible collective action. But this observation is only the starting point of serious and spiritually vital discussion. The problem of the realists is that they misconceive the <u>function</u> of morality in public policy. They conceive of morality as an alternative mode of behavior or an alternative pursuit. They do not consider morality as an inescapable dimension of all behavior, or articulate morality as a set of constraints on all behavior. Thus, they confuse morality with moralism, attributing the exercise and influence of morality in the public arena variously to legalism, hypocrisy, excessive zeal, or intellectual incapacity.

But they succeed only in impugning, not invalidating, morality as a source of restraint on the statesman as well as the private individual. In short, the realists leave the problem where they found it -- recognizing the incongruous demands, on the one hand, of prudent statecraft and, on the other, of the moral strictures received through our philosophical and legal traditions and imbedded deeply in the action patterns of ordinary individuals. But they do not reach the stratum of analysis where the principle of reconciliation is to be found.

The requirement for a moral policy is both simple and complex. The simple component remains this: that the morality of state action must be comprehensible in the ordinary terms of the morality of the individual. This is a crucial long-run basis for the legitimacy of government -- where individual citizens delegate their functions to government, and government exercises the authority to compel the support of individual citizens.

The complex component is this: that the moral antinomy between the conduct of the individual and the conduct of the state is derived from, and "necessitated" by, the conditions of the environment of the state. In this limited sense, those theorists who rationalize the amoral behavior of the statesman as necessary in a power-dominated system are right -- as long as the maintenance of a certain structure of power in the international system is seen as the condition for the life of the state. So we must approach the moral question from a <u>systemic</u> perspective. If each of several powerful states attempts to pursue its own

177

safety through ordering or dominating the international system, then it is likely -- through obstruction or preemption by other states --that the entire system will be characterized by aggressive behavior imposed by reciprocal necessity; the safety of each state will, practically, be severely circumscribed.

Therefore, for the exercise of morality even to be feasible, the strategic conditions must exist -- and must be perceived to exist -- in which morality is viable. Two-tier morality is the inevitable concomitant of foreign policies of control and international systems of enforced order, whether condominium and collective security, bipolar confrontation, or the multipolar balance of power. So the causal circle is joined. The two-tier attitude toward morality is perpetuated by the types of world order we have constructed and the types of national response we have pursued.

Morality vs. Moralism

We should not be seeking a principle that leads immediately and singly to the "good." Morality, in the context of the international behavior of nation-states, does not immediately mean doing "good" and sponsoring "worthy" objects of policy. Such a pursuit of values as a motive multiplies the instances in which the state might exert its power, particularly through intervention. This is not morality, but moralism; it affords a pretext for expanding, rather than restricting, the occasions for general harm.\19 But ethical principle in the service of nonintervention becomes a limit on national action.

It is important that morality be treated as a constraint -- a limiting rather than an enabling principle. And it is important that nonintervention be regarded as the dominant constraint (corresponding to the fact that intervention/nonintervention is the dominant "dimension" of national action). Moralism is a perversion of morality precisely because it represents the widening or removal of the dominant constraint of nonintervention for the sake of a "worthy" objective. (Amoralism is simply the removal of the constraint of morality, creating a different style of foreign policy-making but leaving certain prudential constraints on intervention.) Moralism becomes the active pursuit of morality in national action, allowing -- sometimes causing, even requiring -- intervention, and paradoxically creating the general conditions for widespread immorality. Indeed, the irony is that the more "moral" are perceived to be the ends, the more egregious are permitted to be the means.

In today's context of corporate, remote, and mechanized violence, a painful dilemma presents itself: Philanthropic, expansive attitudes are not automatically systemic or policy virtues. Quite the contrary: Individual virtues are often collective vices. Thus, there is no symmetry in the attempt of a state to project the virtues of the individual. A state should incorporate the restrictive morality of the individual, refraining from destruction and harm. But it should not enforce moral principles by intervening beyond its borders, exporting force, and mobilizing some of its constituents to fight the battles and prosecute the causes of others.

Several kinds of morally based principles are expansive when applied to state action, even if they appear in the guise of qualifications or limitations. One is the justification of intervention to reinforce or establish "freedom" or "justice," or to vindicate rights or claims such as "self-determination." These principles might require intervention in the affairs of another sovereign state to bring about freedom or justice or self-determination for a portion of the population of that state. Therefore, these principles do not reduce, but rather expand, the "policy space" for intervention. Moreover, when such principles require a more interventionist posture, then the higher the value we place on them, the wider yet will be the scope for acts of intervention.

Another principle that becomes expansive is the "national interest" criterion. In conjunction with moral sympathies, it extends, rather than limits, the exercise of intervention; for moral affinities become additional interests, rather than constraints. We would intervene not only in those cases where American security interests were threatened, but also where we had a moral affinity with some nation, even if it were outside our sphere of security concerns. On the contrary, we should recognize only those moral affinities that operate inside the primary constraint of nonintervention -- that is, those moral imperatives that impose a double limit on national action.

Yet another expansive moral principle, which poses as a limiting principle, is that of the "just war." I do not intend here to review the traditional defini-

tions and conditions of the just war.\20 Rather, I
stress the general form of the rationale of the just
war: The decision to wage or risk war is justified by
the greater costs that would otherwise be incurred and
the probability of incurring those costs. So the just
war involves an allocation of costs: There is the
unavoidable weighing of some death and destruction
against other death and destruction. This calculus is
most poignant in the prosecution of limited wars "to
prevent larger wars," either through reinforcing deterrence by demonstrating capacity and will, or through
anticipating and preempting a feared future attack. In
the nuclear age, limited war is the normal case of the
just, or justified, war.

But the justification for limited war to prevent
war is, at base, the trade-off of present lives for
future lives, or some lives for other lives. The acceptance of such a trade-off depends on a utilitarian
conception of value. For usually the "wrong" people pay
for a war, whether across space or across time. In
essence, the mobilization of all to fight the battles
of a few, or some to fight the battles of others, is
the same as the infliction of limited war on a present
generation to prevent the possibility of greater war
for a future generation. The specific strictures of the
just war doctrine do not mitigate this problem.

The validity of this essentially utilitarian calculus rests on its blindness, its abstraction, and its
homogeneity -- the extent to which we do not know the
"name on the bullet." The closer one gets to identification of the actual individual casualty, the closer
the trade-off comes to deliberate and particular sacrifice -- a notion the progressive rejection of which
provides a key to the advance of civilization.

A Meta-Strategy For Morality

We do not gain much intellectual advantage by asking
the obvious "first order" question, "What is moral
conduct?" and then attempting to infuse this conduct
into the purposes and processes of a nation. Morality,
in the context of the international behavior of nation-
states, does not immediately mean doing "good" and
sponsoring "worthy" objects of policy. The trouble is
that conceptions of morality differ substantively among
nations, and some, such as communism, are as impera-
tively universalistic as ours is alleged to be.\21 If
we entertain morality as a motive, an object, or a

style of foreign policy, we only encourage expansive and interventionist behavior. Proliferated throughout a system of nation-states with diverse moralities and roughly equal capabilities, this is a prescription for unending conflict.

We are led to a more structural definition of morality. We must envisage morality in its appropriate and necessary setting -- an international system in which diverse, even conflicting, moralities can co-exist. We should be seeking a system, and a direction of national conduct within that system, that severely limits the occasions for conflict and the "necessity" for intervention. Nations must be able to afford moral foreign policies, and they must build certain consistent orientations, or presumptions, into their foreign policies, so they can make moral responses. This implies that nations should be alert to the possibility of meta-strategies that would transform the international system and condition their own structures of choice, so that morality is feasible, safe, and even profitable.

One can project the general consequences of two opposing meta-strategies toward moral conduct by nations. On the one hand, one can posit interventionist behavior by each nation in the defense and furtherance of national interests -- even admitting that the perceptions of interests are genuine and wholesome, and that the measures to secure and preserve those interests are decent and proportional. On the other hand, one can posit the situation in which each state in the international system lives within a self-denying ordinance of nonintervention. It is not hard to imagine which meta-strategy would produce less conflict, more harmonization of conduct, and ultimately a more pervasive climate for morality.

This device of a meta-strategy toward morality is the only way of breaking out of the strictly logical implications of the "Prisoner's Dilemma," the general situational predicament constructed by game theorists. This game starts with a situation where neither of two parties (originally, separately interrogated suspects) can either trust or communicate with the other, and each must make the decision to engage in, or abstain from, preemptive conduct (originally, confession and implication of the other), where (1) the consequence of abstention by oneself and not the other is extensive destruction to oneself and avoidance of destruction to the other, (2) the consequence of preemption by oneself

181

and not the other is avoidance of damage to oneself but destruction to the other, (3) the consequence of attempted preemption by both simultaneously is moderate damage to both, and (4) the consequence of abstention by both is avoidance of damage to both. Rationally -- that is, in the strict rationality posited by the game itself -- each party must adopt the third, compromise, strategy (a "minimax" strategy, minimizing the maximum damage to oneself), which, though less advantageous than the fourth, or "ideal," solution, is nevertheless "necessary" within the stringent terms of the game.

Prisoner's Dilemma -- mitigated by some communication and some chance to build mutual trust -- is the situation that might face all in an international system of autonomous, nuclear-armed, and self-interested states. The only escape is a meta-strategy of deterrence (which tends to the mutually destructive solution). In a strict, single play of Prisoner's Dilemma, such a constructive meta-solution is not "available."\22 But in a relaxed version, particularly an ongoing, many-round version, a meta-strategy of avoidance of conflict, based on indifference to strategic advantage, can lead to the ideal solution for all parties; whereas meta-strategies of deterrence, based on preservation of advantage, can lead all parties to ruin.

There is a certain convergence of the two meta-strategies, in that either, if perfectly executed by all parties, will lead to universal peace. The difference is that the universal threat of intervention is held to be, and must be, a self-executing policy, producing mutual, or (in a balance-of-power system) multilateral, deterrence.\23 Whereas universal nonintervention is somewhat more speculative -- at best, more like a self-fulfilling prophecy. The difference becomes evident if the systems break down: Universal deterrence operates on other parties, but _if_ it fails, it produces expanding disaster. Universal abstention operates only by each party on itself; if it is breached, at least the damage may be more contained.

The Kantian Leap

Escape from the general form of Prisoner's Dilemma requires not a blind leap of faith, with no structured hope of a satisfactory result, but a meta-strategy, by each nation, of rigorous, consistent nonintervention. This would amount to a "Kantian leap" to a universal regime of self-restraint and conflict avoidance.

In principle, such a meta-strategy is built on the presumption that each state will -- indeed, "must" in the case of destructive strategies -- reciprocate the behavior of each other state in adopting a certain orientation toward the international system.\24

Admittedly, the abstention of certain powerful nations from the defense and enforcement of right and justice might, empirically, seem to produce a system that would be either war-ridden or dominated by one or a few mighty, uninhibited, and immoral states. But such an empirical judgment might be premature; certainly it misses an important point: Systems such as the international order are not deterministic -- that is, they are formed by the deliberate decisions and actions of each member. The point is that, in a fragmented system of autonomous nation-states, war avoidance lies in the prescription by each state, for itself, of that action that decreases its propensity, and exposure, to conflict. The proper question is whether a rule of conduct, if adopted by individual nations, leads to an undisturbed, peaceful system or to a tension-ridden, war-prone system.

In the first "round," a restrictive concept of morality in national conduct would encourage considerable strategic indifference, and would risk the loss of certain objects that had been considered strategically necessary or morally worthy. In a later round, however, the entire international system should settle down to the revised pattern of actions and expectations. At the very minimum, the pursuit of such a meta-strategy should leave the state no worse off in its own basic security requisites. An assumed attitude of indifference to strategic objects would keep a nation out of peripheral conflicts -- at the expense of also keeping that nation out of conflicts provoked by attacks on important allies, seizures of strategic territories or passages, and control of areas of industrial strength.

But the contrary projection, which one might call the "Machiavellian" projection,\25 is a situation of overlapping interests, intervention, and mutual preemption, which arrives at mutual damage -- saving, of course, the tenuous assumption of perfect mutual deterrence. But a deterrence system, which purports to be a third, alternative, projection, is really a suspended form of the Machiavellian projection. It may be stable from day to day, in practice, but its stability is based on partial trust, partial limitation of capabilities, partial information, and partial communication. If it breaks down -- if deterrence fails -- the situation is likely to be transformed into a Prisoner's Dilemma; whereas, if the assumptions of the Kantian leap to self-restraint break down, there are still likely to be some damage-limiting -- or, more accurately, damage-avoiding -- options and mechanisms.

IV
Conclusion:
Nonintervention as a Moral Ground

In sorting out the competitive or reinforcing claims of strategic and moral factors, we should adopt the rule that more tightly limits the possible destructive actions of state. This would be the rule that accepts either nonintervention or morality, whichever is the least permissive principle. Then morality -- not moralism -- becomes not a pretext for, but a reinforcing guarantee against, war. We are also led to a construction of moral behavior that, in apparent irony, turns on official "indifference" toward what could otherwise be extensively adopted as objects of national strategy. Opportunities for moralistic intervention would be ignored, and the choice of objects of defense on moralistic grounds would be passed up. But nations might still make noninterventionist moves (defining intervention in the strict sense of the destructive use of armed force across national borders) for moral reasons and toward moral objects. Certain kinds of international pressures would still be permissible in a noninterventionist system. And such a system would promote a panoply of normal international functions -- commercial, financial, cultural, environmental -- as well as private nongovernmental relations.

This restricted, asymmetrical application of morality to qualify intervention leads to some conclusions about the related notions of justice, order, and law. This conception would be negative toward the claims of justice, insofar as justice were taken to mean the vindication of groups or nations, and skeptical of the requirements of order, insofar as order were taken to mean the preservation of structure and control, but positive about the strictures of law, insofar as law were taken to mean self-restraint and consistent, predictable behavior.

184

We would arrive at a world of buffers and restraints. With regard to nuclear strategy, restraints consist of the doctrines of targeting and precedence of use, and insulation is achieved by relinquishing extended deterrence and confining deterrence to the finite essential objects that constitute a nation's territory, the lives and domestic property of its citizens, and the integrity of their political process.

In the last analysis, it takes a noninterventionist stance to eliminate the conditions for manipulating nuclear threat or escalating to nuclear attack or counterattack. In short, to have a finite posture and strategy, we must have finite objectives, not the indefinite protection of objects of policy and the open-ended matching of the Soviets in some category of force or influence. In this respect, a succession of American administrations has had indefinite objectives and an open-ended strategy. Many of their critics in the "arms control community," concerned primarily with the stability of deterrence and the cost of defense, would still like to have the first (indefinite objectives), but without the second (open-ended strategy) -- and this might create a serious strategic contradiction and possibly lead to the most immoral position of all (inordinate reliance on the threat of nuclear retaliation). The approach I have proposed here can contemplate a finite posture and strategy because it encompasses finite objectives.

Foreign policies will not be sound until they resolve the tension between morality that is comprehensible to the individual and action that is necessary for the state. But the tension cannot be resolved simplistically in favor of one or the other. If we are to have morality in statecraft, we must have an international system and a foreign policy that permit its exercise and influence.

Notes

1. An elaboration of this and related arguments appears in Earl C. Ravenal, "Counterforce and Alliance: The Ultimate Connection," International Security, Spring 1982, and in the Report of Panel Three, "Rethinking Essential Equivalence," in Rethinking U.S. Security Policy for the 1980's, Seventh Annual National Security Affairs Conference July 21-23, 1980 (Washing-

ton, D.C.: National Defense University, 1980).

2. See, for example, General Daniel O. Graham; Max Kampelman, Zbigniew Brzezinski, and Robert Jastrow, op. ed., New York Times, January 26, 1985; and James Schlesinger.

3. We would have somewhat fewer targets, if we determine that the consequences of this scale of destruction would include a global, or Northern Hemispheric, "nuclear winter." We would also have to develop, and limit ourselves to, weapons and detonation tactics, such as airbursts, that would have the discrete and contained effects necessary to eliminate the military targets without causing excessive fallout, debris, and smoke that would rise into the atmosphere and cause occlusion of sunlight and destruction of the ozone. We would also have to design, and circumscribe, our entire retaliatory counter-military attack so that its total weight -- immediate and over time -- would be well under the threshold of massive and irreversible global ecological damage. Concern for ecological effects especially reinforces the doctrine of avoiding cities. It also contributes, in a way, to the case for some strategic defense, even if porous or partial.

4. "Nuclear Weapons and the Atlantic Alliance," Foreign Affairs 60:4, Spring 1982, pp. 753-68.

5. But American disengagement from Europe -- which, in any case, would be accomplished only over a ten-year period -- is not tantamount to the loss of Europe to Soviet aggression. Western Europe, even without American protection, would not be automatically overrun by Soviet forces, or intimidated into political subservience to the Soviet Union. The countries of Western Europe, even if not formally united in a new military alliance, have the economic, demographic, and military resources, and the advantage of natural and man-made barriers, to defeat or crucially penalize a Soviet attack. See the more ample treatment of this point in Earl C. Ravenal, NATO: The Tides of Discontent (Berkeley: University of California, Institute of International Studies, 1985).

6. In an independent American strategy of disengagement and conflict avoidance, arms control has an important, but ancillary, role. Not all aspects of arms control are designed to enhance stability; some serve the additional purposes of reducing the cost burden of preparing for war and reducing the contingent destruc-

tion of war, and in other ways conduce to a more benign international system and a more moral exercise of foreign policy. These other virtuous purposes should not excessively be traded off against stability. Arms control agreements should be sought across a wide range of situations and functions and should cover both strategic and conventional arms. For a more extensive treatment of arms control, see Earl C. Ravenal, Toward World Security: A Program for Disarmament (Washington, D.C.: Institute for Policy Studies, 1978).

7. This is a position taken in the early 1970s within the United States Catholic Conference by Rev. J. Bryan Hehir, S.J. Father Hehir himself, in contributing to the drafting of the National Conference of Catholic Bishops' pastoral letter on nuclear war in 1983, shifts the locus of this critical distinction, now placing it between threatening nuclear retaliation (illicit) and possessing a retaliatory nuclear force (licit).

8. See National Conference of Catholic Bishops, The Challenge of Peace: God's Promise and Our Response (Washington, D.C.: United States Catholic Conference, 1983).

9. The traditional doctrine of the just war invokes the jus ad bellum (the initiation of war) and the jus in bello (the conduct of war). The first stipulates that war must be waged by legitimate authority, be in a just cause, be undertaken with the intention of achieving a just and lasting peace, be undertaken as a last resort, and have a reasonable expectation of success. The second stipulates that hostilities must be proportionate to the evils opposed and discriminate in avoiding the killing of noncombatants.

10. Viz. Michael Novak et al., "Catholicism in Crisis," pamphlet, March 1983; and William V. O'Brien, "The Peace Debate and American Catholics," The Washington Quarterly, Spring 1982.

11. See Schlesinger's press conference of January 10, 1974; a transcript appears in Survival, March/April 1974, pp. 86-90. Of course, the decision by the Nixon administration to implement a new targeting doctrine had been taken nine months earlier; see George Sherman, "Debate Mounts on Schlesinger Nuclear Policy," Washington Star-News, April 15, 1974. And a series of presidential State of the World messages from 1970 stressed the need for more selective use of nuclear weapons and more flexible targeting; see Earl C. Ravenal, "The

Political-Military Gap," Foreign Policy 49:1, Summer
1971. Ikle's article is "Can Nuclear Deterrence Last
Out the Century," Foreign Affairs 51:2, January 1973.
Ikle's statement, in itself, is not yet "counterforce"
in either the original preemptive silo-busting sense or
even the second-strike damage-limiting sense of the
early 1960s.

12. See "Solution to Counterforce: Land-Based
Missile Disarmament," F.A.S. Public Interest Report,
February 1974; interview, with Ikle, February 1, 1974,
reported by Michael Getler, "U.S. Urged to Retire Land-
Based ICBMs," The Washington Post, February 2, 1974.

13. There is an alternate formulation of the nature and relationship of these types of moral rule -- a
sort of systematic statement: If one starts from the
moral point of view in designing a nuclear force structure and doctrine, one is concerned to minimize the
possibility of use and to minimize innocent casualties
if used -- both of which outcomes must be compared
against the criterion of expected losses. This appears,
then, as an "objective function," since it is expressed
in terms of minimization. But there is also another
criterion, which is absolute and therefore appears as a
"constraint," and that is the deontological or fundamental restriction that under no circumstances must one
target or intend to take the lives of innocent civilians (even though, of course, some collateral fatali-
ties might be the result of a certain strategy). The
two kinds of "equation" or "inequality" would still
have to be composed, in this case by a process analogous to "linear programming."

14. The nuclear strategy offered here differs from
that of such complete minimalists as Philip Green. See
Philip Green, Deadly Logic: The Theory of Nuclear Deterrence (Columbus: Ohio State University Press, 1966),
and his chapter in Morton A. Kaplan et al., Strategic
Thinking and Its Moral Implications (Chicago: University of Chicago Press, 1973). Green draws out the moral
logic of the nuclear situation, in the event of a
failure of deterrence, in the direction of surrender,
rather than retaliation against cities or further damage limitation against military targets. I do not believe it is necessary to go so far as to exclude military targets -- that is, to carry out the moral principle to the exclusion of any strategic benefit. (Also,
of course, minimum deterrence, coupled with a noticeable disinclination to implement even this, would
amount to very little deterrence at all.) Green's posi-

tion bears a certain resemblance to that of at least earlier drafts of the Catholic bishops' pastoral letter.

15. In other words, I dissent from the formulation of Woodrow Wilson, which is only superficially similar to the one I advance here: "We are at the beginning of an age in which it will be insisted that the same standards of conduct and of responsibility for wrong done shall be observed among nations and their governments that are observed among the individual citizens of civilized states." (From Wilson's War Message, April 2, 1917.)

16. For an extended critique of utilitarianism, see Stuart Hampshire, "Morality and Pessimism," The New York Review of Books, January 25, 1973. Hampshire favors a disaggregated, discontinuous evaluation of acts and an absolute proscription of certain acts such as the taking of life. I agree with Hampshire that a true morality requires a disaggregated view of moral constraints and that the primary fault of utilitarian doctrine is the reduction of all moral imperatives to a calculus of "commensurable gains and losses along a single scale," permitting illicit trade-offs of values. My scheme of morality in the policy process would allow -- theoretically, as well as practically -- the positing of a number of disparate moral constraints, or reserved values. In a formal "model" of the policy process, approximating a "linear program" model, these several moral constraints could be expressed as a series of separate limiting inequalities.

17. These citations are from Christianity and Power Politics (New York: Scribner's, 1940), pp. 8-18. Niebuhr's seminal work is Moral Man and Immoral Society (New York: Scribner's, 1932). Another of his texts on the same theme is The Irony of American History (New York: Scribner's, 1952). The theologian Paul Ramsey puts the case even more graphically: "...there may be modalities of morality in the use of power and in the art of government which moralists should discern that are specifically yet not generically different from the right and the good to be shown forth and accomplished in other sorts of human behavior....The covenant with Noah placed in man's hands the awful instrument of rightfully shedding the blood of any man who sheds man's blood. That legitimates government's use of evil to restrain greater evil, which evil would be limitless but for the constraints of government authority, punishment, enforcement, and countervailing interstate

encounters." ("Force and Political Responsibility," in Ernest W. Lefever, ed., Ethics and World Politics (Baltimore: Johns Hopkins University Press, 1972), pp. 44, 60.)

18. Arthur Schlesinger, "National Interests and Moral Absolutes," in Ernest W. Lefever, ed., Ethics and World Politics, op. cit. Not quite comfortable with the exclusion of morality from the area of foreign policy, Schlesinger hedges by inserting qualifying adjectives: "simple moral verdicts," "the facile intrusion of moral judgment into foreign affairs," "the easy applicability of personal moral criteria to most decisions in foreign policy," "excessive righteousness," etc. (emphasis added).

19. Without introducing the dominant dimension of intervention/nonintervention, it is impossible to make sense of the various positions on international morality, and their consequences for foreign policy. An example of the poverty of one-dimensional analysis is Ernest W. Lefever, "Morality Versus Moralism in Foreign Policy," in Ernest W. Lefever, ed., Ethics and World Politics, op. cit. Lefever restates Reinhold Niebuhr's dichotomy of "rational idealism" and "historical realism." He also characterizes Woodrow Wilson as the classic manifestation of the former. I would have to reject the analytic scheme of both Niebuhr and Lefever, since I wish to reject both "historical realism" and "rational idealism" -- if the latter implies adherence to the expansive moralism of Woodrow Wilson. Within his deficient scheme, Lefever is unable (pp. 4, 5) to define "moralism" analytically, and unable to attribute it univocally either to realism or idealism. What he calls "soft moralism" is nothing but noninterventionism.

20. This has been done comprehensively by Robert W. Tucker in The Just War: A Study in Contemporary American Doctrines (Baltimore: Johns Hopkins University Press, 1960), and in his chapters in "The Rationale of Force," Part II of Robert E. Osgood and Robert W. Tucker, Force, Order, and Justice (Baltimore: The Johns Hopkins University Press, 1967).

21. Henry Kissinger, in his Nobel Peace Prize acceptance address said: "Some common notion of justice can and must be found, for failure to do so will only bring more 'just' wars" (reprinted in Department of State Bulletin, December 31, 1973, p. 782). Unfortunately, this can be taken as another piece of occa-

sional rhetoric, exhibiting more appropriateness than conviction. Moreover, Secretary Kissinger is wrong empirically and prescriptively: It is unlikely that any common notion of justice will be found, and it is just as unlikely that such an invention would obviate "just" wars -- just as Kissinger ignores the converse possibility of a world "order" built on agnosticism about justice and abstention from its pursuit.

A confluence of laws is empirically unlikely. See Adda B. Bozeman, The Future of Law in a Multicultural World (Princeton: Princeton University Press, 1971), for a pessimistic analysis of the basic, growing, and irreconcilable divergence among Islamic, Asian, and Western concepts of law and politics, particularly the state, war and peace, and human rights.

22. This point is made by John C. Harsanyi in a review of Nigel Howard, Paradoxes of Rationality: Theory of Meta-games and Political Behavior (Cambridge: MIT, 1971), in American Political Science Review, June 1973, pp. 599-600.

By now there is a considerable literature on the relevance of the classic game of Prisoner's Dilemma to our situation in the real world. There is even a body of experimental data; see Anatol Rapoport and Albert M. Chammah, The Prisoner's Dilemma, A Study in Conflict and Co-operation (Ann Arbor: University of Michigan Press, 1965), in which two results are particularly supportive of my discussion here. First, after a period of testing of the situation, the structure of the game and its payoffs, and the attitudes of the opponent (about 50 games), the contestants have come to cooperate less and suffer more, commonly; but after about 200 replays, they arrive at a preponderance of cooperative behavior (about three-quarters of the time). Second, constantly reminding the players of the payoff matrix doubles the frequency of mutually cooperative behavior. These findings are discussed by Karl W. Deutsch, Nationalism and Its Alternatives (New York: Knopf, 1969), pp. 160-62, and they form part of the basis for his guarded hope for gradually self-corrective actions by individual states, leading to "a pluralistic world of limited international law, limited, but growing, international cooperation, and regional pluralistic security communities" (p. 190). See also Robert Axelrod, The Evolution of Cooperation (New York: Basic Books, 1984).

23. In this regard, it is important to recognize that collective security -- particularly the regime

envisaged by Woodrow Wilson in Article X of the Covenant of the League of Nations -- epitomizes a system of universal intervention: "...every member of the League, and that means every great fighting power in the world...solemnly engages to respect and preserve as against external aggression the territorial integrity and existing political independence of the other members of the League. If you do that, you have absolutely stopped ambitious and aggressive war..." (Wilson's speech in support of the League, Indianapolis, September 1919, quoted in Arthur S. Link, Wilson the Diplomatist: A Look at His Major Foreign Policies (Baltimore: Johns Hopkins University Press, 1957), p. 142. This is another illustration of the tendency of "morality," when qualifying interventionism, to expand, rather than limit, intervention and thus to become moralism.

24. The treatment of moral propositions advanced by Immanuel Kant in his "categorical imperative" makes them "testable" by imagining them as universally binding. Though this criterion is clearly not utilitarian, it is just as clearly not unempirical. Kant defines his categorical imperative in Foundations of the Metaphysics of Morals, sec. II; see the translation by Lewis W. Beck (Indianapolis: Library of Liberal Arts, Bobbs-Merrill, 1959).

My invocation of Kantian principles refers to the reasoning that underlies his categorical imperative as a general standard for the correctness of moral principles, not to the specific prescriptions and requisites of his Perpetual Peace (1795); see the translation by Helen O'Brien (London, 1927). Here, Kant states that enduring world peace must be based, among other conditions, on the existence, in every state, of republican institutions and the "ultimate sanction of the citizens" on the question of "whether there shall be war or not" (pp. 26-27). Actually, Kant's specific prescription for world order amounts to a regime of collective security -- a union of states that falls short, politically, of a confederal world, an intermediate solution between unattainable world government and unacceptable international anarchy. See the discussion of Kant's theory of international order in Kenneth N. Waltz, Man, the State, and War (New York: Columbia University Press, 1959), particularly pp. 84, 162-65. Waltz is respectful but skeptical of Kant's argument.

For my analysis the most important intellectual thrusts of Kant's ethic are: the process by which it enjoins moral conduct on states by objectifying the criteria of moral conduct (and does this on a single, not a two-tier, plane of ethical analysis); and the process by which it proceeds from the moral conduct of each individual member of the system to the definition of morality and order for the system as a whole. The flavor of these processes is caught by the phrase "as if" (as in: Nations should act in a certain way, as if the principle of their own conduct were the principle of the conduct of all others in the system). "As if" is emphatically not the same as "if" (as in: Nations should act in a certain way, if the principle of their own conduct is also the principle of the conduct of all others in the system). The latter is a principle of pure prudence, that makes a state's actions contingent on the actions of other states. To the contrary, the essential point in an international moral order based on the Kantian categorical imperative is that the conduct of each state is not contingent on the actual (or predicted) conduct of all others, but rather is conditioned on the validity of its conduct as prescribed for all others -- and thus, somewhat paradoxically, is unconditional, or "categorical." In that way, the correct conduct of each state, as if by all, leads to the correct conduct of all. Therein lies the bridge from conditionality to unconditionality, and from an aggregation of individual actions to a universal state of affairs. That is why I characterize this process as a "leap," and why I characterize the generation of world order out of this aggregation of ideal national conduct not as a "self-executing policy," but as a "self-fulfilling prophecy."

An important contemporary approach to an ethic that is appropriate to man's condition is Glenn Tinder, "Transcending Tragedy: The Idea of Civility," American Political Science Review, June 1974.

25. After Raymond Aron's distinction between the "Kantian" and the "Machiavellian"; see Peace and War: A Theory of International Relations (New York: Praeger, 1968), p. 577. In contrast with Aron, however, I do not equate Kantian "idealism" with the "contractual" motive, which posits the elimination of war through the explicit, collective behavior of states in an international order or organization. In my view, the Kantian solution is a tacit resultant of the behavior of each state, for itself.

Chapter 6

THE SCIENTISTS' DILEMMA

Sidney D. Drell

Over forty years ago the dawn of the nuclear age burst upon us as the fireballs rose over Alamogordo, Hiroshima, and Nagasaki. And with that dawn, scientists acquired a heavy responsibility for having created and unleashed unprecedented power to alter the human condition -- if not destroy the human race. The new fact that the fruits of our learning threaten the existence of all of humankind presents an acutely heightened dilemma to scientists and to society as a whole. Our predicament is precarious because we have so little, if any, margin of safety.

It is, of course, not at all new for scientists to be involved in warfare and developing weapons of death.\1 Archimedes designed fortifications and instruments of war, including a great catapult, to help thwart the Romans besieging Syracuse in the third century B.C. Leonardo da Vinci was renowned as one of the greatest military scientists of his time. He wrote to Ludovico Sforza, ruler of the principality of Milan, offering to provide any instruments of war that Sforza could desire -- military bridges, mortars, mines, chariots, catapults, and "other machines of marvelous efficacy not in common use." Michelangelo was at one time engineer-in-chief of the fortifications of Florence. So there is a very distinguished honor roll of those who have designed and built weapons.

But never before have scientists dealt with weapons of absolute destruction whose use could mean the end of civilization as we know it, if not of humankind itself. And never before has the gap been so great between scientific arguments -- even the very language of science -- and the political leaders whose decisions will shape the future. Former British Prime Minister Harold Macmillan lamented this fact in his book Pointing the Way:

> In all these affairs Prime Ministers, Ministers of Defence and Cabinets are under a great

handicap. The technicalities and uncertainties of the sophisticated weapons which they have to authorize are out of the range of normal experience. There is today a far greater gap between their own knowledge and the expert advice which they receive than there has ever been in the history of war.\2

I will confine my remarks here to the danger of nuclear holocaust, but advancing frontiers of knowledge in other areas of science, such as genetic engineering and environmental modifications, have also given human-kind unprecedented powers to alter the human condition. They too, have caused alarm and pose a special burden on scientists, individually and collectively.

One way to pose the scientists' dilemma in its sharpest form is to recognize that we are trained to approach issues such as the danger of nuclear weapons as a technical issue. We bring important physical in-sights to an understanding of the significance of a nuclear explosion, the meaning of a megaton, and the reality of radioactive fallout and its deadly human consequences. These facts must be understood because they limit the range of practical policies for facing the nuclear danger and seeking to avoid conflict. But at its most fundamental level, in dealing with nuclear weapons we are facing a profound moral issue. And to this realm the scientist brings no special expertise! Furthermore, outside the laboratory the scientist en-ters a world of policymaking and politics where shift-ing and seemingly irrational rules of politics and social interaction replace the familiar: the disci-plined study of fixed, rational, and (when fully under-stood) beautiful laws of nature. In the more turbulent realm of politics, the scientist often ends up disillu-sioned, if not injured and embittered. It was Einstein who said so appropriately that "politics is much harder than physics." But do we -- collectively as a community -- have a choice to ignore the world and the problems it faces, now that we have created these weapons of absolute destruction?

At the outset scientists recognized and warned of the moral challenge posed by the nuclear weapons of mass destruction. Physicists Enrico Fermi and I.I. Rabi powerfully summarized this moral dimension in their personal addendum to the 1949 report of the General Advisory Committee of the Atomic Energy Commission on the decision whether to develop the first thermonuclear weapon, the "super":

It is clear that the use of such a weapon cannot be justified on any ethical ground which gives a human being a certain individuality and dignity even if he happens to be a resident of an enemy country....

The fact that no limits exist to the destructiveness of this weapon makes its very existence and the knowledge of its construction a danger to humanity as a whole. It is necesssarily an evil thing considered in any light.\3

Two of the earliest pioneers of the nuclear age, J. Robert Oppenheimer and Andrei Sakharov, cautioned against the mortal dangers of the atom, which they played so important a role in unleashing. Indeed, they themselves stand as tragic reminders of the wounds and disillusionment suffered by scientists who leave their laboratories to join in a Faustian bargain with governments and policy.

Oppenheimer and his colleagues at Los Alamos were the elite of the scientific world, united in their commitment to build an atomic bomb by their fear that Hitler would acquire one from his own scientific community. Their elation at the success of their efforts was tempered by uncertainty at the wisdom and necessity of the use of the bomb in the closing stages of World War II, following Germany's defeat. As the postwar political climate chilled in a cold war with the Soviet Union, Oppenheimer and many of his colleagues were distressed at the prospects of our moving ahead to the second generation of nuclear weapons. These were the thermonuclear bombs -- today's hydrogen bombs -- for which the fission weapons or so-called atom bombs of Hiroshima and Nagasaki were mere triggers. With the ashes, rubble, and horror of Hiroshima and Nagasaki fresh in their minds, the atomic scientists sought ways to avert growth in the devastating power of weapons by yet another factor of 1,000.

Oppenheimer was chairman of the General Advisory Committee of the Atomic Energy Commission, which advised the Commission and President Truman on the matter of proceeding with the development of the hydrogen bomb. In his 1949 report to Commission, chairman David Lilienthal, on behalf of the entire committee, includes the following recommendations and concerns:

It is clear that the use of this weapon would bring about the destruction of innumerable human lives; it is not a weapon which can be used exclusively for the destruction of material installations of military or semi-military purposes. Its use therefore carries much further than the atomic bomb itself the policy of exterminating civilian populations....

We are all reluctant to see the United States take the initiative in precipitating this development. We are all agreed that it would be wrong at the present moment to commit ourselves to an all-out effort toward its development.\4

After discussing further the advisability of a decision not to develop the weapon, the report continues: "The Committee recommends that enough be declassified about the super bomb so that a public statement of policy can be made at this time."\5

But there was no public debate at that time, and we went ahead with the hydrogen bomb. In the end, Oppenheimer's questioning of the morality of developing the hydrogen bomb was one of the factors which led to his public disgrace as a security risk and left him personally devastated.

The career of Sakharov is even more poignant. His life is a morality play whose theme is the struggle between conscience and principle on one hand and brute political power on the other. We follow his path to becoming a disillusioned dissident through his own writings. Sakharov tells of his initial involvement in the Soviet hydrogen bomb project, motivated by his conviction that the world would be safer if there were a socialist bomb to balance a capitalist one:

A few months after defending my dissertation for the degree of Candidate of Doctor of Science, roughly equivalent to an American Ph.D., which occurred in the spring of 1948, I was included in a research group working on the problem of a thermonuclear weapon. I had no doubts as to the vital importance of creating a Soviet super-weapon -- for our country and for the balance of power throughout the world. Carried away by the immensity of the tasks, I worked very strenuously and became the author or co-author of several key ideas.\6

In fact, the importance of Sakharov's contribution led to his unprecedented election as a full member of the Soviet Academy of Sciences at the youthful age of 32, to his receiving many of the highest awards and prizes in the Soviet Union, and to his deserved reputation as father of the Soviet hydrogen bomb.

Sakharov writes of becoming increasingly involved during the 1950s with a military-industrial complex "blind to everything except their jobs," and he tells of coming "to reflect in general terms on the problems of peace and mankind and, in particular, on the problems of a thermonuclear war and its aftermath." His concern about the harmful effects of radioactive fallout from atmospheric testing of nuclear bombs led Sakharov to begin a campaign to halt or limit testing. He tells of speaking out in an unsuccessful effort to halt the 1958 series of tests. When the Soviets began preparing for their 1961 test series after a three-year moratorium, Sakharov wrote a note to Khrushchev saying: "To resume tests after a three-year moratorium would undermine the talks on banning tests and on disarmament and would lead to a new round in the armaments race -- especially in the sphere of intercontinental missiles and anti-missile defense." As Sakharov describes it, Khrushchev responded in an off-the-cuff after-dinner speech: "Sakharov is a good scientist. But leave it to us, who are specialists in this tricky business, to make foreign policy." He went on to say, "I would be a slob, and not chairman of the Council of Ministers, if I listened to the likes of Sakharov."\7

Sakharov tells of "the feelings of impotence and fright that seized" him when he failed to stop a very powerful and technically useless test explosion, and concludes he was deliberately misled by Khrushchev. But he also expresses satisfaction in having been able to use his position in 1962 to present to a key Soviet official an important idea from a friend, which may have been instrumental in bringing about Soviet agreement to the limited Nuclear Test Ban Treaty of 1963. This treaty banned all but underground tests, thereby removing the hazard of radioactive fallout.

Like Oppenheimer, Sakharov was disturbed by the moral consequences and political use made of his work, and he too became totally disillusioned. While exiled to Gorky and isolated from friends and scientific colleagues, Sakharov continued to caution us about the dangers of nuclear holocaust, as he did in the New York Times Magazine in 1980:

Despite all that has happened, I feel that the

questions of war and peace and disarmament are so crucial that they must be given absolute priority even in the most difficult circumstances. It is imperative that all possible means be used to solve these questions and to lay the groundwork for further progress. Most urgent of all are steps to avert a nuclear war, which is the greatest peril confronting the modern world. The goals of all responsible people in the world coincide in this regard, including, I hope and believe, the Soviet leaders....\8

It is now 44 years since Oppenheimer and his colleagues went to work to build weapons of unparalleled destructive power out of fear of Hitler's Germany. It is 39 years since the young Sakharov pitched in to build a socialist hydrogen bomb to balance a capitalist bomb, and as he then saw it, to contribute to peace and stability through deterrence. In the end they both were officially outcast and bitterly disillusioned. But given the political circumstances at the time of their decision -- and without the benefit of hindsight -- who can say that each man did not make the right choice?

As scientists we are trained and work in a field whose content is without moral values; we study the laws and building blocks of physical nature. But as human beings we must make a moral choice of whether or how to involve ourselves in the political processes that determine the uses of weapons of war.

I personally believe the scientific community would be irresponsible to turn away from this involvement. The nuclear weapons that are the fruits of our labor have radically changed the meaning of security and survival. A major nuclear war would be a catastrophe so far beyond human experience and imagination that the dreadful unknowns dwarf the calculable or predictable effects. It is well known by scientists that much of what we have learned about the effects of nuclear weapons came as surprises from the atmospheric test explosions of single bombs during the 1950s (e.g., EMP (electromagnetic pulse), the Van Allen belt,\9 and distant deadly fallout). How can we even begin to imagine the enormity of the catastrophe of a nuclear war, its long-term and perhaps permanent scars on the earth, and the barriers to the recovery of societies and survivors? In view of the scale of the danger and extent of the unknowns, as a society we face no greater

200

challenge than that of avoiding nuclear war. The primary responsibility, as well as authority, to lead the world away from the brink of a nuclear holocaust lies with the leaders of government and with societies as a whole. But in formulating policies, physical and technical realities must be recognized and respected. Laws of nature cannot be coerced or classified, and scientists must see to it that they are understood and applied correctly. Of course, it will take a two-way effort to close the gap, lamented by Harold Macmillan, between societies and the scientists, but it must be closed.

Government cannot dispense with the scientist. It has an obligation to arrange for the best possible scientific analysis and advice before making its decisions or raising false expectations. Furthermore, scientific advice must be neutral and free of political and doctrinal biases. This is not easy to achieve. As scientists we may be experts, but we are also human. Personal biases occasionally cloud our professional judgment, although some of us manage to control them better than others. A diverse body of experts is needed to provide judgments which are balanced and informed. President Eisenhower understood these issues well when he created, in 1958, the position of a full-time science adviser in the White House and also established the President's Science Advisory Committee, which served the President and the nation well for more than a decade before it was disbanded in 1974. He also showed his wisdom when he responded to a question about the political affiliation of his scientific advisers by saying, "I don't want to know."

The need for sound scientific advice is especially pressing today since President Reagan's famous "Star Wars" speech of March 23, 1983, in which he called on the scientists "who gave us nuclear weapons to turn their great talents now to the cause of mankind and world peace, to give us the means of rendering these nuclear weapons impotent and obsolete," and he held out hope of a world free of the nuclear threat of retaliation. How should we respond to this call?

The President's proposal for a shift from deterrence based on the mutual fear of nuclear retaliation to reliance on defense against nuclear annihilation has strong appeal. The impulse to look to our weapons and armed forces to defend us, rather than threaten others, is a natural and deeply ingrained one with long historical precedent in the era before nuclear weapons.

Throughout history, military analysts have grappled
with the role of offense versus defense. Many instances
in the past can be cited where defense has proven
decisive to the outcome of combat. Today, however, when
we face the staggering destructive power of nuclear
weapons, when just one single, relatively small nuclear
bomb is a weapon of mass destruction, we must recognize
that effective defenses must meet a much higher standard of performance than at any previous time in warfare's history. A 10 percent defense such as that which
won the Battle of Britain -- or even a 90 percent
defense -- against today's threat of almost 10,000
strategic nuclear warheads cannot protect a nation from
nuclear annihilation. So profound has been the change
in the level of destructiveness that simplistic historical comparisons are often misleading. The debate on
defense has been relatively dormant since the ABM Treaty of SALT I was ratified in 1972. Now that the President has rekindled it, it is important to look at the
practical side of the issue of offense versus defense
under the shadow of current nuclear arsenals. He is
calling for nothing less than a fundamental change in
the basic strategic relationship between the United
States and the Soviet Union, which today is based on
the fact that we are defenseless against each other's
nuclear weapons. We live in a balance of terror as
mutual hostages.

It is a physical reality that if either superpower
launches a nuclear attack it faces the risk of a nuclear retaliatory strike that can cause damage sufficiently large as to endanger its own existence. While neither the U.S. nor the Soviet Union has made the destruction of enemy populations in response to enemy
attack an explicit policy objective, it is fully recognized that, should a large fraction of the superpowers'
arsenals be used under any doctrine, under any choice
of attack pattern, or for any purpose, the risk to the
survival of the societies of both countries is very
grave indeed. Mutual assured destruction (MAD) is not a
doctrine promulgated by some misguided policymakers
willing to gamble with the survival of their country.
Although MAD is frequently represented as such, nothing
can be farther from the truth. What we are facing is a
technical condition that I believe cannot be escaped by
technology alone.

Furthermore, in a situation of mutual vulnerability, the principal tool to avoid nuclear war is maintaining the stability of the balance. This means giving
highest priority to avoiding a situation where either

202

the U.S. or the Soviet Union would be tempted to preempt the other in time of crisis, seeing that as preferable to facing a likely attack by their opponent. In other words, crisis stability calls for minimizing the perceived advantage to the party that attacks first.

It is no good to be a target with vulnerable forces. Programs that improve the invulnerability of one's retaliatory forces -- including command, control, and communications (C-3) -- can contribute to stability, and this goes for both the United States and the Soviet Union. Scientists can contribute to stability in important ways, one of which is the creation of national technical means which will make it possible to verify compliance with arms limitation agreements.

The ABM Treaty of 1972 is at the base of efforts to approach stability, avoid nuclear war, and achieve arms reductions. It is more than a set of limitations on a class of weapons developments and deployments, and it is more than a symbol of hopes for future arms control progress. It defines the common premises of the U.S.-Soviet strategic relationship, and these are necessary to the pursuit of agreements on political measures to avoid nuclear war.

It cannot be stressed too strongly that the basic purpose of severely limiting ABMs by this treaty was not to save money, and surely not to achieve mutual assured destruction. No government has ever had a policy of pursuing mutual destruction. Rather, we seek mutual survival by recognizing mutual vulnerabilities. The ABM treaty is the formal recognition that mutual destruction could not be escaped if the superpowers were drawn by accident or design into nuclear war.

The technical and political realities of 1972 led the United States and Soviet Union to endorse the basic principles of deterrence and stability and to negotiate limitations on ABMs. In its broadest dimension the ABM treaty is an early milestone in the political approach to avoiding nuclear war.

In explaining his decision on to forego broad defense of the nation in favor of a limited safeguard ABM system designed primarily to defend U.S. retaliatory forces, President Nixon said the following on March 14, 1969:

Although every instinct motivates me to pro-

vide <u>the American people with complete protec-</u>
<u>tion against a major nuclear attack</u>, it is not
now within our power to do so. The heaviest
defense system we considered, one designed to
protect our major cities, still could not
prevent a catastrophic level of U.S. fatali-
ties from a deliberate all-out Soviet attack.
And it might look to an opponent like the
prelude to an offensive strategy threatening
the Soviet deterrent. (emphasis added)

But this whole approach has now been challenged.
The President's "Star Wars" initiative raises fundamental issues regarding U.S. strategic policy that go to
the heart of the superpowers' strategic relationship.
This applies both to the President's explicit vision to
escape from or to transcend deterrence by achieving a
totally effective defense against strategic nuclear
weapons and also to the more modest goal of enhancing
deterrence through an effective, but partial, ABM defense that is now emphasized by the Defense Department.
I am referring here to the Strategic Defense Initiative
(SDI) program as submitted to Congress in 1984 by the
Department of Defense (DoD) and reaffirmed by a White
House statement in January 1985 in which enhanced deterrence is stated as the central purpose.

Much confusion in the public debate on SDI stems
from the fact that the current DoD program to enhance
deterrence differs from the President's vision. Let us
look at both the President's vision and the current DoD
program separately. Is the President's vision to transcend or escape deterrence realistic? What has changed
from 1972 to 1985 that could now make it possible? In
particular, where do scientists and their new technologies figure in this renewed debate? What follows is a
personal assessment based on long experience and continued work on this problem.

Technology has made major advances since the ABM
treaty was ratified in 1972. These include advances in
sensors, battle-management capabilities, computers,
information handling; and in producing, aiming, and
directing high-power beams for target kill.

However, the challenge to create a nationwide
defense is much more than a technical one. Even if the
ambitious and costly research and development program
proposed by the administration achieves its major goals
extending far beyond presently demonstrated technologies, great operational difficulties will still remain.

It is difficult for a responsible scientist to say flatly that a task is impossible to achieve by technical means without being accused of being a "nay sayer." Indeed, many instances can be cited in which prominent scientists have concluded that a task is impossible only to be proved wrong by future discoveries. One should recognize, however, that the deployment of an impenetrable defense over the nation is not a single technical achievement but the evolution of an extensive and exceedingly complex system that must work reliably in a hostile environment against a determined and uncooperative opponent. Furthermore, one must have continued high confidence in the defense system and its ability to accomplish the enormous task of battle management in very short time frames -- especially against an offense that can adopt a broad repertoire of countermeasures against it -- although it can never be tested under realistic conditions. The system would have to work perfectly the first time it is used, especially in a nuclear environment. This is, to put it mildly, a preposterous requirement.

Protection against ballistic missiles requires many links in a defensive chain, all of which are crucial. There must be sensors to provide early warning of an attack and a command structure with authority to make decisions to commit defensive forces on exceedingly short notice and then to implement those decisions efficiently. This raises the grave question of whether this chain of command, from warning to decision, must be totally automated or may contain human links. The defensive system must also have sensors that acquire and track enemy missiles and then aim and fire defensive devices, whether they are material interceptors, such as chemical rockets or hyper-velocity guns, or directed-energy devices. Sensors must also determine which of the attacking missiles have been destroyed in order to fight secondary or tertiary engagements successfully.

Even the most optimistic protagonist for defensive systems agrees that no single layer of defense could possibly be effective. Thus SDI describes its goal as a multilayered defense of extensive scope, capable of attacking ballistic missiles during the boost phase as they are lifted into space, then during the midcourse of their flight, and finally, during reentry over their targets.

I strongly emphasize that the issue is not whether a specific technology for the interception of incoming

205

ballistic missiles can be demonstrated. There is no question that a single reentry vehicle from a ballistic missile can be destroyed by nuclear explosives lofted by interceptors -- as was shown to be feasible in earlier developments -- or by nonnuclear, high-velocity projectiles -- as was demonstrated by the U.S. Air Force in June 1984. I also believe that a demonstration can be staged in which an ascending intercontinental ballistic missile (ICBM) rocket can be damaged by airborne or spaceborne laser beams. However, such demonstrations of intercepting and destroying cooperating targets hardly have bearing on the feasibility of the overall system or the solution of operational problems. To illustrate an operational difficulty that cannot be avoided, consider the basing of killer beams. If these defensive systems are deployed in space, they will be vulnerable to direct attack from the ground or by space mines.

Furthermore, space-based ABM platforms would be large, expensive, fragile, and more vulnerable than the ICBMs against which they are targeted. They are also inefficient since they are on station above the launch areas of attacking missiles only a small percentage of the time as they circle the earth. As a result, they must be duplicated many times over. I share a judgment given by Edward Teller in testimony to the Senate Armed Services Committee, shortly after the President's 1983 speech, that a space-based laser system does not offer a credible prospect of an effective defensive layer.

To avoid vulnerability, the systems may be ground-based and mounted on missiles poised to launch -- that is, to pop up -- upon notification of enemy attack. One such example is the X-ray laser pumped by a nuclear explosive and designed to attack the rising ICBM during its boost phase. The most important operational difficulty of a pop-up system is the lack of time available for it to reach above the atmosphere and engage the attacking missiles. Such a system would have to be forward-based, because it cannot see over the horizon, and automated for quick response. This poses serious policy problems because the automated processes would necessarily involve decisions of whether and how to respond -- including authorized release of nuclear weapons -- depending on the intensity and tactics of the attack. In addition to these formidable operational requirements, countermeasures technically available to the offensive party can further impede any possibility of a pop-up X-ray laser defense. One countermeasure is simply to redesign the offense with new high-thrust hot missiles that sacrifice only a small fraction of their payload in order to complete their burn at altitudes below the top of the atmosphere.

There are other possible technical remedies, but it is simply not possible to escape all of these problems. It is for these reasons that I see no prospect of building a totally effective nationwide defense against ballistic missiles. This is true against the current Soviet threat, and I see absolutely no present prospect of achieving such a defense against an unlimited offensive threat that can overwhelm it with more warheads, evade it with cruise missiles and bombers which have flight paths entirely within the atmosphere, or directly attack it. I agree with Dr. Richard DeLauer, under secretary of defense for research and engineering from 1981 to 1984, who said to reporters in May 1983: "With unconstrained proliferation, no defensive system will work."\10

If a totally effective defense is unattainable, how about a partially effective one to enhance deterrence? When submitting the five-year program for SDI in March 1984, DeLauer testified before the House Committee on Armed Services that Defense Department studies have concluded that advanced defensive technologies could offer the potential to enhance deterrence and help prevent nuclear war by reducing significantly the military utility of Soviet preemptive attacks and by undermining an aggressor's confidence of a successful attack against the United States or our allies. Program advocates claim that this mission can be met by even a less-than-perfect area defense of population and industry.

It is indeed true that if a potential attacker faces the prospect of attrition of its forces by a defense in addition to the expected retaliatory strike, its confidence in the success of the planned attack would decrease and the complexity of planning such a move would increase. If one could anticipate that this would be the only Soviet reaction to an expanded SDI, one might consider this to be sufficient reason to move ahead toward deployment of a nationwide defense against ballistic missiles. However, the much more likely Soviet response would be to initiate a variety of programs to counteract the effectiveness of such defenses and to retain full confidence in its deterrent. More than likely it would also move ahead with intensified defense programs of its own. The net result of these moves and countermoves would be the addition of yet another component to the arms competition between the superpowers, in both offensive and defensive forces, and the end of the ABM Treaty of 1972, which explicitly prohibits the development and deployment of nationwide ballistic missile defenses. In consequence, the security of the United States would be diminished, not increased.

Unless we first establish an arms control framework by making progress in negotiating and ratifying treaties restraining future weapons developments, testing, and buildup, it is not unthinkable or unreasonable for the Soviets to view our defensive programs, accompanied by our ongoing intensive effort to modernize and improve our offensive forces, as evidence of developing a first-strike capability -- a first strike that would leave them with a weakened retaliatory force against which our defenses, although imperfect, would be relatively more effective. Of course, the same would be true if the roles of the Soviet Union and the United States were reversed. Recall how in 1960 we responded to Soviet MIRVs.

MIRV technology was originally stimulated by the initial limited deployment and anticipated expansion of ballistic missile defenses around Moscow. By substantially increasing the firepower of the offense -- measured in the number of warheads and damage expectancy, not megatonnage -- MIRVs have not made us more secure; they themselves have become the focus of instability by their growing threat to land-based U.S. and Soviet ICBMs. And it was both cheaper and simpler for offensive countermeasures to offset defenses.

To summarize, as I see it, "Star Wars" offers no path to achieving either of the two visions that have given it momentum: the vision to substitute a defensive strategy for deterrence and the vision to create, or even improve, the environment for arms control and reductions. Most likely an accelerated buildup in strategic defense will lead to a more dangerous world by stimulating an arms race, a competition of countermeasures and confrontation, leaving the ABM treaty in its wake as a monument to past hopes. It is a bad idea!

But our judgments about what to do in strategic defense research as a hedge against technological surprises or Soviet actions cannot simply be answered by a yes or no. We have to develop both a diplomatic and technical approach which carefully define what we should and should not be doing -- outlining how to avoid endangering the ABM Treaty and hopes for reductions in offensive weaponry in the Geneva talks, while at the same time protecting ourselves from technological surprises or from dangerous exposure to Soviet actions should they choose to break from treaty restraints. We need to find a position that neither exaggerates nor underestimates Soviet abilities.

As I have tried to illustrate, the "Star Wars" issue is clearly one of such great technical complexity that scientists should play a central role in helping clarify what can and cannot be done, the opportunities as well as limitations of the technology, and the dangers of going ahead with defenses as opposed to remaining defenseless against nuclear terror. Better yet, scientists should explore whether a new path can be paved to a less dangerous world. Science has an important contribution to make here, but if we are to make an effective contribution there is much to do:

--we must study the technology and understand it;

--we must understand the political process;

--we must learn to make ourselves understood as well as credible to people without technical training.

This kind of activity takes patience, work, and training and is rarely, if ever, as exciting as science in the laboratory. It is often frustrating and, as Oppenheimer and Sakharov have learned, can leave you feeling deceived. And it takes humility to work in a political arena that Einstein correctly characterized as more difficult than physics.

In the last analysis, I do not see the path to a safer world paved by technology alone -- or even in large measure. Instead I think the scientific community as a whole bears a major responsibility to work to remove the threat of nuclear holocaust by venturing into the unfamiliar and hazardous political arena. It is our obligation to generations yet unborn.

Notes

1. The following discussion of the scientists' responsibility and dilemma relies on material from the

209

author's Danz Lectures, which were collected in <u>Facing the Threat of Nuclear Weapons</u> (Seattle: University of Washington Press, 1983).

2. Harold Macmillan, <u>Pointing the Way, 1959-1961</u> (London: Macmillan, 1972), p. 250.

3. Enrico Fermi and I.I. Rabi, addendum to the Report of the General Advisory Committee of the Atomic Energy Commission, 1949, as quoted in Herbert Frank York, <u>The Advisors</u> (San Francisco: W.H. Freeman, 1976), p. 158.

4. Herbert Frank York, <u>The Advisors</u>, op. cit., pp. 155-56.

5. Ibid., p. 156.

6. Andrei D. Sakharov <u>Sakharov Speaks</u>, Edited and with a forward by Harrison E. Salisbury (London: Collins/Harvill, 1974) pp. 29-30.

7. Ibid., p. 32.

8. Andrei D. Sakharov, <u>New York Times Magazine</u>, June 8, 1980.

9. A belt of intense ionizing radiation that surrounds the earth in the outer atmosphere.

10. Quoted by Richard Halloran in <u>New York Times</u>, May 18, 1983.

Chapter 7

The Mirrored Image:
How Americans Wrongly Think They Can Make a Safer World
through Arms Negotiations with the Soviets

Henry S. Rowen

Debate about limiting nuclear arms has become a popular
pastime in this country in the last decade. A striking
feature of this discourse is its inward-looking and
moralistic character. We devote much of our energy to
debating the rights and wrongs of such doctrines as
mutual assured destruction (MAD), no first use, nuclear
"freezes," and the pros and cons of the MX, the Midgetman, and other weapons, while sorting out the good guys
from the bad guys by the depth of their commitment to
reaching agreements with the Soviets. Meanwhile, the
Soviets, unperturbed by any domestic debate on these
matters, go on building missiles, bombers, defenses,
and bomb shelters.

The intensity of the debate obscures some important elements of agreement among most people in the
West on the importance of avoiding nuclear war. Disagreements are mostly about how best to avoid nuclear
war and also about the weight that should be given to
other goals (that might possibly, but not necessarily,
conflict), such as protecting Western Europe. This is
true both of utilitarians, who concentrate on the ends
sought (avoidance of major war of any kind, protection
of Europe), and those who focus on the morality of the
means employed (deterrence through the threatened use
of nuclear weapons).

Disagreement about methods marked the debate on
control of nuclear arms in the 1984 presidential campaign. Walter Mondale repeatedly spoke of the "ever-
rising arms race," "this arms madness," and the essen-
tiality of negotiated arms control. The President had
already raised the ante in his March 23, 1983, speech
on ballistic missile defense -- the "Star Wars" speech
-- by posing the ultimate goal of eliminating nuclear
weapons. During the campaign Ronald Reagan also presented himself as an arms controller and as a tougher
negotiator.

Mondale endorsed the position that nuclear weapons have no military utility, that their use would be suicide, and that they exist only to be controlled. He approvingly cited a book by Strobe Talbott, <u>Deadly Gambits</u>, on these themes.\1 According to Mondale, <u>any</u> agreement that "controls" nuclear weapons is good. Those in favor of doing whatever seemed necessary to get agreements are the good guys, while those who hold out for stronger stands are the bad guys.

The Soviet Union hardly figures in Talbott's account, nor does it figure in many other writings on this subject. To the extent that it is does, the Soviet Union is portrayed as a kind of mirror image of the United States in its aims, military posture, and doctrines. Although there are some points of similarity between the U.S. and the USSR, especially in their levels of technology, this is a wild distortion of reality.

Let me be specific on several ways in which this mirror reflects falsely:
- For nearly two decades, from the late 1950s to the late 1970s, the U.S. reduced the scale of its spending on offensive and defensive nuclear forces, while the Soviets increased theirs.
- We virtually abandoned efforts to defend the U.S. from nuclear attack in the early 1960s, while the Soviets expanded their efforts.
- We chose not to build any antiballistic missile (ABM) defenses, while the Soviets went ahead with the one permitted under the ABM Treaty.
- For many years we did little to modernize our nuclear forces in Europe, in contrast to the Soviets.
- We reduced the size of our overall nuclear stockpile and its total megatonnage, while the Soviets increased theirs.
- The Soviets have violated the ABM Treaty and other arms control understandings, while we have not.

These facts are simply ignored by many Americans and Europeans who hang on to dogma about the nature of the Soviet Union, our relationship to that country, and the evolution of the nuclear competition. On this last topic, three beliefs are central: that we are caught up in an ever-escalating arms race; that both sides have a hair-trigger posture that is susceptible to triggering events leading to a nuclear exchange; and that overwhelming destruction would be inevitable if any nuclear weapons were used. This last belief -- total devastation -- is described by some as not a question

212

of choice but simply as a "condition." Not only have these concepts been widely promulgated in the West but, in accordance with the prevailing assumption of symmetry, they are also attributed to the leaders of the Soviet Union. The "fix" for these problems is held to be either mutual agreement on arms or unilateral American reduction (a less widely shared view).

Whatever the evidence in support of such beliefs and whatever their prospects at the time of their formulation in the 1950s and 1960s (and the prospects were small based on what we knew of the Soviets then), those who continue to hold them must confront the evidence of the past twenty years. Enthusiasts for arms control are reluctant to do this, and confronting the evidence was also largely avoided during the 1984 campaign. As in the case of Strobe Talbott and Walter Mondale, agreements are simply assumed to be good.

I summarize the history of American nuclear strategy as follows. Richard Nixon and Henry Kissinger set out in 1969 to do three things: slow the nuclear arms race; lower incentives for a preemptive nuclear strike by reducing the threat to our nuclear forces while keeping populations vulnerable (MAD); and link nuclear arms agreements to detente, which implied restrained Soviet interventions around the world.

What happened was rather different. American real spending on nuclear forces, which peaked in the late 1950s, continued to decline before and after the signing of SALT I in 1972. (Our spending increased significantly only after the Soviet invasion of Afghanistan in 1979.) Meanwhile, Soviet spending tripled to almost twice ours for offensive nuclear forces and three times ours for total offensive and defensive forces. The same happened with nuclear stockpiles -- ours went down and theirs went up. As former Defense Secretary Harold Brown has put it, when we build, they build; when we stop, they build.

As for reducing Soviet incentives to strike our nuclear forces -- in particular, our missile silos -- the American negotiators failed to get the Soviets to specify what they understood to be "heavy" missiles, which were the only ones assumed able to destroy silos. Contrary to the expectations of our negotiators, the Soviets multiplied silo-destroying warheads drastically. And with their increasingly accurate warheads, even smaller warheads on lighter missiles now pose a grave threat to our silo-based missiles and will

213

threaten MX missiles. Our negotiators failed to recognize that guidance technology was following a trend that would make dangerous even a much smaller force of smaller missiles than the sizes agreed upon in SALT I or the lowest level seriously debated for tabling in START.

We also rejected an ABM defense of our missile silos on the grounds that it might be extended to defend our cities. This point bears reflection. In a passion to assure that our cities and people would be exposed to nuclear attack (in accordance with the principle of MAD), we gave up a major option for the defense of our missiles. With a vulnerable land-based missile force, we now find ourselves reduced to a set of dangerous or doubtful alternatives. Meanwhile the Soviets, far from adhering to the MAD concept of leveling off and cutting back on offensive forces and leaving the population undefended, not only stepped up their investment in offensive forces but (exercising their ABM Treaty right) built an ABM defense of the Moscow region. Lately they have been discovered to have departed from our agreements in several ways, including the building of a big radar in the middle of the country, a clear violation of the ABM Treaty. Of course the defenders of arms control and the ABM Treaty contend that Congress never ratified SALT II, so we have no right to complain about their offensive-system "deviations." Besides, the Soviet radar is really only a space-tracking station, and, anyway, we have some peculiar radars too. It makes one wonder how arms control is going to bring stability and peace.

The proposition that nuclear weapons should be directed only against populations, a central tenet of MAD, has received more support than one might have expected given its inconsistency with deeply held Western moral values. For instance, the recent American Catholic bishops' statement on nuclear weapons, although confused and inconsistent on several key matters, was unambiguous on the inadmissability of a policy aimed at killing noncombatants. Moreover, this moral prohibition is not contradicted by arguments of a utilitarian nature, as we shall see below.

As for linkage between arms control and more restrained Soviet behavior around the world, that hope faded with Soviet-backed interventions in Angola, Ethiopia, and Cambodia, and disappeared entirely with the invasion of Afghanistan.

According to McGeorge Bundy, George Kennan, Robert McNamara, and Gerard Smith, writing in a recent issue of _Foreign Affairs_, we should not abandon "the shared view of nuclear defense that underlies not only the ABM Treaty, but all our later negotiations on strategic weapons."\2 But the Soviet leaders have not shared our views. For twenty years, as we built down -- almost eliminating our air defenses, dropping civil defense, and drastically reducing the megatonnage of and spending on offensive forces -- they built up. Moscow has never shared the distinctly American view of arms control. To Moscow, the functions of arms control are threefold: to impede our program where we have a technical advantage (ballistic missile defense in the early 1970s) or where we are behind and are about to catch up or surpass them (anti-satellite weapons and ballistic missile defenses today); to prevent deployment intended to strengthen U.S. ties to Europe (blocking NATO's intermediate-range missiles); and to try to preserve a Soviet advantage ("heavy" missiles in SALT I).

In 1957 Henry Kissinger expressed a view that finds more support in the record than that expressed in the _Foreign Affairs_ article:

> The emphasis of traditional diplomacy on "good faith" and "willingness to come to an agreement" is a positive handicap when it comes to dealing with a power dedicated to overthrowing the international system. For it is precisely "good faith" and "willingness to come to an agreement" which are lacking....\3

The overall strategy of the Soviet Union, of which its arms negotiating position is a part, is focused on expanding its control -- or, in the short run, at least its influence -- near its periphery: Europe, the Persian Gulf, Central Asia, and China. To support this expansion the Soviets want to have more effective -- accurate, protected, controllable -- arms, both conventional and nuclear, than their opponents. The many new Soviet long-range missiles and bombers which naturally preoccupy Americans are intended to deter us from defending Europe and other vital areas. Failing that, these weapons are for actual use against our forces, whether in the areas of direct conflict or here at home. Marshal Ogarkov, former chief of the General Staff, has told his troops: "The possibility is recognized of conducting protracted military operations with conventional weapons alone, and, in individual theaters of military operations, even with the limited use of nuclear weapons."\4 When Soviet spokesmen speak to the West, however, they usually send a different message, such as: "any use of nuclear weapons by one side will inevitably lead to the immediate use of that side's entire arsenals."

But there is no place in Soviet doctrine for unlimited or suicidal nuclear war. Their vast investments in anti-aircraft and anti-missile defense and civil defense (high in quality for elites, low for the masses) do not reflect a belief that the use of one or a few nuclear weapons will end the world. There is a major difference between the two sides in posture and beliefs in this respect. Although many of these Soviet systems might not work, the magnitude of their preparations for war -- and specifically for nuclear war -- is impressive. Another measure of the serious nature of Soviet war preparations is the share of their GNP devoted to nuclear offensive and defensive forces, which is _three_ _times_ that of the U.S. -- about three percent of the GNP for them, and one percent for us. They spend more on defenses alone, active and passive, than we do on offensive forces. This doesn't mean that they take a casual view of nuclear war -- or any kind of war, for that matter. On the contrary, they are more serious about it than we are.

There are growing signs that the Soviets recognize that there are limits to the coercive threats of nuclear war and that the risks associated with their actual use could be very high. For some time, some Soviet authors have been emphasizing the importance of having a powerful capacity to wage war at the non-nuclear level; Soviet investments in conventional forces reflect this perspective. But it is also true that the Soviets have not visibly scaled back their nuclear investments either.

The Soviets want to extend their influence, and the U.S. is the biggest roadblock in their way. Therefore, a primary Soviet aim in negotiating, as well as in arming, is to weaken and fragment our alliances. In 1984 the main Soviet negotiating effort was directed at preventing any deployment of our missiles in Europe. It failed. In 1985 they concentrated on stopping the President's Strategic Defense Initiative (SDI). They also persisted in trying to slow or stop the European missile program; recently they proposed a freeze on these deployments at a level which gives them about a ten-to-one advantage in warheads.

In negotiating Moscow has learned that it can get help from dedicated Western believers in MAD who work to kill troublesome U.S. programs, such as those for the construction of highly accurate long-range cruise missiles, while the USSR pursues such programs with unrelenting vigor. Now there are protests that we must not do anything in the SDI program that could conceivably be construed as violating the ABM Treaty, such as developing a defense against medium- or short-range missiles threatening our military units in Europe (even though the Treaty clearly prohibits a defense only against "strategic" weapons). Meanwhile, the Soviets are violating the treaty as well as other understandings.

It should be clear that the alternative is not an uncontrolled nuclear arms race in which both sides build increasingly threatening weapons and spend more money on nuclear arms. We demonstrated the feasibility of unilaterally cutting spending on these arms over an extended period of time. Some people might respond with the observation -- or charge -- that we modernized our forces in the process. Of course there is a continuing evolution and competition in technology. Sometimes this leads to the emergence of weapons of great and indiscriminate destructiveness, as with the fission bomb and especially the early thermonuclear bombs. Also, early long-range missiles equipped with these weapons were very inaccurate, a property which compounded the prospect of vast and indiscriminate damage. But technology can also work in the other direction, toward more precision and less indiscriminate damage. We have been introducing much more accurate weapons with lower yields (as have the Soviets). We have also been making improvements in conventional weapons which sometimes enables their substitution for nuclear ones. Moreover, advancing technology has permitted new and more secure methods of basing nuclear forces and of providing for their more reliable control. Finally, technology is advancing the possibility of defense against ballistic-missile attacks. In these respects, recent trends in technology are coming to the support of the bishops' injunction against killing noncombatants.

In short, the technological competition can yield both troublesome and desirable technologies, or "bad" and "good" ones, if you prefer. This process is not one in which bad, that is, indiscriminate, weapons will necessarily drive out good ones in a kind of military equivalent of Gresham's law. However, I do not want to be understood as suggesting that all is for the best in

this best of all possible worlds; much more should be
done to reduce the destructiveness of nuclear weapons
and our dependence on them altogether.

The main question is how to accomplish this.   We
need to set about making necessary changes, such as
moving more vigorously toward smaller-yield, more accurate reentry vehicles (and away from high-yield vehicles); pursuing technologies for cruise missiles and
smart weapons (mainly for nonnuclear missions); developing stealth technology; and researching ballistic-
missile defenses.

I want to be clear on a key point: It is not just
that the arms control endeavors of the past twenty
years have failed in their goals. These endeavors, or
more accurately, the climate of opinion in the U.S. on
nuclear strategy and forces during this period, expressed both in arms negotiations and weapons decisions, actually helped to <u>worsen</u> our security. For
example, the MX was designed as a large, multi-warhead
missile in part because we had agreed to restrictions
on launchers in SALT I. As a result, we ended up with a
missile which will be vulnerable and have a good silo-
killing capacity, a bad combination for stability in an
acute crisis. The Brooke Amendment of the early 1970s
was directed against improvements in the accuracy of
our missiles. Our 54 Titan II missiles, which became
increasingly vulnerable and unreliable over time, were
kept as bargaining chips in SALT negotiations largely
because they were our only approximation to "heavy"
missiles. Mobile missiles were opposed for a time because they were hard to count verifiably, even though
they would be much less vulnerable to attack. Cruise
missiles have been opposed because it is not possible
to verify whether they contain nuclear warheads. Ballistic-missile defenses have been opposed because they
might be used to protect people in addition to missiles.

When defenders of the arms control enterprise
claim, as they often do, that our agreements have not
prevented us from deploying the weapons that we wanted,
they slide over the question of who "we" are. Many
people other than the President and the secretary of
defense make decisions in the government. These many
subordinates get their cues from the (often discordant)
statements and decisions of their seniors. Sometimes
the alternatives they perceive, or even their decisions, are not visible to those at the top. And members
of Congress have their own instruments of power, such

218

as those enumerated in the Brooke Amendment. In short, it was faulty reasoning about our interests, the nature of the arms competition with the Soviet Union, and how the state would behave that was the common cause of disadvantageous agreements and some bad U.S. weapons choices.

In the past several years attention has been focused on intermediate-range missiles in Europe. Following the deployment of SS-20 missiles by the Soviet Union, which was part of a large build-up of both nuclear and nonnuclear forces, the NATO governments decided in December 1979 to station intermediate-range missiles in several European countries. This NATO force was seen as largely symbolic, one that would help to link the U.S. more visibly to Europe. However, the NATO governments, responding to their domestic antinuclear movements, also decided to pursue an agreement that would do away with these missiles on both sides -- despite the fact that the main cause of the NATO deployment, growing Soviet power, would remain.

After much debate in Germany and other European countries, the decision was made to go ahead with the deployment of these missiles. Then came the Reagan-Gorbachev summit meeting in Reykjavik in which their elimination, and more, was discussed. It now appears that a far-reaching agreement on nuclear delivery systems in Europe will be signed.

Whatever the merits of the Euro-missile issue, it is evident that it has implications for the strategy for Europe's defense which now urgently need to be considered. We need to recognize that the enormous growth of Soviet nuclear strength has eroded -- some would say practically eliminated -- what was a major element in the U.S. strategy for defending allies. That change, together with large increases in Soviet conventional forces, makes Soviet moves on its periphery less threatening. (The Soviet preference in such moves, perhaps a condition of them, is to avoid engagement with the United States, and also naturally to avoid conflict of any kind.) Although stronger conventional forces are essential to prevent or to cope with Soviet moves against areas vital to our national interest, nuclear weapons are also needed mainly to deter Soviet nuclear attack. They also have some residual value in discouraging nonnuclear attack, especially in Europe. The upshot is that we should both steadily reduce our dependence on nuclear weapons and continue to improve our ability to use them -- if we have to -- in more discriminate ways.

This argues for making our nuclear forces as effective as possible against Soviet military forces. The
resources available provide us with about 11,000 nuclear warheads on 2,000 long-range missiles and bombers; 4,000 to 5,000 of these have a good chance of
surviving a well-executed sudden Soviet attack. This
substantial number of weapons, allowing for losses en
route, could destroy a wide range of Soviet targets,
including ground, air, and naval forces, lines of communication, and nuclear offensive forces. We would be
able to hold in reserve a large enough force to give
the Soviets an extra incentive not to make the all-out
attack on our cities that we have feared, but have had
no good reason to believe they have ever planned. This
implies being able to avoid inflicting collateral damage -- as a by-product of attack on military targets --
on Poles, Czechs, Great Russians, and other innocent
civilians. Being capable only of such indiscriminate
damage would not only increase the likelihood of our
being the victims of such damage ourselves, but much
more likely would lead to our political collapse in a
crisis.

We are also short of missiles accurate enough to
destroy key Soviet facilities with confidence, an objective that the Scowcroft Commission described as
being "able to put at risk those types of Soviet targets -- including hardened ones such as military command bunkers and facilities, missile silos...which the
Soviet leaders have given every indication by their
actions they value most."\5 However, bureaucratic iner-
tia as well as the ideology of MAD has kept us from
fully exploiting the emerging technologies of accurate
guidance. For instance, terminal guidance of cruise
missiles creates the potential for accuracy measured by
a few feet. More broadly, our main competitive advantage across all weapon categories is to fully exploit
our technological superiority in making smarter, more
accurate, more controllable, "stealthier" weapons.

Our land-based ICBMs (intercontinental ballistic
missiles) are also highly vulnerable in their silos. It
is not yet clear that any reasonable solution can be
found to basing protected missiles in the U.S., but if
there is a solution, it presumably involves a combination of mobility, hardening, deceptive basing, and
missile defenses. Arms control agreements will not fix
this problem; no feasible constraint on Soviet forces
is going to enable ordinary silo-based ICBMs to sur-

vive, given basic trends in the accuracy of Soviet weapons. Despite all of this, our negotiators are back in Geneva. That being so, we could do worse than have two more years of palaver while each side pursues its own programs. At least that would be better than signing more bad agreements.

Are there no possible agreements of value to both the U.S. and the Soviet Union? We have a few now: the agreement not to poison the atmosphere with radioactivity (the Nuclear Test Ban Treaty); the agreement on avoiding military incidents or accidents (the agreement on "rules of the road" to avoid naval incidents and the "Hot Line" Agreements); and efforts to slow the spread of nuclear weapons (through the Nonproliferation Treaty). I do not include on this list the ABM Treaty, the arms controllers' favorite agreement, for reasons I have given earlier. My answer to the question, "What is the future role of arms control agreements?" is, to quote the old soldier's order, "elevate them sights a little lower." Agreements might be sought on "rules of the road" for military satellites in space (but not by trying to ban anti-satellite weapons, as the Soviets have attempted) and on avoiding a possible global "nuclear winter" from the massive use of nuclear weapons against cities.

Missing here is negotiation to shrink nuclear forces. It is not that all 11,000 offensive warheads of 2,000 delivery vehicles are vital to our survival. The law of diminishing marginal utility applies. We have reduced the number and explosive yield of our weapons, with much of this reduction taking place _before_ arms control negotiation began, and we could unilaterally reduce our stockpiles in the future. But when we try to limit forces by agreement, we get mostly some self-restraint plus the illusion of Soviet restraint. As the illusion is gradually stripped away, as it has been on SALT, we hesitate to react because it is painful to face reality. Notwithstanding the potential for agreements on selected issues, I believe that there is no important U.S. objective related to the balance of nuclear forces -- or the role of these forces in discouraging Soviet moves abroad -- which is attainable through any remotely feasible arms control agreement. Nor will the Soviets agree to anything that either forces them to abandon their aim of splitting our alliances or hinders them in coercing the democracies. If we want a better-protected and more discriminate nuclear force and, if possible, a less costly one, and if we want to diminish the role of nuclear weapons in

our defense strategy, we will have to pursue these
goals on our own.

This conclusion, of course, runs counter to the
popular demand in this country and in Western Europe
that we persist in negotiations. These demands reflect
deeply felt concerns in the West about nuclear weapons.
There are also widely and deeply held values about
preserving freedoms. Reconciling these yearnings is the
continuing and difficult task of statesmanship. There
has also been a marked shift in opinion among elites
toward a position of greater skepticism on the accomplishments of negotiated arms agreements. Perhaps the
key event marking this shift was the failure of the
U.S. Senate to ratify SALT II. There has also been a
noticeable willingness in Congress to appropriate funds
in support of the Carter and Reagan administrations'
nuclear buildup, and European governments are going
ahead with missile deployments.

Thus, the arms control/security debate is amply
supplied with conflicting views, a familiar phenomenon
in democracies. In this situation negotiations are
politically required. But our leaders also have a responsibility -- not adequately met in the SALT negotiations -- to tell the public essential truths on such
crucial matters. In short, public expectations about
what is likely to be achieved should be kept at a low
level, while our negotiators should be alert to possible agreements on specific topics where an increase in
our security might actually be achieved.

Notes

1. Strobe Talbott, Deadly Gambits (New York:
Knopf, 1984).

2. "The President's Choice: Star Wars or Arms
Control," Foreign Affairs, Winter 1984/85, pp. 264-278.

3. Henry A. Kissinger, Nuclear Weapons and Foreign
Policy (New York: Harper, for the Council on Foreign
Relations, 1957).

4. Marshal N.V. Ogarkov, Sovetskaya Voyennaya
Entsiklopediya (Soviet Military Encyclopedia) (Moscow:
Voyenizdat, 1979), vol. 7, p. 563.

        5. Report of the President's Commission on Strate-
gic Forces (Scowcroft Commission), 1983.

Comments by Dennis Ross

Henry Rowen must surely be regarded as one of the deans of American civilian strategy. Few people understand the substance and challenges of strategy in the nuclear era as well. Professor Rowen's views on issues of war and peace, nuclear strategy, and the role of arms control are important, frequently provocative, and always worthy of serious consideration.

His current paper is no exception in this regard. Basically, his theme might be summarized as follows: the U.S. and the Soviets approach nuclear strategy and arms control differently; the arms controllers in our country have not understood this and have instead been blinded by their own tendency to treat Soviet behavior as a mirror image of ours; the gaps in our strategic approaches rule out any meaningful arms control agreements; and therefore, we should take unilateral military steps and not pursue the chimeras of arms control to meet the needs of our security.

I would like to take a brief look at several of these issues. In particular, I will take a closer look at the strategic gaps separating the U.S. and USSR; suggest that these gaps do limit the kinds of arms control agreements that are possible; ask whether such limited agreements threaten our security; and finally, conclude by raising a question about the consequences of dispensing with the arms control process as we know it.

What causes the asymmetries between U.S. and Soviet strategic force postures? Perhaps I should start by noting that I agree with Professor Rowen's view that there are real asymmetries between the U.S. and Soviet force postures and that these asymmetries necessarily limit what can be achieved in the arms control process. Whereas Professor Rowen basically focuses on different manifestations of behavior to highlight the gaps between the U.S. and the Soviets -- e.g., "We observe arms control agreements, the Soviets violate them" -- I prefer to take a more structural approach to account for the differences. By this I mean that I believe one can learn more about the gaps and their implications by looking at the inputs or factors that shape our competing force postures than by looking only at particular behavior or output.

In this regard, it is worth noting that our dif-

ferent force structures have grown out of very different geographical settings and, related to this, different military needs. They have also grown out of different military and bureaucratic traditions, rates of
technological development, and military doctrines.
Unlike the U.S., the Soviet Union has been very much a
continental land power. The Soviet military has traditionally been preoccupied with regional threats, and
their missile forces have been viewed as a kind of
long-range artillery designed to deal with regional
threats by providing fire support en masse. The Soviets
developed bigger missiles in part because of technological limits but also in part because the "big-missile"
design teams had more success and political clout than
competing design bureaus. Even in the nuclear era,
Soviet military doctrine has emphasized traditional
military missions and values -- meaning that the military's job in wartime has been defined as prevailing
over the adversary and limiting the possible damage the
adversary can inflict. The Soviet military takes this
responsibility seriously not because they seek a war or
believe that the horrific consequences of such a war
could be easily contained, but rather because Soviet
experience and ideology make it clear that wars can
happen and they had better be prepared for them.

Clearly, a variety of factors have contributed to
the existence of a Soviet force posture that looks very
different from ours, with the bulk of Soviet nuclear
firepower in ICBMs. As the Soviets began MIRVing their
ICBMs -- equipping them with multiple independently
targeted reentry vehicles -- and as the accuracy of
their warheads dramatically improved, that force posture increasingly threatened the survivability of our
land-based forces.

Not surprisingly, we have sought to use the arms
control process to contain this threat by proposing
deep cuts in ICBM launchers, throw weight, and warheads. The Soviets have viewed our proposals -- which
required much greater cuts on their side, given their
much larger ICBM force -- as thinly veiled attempts to
get them to surrender their most effective weapons and
to develop a force posture that served our needs and
not theirs. We have seen our proposals as offering a
way to create greater strategic stability and convergence.

The basic problem is that arms control has not
been, and is not likely to be, able to produce the
kinds of changes in the force structures of both sides

that would make convergence possible. In the absence of greater parallels in our respective force structures -- so that one side does not have to make the lion's share of the concessions -- the kinds of arms control agreements that are likely are the kinds we have seen to this point, namely, the SALT I and SALT II agreements.

Do these kinds of agreements threaten our security? I would argue that neither SALT I nor SALT II did, largely because they did not really prevent us from doing anything that we might have regarded as important to our security. By the same token, because they did not limit much, they also did not do much to enhance our security. Professor Rowen is surely right when he says that arms control to date has not succeeded in achieving the Nixon/Kissinger objectives of slowing the arms race, lowering incentives for preemptive nuclear strikes by reducing the threats to our respective nuclear forces, and fostering more moderate competition in the Third World.

Professor Rowen believes that the kinds of agreements that have been achieved to date harm our defense because they create the illusion of security. If that were so, however, one might ask why we have gone ahead with our strategic modernization plans. After all, the basic elements of our strategic modernization program -- MX, B-1, stealth, cruise missiles, Trident I and II -- were all initiated in the Ford and Carter administrations. If we had been lulled by the illusion of security created by SALT I and SALT II, we presumably would have scaled down dramatically on these programs.

The reality is, of course, that arms control has not slowed the pace of modernization on either the U.S. or the Soviet side. That is surely one of the reasons that the arms control process as we know it has not achieved very much.

So long as both sides see arms control as a vehicle for attempting to get the other to reduce those weapons it most fears, while preserving the weapons it most values, arms control cannot be expected to get very far. Certainly the fear that one's government will be put at a grave disadvantage if it makes concessions in the military area where it is most competitive makes both sides reluctant to take significant steps in arms control.

Such a phenomenon is not particularly new. Historically, arms limitation negotiations have been characterized by each side attempting to preserve its own advantages while seeking to restrict those weapons or asymmetries that most favor its opponents. Note, for example, that in the various talks in the 1920s, Britain and the United States, as chief naval powers, sought to abolish the submarine and retain battleships and aircraft carriers, while the lesser naval powers sought to limit the latter and retain the former. France, as the major land power, sought to retain tanks and heavy guns, while the lesser land powers sought restrictions on them.

Not surprisingly, throughout SALT and now START, the Soviets have sought to preserve their heavy missiles, while limiting each new U.S. system or development, including MIRVs, cruise missiles, and now SDI. As noted above, we have done the reverse.

The certainty that this behavior will continue is, I believe, one reason that the strategic nuclear relationship is an essentially stable one, where neither side is likely to gain any appreciable advantage. Two other factors make the relationship fundamentally stable. One is the very size of the nuclear arsenals: on each side warheads number between 9,000 and 11,000. The other is the reality that, regardless of how selective one's nuclear targeting options become, neither side will ever be keen on actually carrying out its nuclear threats.

I see signs that the Soviets have come to appreciate the fundamental stability of the strategic nuclear relationship. And these signs are not only limited to leadership statements about the catastrophe of nuclear war that Professor Rowen believes exist only for Western consumption. (In this regard, more and more of the Soviet professional military literature, written for Soviet military consumption, speaks of the inability to guarantee or predict outcomes when conflicts go nuclear. That cannot be a particularly reassuring sentiment for a Soviet military audience when it comes from those charged with ensuring that the USSR must prevail if a nuclear war should occur.)

At a higher level, authoritative statements with operational overtones have been made by the late Defense Minister Dmitri Ustinov and the former Chief of Staff Nikolai Ogarkov. Both spoke of the impossibility of escaping retaliation and, in effect, of the unshakable stability at the strategic nuclear level. Ustinov said that this stability argued for the adoption of a no-first-use pledge, which he also noted required greater operational controls to ensure no accidental or unsanctioned release of nuclear weapons.\1 Ogarkov suggested that the balance at the strategic level and the certainty that it could not easily be shaken argued for the direction of more resources into new technologies, especially at the conventional level.\2

If nothing else, these examples suggest that both sides may well understand the fundamental stability that exists at the strategic nuclear level. That does not mean that either side will simply agree to alter its force structures for the sake of arms control. In fact, there remains considerable commitment on each side to maintaining the shape of its present forces -- witness our commitment to going ahead with the MX in a vulnerable basing mode and the continuing Soviet commitment to their SS-18s and SS-19s at a time when mobile substitutes would have a far greater chance of survival.

Since the existence of basic stability at the strategic level does not remove the asymmetries in the force structures and make arms control more likely, one could ask, Why shouldn't we take the unilateral steps Professor Rowen suggests? If the nuclear equation is basically stable and the arms control process as we know it is not likely to achieve much militarily, then why not adopt this position and basically dispense with arms control?

One could raise a number of problems or questions in this regard, but for purposes of this commentary I prefer to raise just one general concern that Professor Rowen may not have considered fully enough: we cannot approach this whole question as if we had never had an arms control process; we cannot deal with arms control as if we were starting from scratch.

The process has created a set of expectations here and in Europe, and these expectations and images will not go away. They have great political currency and strong moral overtones, and they have succeeded in making President Reagan, among others, a strong devotee of arms control.

Since one of Professor Rowen's major concerns with the current arms control process is that the Soviets will continue to try to use it to split the NATO alliance, it is important for him to consider how the alliance would be affected if it became clear that we were no longer serious about arms control. It seems to me that the adoption of such a posture -- for which Professor Rowen seems to be arguing -- could have the very effect he hopes to avoid.

Notes

1. Marshal Dmitri Ustinov, "Rejecting the Threat of Nuclear War," _Pravda_, July 12, 1982, p. 4. Ustinov was specifically referring to the operational implications that prevention of nuclear war had on the training of troops, on the organization of headquarters, and on which Soviets had the authority to release nuclear weapons.

2. Interview with Marshal Nikolai Ogarkov, _kraznaia zvezda_, May 9, 1984, p. 1.

PART III:
ETHICAL PERSPECTIVES
ON POLICY CHOICES

Chapter 8

ECONOMIC DEVELOPMENT: THE ROLE OF VALUES

Dwight H. Perkins

Do values and beliefs affect economic development around the world? Almost everyone, even economists, would answer that they do, but there would be little agreement over how. Most economists avoid the subject on the grounds that economic tools have little to contribute to an understanding of the role of values in development. Other social scientists are less reluctant to discuss values, but all too often they fail to combine these discussions with an in-depth understanding of the other dimensions of economic development.

Those who study economic growth recognize that there is a major gap in our understanding of the nature of development, but there are considerable differences in the ways they propose closing it. The problem, to be sure, can be posed in conventional economic terms. In the language of growth accounting, the issue is why some countries have such a high rate of growth in total factor productivity while others experience little, no, or even negative productivity growth. There is also the question of why some countries are effective at mobilizing domestic capital and labor resources while other nations are not.\1

The contrast between the fastest-growing region of the world, East Asia, and the slowest-growing region, sub-Saharan Africa, illustrates the problem. The record of Japan and the "gang of four" (South Korea, Taiwan, Hong Kong, and Singapore) is well known. During the 1960s and 1970s, these countries sustained annual GDP (gross domestic product) growth rates of 9 to 10 percent a year (7 to 8 percent per capita); they achieved high rates of capital formation (more than 30 percent of GDP in Japan and Singapore; somewhat lower in the 1960s and early 1970s in South Korea)\2; and their labor forces grew at 2 percent per year (except for Japan which was lower). The increase in these inputs accounts for only about half the rise in production in each country but Singapore. The remainder came from productivity increases or what is sometimes referred to

233

as the "residual."

In sub-Saharan Africa, the labor force also grew
at 2 percent per year in the 1960s and 1970s, and the
rate of capital formation was quite high (averaging 23
percent of GDP in the 1970s).\3 But as the investment
rate rose from under 20 percent in the 1960s to over 20
percent on average in the 1970s, the growth rate of GDP
fell from 4 to 3 percent and the rate of population
increase rose from 2.5 to 2.7 percent. The result was
that per capita GDP hardly rose at all in the 1970s and
actually began to fall in the early 1980s.

There are many reasons for the stark contrast
between East Asian and sub-Saharan African economic
performance. World Bank studies cite the proliferation
of badly designed and implemented projects in Africa,
the mismanagement and excessive number of state-owned
enterprises, and overvalued exchange rates that discriminate against agriculture. Some of the problems
have been due in part to nature -- the ever-present
threat of drought, for example -- but most of the
difficulties have been man-made, the direct result of
inappropriate government policies. There is little
doubt that if the many inappropriate policies were
changed, the situation in Africa would improve. Some
African nations are in fact making the necessary policy
changes, but the question is why so many are persisting
in policies that are so self-defeating in terms of
national development. Part of the answer is that these
societies have often become corrupt or "rent-seeking"
societies, in which powerful figures use their power to
further their narrow self-interests.\4 But even this
does not get at the real heart of the problem -- why
these societies tolerate leaders that behave in this
way. It is not that large numbers of people are ignorant about what is going on, nor is it credible to
suggest that this situation serves the interests of the
industrialized capitalist nations of the West, who keep
it in place (although some individuals in the industrial capitalist countries do no doubt benefit from the
situation).

The major theme of this essay is that governments
and their leaders are allowed to continue in this kind
of behavior in part because there is no shared set of
values among actual or potential holders of power in
those societies that transcends narrow group interests.
And, in the absence of such transcending values, there
is little incentive or capacity on the part of the
political leadership to promote sustained economic

development. This lack of shared values is not handed down through the ages and fixed for all time, but can change quite suddenly if conditions are ripe.

A secondary theme is that the specific content of transcending beliefs and attitudes does matter, but not as much as the ideologues of state planning or the free market would have us believe. The Protestant ethic used to be thought of as an essential ingredient for successful development.\5 More recently the Confucian ethic has been deemed an essential element in East Asia's economic performance. No doubt there are elements in both Protestant Christianity and Confucianism that are consistent with and even supportive of growth-oriented government policies and individual performance; but there are many antidevelopment components to both philosophies or religions as well. The beliefs that affect development policy most are not necessarily those deeply embedded in a society's religious experience, but those that shape how a nation and its leaders perceive their own role -- whether they are there to serve broad national interests as opposed to small group interests. Development policy is also affected by how these leaders perceive the world beyond their borders, i.e., as hostile territory full of dangerous predators where the rules are stacked against a new entrant, or as a place full of opportunity.

I
Unified and Stable Government Policies

It used to be taken for granted -- but now must be stated explicitly -- that governments can and must play an essential role in economic development. Even a policy of pure laissez-faire (and Hong Kong is the only place in the world where true laissez-faire capitalism prevails) requires deliberate acts on the part of the government to provide an infrastructure and institutions supportive of well-functioning markets. In most countries, of course, the role of the government in the economy is far more pervasive than this. Governments frequently own a significant share of the nation's major enterprises, provide a large proportion of development expenditures, set taxes which influence prices (particularly of imports), and much else.

Governments must not only follow policies that are conducive to development, but must do so on a sustained

and consistent basis. To maintain consistency the government itself must remain stable. In fact, an appropriate definition of a stable government is one that
can maintain a consistent set of development policies
over at least a decade and preferably longer. At issue
is not whether the name of the leader changes every two
or three years, as has been the case in Japan, but
whether each succeeding leader moves infrequently and
cautiously to alter inherited development policy.

A striking feature of the most successful Asian
economies is the consistency of their development policies. Japan is democratic and the others are authoritarian; but it is not their authoritarianism that sets
them apart. Most developing countries have authoritarian governments, and many have leaders who have held
office for one or two decades (although the latter
situation is less and less true in Africa as the
"founders" of the newly independent states die off or
are overthrown). What sets the successful developers of
Asia apart is their ability to set development policies
and goals designed to serve broad national interests
rather than the narrower purposes of particularly powerful individuals or groups. Of course corruption does
exist, and members of political coalitions get paid off
in various ways, but somehow these special interests
have not been allowed to submerge the broader national
goals. The reason this was possible, I shall argue, is
that these nations were able to achieve a considerable
degree of consensus or shared values on economic goals
at least -- a consensus that has not been seriously
challenged by any opposition group during the past two
decades.

To emphasize shared values is not to deny that the
state had other resources at its command with which it
could compel compliance with development policies. For
example all of the successful Asian developing states,
except postwar Japan, have relied significantly on
instruments of coercion. Growth, once underway, gave
governments additional means to induce compliance,
including high-paying jobs and opportunities for entrepreneurial profits. However, many nations have been
unable to achieve a stable environment for development
policy with these same instruments available to induce
compliance, including some in the best position to
"buy" stability because of natural-resource wealth --
Nigeria with its oil wealth being a good case in point.

How has this degree of consensus and the resulting
stability been achieved in Asia? And why has a compara-

ble degree of consensus been so difficult to achieve in much of Africa?

East Asia has not always been blessed by the current level of consensus on economic goals. Japan is the one exception in the region: During the nineteenth century the Japanese were able to throw off the feudal shogunate, abolish many of the hereditary privileges of the feudal leadership, and embark on a development program that lasted into the twentieth century. There was only one serious challenge to this program, the Satsuma Rebellion in 1877, which was quickly put down. One reason for this quick transition from feudalism, it has been argued, is that the Japanese were loyal to the lord, the man, not to the system or set of be-liefs.\6 If the lord decided to change the system, the retainer followed with little sense of inner conflict. Unity around economic policy may also have been made easier by the homogeneity of the Japanese people and the fact that the nation had been basically unified, despite its formal feudal structure, for over two hun-dred years. There was also the external threat from the sea in the form of Commodore Perry and his successors.

China, too, faced an external threat and had a relatively homogeneous populace, although less so than Japan. All Chinese who could read and write could communicate with each other, although, unlike in Japan, spoken dialects did differ. The Chinese had a longer tradition of being a unified state than Japan; China, in fact, had not been divided for any length of time for six hundred years.\7 Achieving unity over such a vast area and such a large population was one of the great achievements of Chinese civilization and was largely attributable to the fact that China's governing elite shared a common set of Confucian values carefully nurtured by years of study and a state examination system.

Yet, China's imperial unity collapsed at the turn of the twentieth century, and the discrediting of the Confucian system of government made it impossible to rebuild that traditional basis for unified government. Despite many continuing shared values, and despite the external threat from the imperial powers, China de-scended into the chaos of warlordism from which it did not fully emerge until 1949. Descriptions of the venal-ity of Chinese government and military officials in the period 1900-49 are not unlike those emanating from present-day Nigeria.\8 For large numbers of Chinese, including many of the educated, the highest goal was to serve the interests of their own family. By the late 1940s, the Nationalist government was so undermined internally by such values that it was incapable of pursuing anything but the most feeble defense of its own survival.

Many, perhaps most, Chinese were not happy with this state of affairs and many joined the Communists, seeing them as the only hope of restoring a true national unity based on purposes higher than narrow self-interest. It wasn't just the Communists on the mainland that achieved unity and a sense of national purpose after 1949; the Nationalist government, after retreating to Taiwan, also succeeded in restoring a more transcendent goal than lining its own pockets. Whether it was an instinct for survival or simply that a better group of people were able to gain control after the debacle on the mainland is history still to be written.\9 What is clear is that the government in Taiwan was unified and dedicated to the purpose of systematically strengthening itself.

The mainland Chinese government was able to unify the country around the goals of development for ten years after 1949, until the mistakes of the Great Leap Forward (1958-60) led to a deep split in the leadership of the Chinese Communist Party. That split caused great uncertainty in the minds of Chinese development planners, particularly during the Cultural Revolution period (1966-76), and that uncertainty was an important if indirect reason why China's overall growth rate averaged only 4.5 to 5 percent per year (2.5 to 3 percent per capita) from 1952 to 1979. While that is a respectable rate of growth in historical terms, it is well below that of the other nations of East Asia during this period and probably is well below China's current growth rate.

In contrast, Taiwan had few major internal disagreements over development policy after 1949, and the only significant change in top leadership occurred when Chiang Kai-shek died and was replaced by his son Chiang Ching-kuo. Even some of the key economic ministers, such as K.T. Li, served for unusually long periods of time. If unity of purpose had not been maintained and rapid economic growth not achieved, Taiwan might not have survived as a separate entity. Perhaps the instinct for survival itself created the required unity of purpose, but one suspects there is much more to the story. Shared Confucian values, including respect for and obedience to husband, father, and emperor (or president), presumably also played a role.

What is it that triggers a sudden change from long periods of instability to one of unity and stability? In mainland China it was exhaustion after thirteen years of war and civil war plus the victory of a disciplined party and army. The people were ready and eager for stability, and the party had the internal cohesion and national legitimacy needed to provide it. The case of South Korea, however, may be significant to a greater number of other countries because unity did not evolve out of a decade and more of warfare and exhaustion.

Korea regained its independence from Japan in 1945, and was concurrently split in two by the Yalta agreement. In the South there was low-level guerilla warfare and chaos in national politics. In 1948, Syngman Rhee was brought back from decades in exile abroad to be president. By his own political skills and with the help of the U.S. Army after the advent of the Korean War, he remained precariously in power until he was overthrown in 1960 in the aftermath of student riots. There are many reasons why one would expect unity to be more easily achievable in Korea than in many other nations. Korea had a thousand-year history of unity, the Korean people are racially and culturally homogeneous (minor regional variations in culture notwithstanding), and they speak the same language. The division between North and South initially caused a measure of disunity in the South, but the behavior of the North during the Korean War so alienated those in the South that fear of the North -- and of any renewal of the Korean War -- became a powerful stabilizing force. In addition, land reform and the destruction of private assets in urban areas during the war meant that most people in the South started out more or less from a position of equality; class divisions were thus not an important source of internal political conflict. Yet, the Chang Myon government, which was freely elected in 1960, had great trouble ending low-level violence in the nation and succumbed quickly to a military coup.\10

Park Chung Hee, who came to power as a result of the coup, ruled for seventeen years and was not effectively challenged until the end of that period. How could a military coup create the long period of political stability that proved so instrumental to rapid economic growth? Initially the answer may be no more than that the people were tired of political chaos.

239

The ability of the army to restore and maintain order
was in part due to the fact that it was the one large,
cohesive, and disciplined institution in Korean society. Not all commanders supported the coup; many in
fact felt that the army had no place in politics, but
they didn't challenge the Park government. As the years
passed, the government's claim to legitimacy rested not
so much on its ability to avoid chaos as on its ability
to achieve rapid economic growth. President Park was
even able to win a reasonably open and honest election
in 1967. Under these circumstances, unity and stability
were reinforced by the basic cultural homogeneity of
the Korean people, the fear of the North, and the
comparative lack of sharp class differences. A large
part of the population could share the government's
goal of emphasizing growth because so many people saw
that they were sharing, or might soon have the opportunity to share, in the benefits of economic growth.

In contrast to China, Taiwan, and both Koreas, the
experience of Singapore illustrates that the cohesive
organization that brings unity and stability need not
necessarily be the army. Singapore, on the eve of
independence, was wracked by politically motivated
strikes often led by the Political Action Party (PAP),
which was itself split between moderate and radical
factions. With help from the British, the moderate wing
of the PAP, under Lee Kuan Yew, gained control of the
party. After a brief experiment as part of Malaysia,
Singapore was pushed out of the Malaysian federation
and began two decades of uninterrupted rule by the PAP
and Lee Kuan Yew (who is still in power). In principle
Singapore is a multiracial state, although 70 percent
of the population is Chinese and the leadership is
mostly Chinese. With a population of only 2.4 million,
Singapore is also small. Most Singaporeans see themselves as a tiny and somewhat vulnerable Chinese island. They feel threatened by Malaysia and Indonesia,
their neighbors in the Malay Sea, even if at present
this external threat is seen only as a potential one.
The Singapore government does employ restrictions on
the press and other information sources, but the degree
of coercion is quite mild when compared with many other
states that have had much less success in achieving
stability.
Some generalizations about the sources of unity
and stability can be drawn from the experiences of
China, Taiwan, South Korea, Singapore, and Japan.
China, Taiwan, Korea, and to a lesser degree Singapore
went through periods of extreme instability so that one
cannot make a case that societies based on Confucian

culture are by nature always orderly. In most of these countries, order was initially achieved by a political and/or military organization that was internally unified and well-organized (the Chinese Communist Party, the mainlander group that took over Taiwan after 1949, the South Korean Army, and the PAP in Singapore). Rule was sometimes legitimized by elections, but only Japan had a completely free and open political process, and this not until after World War II. All of these governments strove early on to consolidate and maintain power by bringing concrete benefits to the great majority of their people. All of them (with the exception of one of the two major factions in China in the 1960s and early 1970s) saw rapid economic growth as the principal vehicle for achieving this end.

Because these governments had the strength initially to restore order and unity and because they embarked almost immediately on successful economic development programs, they were able to take advantage of the other unifying elements in their societies: a common cultural heritage, in most cases a common language, a shared perception of an external threat, and a lack of deep class divisions and extreme forms of income inequality. Confucian values of a son's obedience to his father and a father's obedience to the emperor or, in modern terms, the state, may also have reinforced unity and stability.

In contrasting this East Asian experience with the situation in much of sub-Saharan Africa, some of the essential causes of the disunity and instability that have plagued so many African countries become clear. Most of sub-Saharan Africa did not achieve independence until the early 1960s. The new nation-states were the creations of colonial administrations and their political structures bore almost no relation to those which existed in Africa prior to colonization in the late nineteenth century. Previously, the principal form of political organization had been the tribe, and tribal relationships and loyalties still play a major role in how people relate to each other today. Overlaying these tribal differences are differences in religion, with Islam pressing southward across the Sahel, Christianity pushing inland from enclaves on the coast, and with many Africans accepting neither. A second overlay is the culture of the colonial metropole, principally France and England, and to a lesser extent, Portugal and Belgium. Only this last element had much influence on how boundaries were drawn.

The situation in West Africa illustrates the problems caused by these competing influences.\11 If West
Africa were divided along reasonably homogeneous ecological and cultural lines, one would travel through
four distinct regions journeying inland from the coast.
The coastal area is dominated by cash crops grown for
export; it contains the major cities and is primarily
Christian. In the second zone, which is also Christian,
mainly food crops are grown. And, while the third zone
also produces food crops, it is partly Moslem. The
fourth zone is desert, commercial, and nomadic, and it
is primarily Moslem because this was the area most
easily reached by Moslem traders who used the desert
much as sailors did the sea. Thus there are four quite
distinct ecological and cultural areas, and the boundaries between them are reinforced by tribal differences, but the unity within areas is also reduced by
those same differences.

National boundaries, however, show no relation to
these zones. Following colonial administrative lines,
they cut right across them, and in the case of the
larger countries such as Nigeria, cut across all four.
The results of this method of nation-building, which
left nations containing many distinct tribal or cultural groups, have been coups or civil wars based on
cultural or tribal differences, including those in
Nigeria, Chad, Sudan, Uganda, and Angola.

Political instability is not the only result of
this situation; development efforts also suffer. It is
difficult for political leaders to conceptualize and
carry out development programs designed to promote the
welfare of the majority of the people in a nation.
Development, instead, has become a way for leaders to
retain power and control over allocation of the fruits
of political power by rewarding their own ethnic group
and building coalitions with other groups. Formal education has little to do with this process. Ghana and
Nigeria, which had two of the most well-educated populations in Africa, are among the most vigorous practi-
tioners of this kind of politics today. Under such a
system, it is virtually impossible to run state-owned
enterprises efficiently because a primary role of the
enterprises is to reward political supporters. It isn't
easy to run efficient private enterprises either: the
state has numerous measures at its command (e.g., tariffs, quotas, government construction contracts) which
can make inefficiency in the private sector just as
profitable to one's supporters.\12

242

Does it follow that Africa is doomed to continue on this path indefinitely into the future? Certainly there are grounds for pessimism. Unlike the countries of East Asia, African nations are not culturally homogeneous and have not experienced centuries of self-rule within boundaries similar to those that exist today. The African nations that have known long periods of unity and stability are those that are still ruled by their founding fathers -- the individuals who led them to independence from colonial rule, or at least presided over the process. How many of these nations will remain stable after these leaders leave the scene? They cannot be replaced, for each new nation has only one "founding president."

Although there are many grounds for pessimism about Africa's ability to achieve the unity and stability needed for development, it may not be entirely warranted. As the East Asian experience demonstrates, unity and stability can occur quite suddenly under a government dedicated to broad development goals. And once it comes, successful development fosters continued stability -- if large parts of the population receive the benefits -- and that stability makes possible continued development. Unlike much of Latin America, Africa does not have many societies with highly unequal income distribution. Since unequal income distribution, particularly when reinforced by social stratification, tends to limit the extent to which the benefits of development are shared, this may mitigate the causes for pessimism.\13

The development experience of Indonesia may offer a more suitable example than that of East Asia of what could happen in Africa. Like many African countries, Indonesia's population is diverse. Indonesians had a common heritage only in the sense that most were of the Malay race and had lived for a long time under Dutch rule. Their differences were enough to lead to civil war in 1958. Sukarno, the founding father and president of Indonesia from 1945 to 1977, and his associates had helped overcome regional differences by building a sense of nationalism and introducing a common language acceptable to all, but Sukarno had no interest in development. The coup-countercoup of 1965 was not based on regional differences, but it did bring to power the army, some of whose leaders at least saw broad-based national development as a desired goal. At the time of the 1965 coup, two groups in Indonesian society were internally cohesive and well-organized: the Communist Party and the army. The army won control, made Suharto president, and launched a development program that, with the help of OPEC, made possible a sustained increase in the standard of living of the great majority of the Indonesian people.

It is not the purpose of this essay to predict when or if Africa will achieve the kind of political change that will make possible sustained economic development. The point here is a simpler one: economic development is impossible without stability and political leaders whose values or goals transcend the narrow pursuit of their own interests and those of their friends. The specific content of those values and goals is probably less important than the fact that they are shared among the leadership and that they involve more than greed. Unity and stability can take a long time to achieve, even for those countries that seem to be favored by conditions suitable for it, such as those in East Asia with a common Confucian heritage and centuries of self-rule within established boundaries. Japan took hardly any time at all, but China, it could be said, took over 100 years. When unity and stability do come, however, they often come suddenly and with the aid of some organization within society, be it a political party or the army, which is better organized and more cohesive than the society at large.\14 No doubt there are other paths to a similar end. Certainly the path described here doesn't fit well the experience of England, the United States, or, more recently, India.\15 But it is a path that has been taken by many nations, and one suspects that others will probably follow.

It is not easy to predict when a nation will achieve the unity and stability necessary for consistent development policies, but one can say something about the kinds of policies likely to move a nation in that direction.\16 Some nations, associating the unity of Asia with authoritarian controls, may prefer not to move in this direction. However, as indicated above, these controls do not seem to be at the heart of successful development in Asia. The Confucian element in the East Asian experience suggests that shared values can be imparted through formal education, but do you need shared values in the first place before formal education is capable of transmitting a consistent message? Generating nationalist fervor can be effective, as it was in Indonesia and in nineteenth-century Germany, but the cost of this method to a nation and its neighbors can be high. Redistribution of income and wealth can be helpful in eliminating a major source of conflict over the appropriate goals of the state, but redistribution can be very difficult to achieve; in Asia it took sustained, full-scale warfare.

In short, there are measures that governments can take to bring about unity and stability, but most involve heavy costs. It is more realistic to think of allowing historical processes to work themselves out over time than it is to talk about deliberate efforts by government policymakers. The historical processes involved are as much intellectual history as they are political history more narrowly defined.\17 For it is not just a matter of how one group or class of people gain power and hold onto it; it is also how a nation's people come to share ideas and ideals about where their nation should be going.

II
Where Do Policies Come From?

Up to this point in the essay, the specific content of development policies has been neglected, as if all that was needed for growth to take place were unity and sta-bility around some set of reasonably consistent poli-cies. But policies, of course, do, matter and if they are misguided enough they can bring growth to a halt altogether. This is not the place to prescribe poli-cies for particular circumstances. The East Asian expe-rience demonstrates that development can take place under policies ranging from autarkic central planning (China and North Korea) to laissez-faire capitalism (Hong Kong and, to a lesser degree, Singapore), with state-influenced market economies in between (South Korea, Taiwan, and Japan). My purpose is to examine why countries pursue policies that fail to achieve develop-ment when alternative policies are available.

There are at least three possible explanations. First, those making policy simply do not understand economics and fail to listen to advisers who do; or they do not have the ability to judge which advisers are most knowledgeable. Second, vested interests stand behind undesirable policies and are in a position to block change. Third, the values and beliefs of politi-cal leaders predispose them toward certain sets of policies whether or not those policies serve their self-interests, narrowly defined. (While in principle the propositions stemming from these beliefs are often subject to empirical verification or refutation, such analysis frequently has nothing to do with how policies are decided, even when technically well-trained economists are the decision makers.) The third explanation relates most directly to the relationship between values and beliefs and economic development. Still, a brief discussion of the other two is in order.

The first explanation -- that lack of understanding has led to mistaken economic development policies -- probably applies best to the immediate post-World War II period when most developing nations achieved independence. At that time, the field of economic development had been virtually dormant for 70 years, and everyone, economists as well as prime ministers, was groping for solutions to what was, for all of them, a new problem. Since then, however, experience has gone a long way to prove which policies work and which don't, and fewer and fewer government planners are making the more horrendous errors of the past (pushing autarkic growth for small countries, levying prohibitive tariffs to mobilize the underemployed domestic labor force, etc.). There is still a bias against free, open markets in some developing countries, and this is due to a lack of understanding of how markets work. But such bias is far less evident today than it was a decade or two ago.

In contrast, the second explanation for the persistence of poor development policies -- that vested interests block sound policy -- is quite applicable today. The role of vested interests is pervasive, and there is no real sign that their influence is slackening. In fact, one of the most serious costs of past policy mistakes is that they created vested interests that are now making it difficult to change policy for the better. The seemingly innocuous urban grain subsidy of yesterday has often become a major budget drain today, continued because the government is not willing to risk the rioting that may follow its revocation. And a tariff or quota designed to promote a domestic industry cannot be removed, even though the industry never became competitive, because it would put too many people out of work and the owner is someone's brother-in-law.\18 The subject, however, is vast and cannot be dealt with systematically here. Suffice it to say, if the political process is dominated by individuals primarily interested in creating opportunities of this type, development is impossible.

Because of its relevance to the relationship between values and development, I will focus on the third explanation for the persistence of poor development policies. What is meant when one says that values and beliefs predispose policymakers toward certain sets of policies? This subject is best illustrated by looking at a concrete example. One of the most fundamental economic policy decisions facing any developing country is how to handle its external economic relations. Should the nation seek to promote exports and expand its role in international trade, or should it push for as much import substitution as possible in order to minimize its dependence on external markets? By accepting foreign direct investments, credits, and foreign aid, is a nation expanding the capital resources available for development, or is it becoming entangled with the interests of advanced, capitalist nations in ways that will ultimately stifle development?\19

In principle, these questions can be answered through systematic economic analysis and empirical inquiry. For example, an important issue in the export-led versus import-substitution paths to growth is whether the demand for a developing nation's exports is income and price elastic: will a lowering of prices to levels that are competitive worldwide open up a vast overseas market for these exports, or will that market be very limited in size? Whether the product is shoes, textiles, or copper, there is nothing inherently difficult about finding a concrete answer to this question. There will be elements of uncertainty and risk, to be sure, but these, too, can be dealt with systematically.

It is my contention, however, that in practice development questions are seldom decided in this way. What really determines a nation's orientation toward the international economic system has more to do with the philosophical disposition of that nation's leadership than it does with anything that can parade under the term analysis. If analysis is used at all, more often than not it is used to support existing philosophical predispositions, not to change them.

In the vernacular of economic analysis, the issue of whether to push exports or concentrate on protecting domestic industries is a debate between "elasticity optimists" and "elasticity pessimists." Optimists believe that there is a vast market for their goods just waiting to be tapped if they can lower the costs of their domestic industries enough and set their exchange rate at an appropriate level. Pessimists believe that

the potential market is small and that efforts to tap
it will run into sharply declining prices for export
products (worsening terms of trade) and/or large-scale
unemployment in domestic industry, because the price of
imported inputs has been raised to prohibitive levels
by devaluation.\20

One side or the other, the optimists or the pessimists, usually dominates the debate in a given country.
For example, the typical attitudes of political leaders
and economists in Japan, South Korea, Taiwan, and
Singapore has been in sharp contrast to attitudes found
in India, Bangladesh, and until recently, China. Do
these differences in attitude reflect differences in
fundamental economic conditions? In some cases they
may, but that does not appear to be the major reason
for the differing attitudes found in Asia.

The point can be illustrated by comparing the
situation in Bangladesh in the early 1980s with that in
Korea in the early 1960s. The figures presented in
Table 1 show that both countries were dependent to an
extraordinary degree on external aid for survival during these periods. Bangladesh received remittances from
its citizens working in the Middle East, and Korea
received payments as a result of the U.S. forces sta-
tioned there (a figure not included in Table 1).
Exports paid for only 27 percent of imports in Bangladesh and a miniscule 14 percent in Korea. Both countries were extremely densely populated and imported
large quantities of grain. Agricultural products were
the main traditional exports, but, given the poor land
endowment, rapid expansion of these exports was difficult at best. Neither country had any natural resources
to provide exports other than land. The per-capita
income in Bangladesh in 1981 was $140. Korea's in 1962
in comparable prices was considerably higher -- over
$400. (It had been well below this level right after
the Korean War but was still above that of Bangladesh.)

Bangladesh and Korea, and other countries in similar situations, really have two choices. They can either continue to be dependent on aid indefinitely,
fighting for a large share of the available aid, or
they can promote exports in an effort to generate the
foreign exchange needed to pay for imports. Import
substitution can also take place -- both Bangladesh and
Korea pushed it during these periods -- but there is no
prospect whatsoever that import substitution, as a
primary strategy, will ever reduce aid dependency in
such situations.

Table 1

The Balance of Payments
Of Bangladesh and South Korea\21
in millions of dollars (U.S.)

	Bangladesh (1981-82)	South Korea (1962)
Exports	594	55
Imports	2,200	390
Remittances	315	--
Aid, loans, donations (net)	1,162	219

Given this basic choice between export promotion or continued aid dependency, political leaders rarely prefer the latter. Aid dependency means having to listen to, and to some degree, follow the dictates of the foreign states giving aid. And because aid levels worldwide have stagnated, aid dependency is a formula for limited or no growth.

It was the compelling logic of this argument that drove the South Korean government in the early 1960s to push an export drive, which ultimately proved highly successful. The military leaders who ran the government knew that they faced stagnant or declining levels of aid, and they considered American attempts to use aid to dictate how they should run their country as an affront to their nationalism. Initially, Park Chung Hee probably had little idea of how to promote Korean exports or if such an export drive would be successful, but he soon reached the conclusion that Korea had to try.

Why hasn't Bangladesh followed this logic and taken a similar path? Some would argue that vested interests in maintaining existing controls and distortions make export growth difficult. But vested interests in Korea in the early 1960s were also on the side of continuing controls, and Korea's exchange rate under Syngman Rhee was as overvalued as any. Others point to the fact that Korea is a "hard" society, using Myrdal's terminology,\22 hence the government had the strength and will to overcome these special interests, whereas

Bangladesh is a "soft" society whose government lacks such power. Yet no one would have called the Korea of the late 1940s or the 1950s a hard society; somehow Korea managed to change from a soft to a hard society in a few short years.

Why then is Bangladesh continuing policies that will keep it in its present situation indefinitely? Talking to policymakers and economists in Bangladesh gives one the impression that they don't really believe the people of Bangladesh are capable of launching an effective export drive. The excuses are many -- some say Bangladesh has few entrepreneurs, others that the conditions that made East Asia's performance possible are no longer valid -- but rarely are these views based on systematic analysis. Instead, they reflect a deep pessimism about the nature of the outside world and of their own capacities.

Is this pessimism deeply rooted in Islamic values or Bengali culture? Possibly, but I doubt if this is the major explanation. Is it Fabian socialist values imported from Britain, or perhaps simply that extreme poverty and the lack of any real experience with suc- cessful development reinforces attitudes that keep a country in such a state? Bangladesh looks toward India where it sees many of its own attitudes reinforced; Korea, at least, had the advantage of being geographi- cally and culturally close to Japan, which presented a very optimistic picture of what was possible. The geo- graphic and cultural proximity of the East Asian export experience clearly had something to do with China's dramatic turn after 1976 from an autarkic, import- substituting nation par excellence into a vigorous export promoter.

Values, attitudes, and beliefs have a great deal to do with a country's choice of economic development policies. Some would say it is ideology that determines policies, with believers in communism favoring one set and advocates of capitalism another. There is no evi- dence, however, that the Chinese have given up Marxist- Leninist political principles or their belief in the virtue of state ownership of the means of production just because they are now promoting the export of manufactures.\23 Neither is it apparent that the doc- trines of Confucianism are more compatible with export- led growth than those of Hinduism or Islam. One sus- pects that the values involved are more the result of the culture of extreme poverty than any specific set of religious or political beliefs.

III
Values, Work, and Entrepreneurship

I have concentrated on values that affect governments' development policies and the very ability of those governments to implement consistent economic development policies over a period of a decade or longer. However, most of the literature on values and economic development is concerned with how values directly affect the performance of the principal economic actors: entrepreneurs, managers, and workers. For well over a century, scholars have been fascinated by the question of why some societies produce capitalists and entrepreneurs who lead a nation into a period of dynamic economic growth. The most eloquent writer on the relationship of values to the creation of a capitalist or entrepreneurial class was Max Weber, whose The Protestant Ethic and the Spirit of Capitalism first appeared in 1904-5.\24 As predominantly Catholic nations entered into sustained periods of economic development, it soon became apparent that ascetic Protestantism had no monopoly on values that were consistent with successful entrepreneurship. In recent decades Confucianism has been put forward as a value system that appears to be particularly well-suited to producing successful capitalists.

It is difficult to establish any clear relationship between religious or philosophical doctrine and entrepreneurship, and the debate over the relationship of Confucian beliefs to the entrepreneurial spirit is a good example. Prior to 1970, the most common view of Confucianism was that it was a block to development. Confucianism looked to the past, not to the future: any policy that could not find an appropriate precedent from some earlier dynasty was by definition not rooted in Confucian values. Similarly, the Confucian emphasis on the family was seen as antagonistic to the kind of rational calculations so essential to modern capitalist enterprises. Instead of hiring the most qualified people, Chinese enterprises were riddled with nepotism and therefore were hopelessly inefficient.\25 Chinese enterprises were also small because entrepreneurs found it impossible to establish a basis for trust beyond the ties of family; the large, limited-liability corporation of modern capitalism could not exist in a Confucian setting.

There is some truth to these charges, but as the performances of Singapore, Hong Kong, and Taiwan make

251

clear, the argument is fundamentally flawed. Chinese firms do practice nepotism and do tend to be small, but family ties mean that members of one's own family can be expected to work loyally and with unusual dedication.\26 Nepotism didn't work this way in nineteenth-century government agencies because neither the head of the agency nor his hired relatives had any real incentive to push for efficiency. Small size, far from being harmful, may have been the most appropriate structure for the kind of export-oriented industrialization that has characterized these states in recent times. In any case, Korea (as Confucian a state as any) demonstrated that large conglomerates on the Japanese model were possible. (For that matter, the Japanese too shared many Confucian values.) As for looking to the past for precedent, Liang Ch'i-ch'ao and Kang Yu-wei demonstrated as early as the 1890s that one could justify efforts to modernize by reference to the classics. Contemporary government figures in East Asia -- whose political style is often quite Confucian -- would find the notion that Confucian precedents inhibited industrialization to be almost incomprehensible. Like most living value systems, Confucianism has adapted to the changed environment of the industrial era while retaining its core beliefs.

Others who have tried to explain entrepreneurship have turned more to psychology than to religion or philosophy. The two best-known writers in this area are David McClelland and Everett Hagen.\27 McClelland argues that individuals are educated from early childhood in values that either promote or inhibit the need for achievement. School primers which stress the rewards gained from winning a race or some other achievement are seen to be consistent with the requirements of an entrepreneurial society; those that stress cooperation over competition and other similar values are not. Few would dispute that some drive to achieve is necessary for anyone attempting to build a modern enterprise or even climb the organizational ladder of a modern corporation; the hard part is finding contemporary societies that lack people who have this kind of drive. It is not necessary for everyone to have these values; only a small minority of entrepreneurs is required. And for those societies that lack a need for achievement, we must question whether it is because they have deeply held values that inhibit this need or whether the society provides few opportunities for achievement.

The early development of the Malayan tin mines illustrates the latter point. The mines themselves were deep in the jungle-covered interior of peninsular Malaya. The Malay population lived principally on the coast, making a living from fishing and farming, and showed no interest in going inland to gain riches by meeting the growing world demand for tin. Development of the mines, therefore, fell to the desperately poor migrant workers from South China. As time passed, some of the Chinese accumulated money from working in the tin mines, went into commerce with the British, helped develop the cities of Malaya, and became rich entrepreneurs. What developed was a classic clash of cultures between one that was compatible with modern economic growth and another that was not.

The missing detail in this story is that the jungles surrounding the tin mines were infested with malaria, and many of those who went into them died. Even for those who didn't die, conditions were harsh and only a handful ever found their fortune. While such conditions were acceptable to the desperately poor of South China who had no other way to accumulate enough money to even consider marriage, they presumably made much less sense to a Malay farmer or fisherman who could meet most of his basic needs without taking such a high risk. When life in the interior became more attractive, and when there were scooters, television sets, and other consumer goods to buy with the money acquired, Malays began flocking to the cities in search of economic opportunity as well. Developing successful entrepreneurs among the Malayan workers, however, has taken longer, in part because the Chinese were there ahead of them and had more than half a century of experience behind them.

This is not the place to critically review all the theories put forward to explain entrepreneurial behavior. Surprisingly, much less has been written by development specialists about why workers in some countries are diligent and disciplined while those in others are not. Do these differences result primarily from inherited values? The issue is worth serious empirical investigation, but the probable answer is no. A great deal has been written about how different material and nonmaterial incentive systems affect worker performance within already industrialized nations. While the appropriate incentive system may vary due in part to differences between nations in underlying cultural values, most cultures that have tried have been able to find some incentive system that elicits the required effort. Is there anything in the East Asian experience to suggest that traditional values and work effort are closely related? The image of the hard-working Chinese has given some credence to the notion that Confucianism has some influence.\28 On the other hand, the experience of Hong Kong plant managers with the poor work habits of recent immigrants from the People's Republic of China -- as contrasted to the great diligence of Chinese refugees from Vietnam -- suggests that something besides Confucian values is at work. Communism in China has not destroyed Confucian values, but it has undermined worker discipline and effort by awarding permanent employment and fixed wages that change little whether or not the worker performs. If the Chinese of Southeast Asia also had an "iron rice bowl," they might not work very hard either.

The point is not that values play no role in an individual worker's level of effort. It is that, in examining why people work hard, one needs to start with more conventional reasons and then work backward to see if there is some residual that cannot readily be explained by the nature of incentive systems provided to the workers. It is to explain this residual that one should look more closely at the Confucian or Protestant work ethic.

IV
Conclusions

As the previous section indicated, it is difficult to make any broadly applicable statements about how values affect human behavior in ways that promote economic development by creating the right kinds of entrepreneurs, managers, and workers. There may not be much to be said that is relevant to whole nations and regions of the world or that will stand up to rigorous analysis and empirical verification. That does not mean that values play no role, only that to understand that role, the analyst must explore the issue in a specific context, during a particular period, in order to incorporate the inevitable complexities. The anthropologist, therefore, is more likely to have something to say on the subject than the economist, the psychologist, or the research sociologist.

On the other hand, values appear to play a more transparent role in the way political systems operate. Since political systems have a major effect on whether economic development takes place, values clearly -- if indirectly -- affect development. The values that matter, however, are not those arising out of the specific doctrines of one religion or another. They are rather the commonly shared values that provide a basis for achieving national unity behind some broad development program. Nationalism is one such value, but alone it may not be sufficient to overcome regional and ethnic differences and achieve the required unity, unless it is reinforced by other shared values, such as those provided by Confucian culture.

Finally, development is made easier if government policymakers possess values that lead them to try policies that work. Since the 1960s these values have included a willingness to exploit international comparative advantage through the development of exports, rather than turn inward. In many countries they have also included a belief that farmers and workers usually know what is best for them and can properly exercise freedom of choice through both the market and the political process if given the opportunity. The alternative view -- government paternalism -- has also had a role to play, but all too frequently has become an excuse for controls whose only real purpose is to enhance bureaucratic power and maximize benefits for a few.

Some may disagree that these are the correct values to pursue in the push for economic development. But whatever the necessary values may be, whether a government will incorporate them into an overall development policy is as dependent on the value systems of leading policymakers as on the theorizing and empirical analyses of economists. But economic theory and analysis do have a role; the values and beliefs underlying any development policy will not survive if analysis and experience continually indicate that those values and beliefs are based on false premises.

Notes

1. Development as contrasted to growth also includes structural change in the economy (industrialization, urbanization, etc.), participation by citizens of the country in development of the modern sector, and participation by them in consumption of the gains from growth.

2. Gross domestic investment as a percentage of GDP was consistently more than 30 percent for Japan, was in the high 30 percent range in the 1970s in Singapore, and was around 27 percent in South Korea in 1970 and 1981. The World Bank, World Tables, 3d ed. (Washington, D.C.: The World Bank, 1983), vol. 1, pp. 504-06.

3. Elliot Berg et al., Accelerated Development in Sub-Saharan Africa: An Agenda for Action (Washington, D.C.: The World Bank, 1981), pp. 144, 147. By 1982, the capital formulation rate had fallen back to 19 percent; see Stanley Please et al., Toward Sustained Development in Sub-Saharan Africa: A Joint Program for Action (Washington D.C.: The World Bank, 1984), p. 61.

4. The term "rent-seeking society" refers to countries where officials create artificial barriers to trade and competition that have the effect of driving up prices and creating artificial windfall profits for selected individuals or groups. See, for example, Anne O. Krueger, "The Political Economy of the Rent Seeking Society," American Economic Review, no. 3, 1964, pp. 291-303; Gunner Myrdal, Asian Drama: An Inquiry into the Poverty of Nations (New York: Pantheon, 1968); and Robert Bates, Markets and States in Tropical Africa: The Political Basis of Agricultural Policies (Berkeley: University of California Press, 1981).

5. The seminal work on this subject, of course, was Max Weber, The Protestant Ethic and The Spirit of Capitalism.

6. An early statement of this argument can be found in Mary Wright, The Last Stand of Chinese Conservatism (Stanford: Stanford University Press, 1957), chap. 8.

7. China was divided during the warlord period of 1918-31 and the Japanese invasion, 1931-45, and also during the decades of transition from the Ming to the Qing dynasty in the mid-seventeenth century. But the last time China was ruled by more than one government, each controlling substantial amounts of territory for more than a decade or two was in the Song dynasty which ended in the thirteenth century.

8. See, for example, the account of how Chinese officials handled the Honan famine in Theodore H. White and Annalee Jacoby, Thunder Out of China (New York: William Sloane, 1946), chap. 2.

9. There is a growing literature on what the leaders of the Taiwan government did to promote economic development, but little has been written on why they undertook these policies after 1949 when they failed to do so before.

10. Many of these issues are discussed at greater length in E.S. Mason et al., The Economic and Social Modernization of the Republic of Korea (Cambridge: Harvard University Press, 1980).

11. The discussion in this and the following paragraph is based on that of Keith Hart, The Political Economy of West African Agriculture (New York: Cambridge University Press, 1982).

12. There are a number of able studies of African economic development over the past decade or two, including Michael Roemer, "Economic Development in Africa: Performance Since Independence and a Strategy for the Future," Daedalus, Spring 1982, pp. 125-43; and Tony Killick, Development Economics in Action: A Study of Economic Policies in Ghana (London: Heinemann, 1978).

13. This statement is based more on impressionistic evidence than on hard data. A major effort to pool what is known about income distribution throughout the world makes it clear that Latin America shows high income inequality (10 of 15 countries for which data were available were in this category). We know much less about Africa; of the 45 states in sub-Saharan Africa, data were available for only 13 (6 of which were in the high inequality category), but the quality of even these figures is low, to put it mildly. H.B. Chenery et al., Redistribution with Growth (Oxford: Oxford University Press, 1974), pp. 8-9.

14. The basic point being made here has much in common with Alexander Gerschenkron's view that ideology and strong central government played a primary role among the large developers of Europe (who used that ideology and the state to break down barriers to development). See his Economic Backwardness in Historical Perspective (Cambridge: Harvard University Press, 1962), chap. 1, and his Europe in the Russian Mirror (Cambridge: Harvard University Press, 1970).

15. Indian unity and stability has rested on a combination of democratic institutions which balance and diffuse the many conflicting elements in Indian

society plus the charismatic leadership of Nehru and his descendants. Development policies and programs more often than not reflect the requirements of political coalition-building than a systematic effort to achieve rapid and sustained economic growth, although the two goals are not necessarily in conflict.

16. In essence, this question is the same as that asked by Warren Ilchman and Norman Uphoff, "How would we advise Colonel Yukubu Gowon of Nigeria on how to achieve political stability, national unification, and economic and social development?" See their The Political Economy of Change (Berkeley: University of California Press, 1971). They go on to argue that political science to that point had few answers to this question.

17. Some of what is argued in this essay fits within the framework of what some refer to as the "structuralist" school of sociology or politics (Marxist and non-Marxist). See the typology in A. Eugene Havens, "Methodological Issues in the Study of Development," Sociologia Rurales XII:3/4, 1972 pp. 252-72. But the emphasis here is on ideas and values, some of which may be facilitated by structural change, but which can also arise quite independently of changes in social structure.

18. There is a large body of literature on the economics, costs, and benefits of import substitution as a development strategy, and much of this literature also deals with the politics involved. See, for example, Anne Krueger, Foreign Trade Regimes and Economic Development: Turkey (New York: Columbia University Press, 1974); Albert O. Hirschman, "The Political Economy of Import-Substituting Industrialization in Latin America," in A Bias for Hope (New Haven: Yale University Press, 1971), pp. 85-123; and Ian M.D. Little, Economic Development: Theory, Policy and International Relations (New York: Basic Books, 1982), part VI.

19. The literature on this subject is vast from Hobson and Lenin to Paul Baron, Andre Gunder-Frank, and many others.

20. There is, of course, much more than elasticity optimism and pessimism involved in the attitudes of policymakers toward involvement in international markets. A useful analysis of the role of ideology in determining development strategies in Latin America is found in Albert O. Hirschman, "Ideologies of Economic Development in Latin America," in A Bias of Hope, op.

cit., pp. 270-311.

21. The Bangladesh figures were converted into dollars at the official exchange rate from Bangladesh Bureau of Statistics, Statistical Pocketbook of Bangladesh, 1982 (Dhaka: Bangladesh Bureau of Statistics, 1983), p. 235. The Korean Figures are from Economic Planning Board, Handbook of Korean Economy 1980 (Seoul: Economic Planning Board, 1980), pp. 95-99.

22. Gunner Myrdal, Asian Drama: An Inquiry into the Poverty of Nations, op. cit.

23. A fall 1984 article in Beijing's Renmin Ribao (People's Daily) was widely interpreted by the press as implying a rejection of Marxism-Leninism, but in reality the article was criticizing those who follow Marx and Lenin dogmatically.

24. See the more recent edition published by Charles Scribner (New York) in 1958.

25. Probably the most influential article in this vein was one by Marion Levy and Shih Kuo-heng, "The Rise of the Modern Chinese Business Class," (New York: 1949).

26. An interesting analysis of the relationship between these elements and the values of Sinic culture is by Gordon Redding and Gilbert Wong, "The Entrepreneurial Factor: Ingredients in the Asian Experience," in The Asian Development Model and the Caribbean Basin Initiative (New York: Council on Religion and International Affairs, September 1984).

27. David McClelland, The Achieving Society (Princeton: Van Nostrand, 1961), and Everett Hagen, On the Theory of Social Change: How Economic Growth Begins (Homewood: Richard Dorsey, 1962).

28. D.H. Perkins, China's Modern Economy in Historical Perspective (Stanford: Stanford University Press, 1975), introduction.

Chapter 9

KEEPING THEM OUT:
ETHICAL DILEMMAS OF IMMIGRATION POLICY

Aristide R. Zolberg

How many altogether, nobody knows for sure; but there
is little doubt that they are pouring in. Year in and
year out, under its present laws the United States
admits more immigrants and refugees for permanent resettlement than all the rest of the world's countries
combined. But the lines of applicants are getting longer, and in addition to the traffic through this relatively open legal door, more people enter or stay
surreptitiously than anywhere else as well.

Amidst proliferating assertions to the effect that
an unruly flow of poor aliens from the Third World
imposes unmanageable economic, social, and political
burdens on the American people, the United States in
1979 undertook a comprehensive recasting of its immigration and refugee policy. Out of this emerged the
"Simpson-Mazzoli" bill which, after several deaths and
metamorphoses, was reincarnated in the Ninety-ninth
Congress as "Simpson-Rodino." The bill looked like it
was becoming a corpse once again, but -- as Sen. Alan
Simpson inimitably put it -- it was "jump-started" back
to life against all odds in the final days of the
second session and was ultimately signed into law by
President Reagan on November 6, 1986, as Public Law 99-
603. Despite multifarious controversies over particulars, which account for this rocky legislative history,
there was broad consensus from the outset on the policy's general orientation. As set forth in the staff
report of the commission appointed by President Carter,
one of the "first principles of immigration reform" is
that "the open society does not mean limitless immigration. Both quantitative and qualitative limits are
needed to serve the national interests of the United
States." However, the report adds, "those limits must
never be imposed by reason of color, nationality or
religion; and once admitted to the United States,
aliens should be welcomed and encouraged to be a part
of the country and contribute to its well-being."\1
These words constitute a succinct statement of the

doctrine widely accepted by political liberals in the
United States in the sphere of immigration policy. But
what is the warrant for asserting that "the open society does not mean limitless immigration"? Interest in
this question arises today not only because immigration
has become a prominent issue throughout liberal industrial societies, but as a consequence of the growing
concern of theorists with problems of social justice at
the international level. Although much of the initial
discussion centered on issues of foreign aid, more
recently the sphere of immigration has emerged as another critical area for consideration of these matters,
as it is evident that the relocation of population from
less-favored to more-favored states is to some extent
an alternative to global redistribution by way of relo-
cating goods and benefits.

Is the prevailing doctrine consistent with liberal
theory? The classics of that tradition have little to
say on the matter because, despite the fact that most
constituted societies have experienced significant
immigration and emigration during some segment of their
historical existence, political and social philosophers
have viewed them tacitly as self-contained population
entities. Empirical theorists have generally followed
suit. Why that should be so is in itself an interesting
question, which must be left to another occasion.

Guidelines for the making of immigration policy
consistent with liberal principles must therefore be
derived indirectly. However, efforts to do so have
proved inconclusive; at worst they lead in opposite
directions. For example, the author of a recent overview of what different philosophers might have to say
on the subject of immigration from developing to developed countries comes up with an array of prescriptions
ranging from a wide-open door to severe restrictions.
He concludes that variation in the recommendations each
philosopher would make has little to do with the usual
differences in outlook -- utilitarianism, the difference principle, the minimal state, and the like -- but
that "a much more critical issue is whether one applies
whatever principle one adopts to the internal affairs
of the nation-state or to the world as a whole."\2
Indeed, this was already evident nearly a century ago,
when Henry Sidgwick observed, concerning the imposition
of limits on immigration: "The truth is, that when we
consider how far the exercise of this right of exclusion is conducive to the real interest of the State
exercising it, or of humanity at large, we come upon
the most striking phase of the general conflict between

the cosmopolitan and the national ideals of political organisation, which has more than once attracted our notice."\3

Sidgwick's distinction may be briefly recalled:

> According to the national ideal, the right and duty of each government is to promote the interests of a determinate group of human beings, bound together by the tie of a common nationality -- with due regard to the rules restraining it from attacking or encroaching on other states -- and to consider the expediency of admitting foreigners and their products solely from this point of view. According to the cosmopolitan ideal, its business is to maintain order over the particular territory that historical causes have appropriated to it, but not in any way to determine who is to inhabit this territory, or to restrict the enjoyment of its natural advantages to any particular portion of the human race.\4

But which of these perspectives is more appropriate for the determination of immigration policy?

Since recent discussion of the distinction and its general implications are available, I shall limit myself to an examination of the relevance of each perspective for the determination of immigration policy, introducing this with a brief overview of some empirical matters pertaining to the costs and benefits of international population movements. As the Carter Commission's statement indicates, in the United States the prevailing doctrine is founded on the national principle, and it is quite evident that this is the case within the world of liberal states as a whole. Yet I believe it can be demonstrated that liberal theory requires us to give precedence to the cosmopolitan principle. That being established, however, there is no gainsaying the validity of some of the grounds for restricting entry that arise when immigration is considered from a national perspective. In effect, these may be invoked to modify somewhat the policy that would be adopted on the basis of the cosmopolitan perspective, without violating its spirit. To simplify matters, the emphasis will be on U.S. immigration policy, but most of what is said applies, _mutatis mutandis_, to the world of liberal states in general.

I
International Population Movements:
A Balance Sheet

As with other fields of public policy, controversies in the sphere of immigration often involve varying estimates of costs and benefits, both of the status quo and of proposed alternatives. Although it is impossible to settle these empirical matters here, largely because many of the relevant questions remain unanswered and some are perhaps unanswerable, the quality of ethical discussion might be improved and its relevance to policy enhanced by a more precise understanding of what such calculations entail.

Contemporary international migrations can be divided typologically into two distinct streams, with some empirical overlap between them. The first is a movement of manpower which originates largely in less developed countries, including Mediterranean Europe and most of the Third World, and is directed toward developed capitalist societies and some of the richer countries of the Third World itself. Most of the migrants begin as recruited or self-marketed temporary workers, but often end up seeking to settle in the receiving country. They include a large mass of low-skilled workers, with a smaller component of highly skilled workers and professionals ("brain drain"). To the extent that it leads to settlement, this labor migration tends to generate a secondary stream of dependents.

The second major stream consists of refugees, defined here as people who have fled their country in the face of direct danger to their lives by way of persecution or other forms of violence, or who are recognized by international organizations or some states as refugees.\5 People in this category also originate overwhelmingly in Third World countries, together with a small number from the Soviet Union and Eastern Europe. Although most Third World refugees go to other countries within the region of origin, some end up being resettled in affluent liberal states.

Much of the current discussion of costs and benefits of international migration focuses on economics. Yet because the globe is divided into territories governed by states that exercise mutually exclusive jurisdiction over them, international population movements do not entail only the physical relocation of persons and the work they perform from one place to another;

they involve political action -- at least a temporary
and partial change of jurisdiction, but possibly as
much as a total change of membership from one political
community to another.\6 By the same token, emigration
and immigration are two sides of the same coin: emigration cannot take place in the absence of a concomitant
possibility of immigration and vice versa. It follows
that discussions pertaining to either aspect of the
process cannot be conducted without keeping in mind
that that aspect has implications for the other. It can
be seen that one of the reasons why it is so difficult
to achieve agreement on estimated costs and benefits of
immigration is that a proper calculation should take
into account the country of origin as well as the
country of destination. Moreover, it is by no means
clear to which of these collectivities one should attribute the costs and benefits experienced by the migrants themselves.

Within this global structure, individuals can be
thought of as being born by chance in one state or
another. Given a world organized into bounded territorial states marked by wide differences of political and
economic conditions, in which there are no institutionalized mechanisms for redistribution of benefits between countries, and where in the short to medium term
prevailing conditions are relatively immune to change
through individual effort, it makes sense for individuals to maximize benefits by living and working in the
states where better conditions prevail. Those not fortunate enough to have been born in good conditions can
achieve them by moving. People from poor countries
aspiring to relocate indeed constitute a growing pool.
In addition, the various regions of the Third World are
prone to violent upheavals which tend to trigger flows
of refugees, some of whom aspire to resettlement in the
United States as well as other Western countries. Hence
in the foreseeable future, the affluent liberal states
are likely to continue to face immigration pressures.

Different estimates of the costs and benefits of
emigration are thus possible, depending on whether the
unit of reference is the original collectivity or particular sets of individuals. Much of the debate on
"brain drain," for example, hinges on that distinction:
there is little doubt that Third World professionals
are better off if they move to affluent countries, or
that these countries benefit from their presence; but
the country of origin undoubtedly incurs some sort of
loss. How should this figure into the calculation?
Matters are further complicated by the necessity of

taking into account not only the economic impact of
emigration, but also its political effects on the individuals and collectivities involved. Individuals are
undoubtedly better off when moving from an authoritarian to a liberal state; but the departure of enlightened potential leaders might reduce the likelihood that
the state of origin will develop in a liberal direction, and hence constitutes a political cost for those
who are left behind. Although empirical findings concerning these matters are inconclusive, it is not far-
fetched to assume that the overall balance -- for those
who move and for those who stay behind -- is at best
positive and at worst indifferent. I shall adopt this
assumption so as to maximize the ethical problem posed
by restriction on the entry side.

One of the most tangible consequences of immigration pressure on the receiving countries has been the
proliferation of research concerning the impact of
immigration. (This observation is one of the few pertaining to the subject under consideration that is not
subject to doubt.) Overall, the following is probably a
good approximation of reality with respect to the economic side.\7 It is generally reckoned that a flow of
immigrants from the Third World at the ongoing level
tends to stimulate overall growth, but there is reasonable evidence that it has a slightly negative effect on
the income of the lowest stratum of the indigenous
labor force in the receiving country. For purposes of
the present discussion, however, the receiving country
will be considered as a single unit, and it will be
assumed that any injustice in the distribution of costs
and benefits among various groups (or localities) can
be dealt with by means of internal redistribution
rather than by limiting immigration.

Nevertheless, there is little doubt that a very
large flow -- say, of six million per year in the case
of the United States (approximately twice the proportion in relation to current population as arrived in
the all-time record year of 1907) -- would impose in-
tolerable economic costs on the receiving society as a
whole. This is mainly because it would exceed the
capacity of its capital resources to absorb so much
additional labor all at once and would bring about
brutal overuse of its collective goods (e.g., welfare
system) in the short term, with other catastrophic
consequences following in the wake of inadequate provisions for welfare.

However, the consequences of immigration are not

limited to the economic sphere. Given that in the world as a whole cultural variation increases with geographical distance and that states tend to promote the formation of distinct national cultures, international migration usually entails an encounter between different people hitherto separated by space. The degree of difference is magnified if, as tends to be the case, the movement is shaped by the unequal structure of the world economy, and the social and economic conditions that govern the lives of the newcomers in the receiving society tend to perpetuate their distinctiveness. Therefore, immigration also has the effect of altering the composition of the receiving country's sociocultural community. To the extent that it involves permanent settlement and admission to citizenship, it modifies the political community as well.

Since the reactions of receivers in this regard are largely shaped by prejudicial stereotypes which antedate the arrival of the immigrants, much of what is said concerning the danger immigrants pose to the political community should be discounted. But even when considered in the most objective perspective, the incorporation of any new population presents difficulties and will occasion some sort of strain for the receivers. It stands to reason that the degree of strain will grow with the size of the immigrant group and the concentration of the flow over time, as well as with the cultural distance of the immigrants from the mainstream of the receiving society. Albeit distinct from economically grounded objections to immigration, reactions pertaining to membership tend to be exacerbated by cyclical downturns which trigger more vociferous efforts to stem the alien tide or, in the more extreme case, to reverse the flow.

It is quite evident that the world of industrial capitalism is currently in the restrictionist phase of a cycle that began with the generalization of labor importation in the 1960s. International borders have thus been turned into a cosmic arena where the fortunate few confront the disadvantaged many. The confrontation takes on a particularly dramatic aspect in North America because the United States shares a long land border with one Third World country, and its southeastern coast is within short reach of many others. It is taking place in the white Commonwealth countries and in Europe as well, where the tendency of "guestworkers" to turn into permanent settlers has provoked a racist backlash which has, in some cases, stimulated the revival of an authoritarian right.

267

II
The Cosmopolitan Perspective

As a statement of the cosmopolitan perspective on immigration, one can hardly surpass the poignant plea of Herman Melville. Writing in 1849, at a time when the huge wave of arrivals from famine-ridden Ireland exacerbated anti-Catholic feelings and propelled the issue of immigration for the first time to the center of the American political arena, contributing to the collapse of the second party system, he exclaimed:

> Let us waive that agitated national topic, as to whether such multitudes of foreign poor should be landed on our American shores; let us waive it, with the one only thought that if they can get here, they have God's right to come; though they bring all Ireland and her miseries with them. For the whole world is the patrimony of the whole world; there is no telling who does not own a stone in the Great Wall of China.\8

The cosmopolitan perspective is thus quite straightforward. Bruce Ackerman has argued more formally that the notion of equal moral worth, which lies at the heart of liberal theory, leads inexorably to the conclusion that there are no justifications for highly restrictive immigration policies such as now prevail throughout the liberal world. In his dialogue, "Explorer" attempts to deny citizenship to "Apollonian" by virtue of prior arrival, but fails to provide a justification for doing so once he admits that Apollonian is as good as himself. Ackerman follows this up by pointing out that

> Quite unthinkingly, we have come to accept the idea that we have the right to exclude nonresidents from our midst. Yet, unless something further can be said, the dialogue between Explorer and Apollonian applies equally to the conversation between a rich American and an impoverished Mexican who swims over the border for a talk. The American can no more declare the intrinsic superiority of the first occupant than the Explorer can.\9

The point can perhaps be made even stronger if instead of a confrontation between a rich American and an impoverished Mexican, we imagine one between an impoverished Mexican who entered the U.S. surreptitiously but meets the deadline for legalization as a permanent resident under an amnesty program (such as was recently enacted) and his neighbor in the barrio of an American city who came a day later and hence faces deportation.

Ackerman concludes that "only a very strong empirical claim...can permit the American to justify exclusion of the foreign-born from his liberal state."\10 Again he casts his argument in the form of a dialogue, this time between a rich westerner and a poor easterner. The former points our that "we in the West are far from achieving a perfect technology of justice; if we admit more than Z newcomers, our existing institutions will be unable to function in anything but an explicitly authoritarian manner."\11 The justification for violating the neutrality principle (which requires that all be treated alike) is that if the Easterner is allowed to move to the West, this will "destroy the entire liberal conversation that guarantees the rights of all existing citizens." Since such upheavals cannot be predicted with accuracy, the requirement of social justice is met when "statesmen set an overall Z conscious of an immigrant's prima facie right to demand entry into a liberal state."\12

Joseph Carens reaches a similar conclusion by way of John Rawls's "veil of ignorance."\13 No restrictions would be permitted unless they could be shown to be essential to the maintenance of the total system of equal basic liberties. Paralleling the case of religious toleration, the limitation would be chosen in the original position because "the disruption of these conditions is a danger for the liberty of all." Restrictions could be imposed only if it could be demonstrated that the immigration under consideration carried a high probability of bringing about chaos.

Quite independently of any considerations arising from justice, the cosmopolitan perspective imposes itself because of what liberal theory has to say with respect to exit. Liberal principles, regardless of whether one adopts the cosmopolitan or national perspective, prescribe the almost unqualified right of individuals not only to leave their country physically, but even to relinquish membership in their political community of origin. This has come to be generally acknowledged as a desirable norm at the level of the international community, even by states which violate it in practice. However, no such consensus exists on the right to enter.

Is this peculiar asymmetry compatible with liberal theory? There is reason to doubt that this could be the case. Upon reflection, it is evident that the asymmetry is grounded in a more fundamental one involving the rights of individuals and collectivities. Whereas free exit is a concomitant of the priority accorded in liberal theory to the rights of individuals -- regardless of the impact the exercise of these rights might have on the collectivity of origin -- when it comes to entry, priority is accorded to the national interest of the collectivities of destination.

But as we have seen, given the social organization of the globe, emigration is impossible in the absence of a place to enter. The implications of the asymmetry under these conditions are highlighted by a not-so-far-fetched hypothetical situation. Currently there are some indications that regimes which hitherto imposed a nearly absolute prohibition on exit are modifying their position somewhat. At the same time, however, the general trend in immigration policy within the world of affluent liberal societies is toward more severe restriction. Should both trends prevail, citizens of the formerly no-exit states would remain immobilized because they would have no place to go.

Liberal states are thus under collective obligation to provide at the least a sufficient number of entries to foreigners so as to enable them to exercise their right of exit. How many cannot be established precisely, but it surely must be significantly above zero for any of the states under consideration for entry. It is within the context of the cosmopolitan obligation to keep the door open to some foreigners that we must examine the validity of grounds invoked to restrict entry.

III
The National Perspective

Sidgwick not only introduced the distinction between the cosmopolitan and national perspectives in liberal theory, he went on to argue that the national perspective was a more appropriate guide for the formulation of immigration policy. Although the position is set forth in the course of a more general discussion of the

270

relation of national interest to international duty, it rests on elements spelled out in connection with a discussion of membership of the state.

Sidgwick establishes that "a modern State is normally a determinate and stable group of human beings, whose government has a practically undisputed right of regulating the legal relations of human beings over a determinate portion of the earth's surface."\14 The question then arises of "how new membership of such a society is to be acquired." It cannot be by mere habitation, he argues, because "the inevitable result would be either to dissipate the sentiment of nationality which which we have recognised the importance of maintaining, or to hamper intolerably the intercourse between nations." The alternatives are by way of birth -- to parents who are members of or are residing within the territory -- and by way of consent. The former is relatively unproblematic and of little relevance to the present discussion. As for consent, two steps are involved: admission to residence and admission to citizenship. Sidgwick suggests that the residence of a large number of persons permanently excluded from citizenship within the territory of any community involves an obvious danger of weakening the internal coherence of the community. "Accordingly, if a State permits the free immigration of foreigners, it seems expedient that admission of citizenship should be generally open to those resident aliens" provided they have demonstrated "that they will adequately perform the duties of citizenship."\15 This enhances the critical nature of the first step -- admission to residence -- a question which he believes "cannot well be separated from the discussion of the external relations of States...."\16

It is in consideration of the principles of international duty that Sidgwick introduces a distinction between the two fundamental principles mentioned, whose applicability he then examines with respect to trade, immigration, and the occupation of new territories. On the first of these Sidgwick asserts that the economic argument on behalf of free trade "is now generally admitted as decisive" when the matter is considered from the cosmopolitan point of view, and that the principle should be adhered to, apart from limited military considerations to the contrary.\17 To the extent that it involves the movement of labor, immigration is an aspect of trade, to which the same rule would apply. In keeping with this, free immigration "is a recognised feature of the ideal which orthodox political economists have commonly formed of international

271

relations," since in order to fully realize the advantages of freedom of exchange "it is necessary that labour should move with perfect ease from country to country to meet the changes that are continually likely to occur in the industrial demand for it."\18

However, Sidgwick himself at this point abruptly rejects the "cosmopolitan point of view" on behalf of the "national ideal." His justification for doing so is grounded in the earlier discussion of membership and his conception of what a social scientist of the functionalist persuasion might term the prerequisites of a national society. He goes on to suggest that the cosmopolitan position "is perhaps the ideal of the future; but it allows too little for the national and patriotic sentiments which...appear to be at present indispensable to social well-being...." Because sentiments of common humanity are not widely shared, "the casual aggregates that might result from perfectly unrestrained immigration would lack internal cohesion." Under these circumstances, "the governmental function of promoting moral and intellectual culture might be rendered hopelessly difficult by the continual inflowing streams of alien immigrants, with diverse moral habits and religious traditions," and "a large intermixture of immigrants brought up under different institutions might inevitably introduce corruption and disorder into a previously well-ordered State."\19

In the original version of his work, published in 1891, Sidgwick also argued that free movement might interfere with efforts to raise the standard of living among the poorer classes of a particular country; but this justification for the national perspective no longer appears in the 1919 edition.\20 Why the deletion? Perhaps Sidgwick himself became aware of the point that Walzer later makes in this regard, namely that "it is at least dubious that the average standard of living of the poorer classes throughout the world would decline under conditions of perfect labor mobility." But it is also possible that Sidgwick sensed that an emphasis on the economic consequences of immigration in fact weakened his overall justification for restrictions. He was well aware that the process impinged on the political sphere as well as on the economic, as indicated by the fact that his first reference to immigration occurs in his discussion of membership in the state. On the basis of this we can elaborate a more explicit statement of the difference between the international movement of persons and international trade: Although persons, qua labor, constitute a factor of

272

production, it is impossible to consider them -- nor will they allow themselves to be considered -- in that capacity alone.

That the immigration of persons differs from the importation of goods, however, does not in itself justify the application of the cosmopolitan principle in the second case and of the national in the first. As Walzer sees it, although Sidgwick presents his arguments as a series of consequentialist considerations that weigh against the economic benefits that might be afforded by free international movement of labor, the various arguments draw their force from a nonutilitarian conception of the importance of societal cohesion. For "it is only if patriotic sentiment has some moral basis, only if communal cohesion makes for obligations, only if there are members as well as strangers, that state officials would have any reason to worry especially about the welfare of their own people...and the success of their own culture and politics."\21

Walzer proceeds to make this position his own and reinforces the argument by way of an empirical claim that "if states ever become large neighborhoods, it is likely that neighborhoods will become little states. Their members will organize to defend the local politics and culture against strangers."\22 More generally, "the distinctiveness of cultures and groups depends upon closure and cannot be conceived as a stable feature of human life without it. If this distinctiveness is a value, as most people...seem to believe...then closure must be permitted somewhere."\23 States are not like neighborhoods but rather like clubs in that they can properly control the admission of members but not prevent them from resigning.

For neither Sidgwick nor Walzer do moral considerations end with the establishment of the right of a liberal state to restrict immigration. Sidgwick makes it clear that he has in mind some quantitative threshold: restrictions would be warranted "if ever [immigration] should threaten to take such dimensions" as to bring about the consequences specified earlier.\24 He is careful to specify that his prescriptions should not be taken as a warrant for excluding people categorically on the grounds that they are different. "Apart from these mischievous consequences, the free admission of aliens will generally be advantageous to the country admitting them," partly for reasons similar to those justifying free trade, but "partly as tending to the diffusion of mutual knowledge and sympathy among nations," and further because "the union of diverse races under a common government seems to be an almost indispensable condition of economic progress and the spread of civilisation; in spite of the political and social difficulties and drawbacks that this combination entails."\25 It is noteworthy that heterogeneous immigration is to be welcomed because of its beneficial effects on the political community, i.e., on the basis of the very principle which provides a warrant for the exclusion of very large numbers.

Walzer similarly specifies that if states are like clubs, this is not to say that any particular set of immigration restrictions is right: Rules of admission "are subject to constraint...."\26 The first constraint arises because, with respect to their moral life, states are more like families in that "citizens often believe themselves morally bound to open the doors of their country...to a particular group of outsiders, recognized as national or ethnic relatives."\27 Another constraint arises because countries possess jurisdiction over territory, a feature that carries with it certain obligations. Although no alien has a right to be a member of a club or family, "it is possible...to describe a kind of territorial or locational right," in terms of which "the state owes something to its inhabitants simply, without reference to their nationality."\28 In this perspective, even people who have come illegally can stay if they have no place to go.

Most important to Walzer, "the control of territory opens the state to the claim of necessity." This entails the principle of mutual aid or Samaritanism which requires, among other things, giving up such luxuries as superfluous space and wealth to necessitous strangers. In a world of members and strangers, "Farther than this we cannot go."\29 Albeit demanding, mutual aid does not require us to redistribute space and other goods in equal amounts to every person on the globe. Nor does it require us to always take in necessitous strangers, as there is often the alternative possibility of giving up some of the space we control for them to constitute a community of their own, or to provide them with material aid in situ. But we are obligated to take in persons whose need "is for membership itself, a nonexportable good" -- i.e., people whose politics or religion are not tolerated where they live."\30 This is what defines "refugees" as a distinct group of victims. Yet Samaritanism is itself tempered by the considerations mentioned previously.

Walzer concludes that "actually to take in large numbers of refugees is often morally necessary; but the right to restrain the flow remains a feature of communal self-determination."\31

In the course of criticizing my own endorsement of the cosmopolitan perspective, Gerald Dworkin has elucidated the more general principle involved.\32 Seeking to exorcise the "spectre of impartiality," he argues that, contrary to Ackerman and Carens, "equal moral worth" by no means rules out giving preference to ones own. It is proper to favor members of one's own family because living together and other contingent facts give rise to claims that deny things to others that they might claim on the basis of an application of universal rules. Although there are differences between families and nations and between specific individuals and communities, the same sorts of considerations apply to the two levels. It is on this basis that members of a community have a right to determine the membership conditions for their community.

Is it possible to extricate morally legitimate concerns regarding the impact of immigration on membership from the morass of prejudice that prevails in this sphere of discourse? Quite aware of the danger involved, Dworkin specifies that it does not follow from the right to determine conditions of membership that a community can exclude others on grounds such as that the others are not quite human. To exclude for such reasons, he points out, is contrary to the injunctions of liberal theory in that it denies equal moral respect.

The resulting position is very well represented by the Carter Commission's statement that quantitative and qualitative limits are justified but "must never be imposed by reason of color, nationality, or religion...." But on what might the limits then be based? Since limits entail selection, what criteria would be acceptable? To clarify these matters, I shall briefly review the historical emergence of immigration policy in liberal states in order to examine how the considerations discussed have entered in and to establish whether other valid grounds exist for limiting immigration.

IV
The Emergence of Restriction in Liberal Practice

In light of Sidgwick's statement that the cosmopolitan principle with respect to immigration is "perhaps the ideal of the future," one would assume that the cosmopolitan ideal had not yet been applied to immigration policy at that time. On the contrary, there had been a case of a state which, in light of the prescriptions of liberal theory, had relinquished legal barriers on immigration. That the case was not the United States but the United Kingdom makes Sidgwick's comments particularly puzzling.

Traditionally, under common law the sovereign exercised control over the entry of foreigners in the realm. Heightened concern for political security in the era of the French Revolution prompted the adoption of an Alien Act in Britain that enabled authorities to police entry more systematically. But this statute was revoked in the late 1820s when doctrines of the political economists reached the height of their influence on legislation, leaving no legal obstacles whatsoever to immigration. It is noteworthy that at the same time Britain also removed the remaining mercantilist obstacles to emigration of its own subjects. As late as the 1870s, British officials cited the absence of restrictions on entry as the hallmark of a liberal state.\33

At that time, few foreigners were in fact settling in Great Britain. The most prominent inward population movement was that of the southern Irish who, despite their lack of civil and political rights prior to Catholic Emancipation, were British subjects with the right to move freely from one island of the United Kingdom to the other. True immigration remained negligible until the early 1880s, when Britain began receiving a substantial flow of Russian Jews. Although most of them were in transit to America, some remained behind and settled for the most part in the working-class neighborhoods of London's East End. It is in relation to this wave that the established liberal position came to be questioned and that efforts were launched to limit immigration.\34 The campaign was blatantly anti-Semitic; led by nationalist Conservatives, it mainly argued that Britain must be preserved from corruption by a racially suspect alien presence so that it could maintain its moral authority over the Empire. This resulted in the Aliens Act of 1906 which empowered officials to prohibit the landing of persons

who appeared unable to support themselves, thereby
effectively barring poor immigrants. While in the minority, the Liberals fought restriction to the bitter
end as incompatible with Manchesterian principles, but
after they came to power, they refrained from abrogat-
ing the law. The 1906 statute turned out to be the
first step in the elaboration of an increasingly restrictive policy, in consequence of which Britain had,
as of 1930, a lower proportion of foreign-born residents than any other industrial country in western
Europe.

In 1891, when Sidgwick first addressed himself to
the question of immigration, British policy in fact
constituted a close approximation of what would be
adopted according to the cosmopolitan ideal. Was he
being disingenuous in consigning this perspective to
the future? The controversy leading to the 1906 act had
gotten underway some time before he published his remarks, and it is not unrealistic to assume that he was
aware of its terms. His own contribution to the contem-
poraneous debate appears to have been judiciously balanced: His demonstration that restriction is justifiable within liberal theory is tempered by a positive
argument on behalf of immigration as a source of
healthy heterogeneity. However, the overall thrust of
his comments is clearly to foster the development of
liberal theory in a national rather than cosmopolitan
direction, with the effect of justifying restrictions
directed quite openly against the admission of poor
Jews from Russia.

In the course of the turn-of-the-century immigration controversy, British advocates of restriction
responded to the argument that a liberal state could
not impose limits on immigration without violating its
principles by pointing to the example of the United
States. Sidgwick undoubtedly had that country -- as
well as others which later constituted the "white commonwealth" -- in mind when he remarked, "I cannot concede to a State possessing large tracts of unoccupied
land an absolute right of excluding alien elements."\35
The case of the United States is particularly revealing
because immigration constituted a key process in the
development of its state and society, and institutional
traditions rendered it necessary to justify legislative
enactments concerning this process on deeper grounds.

At the time of publication of Sidgwick's book, the
United States had recently prohibited the entry of
Chinese coolies and contract workers of any kind for a

277

ten-year period; and in 1882, Congress had enacted the
first general federal immigration law, which provided
among other things for the exclusion of persons likely
to become a public charge, of felons, and of various
other "misfits." Although these laws were of recent
vintage, the restrictions themselves were by no means
new.\36

At the time of its founding, the U.S. was faced
with a world of mercantilist states whose sovereigns
prohibited the exit of valuable subjects, and the Americans were particularly intent on asserting their right
to receive immigrants and to naturalize the subjects of
foreign sovereigns. Strong language to this effect can
be found in the Declaration of Independence. However,
they also issued pronouncements asserting their right
to exclude newcomers.

Although immigrants were desirable, considerations
arising from the relationship between land and labor in
an economy already articulated by the dynamic of capitalism dictated limits to what the United States could
or would do to attract Europeans. Had the goal been
merely demographic growth, America might have achieved
it by distributing freely to the land-hungry masses of
Europe the immense hinterland to which the several
states had gained title under international law upon
implementation of the Articles of Peace in 1783 and
subsequent treaties. However, the "free soil" policy
was rejected for evident reasons: It would drastically
reduce the value of land already held in private hands
and do away with the major source of public revenue and
of capital formation. Concurrently, it would wreak
havoc with nascent industry by providing East Coast
workingmen with an attractive alternative to wage work.
For these reasons, it was imperative that Americans
collectively assert their ownership of the vast spaces
at their disposal, and this required exclusion. One
pronouncement to this effect, presented "at the home of
Dr. Franklin" in Philadelphia in 1787, argued that
"having obtained possession of a certain territory, any
collection of men have a right to exclude all men from
settling in so much of that territory as is necessary
for themselves," a principle in which necessity is "to
be determined upon reasonable principles" related to
the nature of their economic activities.\37 The anonymous author goes on to specify that hunters need more
land than agriculturalists and that the latter in turn
require more than merchants or manufacturers.

What is being stated here might be termed a Lockean justification for exclusion: Property rights are an essential foundation of the polity, and such property rights cannot come into existence or be maintained under conditions of free access. Of course this does not provide a warrant for excluding particular individuals or categories of them, nor even to impose some quantitative limit on immigration. But it does amount to a "primitive" right of exclusion in that the conditions for a society founded on property cannot be met unless access is controlled in some fashion, if only by placing some value on the land itself -- as the United States indeed proceeded to do in 1785. The Founding Fathers might have agreed with Sidgwick's later pronouncement -- "I cannot concede to a State possessing large tracts of unoccupied land an absolute right of excluding alien elements" -- but would have undoubtedly emphasized, as I do here, that "possessing" would be impossible in the absence of control over immigration. In the same vein, these matters of property might be considered to be additional "strong empirical claims" on the basis of which Ackerman's Explorer can assert some conditions for the admission of Apollonian.

Concern with the impact of immigration on the composition of the political community was manifested during colonial times by the enactment of a variety of restrictions on the settlement of religious deviants: dissenters, Quakers, and particularly Catholics. Founded on traditional intolerance, these measures are now of little significance. Of much greater interest is Thomas Jefferson's general caution against a large flow of culturally heterogeneous newcomers from Europe.

After the outbreak of conflict with its American colonies, Britain prohibited the departure of valuable subjects to the rebel land. This had the effect of extinguishing the trade in bonded servants from the United Kingdom (mostly Scots and Irish), as well as of sharply reducing general immigration. The most widely considered solution to the ensuing labor shortage was the massive importation of German peasants under a form of limited bondage known as the "redemptioner system." Advocates of abolition of the slave trade also suggested German redemptioners as substitutes for Africans. It was against this background that Jefferson wondered in 1782 whether the desire of America to import large numbers of foreigners "was founded on good policy" and whether there were "no inconveniences to be thrown into the scale against the advantage expected...."\38

Foreshadowing Sidgwick and many others down to our

own times, Jefferson acknowledged the advantages of an increased labor supply, but pointed out that immigration would bring about serious political problems.

> It is for the happiness of those united in society to harmonize as much as possible in matters which they must of necessity transact together. Civil government being the sole object of forming societies, its administration must be conducted by common consent. Every species of government has its specific principles. Ours perhaps are more peculiar than those of any other in the universe. It is a composition of the freest principles of the English constitution, with others derived from natural right and natural reason. To these nothing can be more opposed than the maxims of absolute monarchies. Yet from such we are to expect the greatest number of emigrants. \39

It is evident that Jefferson did not have unbounded faith in the regenerative effects of the Middle Passage, since he believed early socialization into a "subject" rather than a "civic" political culture would determine the immigrants' subsequent political behavior: "They will bring with them the principles of the governments they leave, imbibed in their early youth...."\40 Moreover, the transformation they would undergo after coming to America would likely be for the worse: "...if able to throw them off, it will be in exchange for an unbounded licentiousness, passing, as is usual, from one extreme to another. It would be a miracle were they to stop precisely at the point of temperate liberty."\41 Nor does he put any trust in the operation of an American melting pot: "These principles, with their language, they will transmit to their children."\42 Despite his concerns, however, Jefferson did not go so far as to advocate positive restrictions, believing that under prevailing conditions a laissez-faire policy with respect to mass immigration from Europe would effect a beneficial selection of suitable persons.

At first thought, Jefferson's position appears to contradict his stance as the author of Virginia's liberal naturalization law, which reduced the waiting period to a mere three years, and as the forceful opponent of the restrictive naturalization law and anti-alien measures devised by the Federalists in the 1790s to protect the United States against Jacobin

280

infection. But the contradiction disappears as we understand that for him, as for Sidgwick and Walzer, immigration was a prelude to incorporation into the body politic. Under the conditions set forth, should this occur, "In proportion to their numbers, they will share with us the legislature. They will infuse into it their spirit, warp and bias its directions, and render it a heterogeneous, incoherent, distracted mass."\43 Somewhat paradoxically, the adoption of a principle according to which immigrants should not be kept from becoming citizens has the consequence that persons whose suitability as citizens is in doubt should not be allowed to enter in the first place. It should be noted as well that the very first Congress restricted naturalization to free whites, thereby barring from membership not only African immigrants but, as interpreted later, also Native Americans (from Canada) and Orientals.

Jefferson's admonition against massive immigration would be perennially invoked later whenever Americans felt threatened by a new wave of immigrants who deviated, by virtue of their religious or ethnic character, from the established norms: Irish and German Catholics through the first half of the nineteenth century, Chinese from the 1850s onward, southern and eastern Europeans in the late nineteenth century. In retrospect, it is evident as well that the prohibition on the importation of slaves, enacted when the constitutional delay expired in 1808, was designed as much to prevent the landing of black persons -- whom Jefferson and his contemporaries considered unfit for membership in the body politic by virtue of the historical experience to which they had been subjected -- as to end American participation in the Atlantic slave trade. In only slightly updated language, the very same concerns over the impact of a massive inflow of immigrants imbued with a different culture which "with their language they will transmit to their children" are being voiced about the Hispanic immigration today. And they are contributing to the resurgence of restrictionist sentiment.

Even granting the validity of Jeffersonian concerns, there is good reason to be strongly skeptical of assertions that this or that group is incapable of acquiring the qualifications of membership, or at least is unlikely to do so within a generation or two. Not only does "equal worth" require us to give fellow humans the benefit of the doubt in this regard, but the experience of the United States itself suggests there are hardly any limits to the possibilities of sociocultural adaptation.

Americans also wished to exclude criminals and paupers who, it was widely believed, were being willfully dumped on their shores by malicious European schemers. The most explicit justification of restriction in American constitutional doctrine appears in City of New York vs. Miln, decided by the Supreme Court in 1837, a time when the arrival of a vast mass of destitute Irish immigrants in the midst of a depression provoked considerable agitation and triggered efforts to reduce the flow.\44 The case involved an 1824 state law designed to prevent the landing of foreigners deemed incapable of maintaining themselves by requiring shippers to post bond on behalf of their passengers. This was challenged by a shipping company on the grounds that the state lacked the right to regulate interstate and international commerce. Under the leadership of Roger Taney, the Court bypassed the commerce issue altogether and upheld the law on the basis of the state's police powers, an outcome which, incidentally, signaled a reversal of the Court's steadfast support of the growth of national power and a turn toward states' rights more generally.

The Court went out of its way to specify that the power of any state to regulate entry was a concomitant of sovereignty, originating in the law of nations, and hence preexisted any written constitution or statute. On this Justice Barbour quoted Vattel, the standard authority: "The Sovereign may forbid the entrance of his territory, either to foreigners in general, or in particular cases, or to certain persons, or for certain particular purposes, according as he may think it advantageous to the state...."\45 And further: "Since the lord of the territory may, whenever he thinks proper, forbid its being entered, he has, no doubt, a power to annex what conditions he pleases, to the permission to enter."\46 American states therefore possessed this authority before the adoption of the Constitution, and being in the realm of police, it was not taken away from them in 1787.

The Justice also commented explicitly on the substantive problems which prompted New York to enact the measure under consideration, problems which are often invoked today as well. The act was "obviously passed with a view to prevent [New York's] citizens from being oppressed by the support of multitudes of poor persons, who come from foreign countries without possessing the means of supporting themselves. There can be no mode in which the power to regulate internal police could be more appropriately exercised."\47 And in his peroration, he moved beyond the realm of economic costs toward broader cultural and political concerns. Restriction of entry was the moral equivalent of quarantine: "We think it as competent and as necessary for a state to provide precautionary measures against the moral pestilence of paupers, vagabonds, and possibly convicts, as it is to guard against the physical pestilence, which may arise from unsound and infectious articles imported, or from a ship, the crew of which may be labouring under an infectious disease."\48 In a concurrent opinion, Justice Thompson was even more emphatic:

> Can anything fall more directly within the
> police power and internal regulation of state,
> than that which concerns the care and manage-
> ment of paupers or convicts or any other class
> or description of persons that may be thrown
> into the country, and likely to endanger its
> safety, or become chargeable for their mainte-
> nance?...[I]f all power to guard against these
> mischiefs is taken away, the safety and wel-
> fare of the community may be very much endan-
> gered.\49

Founded on the national principle, the Supreme Court's multifaceted justification for restriction anticipates the economic and political arguments formulated by Sidgwick and Walzer, but goes beyond them to include the issue of security. The reference to the law of nations is crucial in this respect: Control over immigration is a concomitant of the exercise of sovereignty because, unless states can restrain the movement of persons across their borders, there is no way for them to prevent any potential invader from marching in by posing as an immigrant. Although this might be thought of as a preliberal principle, it cannot be ignored by liberal theory so long as liberal states exist in a world that is organized into a multiplicity of states. This matter of security arises whether one adopts a cosmopolitan or a national perspective. It will be remembered, for example, that Sidgwick endorses the cosmopolitan principle with respect to trade, but grants it might be limited on military grounds.

Pressures to reduce the size of immigration and to restrict the flow from eastern and southern Europe mounted steadily from the 1880s onward, but it was only in 1921 that the United States imposed for the first time a quantitative limit on the main component of the incoming flow. Although this constituted a major policy turning point, justification for it was founded on established grounds.

Organized labor maintained that poor immigrants competed unfairly with native American workers accustomed to a higher standard of living and that immigration restriction was required on grounds of fairness, as it would give labor the sort of protection capitalists already received from a high tariff. Despite the interest of capitalists in maximizing the labor supply, social and political elites opposed the massive "new immigration" from outside northwestern Europe on Jeffersonian grounds, i.e., as undermining the viability of the American republic by way of their unsuitable prior socialization. The only added element was a systematization of the argument and its justification on the basis of what passed as "science." The urgency of restriction in the postwar years was compounded by the outbreak of revolution in eastern and central Europe, which appeared to confirm that people brought up under authoritarian rule would throw this off only "in exchange for an unbounded licentiousness" and exacerbated fears of political contagion.

As institutionalized in 1924, the new U.S. policy excluded Asians altogether, limited immigration from Europe to about 150,000 per year, and allocated these numbers according to national-origin quotas designed to reduce the flow of "new immigrants" from eastern and southern Europe. In addition, applicants had to meet a variety of qualitative requirements, including literacy and the absence of contract. The entry tax was raised to a higher level as well. Immigration from the independent countries of the Western Hemisphere was not subject to numerical limitation; however, since very few from Latin America and the Caribbean could meet the qualitative requirements, the system in effect erected a barrier against legal entry of the populace from those regions. The flow of documented immigrants was thereby reduced from 800,000 in the last unlimited year to an average of about 300,000 in the remaining years before the Great Depression. It should be noted that no provision was made for special consideration on behalf of political refugees or others in urgent need. After 1929, admissions were further restricted through administrative practices on grounds of unemployment. Efforts to breach the paper walls on behalf of European victims of persecution met with very little success. After full employment was achieved during World War II, refugees were denied admission on grounds of national security. \51

In the aftermath of World War II, political liberals -- who often represented "new immigrant" constituencies -- mounted a campaign for reform, seeking to eliminate the national-origin quotas as well as Asian exclusion and to open the door somewhat wider to the relatives of U.S. residents and to political refugees. Despite their efforts, the 1924 system was reenacted with some modifications as the "McCarran-Walter Act" of 1952. However, the liberal camp did succeed in creating a side door for surviving European victims of World War II persecution as well as others displaced as a consequence of the conflict and later for newer refugees as well, i.e., persons originating in countries under Communist rule.

However, the most significant development in the postwar period was that, as indicated by their legislative proposals, the liberal reformers in effect joined the restrictionist camp with respect to the most fundamental feature of immigration policy, numerical limitation. After quantitative restrictions came into being, there was never any debate over whether to maintain the practice, but only on what specific numbers were appropriate; and the discussion of annual size was steadily narrowed to a consensual range.

The racial and ethnic features of U.S. immigration law were finally eliminated in 1965, the year of the Civil Rights Act, but the "Kennedy-Johnson Amendment" which brought this about also confirmed numerical limitation as a permanent element of policy. The annual total from the "Eastern Hemisphere" (now encompassing Asia and Africa as well as Europe) was raised slightly to 170,000, and certain categories of close relatives were admitted beyond this quota. But the law imposed for the first time an annual limit of 180,000 on immigration from the Western Hemisphere. As modified later, the system provided for 350,000 quota admissions for the world as a whole, with a maximum of 20,000 from any given country. The bulk of entries (72 percent) were allotted to family reunion, some to the procurement of skilled workers, and 6 percent were reserved for refugees -- still defined in effect as people originating in Communist countries exclusively.

Enactment of this legislation was considered a liberal victory. However, the new system was definitely

285

more restrictive with regard to Latin America and the Caribbean than the one devised by the restrictionists in the 1920s. It can be argued that this was also true with U.S. immigration policy in general, if the total number of legal admissions is considered in relation to the vastly increased size of U.S. and world population in the intervening period. The removal of racial barriers and discriminatory provisions had the effect of opening up the United States to substantial immigration from Asia for the first time in the twentieth century and from Africa for the first time since the slave trade was abolished. But since applicants without relatives in the U.S. usually qualify for admission on the basis of scarce skills, this has fostered a brain drain from the Third World of dubious ethicality.

The contrast is often drawn between the American legal tradition of immigration, whereby aliens are admitted as permanent residents with the possibility of naturalization through routine procedures, and the system in most of continental Western Europe under which foreigners are initially admitted for a limited time period, with no guarantee that the authorization will be renewed or that prolonged residence will lead to citizenship. In spite of these formal differences, however, a guest-worker system has in effect been institutionalized in the United States as well.

At the end of the nineteenth century, when Chinese and other Orientals were excluded, western agricultural employers turned to neighboring Mexico, whose populous regions had recently been brought within reach by the railroad. Proximity fostered the development of a system of long-term commuting. Further, on the eve of World War I, approximately a third of new arrivals from the less developed countries of Europe were "birds of passage," people who came to the United States to work rather than settle and returned to their country of origin as soon as they had accumulated an appropriate nest egg. After the new immigration system of the 1920s brought the process to an abrupt end, industrial employers, too, resorted increasingly to using workers from neighboring countries of North America -- Canada (more specifically, Quebec) and Mexico -- who were often undocumented and under prearranged contracts, in double violation of the law.

At the beginning of World War II, the procurement of guest workers from Mexico was formalized into a "bracero" program, which was revived in somewhat modified form at the outbreak of the Korean conflict. East

Coast growers also secured the institutionalization of a small guest-worker program (the "H" visa) which has survived to the present. Throughout the postwar period, however, U.S. employers concurrently recruited undocumented workers from Mexico when economic conditions warranted. After the bracero program was abolished in the early 1960s, under pressure from organized labor, the flow of undocumented workers rapidly escalated. This should be recognized as a form of institutionalized labor procurement, made possible by the benevolent neglect of government authorities in the collective interest of U.S. employers. Statistics on the flow of international migrants are notoriously unreliable and highly controversial; the most reasonable view is that the migrants make repeated moves of temporary duration, which result over the long term in some permanent settlement beyond legal immigration.

By the late 1970s, legal immigration amounted to approximately twice the annual quota because of the "chaining effect" of recent arrivals on non-quota relatives, and because of the exercise of executive discretion in the admission of refugees. In March 1980, the United States enacted a new refugee law which, in accordance with the wishes of liberal reformers, removed refugees from the ordinary immigration quota, increased annual admissions to 50,000 -- with the possibility of a larger number if warranted -- and broadened the definition to include victims of persecution more generally, in keeping with the widely accepted U.N. Protocol on the subject. However, 1980 was the year of a "refugee crisis," triggered initially by the resumption of a massive exodus from Indochina in 1979, and compounded by the sudden influx of "marielitos" from Cuba (April-October 1980), admitted under the ambiguous status of "entrants." Considerable publicity was also given to the arrival of a much smaller number of extremely destitute "boat people" from Haiti, who sought recognition as refugees as well.

By the time the Carter Commission completed its work in 1981, there was a widespread feeling that the United States had lost control over its borders. The "end of growth" crisis fostered widespread talk of a horde of illegal aliens taking scarce jobs away from Americans; and the distinction between legal immigrants, undocumented aliens, and refugees was largely lost on the general public that, in the words of one legislator, suffered from "compassion fatigue." Although the Commission addressed itself to a broad spectrum of issues, its major concern was the massive flow of undocumented workers, concerning which it recommended the enactment of a pair of measures: one that would grant permanent residence to many of the aliens now illegally in the country (an "amnesty"), and another that would impose sanctions on employers of illegal aliens to deter job-seekers from entering or staying illegally by denying them access to the labor market.

In somewhat modified form, these proposals were subsequently included in a bipartisan legislative package, named for its Senate and House sponsors as "Simpson-Mazzoli." On balance, this can be thought of as a mildly restrictionist measure which -- if the deterrent is successful -- would have the net effect of reducing overall immigration, particularly of poor people from the Western Hemisphere.

Although the proposal benefited from considerable support among the general public, as indicated by opinion polls, and from leading organs of elite opinion such as the New York Times, it failed to pass in two successive Congresses because the coalition necessary for its enactment kept unraveling.\52 The strongest objections came from Hispanics and civil libertarians, who believe the institutionalization of identity checks on immigration status as an adjunct of employer sanctions would have a discriminatory effect. They were joined by employers, in general, who object to sanctions and the agricultural sector, specifically, which seeks to compensate for the anticipated loss of undocumented workers by expanding the small "H" program into a full-fledged guest-worker system. However, to the extent that legislative proposals were modified in this direction, they evoked opposition from organized labor. Despite their previous failures, advocates of "immigration reform" tried again in the Ninety-ninth Congress. By this time, a more restrictionist mood had set in, prompting those on the opposite side to adopt a more compromising stance. The legislation was finally enacted after the conflict between labor and growers was resolved by way of the "Schumer Amendment," a compromise package drafted on behalf of the Democratic house leadership after months of negotiation, which provided a special agricultural worker program for growers of perishable commodities, but extended to these workers the possibility of becoming permanent immigrants.

Concurrently, a controversy has emerged with respect to refugee policy. Despite formal adherence to the more universalistic United Nations definition of "refugee," the United States continues to accord favored treatment to people originating in Communist countries, particularly Vietnam, Cambodia, and Cuba. Nearly all the "marielitos" of 1980 were ultimately admitted for permanent settlement. In the intervening period, however, several hundred thousand people from violence-torn El Salvador have entered without documents, in search of peace and work, but American authorities have consistently denied them asylum on the grounds that they cannot demonstrate legitimate fear of persecution. Tens of thousands have been deported to their country of origin where, according to reliable observers, many have fallen victim to the violence that had prompted their flight.

V
Conclusions

Although I have not participated in the ongoing debates about liberal theory, I have examined them in search of guidance for establishing immigration policy on sound ethical grounds which are consistent with social justice in a liberal state. I am impressed with arguments on both the cosmopolitan and the national sides. The two positions actually have some important points in common. With either policy as a basis for planning, we come to the crucial matter of a threshold that is conceptualized in much the same way: in both instances, a liberal state can legitimately deny admission by establishing that the next entrant would somehow jeopardize its continued operation as a liberal state. Nationalists and cosmopolitans might differ in what they would tell that unlucky applicant, with the latter undoubtedly explaining that he is not being excluded outright but merely being made to wait. But in practice, the result is the same: no entry.

Gerhard Casper has pointed out that it does matter which policy is adopted.\53 Whereas the cosmopolitan perspective puts the burden of justification on the would-be restrictionists, the nationalist perspective places it on the applicant for admission. I would argue that since we are principally dealing with migration from poor countries with oppressive political regimes to rich countries with liberal ones, justice requires that we choose the cosmopolitan perspective as the starting point. In addition, I have shown that the cosmopolitan perspective must also be adopted if one gives priority to freedom.

Once the precedence of the cosmopolitan principle is accepted, the two perspectives can be thought of as complementary. Given the cosmopolitans' commitment to the preservation of freedom, they have no choice but to acknowledge that immigration must be stopped in the face of impending chaos (as might be caused, for example, by the impact of a very large immigrant flow on the economic and political life of the receiving country). Furthermore, a review of the U.S. immigration experience reveals some additional justifications for restriction that appear valid. One of them is preliberal, deriving from the right of self-defense under the law of nations but compatible with both perspectives of liberal theory; the other is very much within the liberal tradition, arising from a Lockean concern with property.

Let us assume that the protagonists for the cosmopolitan and national policies are reasonable persons who can eventually reach agreement on the empirical facts of a given situation. It would seem to follow then that they would also agree on very similar levels of immigration as the maximum beyond which chaos threatens. Since it is evident that this level has not been reached in the United States or in any of the other affluent liberal societies, there is no warrant for those states to reduce immigration below current levels. On the contrary, even if their policy is founded on a concern for the preservation of the existing membership group, under present world circumstances Samaritanism dictates more generous admissions rather than restrictions on admission.

Since it is unlikely that the agreed-upon level would accommodate all candidates for admission, the most important ethical questions concern the criteria for selecting from among the applicants. In practice, immigration policy must be designed to effect a triage through a system of negative and positive rules: some categories of people will be excluded; others will be assigned various priorities in the queue that is forming at the gate. The only valid ground for exclusion is unsuitability for membership in a liberal state. Immigration laws are replete with such categories. In the United States over the past two centuries they have included slaves and homosexuals, paupers and prostitutes, fascists and Asians of any kind, hunchbacks and Communists, felons and the feeble-minded. The grounds for exclusion must be restricted to those validly invoked to disqualify persons within the state from the exercise of citizenship rights, temporarily or permanently.

We will then be left with a very large pool of eligibles. Neither the cosmopolitan nor the national principle provides a warrant for what might be termed "acquisitive" criteria in an affluent liberal state's immigration policy. This would mean, for example, that the preference currently given to people with very scarce skills must be relinquished or -- what amounts to the same thing -- reduced to a very low level after all our obligations have been met.

The most difficult choice, in practice, involves the competing claims of relatives and refugees. Walzer and Dworkin emphasize the special obligations we owe members of our family, including our extended ethnic kin. Contemporary immigration policies generally do, in fact, attribute the highest priority to these categories. In the United States the problem is that relatives take up so many of the available places that few are left for needier others. The Kennedy-Johnson Amendment of 1965 was nicknamed the "brothers and sisters act" because it grants a high priority to married brothers and sisters of U.S. residents. Since each of the in-laws is in turn entitled to bring in close relatives, this results in a "chaining effect" which inflates the immigration backlog and virtually rules out immigration of people without relatives in the United States, unless they are admitted as refugees. The Carter Commission recommended reducing this priority, a suggestion that was incorporated into the Simpson-Mazzoli proposal. But it was vehemently fought by members of Congress who were responsive to constituency pressures. Family undoubtedly should be given some priority, but given the grave injustices caused by the general principle, it behooves us to keep it within bounds.

Attribution of priority to symbolic kin -- i.e., members of one's own race, nationality, or ethnic group -- is of very doubtful validity. In retrospect, U.S. national-origin quotas were based precisely on this sort of principle: Those most like us, according to a certain historical baseline, were most welcome. The burden of justification here must fall on those who would invoke the principle. For example, its use by Israel as a foundation for the "law of return" can be justified on the basis of historical contingencies; but in contemporary Britain, the principle of symbolic

kinship provides the foundation for a highly discriminatory policy which grants nearly unconditional entry
to "patrials" -- people of British descent who are
citizens of the white Commonwealth -- while excluding
most other applicants, including among them the close
relatives of black citizens of the United Kingdom.

There is widespread agreement among liberal theorists on attributing a very high priority to political
refugees ahead of the economically deprived. There are
two types of reasons for this: the priority attributable to freedom (Carens), and the impossibility of
exporting relief in the case of the refugees (Walzer).
The latter criterion is particularly persuasive. It
rests on the assumption that if we were the only other
country in the world, we would be under obligation to
admit people who can be helped only by being relocated
beyond the reach of harmful agents or situations in
their country of origin. In contrast, those suffering
from extremely severe economic deprivation could be
helped _in situ_. But to refuse them admission on such
grounds would create a concomitant obligation to provide appropriate assistance where they are.

In practice, there is a great deal of disagreement
over who is, in fact, a refugee. Nearly all liberal
states now adhere to the United Nations Protocol which
defines refugees as persons outside of their country,
deprived of its protection, and in legitimate fear of
persecution on a variety of grounds. But adherence to
the Protocol does not entail an obligation to admit all
the persons to whom recognition as refugees has been
granted. As mentioned, the determination of refugee
status in the United States is based on foreign policy
criteria. This is so obviously in violation of liberal
principles that it requires no further elaboration
here.

However, even when administered fairly, the definition in the U.N. Protocol leaves something to be
desired. Focusing on "persecution," it assumes some
identifiable agent, usually the state, whose nefarious
activities are directed against a target group -- an
approach which is based on European experience in the
twentieth century.\54 Although cases of this sort are
not unknown today, most of the Third World populations
that flee their countries now are in reality not targets of persecution, but rather victims of violence
fostered by civil or international conflict, or commonly by some combination of both.\55 As they too cannot
be helped _in situ_, they should be considered refugees

292

in some sense as victims of persecution. For reasons of international politics, however, it is unlikely that the United Nations definition will be extended to encompass this sort of situation; liberal states should therefore do so on their own, or they should design their immigration policies so as to provide at least temporary haven for the victims in question.

Within the guidelines provided by the _in situ_ principle, special consideration must be given to persons whose flight is occasioned by economic deprivation rather than persecution or violence, but where deprivation is itself attributable to state policies that are gravely inconsistent with liberal principles -- as when extreme inequality of land or wages is maintained by the potential or actual exercise of naked force. A classic instance is that of the Catholic Irish, whose starvation in the mid-nineteenth century stemmed from the land policies and penal laws imposed on Ireland by the victorious Whigs after 1690. Although the question did not arise at the time, there is no doubt that had current criteria prevailed, the United States would have denied them recognition as refugees because they would have been the subjects of a liberal state with which it maintained friendly relations, and they could not have demonstrated legitimate fear of persecution. Since they also would not have met the priorities established for the immigration queue either, the Irish would have been refused authorization to land. The principle that we must allow people in dire need into our own territory if they cannot be helped _in situ_ demonstrates why the current policy is unacceptable.

The ethical shortcomings of current U.S. policy in light of liberal theory are quite flagrant. For the time being, since we have not reached the point where chaos threatens, the issue of whether to grant the last available admission to a relative or a refugee does not arise. But precisely because the ark is far from full, we cannot shirk our obligations toward the needy on the grounds that we are being crowded by our sister-in-law's parents. Fortunately, at least some of the people in the Western Hemisphere who are the victims of generalized violence or of extreme exploitation manage to find a haven in the United States -- largely by simply admitting themselves, with the help of some friends. In the absence of persuasive evidence that they cause harm to the receiving society, let the Melville principle prevail: "If they can get here, they have God's right to come...."

293

Notes

1. U.S. Policy and the National Interest, Staff Report, Select Commission on Immigration and Refugee Policy, April 30, 1981, pp. 83-84.

2. Timothy King, "Immigration from Developing Countries: Some Philosophical Issues," Ethics 93:3, April 1983, p. 532.

3. Henry Sidgwick, Elements of Politics, 4th ed. (London: Macmillan, 1919), p. 309.

4. Ibid.

5. This awkward wording is required to cover complex issues pertaining to the consequences of varying legal definitions of "refugee." For a discussion of some of the matters involved, see Aristide Zolberg, Astre Suhrke, and Sergio Aguayo, "International Factors in the Formation of Refugee Movements," International Migration Review 20:2, Summer 1986, pp. 151-69.

6. For an elaboration of this, see Aristide Zolberg, "International Migrations in Political Perspective," in Mary M. Kritz, Charles B. Keely, and Silvano M. Tomasi, eds., Global Trends in Migration: Theory and Research on International Population Movements (New York: Center for Migration Studies, 1981), pp. 3-27.

7. Much of the ground from various points of view is covered in Mary M. Kritz, ed., U.S. Immigration and Refugee Policy: Global and Domestic Issues (Lexington: D.C. Heath, 1983). See also Michael S. Teitelbaum, "Right versus Right: Immigration and Refugee Policy in the United States," Foreign Affairs 59:1, Fall 1980, pp. 21-59.

8. Herman Melville, Redburn (Harmondsworth: Penguin Books, 1976), p. 382.

9. Bruce A. Ackerman, Social Justice in the Liberal State (New Haven: Yale University Press, 1980), p. 90.

10. Ibid., p. 93.

11. Ibid., p. 94.

12. Ibid., p. 95.

13. Joseph Carens, "Aliens and Citizens: The Limits of Liberal Theory," unpublished paper, 1983. See also John Rawls, A Theory of Justice (Cambridge: Harvard University Press, 1971).

14. Sidgwick, Elements of Politics, op. cit., p. 230.

15. Ibid., p. 232.

16. Ibid., p. 231.

17. Ibid., p. 303.

18. Ibid.

19. Ibid., p. 309.

20. See Michael Walzer, "The Distribution of Membership," in Peter G. Brown and Henry Shue, eds., Boundaries: National Autonomy and Its Limits (Totowa, NJ: Rowan and Littlefield, 1981), p. 19.

21. Ibid., p. 8.

22. Ibid.

23. Ibid., p. 10.

24. Sidgwick, Elements of Politics, op. cit., p. 310.

25. Ibid.

26. Walzer, "The Distribution of Membership," op. cit., p. 11.

27. Ibid., p. 12.

28. Ibid., pp. 13-14.

29. Ibid., p. 18.

30. Ibid., p. 20.

31. Ibid., p. 23.

32. Gerald Dworkin, Oral comments at a lecture given by author at the University of Chicago, May 1, 1984, sponsored by the Carnegie Council on Ethics and International Affairs.

33. Richard Plender, <u>International Migration Law</u> (Leiden: A.W. Sijthoff, 1972).

34. Bernard Gainer, <u>The Alien Invasion</u> (London: Heinemann Educational Books, 1972).

35. Sidgwick, <u>Elements of Politics</u>, op. cit., p. 309.

36. The following observations concerning the history of U.S. immigration policy are based on work in progress, summarized in part in Aristide Zolberg, "Contemporary Transnational Migrations in Historical Perspective: Patterns and Dilemmas," in Mary M. Kritz, ed., <u>U.S. Immigration and Refugee Policy: Global and Domestic Issues</u>, op. cit., pp. 15-51.

37. Edith Abbott, <u>Historical Aspects of the Immigration Problem</u> (Chicago: University of Chicago Press, 1926), p. 703.

38. Thomas Jefferson, <u>Notes on the State of Virginia</u> (Chapel Hill: University of North Carolina Press, 1955), p. 82.

39. Ibid., p. 83.

40. Ibid.

41. Ibid.

42. Ibid., p. 84.

43. Ibid., p. 86.

44. <u>New York v. Miln</u>, 2 Paine 429; 8 Peters 120 (1834); 11 Peters 102 (1837). The background and context of this case are discussed in Edward F. Tuerk, "The Supreme Court and Public Policy: The Regulation of Immigration, 1820-82," M.A. thesis, Department of Political Science, University of Chicago, 1951.

45. <u>New York v. Miln</u>.

46. Ibid.

47. Ibid.

48. Ibid.

49. Ibid.

50. Maldwyn Jones, American Immigration (Chicago: University of Chicago Press, 1960).

51. David S. Wyman, The Abandonment of the Jews (New York: Pantheon, 1984).

52. For a summary of the legislative history, see Joyce C. Vialet, "Immigration Issues and Legislation in the 99th Congress," Issue Brief (Washington, DC: Congressional Research Service, February 18, 1987).

53. Gerhard Casper, oral comments at a lecture given by the author at the University of Chicago, May 1, 1985, sponsored by the Carnegie Council on Ethics and International Affairs.

54. Aristide Zolberg, "The Formulation of New States as a Refugee-Generating Process," in The Annals of the American Academy of Political and Social Science 467, May 1983, pp. 24-38.

55. Aristide Zolberg, Astre Suhrke, and Sergio Aguayo, "International Factors in the Formation of Refugee Movements," op. cit.

Chapter 10

WAR IN THE FIJI ISLANDS:
THE FORCE OF CUSTOM AND THE CUSTOM OF FORCE

Marshall Sahlins

> Toward the end of the feudal period (Warring
> States), there developed powerful suzerainties
> animated by a new kind of spirit. Their chiefs
> were warriors, indifferent to the glory be-
> stowed by respect for etiquette and measure,
> but avid for conquests, genuine powers (and)
> riches....It was an epoch of sumptuous compe-
> tition, of surpassing ambitions and of annexa-
> tions.\1

As an anthropologist it is with some embarrassment that
I comment on ethics and foreign policy, precisely because in the societies I know best, there is no ideological difference between ethics and policy. Indeed,
even supposing we could define "the political" func-
tionally, it would not be institutionally distinguished
from the religious, the economic, or the philosophical.
For the Fiji Islands in the nineteenth century, which I
shall discuss here, it mainly comes down to the one
question of who was eating whom. The whole exercise,
then, might amount to a bit of exotic relief, were it
not that this total embeddedness of the political in
the cultural, or at least the cannibal, offers a unique
vantage point for understanding the ethics of war and
peace.

I can also offer some comparative asides, perhaps
not without interest to social scientists concerned
with historical problems of state and empire. These
parochial conflicts of Fijian kingdoms are in many ways
analagous to events that worldwide have marked the
formative epochs of famous civilizations. They are more
than something like the feudal struggles of the Warring
States period in Chinese history, the pre-Sumerian
battles of Mesopotamian city-states, or the "flower
wars" between Aztecs and rival kingdoms of Mexico con-
tending for human sacrifices and political hegemony. On
a point of method, I shall even have something to say
about the history of classical Greece.

299

All these comparative allusions, moreover, evoke an intriguing and recurrent issue of our own history: the relations between main force and a decent respect for the opinions of others or, more generally said, between realpolitik and received institutions, coercive strategies and constituted forms. By drawing attention to culturally remote versions of these classic antinomies in places such as Fiji, we might be able to question our own ethnocentric perception of them. It is not that the one, realpolitik, is merely practical and the other ethical or ideological -- an opposition between the naked interests of power and a customary morality. I shall try to show that the outrageous ambitions of heroic kings were just as much grounded in the cultural order as were the moral imperatives that put an end to their imperial dreams. My topic is Caesarism and Society; it is not Caesarism _versus_ Society, but Caesarism _as_ Society.

As usual, then, the anthropological excursion confronts us with our own homebred dilemmas. "Force," says Marx, "is the midwife of every old society pregnant with a new one."\2 But then force is a coercive rupture and not an established structure; hence, one is compelled to ask, with Rousseau, in what sense can obedience be a duty? "Might" is a physical constraint to which "the word Right adds nothing," Rousseau observed, since as soon as we are able to disobey, our disobedience becomes legitimate. All power comes from God, but so do all ailments; does this mean we should never call a doctor? (Well, perhaps not a doctor of philosophy.)

> Were I considering only force and the effects of force, I should say: "So long as a people is constrained to obey, and does, in fact, obey, it does well. So soon as it can shake off its yoke, and succeeds in doing so, it does better.\3

Marx argues that force makes, or at least mediates, structure. Rousseau in effect claims it is the other way around, insofar as some structure is a priori necessary to make Might Right.

Fijians complicate the problem because for them the same word (_rere_) may signify what we distinguish as "fear" and "respect." One therefore fears/respects (_rerevaka_) the ruling chief. This is what I mean by the liberating value of considering something completely different, a system where the political is embedded in

300

the cosmological. What connects fear and respect for Fijians, we shall see, is a certain idea of force as divine.

I
The Force of Custom

The exotic history I recount thus synthesizes Marx and Rousseau, even if by way of an anthropology neither had exactly envisioned. In the mid-nineteenth century, the enterprising kingdom of Mbau in central Fiji was preg- nant with a form of society structurally unknown to its traditional rivals. For decades the Mbau dynasty of warrior-kings had been expanding its boundaries by feats of military terror that were not only unprece- dented but were a scandal to ancient Fijian standards of propriety and aristocracy. Still, the structures of Mbau's domination were not altogether unique.\4

Mbau was a kind of negative image of classic Fijian society, thoroughly and uniquely organized for war. In Mbau certain transcendent warriors had traded places with the supreme priest-kings of the traditional Fijian polity. In the customary system -- of which the kingdom of Rewa, Mbau's greatest adversary, has been described as "the most perfect example"\5 -- the war- rior is the subordinate figure of a characteristic dual kingship. He represents a delegated function of sover- eignty, deployed to the capture of human sacrifices in battle with rival people; whereas, the reception and consumption of the warrior's victims by the sacerdotal king testified to the latter's ascendency and divinity. Structuralists might speak of an inversion of the diar- chy in Mbau, or a (logically) motivated transformation. Indeed, I will argue that the creative energies of Mbau's imperial projects had not arisen de novo but were unlocked from a traditional logic and form of domination.\6

Yet Mbau had also unlocked the ancient legitima- cies of domination. Its militant war-kings were bent on achieving unparalleled forms of hegemony. By sheer force and massive terror, they sought to transform the customary alliances with border kingdoms -- those that Fijians call "honored allies" -- into the equally tra- ditional but much more despised categories of "tribu- tary subjects" (gali). Beyond that, in the mid-nine- teenth century the Mbau kings conceived the original

idea of ruling the entire Fijian group. Enter here
Rousseau -- together with certain foreign traders representing less exalted ideals of the European Enlight-
enment. So soon as the peoples on the peripheries of
Mbau's conquests could shake off their yoke, they did
so, a freedom many were historically able to achieve by
appealing at once to the established force of a traditional morality and the oncoming force of the European
presence.

Needless to say, the Fijians thus traded their
temporary liberty for a more lasting colonial subjugation. But I shall only touch on that story, concentrat-
ing rather on the period when the course of events was
still governed by an autonomous logic of Fijian politics. For a long time, Mbau had managed to assimilate
even the European merchants as agents of its own _im-
perium_, sometimes with Fijian titles. The denouement
came during its prolonged war with Rewa, from 1843 to
1855, which Mbau finally won, only to discover that its
ambitions had been frustrated internally and superceded
externally. By the time peace was declared, the Fijian
system had been included in the "world system."

Yet if Fiji alone were the world -- as until
recently Fijians had fair reason to believe -- this was
a World War.\7 In the beginning (1843), the cockpit of
battle had been the great alluvial delta of the Rewa
river which, with its 40,000 people in its 96 square
miles -- all embroiled in nearly continuous strife for
twelve years -- was world enough. Yet the conflict
would be fought on sea as well as on land, with riches
mobilized from all over maritime Fiji and fighting men
from as far away as the Tongan Islands. No wonder that
"the idea of universal domination of the Fiji Islands"
was growing in Mbau, as an English missionary reported
during the earlier phases of the war.\8 Mbau's warrior-
king, Thakombau, was then claiming victory after victory in the Rewa Delta, while at the same time making his
presence felt economically all over the islands of
eastern and northern Fiji. In the end (1855), however,
Mbau's success fell far short of the "idea of universal
domination." Still, it had been the greatest war -- the
most organized, the most prolonged, and the most deadly
-- ever fought by indigenous peoples in this ocean.

With all due apologies to Thucydides, one could
even write a history of "the Polynesian war." (To
compare small things with great ones, it is obvious
that the position on ethics running through this paper
is radically different from a Thucydidean political

302

science of interest and desire. But this makes the allusion to famous battles all the more interesting.) Mbau, a great sea power, confronted in Rewa a great land power, and each of the two principal antagonists headed an extensive league of dependent and allied polities (such as the Fijians call <u>vanua</u> or "lands"). Rewa, a town of perhaps 3,000 people, was situated near the mouth of the Delta. Rewa was protected on the land side by the strongly fortified villages of the Rewan confederacy. The settlements of the Rewa Delta were set amidst a labyrinth of canals, drainage ditches, and causeways, supporting intensive cultivation of the so-called giant swamp taro. This was a unique agricultural development, traditionally ascribed to the famous farmers who were original settlers of the area and now formed the bulk and bulwark of Rewa's subjects. According to one archaeologist, the population of the Delta, over whom Rewa largely reigned, was "probably the largest concentration in the South Pacific at this time."\9

In contrast to land-based Rewa, Mbau is just a tiny islet of about 21 acres off the northeast coast of the Rewa Delta. In the mid-nineteenth century it was crowded with 2,000 to 3,000 people who lived on foods delivered by dependent clans on the adjacent mainland and the nearer islands. Surrounded by impressive megalithic canoe jetties and boasting a large complement of fisher-warriors, Mbau was little more than an offshore naval base. Its fleets of canoes, manned by sailor-subjects (in contrast to Rewa's farmers), articulated a far-flung series of subordinate and allied places. They brought not only food and goods from the central Koro Sea, but also native Fijian wealth from the distant kingdoms of eastern Fiji: Lau, Thakaundrove, Mbau, Macuata, and elsewhere. Nominally independent, these kingdoms were in fact tributary to Mbau, at least as long as they were "constrained to obey," and their tributes supported Mbau's military operations in the Delta.

Hence an analogy may be drawn to Sparta (Rewa) and Athens (Mbau) -- although in this case the sea power won. To take the analogy a bit further: Just as Thucydides claimed of the Peloponnesian War, the truer causes of this Polynesian war did not lie so much in the immediate incidents that set it off as in the sinister growth of Mbauan power. In the traditionalist view, Mbau was an upstart kingdom, and for some time it had been a demonstrable threat to the long-established states of maritime Fiji. In the late eighteenth and early nineteenth centuries (thus beginning before European contact), Mbau had wrested its domain by military exploits from the ancient kingdom of Verata on the coast of Great Fiji (Viti Levu). Verata had been, and still is, the noble land of coastal Fiji -- the ancestral home of its ruling dynasties, a kind of sacred source. The kings of Rewa, Mbau's great nineteenth-century rivals, were themselves younger brothers of the Verata lineage, hence their own claims to divinity. But the founding kings of Mbau descended from a sister's son of the Verata ancestor. And in Fiji, as we shall see, the sister's son is the archetypal usurper.\10

In Fiji, as everywhere, foreign policy is never altogether "foreign"; it is not dealings with unrelated peoples. Hence it is never entirely or simply a question of interest, but of interest as organized in a relative cultural mode. The contention between Mbau and its noble enemies was encoded in genealogical and mythological arguments that represented a continuous wellspring of moral outrage. Usurper of the original Fijian royalty, Mbau was as outrageous mythically as it was distinctive structurally. According to certain versions of legend, the heroic founder of the Mbau kingship was accorded supremacy over his royal maternal relatives of Verata and Rewa by the indigenous creator-god of Fiji in return again for <u>military</u> accomplishments -- a famous victory achieved over rebellious subjects of the god. The battle was waged in the mountains of northern Great Fiji, whence the Mbau conqueror migrated via inland waterways to the southeast coast, and then to the present island site of the kingdom. Mbau's later war-kings were likewise migrants through the interior. All this is in pointed contrast to the Verata aristocrats, who had earlier reached their own capital by traveling along the coast. The advent by sea, as well as the greater age of Verata, is further testimony, according to Fijian thought, of superiority in descent. In myth as in practice, Mbau was the incarnate Fijian consciousness of the dangers posed by force to the order achieved by lineage.

The rival kings of maritime Fiji knew such dangers only too well, since they were once the foundation of these kings' own legitimacy. Throughout eastern Fiji -- including Rewa, although not Verata -- divinity and sovereignty begin in draconic exploits of usurpation. In the characteristic dynastic myth, the kingdom is founded by a powerful voyaging prince, a stranger, whose threat to the native clans is resolved when he marries one or more of their ranking women.\11 Henceforth, his successors will stand as sister's sons of

304

the indigenous people -- which is why, in Fijian times, the king is their "god-man" (<u>kalou</u> <u>tamata</u>).

The great privilege of the sister's son is to forceably seize the offerings made to the god of his mother's people. In the archetypal rituals, the maternal relatives nonetheless resent the transgression and retain the privilege of pummeling their audacious nephew. Yet this antagonism is already a kind of piety, since by consuming the offerings, the uterine nephew takes the place of the invisible god of his mother's people. His unlawful act of violence makes him the god in living form.\12 Nor is all this just "ritual" or "superstructure," for in Fiji almost everything we call "trade" and "tribute" is in the first place a sacrifice to the invisible gods. If the offering -- in other words, control of the economy -- then falls to the king, it is by his divine right as sacred nephew to the land.

It is not necessary to believe these legends, but only to mark the integration of the political and the economic in the cosmological. Even if we choose to believe that such cosmic fancies originated in practical events as some mystification of realpolitik, they go on, in the way of a sedimented system, to become the order of practice itself. If Mbau and Rewa were related as sister's son to mother's brother at the level of ancestral lineages, the war between them was centuries old before it began. It repeated as historical event the categorical oppositions of ancient memory between people of the interior and people of the sea, between terror and descent, between the <u>arriviste</u> warrior and his deposed predecessor.

Therein lies a final use I will make of classical metaphors. It is a historiographic point about the role of culture in understanding our Polynesian war. In his preface to <u>The Peloponnesian War</u>, Thucydides tells how, upon gathering information from the participants, he scrupulously eliminated all elements of the marvelous from their tales. His own history was not designed to impress an overly credulous public; rather, as he modestly explained, it was a piece of writing meant "to last forever." And so it has; or at least as long as a certain hard-headed surrealism continues to celebrate this great triumph of <u>logos</u> and <u>mythos</u>. It is curious that the birth of Western historiography is tainted by the ethnographic cardinal sin of ignoring what the people think important.

I had asked the people of the Kamba Peninsula why, in 1854-55, they turned against the warrior-king of Mbau, Thakombau, and joined his enemies, even though they were of his very lineage. One of Thakombau's titles was "King of Kamba," Tui Kamba. The Kamba people allied with a rebellious faction within Mbau, led by Ratu Thakombau's collateral brother, Ratu Mara Kapaiwai. The Kamba peninsula became the fortified center of the rebellion and the site of the decisive battle of the Mbau-Rewa war, where the rebels were defeated by the combined forces of Thakombau and the Christian King of Tonga on April 7, 1855.\13 An old man told the story that everyone agreed was the "true cause" (vu dina). He began by saying, "Brother marrying sister, like the Tui Kamba." He followed this well-known proverb about royal incest by another, by way of sequitur: "treachery à la Mbau" (vere vaka-Bau), referring to a famous disposition of Mbauan politics (the more modern version is "politics à la Mbau" (politiki vaka-Bau)).

Elaborating on this explanation of Kamba's defection, the elder launched into the local origin myth of the Mbau ruler's title. He told how the ancestor of Thakombau had committed incest with his full sister, how they were thrown out of the Kamba Peninsula by their father, the god of the lineage, how the exiled criminal had then seized power in Mbau Island from the old divine king, and so on. "We never use the language of obeisance to that chief," he concluded. "We just say to him, 'Heh, child.'" So goes the current understanding of a turning point in the Mbau-Rewa war.

I have had enough of these experiences to convince me that the enchanted stories Fijians tell about the war reflect its truths (structurally), even when they seem beside the point or manifestly inaccurate (factually). In this instance, the archival records and Western historians have afforded a different explanation, a lot more consistent with our own empiricist folklore. Earlier in the war, the Mbau ruler (Thakombau) had imposed heavy levies in labor and goods on his Kamba grandfathers, not to neglect the sorties of Mbau fisher-assassins in Kamba waters, who were searching for the obligatory human sacrifices of temple rituals. Yet as the "cause" of Kamba's defections, this could be equally metaphoric, or at least enigmatic, since many other Mbauan lands had suffered worse from Thakombau and still remained loyal. But they were not the "grandfathers" of the king, ancestral lineages privileged to say, "Heh, child." Putting it all together, Thakombau had leaned materially on a specific relationship that structurally could not bear the weight.

The point is that kingdoms such as Mbau were made up of a complex set of traditional relations and alliances of various social kinds and strengths. These relations are known and expressed as myths of origins, at once sociological and cosmological -- implying also appropriate material considerations. In combination then with pragmatic contexts, the legends symbolically organize the shifting fortunes of bloody war. For in Fiji almost every myth is told in connection with some custom still observed, as A.M. Hocart says somewhere. So political history unfolds as the projection of ancient myth as mediated by current practice. True, the myths are selectively adapted to real-politics; but this means that practice is transformed into the logic of a mytho-categorical argument.

I shall try now to expand these cultural understandings into a more systematic account of Mbau's victories and defeats.

The structure, first of all, has a cosmic geography -- an opposition of relations on land and sea -- that ensured Mbau's policy of main force would be more effective in the inland battles of the Rewa Delta than were its larger projects of maritime domination. Moreover, the two arenas were interrelated -- the wealth of the outer islands being the means of sustaining Mbau's successes in the Delta -- so that the ultimate check on the maritime periphery set the limits of its expansion.

The reigning dynasties of the maritime states, as we have seen, descend from the high Fijian aristocracy (centered in Verata). Their immigrant kings are associated with a seaward origin, and often also with some Tongan connection -- "Tonga, the sun" (_Tonga matanisiga_), as Fijians say. Seaward and the east are the source of the life of the kingdom. Death, however, was the special work of the western peoples, notably the interior "lands" (_vanua_) of Viti Levu. The inland groups were often similarly organized in powerful principalities, but these were established by migrations along interior waterways from the homeland of autochthonous gods in the mountains (_Nakauvadra_). As a category, the peoples of the inland marches were the "border" (_bati_) relative to the maritime "chiefs" (_turaga_). The term for border (_bati_) literally denotes "tooth [that bites the cannibal victim]"; hence, most generally it signifies "inland warrior-allies."

This contrast between chiefs and inland warriors entails a great series of complementary exchanges between them. For all Fijian goods -- foods, ornaments, weapons, clothing, utensils -- are likewise divided into sea-things and land-things, and coastal and interior peoples are accordingly responsible for provisioning each other with their respective specialties.\14 The exchanges, however, are hierarchical rather than strictly symmetrical. The coastal kings in particular provide the higher status -- sea-things -- to the fighting-men of the interior in a way designed to secure the warriors' allegiance.

The most valuable of the chief's gifts were certain of his own daughters accorded to the rulers of the border lands, in return for which came a flow of sacrificial _cum_ cannibal victims taken by the warriors on the chief's behalf. In Fijian terms, this was an exchange of raw men for cooked women, since the daughters of the divine king had been ceremonially baked according to the rituals of the noble births.\15 The cooking represented a certain humanization, or a diminution of divine value, consistent with the passage of the women into the interior where they would become ancestresses of border chiefs. But then, as descended in the maternal line from coastal kings, the inland warrior-rulers were uterine nephews (of a kind) and had to be treated with some respect. The inland allies were, as Fijians put it, "honored men" (_tamata dokadokai_). They could not be summarily requisitioned for food, a rule insuring that local production was locally consumed rather than drained off as surplus to the coast. The effect was a specific structural demography: The fighting borders were often densely populated -- more powerful in fact than the superior kingdoms of the coast. And the services of these powerful warriors (honored men) had to be ritually requested and rewarded by gifts or feasts, royal in scale and maritime in provenience. This illustrates the military significance of Mbau's influence in the eastern islands, whose tributes it parleyed into fighting strength within the Rewa Delta.

In sum, the geopolitical meaning of the chief-border relation determines a mode and direction of confederation, built into the Fijian system. The maritime kingdoms acquire military strength by opening relations with the interior. I stress the term "opening": The expansion of kingdom alliances takes the specific form of _negotiation_. It is initiated and maintained contingently, by transactions of appropriate goods, persons, and courtesies. Yet these objects of exchange, by their categorical meanings, signify and precipitate a <u>traditional</u> system of alliance between king and border. Not everything in the contract is contractual, as Durkheim taught. The adventitious contract is intrinsically a conveyance of established customs.

Now it is this possibility of making legitimate relationships out of negotiated transactions that allowed Mbau to use force as the midwife of structure, <u>in the Rewa Delta</u>, i.e., on its "land side" in particular. Contemporary missionary observers, as also later European historians, remarked repeatedly on two complementary features of Mbau's successful campaigns in the Delta. On one hand, they spoke of the cupidity of the warrior-rulers of the borders. Ready to offer their allegiance to the highest bidder (to "turn over" (<u>vukica</u>), as Fijians put it, from Rewa's side to Mbau's), their disposition toward the main chance seemed matched only by their capacity for treachery. On the other hand, though, were the curious military tactics of the Mbau ruler, Thakombau, who was more concerned with terrorizing Rewa's allies than with taking Rewa itself. (In the following paragraphs I take some exception to the received tradition that, in this "war of chiefs," Thakombau's objective was simply the destruction of the Rewa king. Mbau was at the gates of Rewa within months of the opening of hostilities, but failed to attack. The brilliant campaign of 1843-45, lauded by A.R. Tippett, was quite wasteful from the point of view of an assault on Rewa itself, which suggests that the strategy of assimilating Rewan lands in the Mbau state [<u>matanitu</u>] was at least as important.\<u>16</u>)

Throughout the first half of the war, Thakombau chose to forego an easy victory by direct attack on the Rewa capital, i.e., by using his great canoe fleets to come up the Rewa River from the south. (See Map 1, appended.) He contented himself instead with deliberately drawn-out marches from the north, through the whole extent of the Delta, directed thus at the fighting lands of Rewa. The Mbau campaigns involved a judicious combination of economic attrition, guerrilla harrassment, and political conspiracy, punctuated by an occasional massive assault involving an army of thousands. The mass battles, however, were the complementary or secondary tactic. Against the strongly fortified towns of the Rewan allies, frontal attacks were generally indecisive -- except for the might they displayed and the fear they inspired. Coupled with the sustained harrassment, however, they opened the field for "conspiracy à la Mbau" with the beleaguered border lands of Rewa. By secretly negotiated promises of royal women and sumptuous compensations in native wealth, Thakombau could then dismantle the Rewan confederacy. The strategy was to transform the system of alliances in the Delta in Mbau's favor. Erstwhile fighting towns of Rewa were drawn into the government (_matanitu_) of Mbau by military pressure. By the appropriate exchanges, they then became the honored warriors of Mbau. As one missionary observer commented, "the riches of Mbau were too much for them."_17_

The political effects were more lasting than the occasional crushing defeats inflicted on Rewa itself. Culminating two of these long marches through the Delta, the Mbau armies sacked and burned the enemy capital in 1845 and again in 1847, on the first occasion killing the Rewa king together with so many hundred others that fresh forces had to be called in to help eat them. Yet just as often, the kingdom of Rewa arose from its own ashes; the conquests did not prove permanent. More permanent were the effects on Rewa's peripheral allies. To this day, certain of them are reckoned and act as "Mbau lands" (_vanua vaka-Bau_). In the years after the war and into the colonial period (post-1874), with that disregard for the proprieties so typical of Mbau warrior-kings, Thakombau attempted to increase his domination of the conquered allies (ex-allies of Rewa) by demanding uncustomary tributes from them. The attempt was intelligible, if not completely successful, because of a structural ambiguity in these relationships: True, the former warriors of Rewa were now "honored men" of Mbau, but they had become so virtually by conquest, and in that respect they could be despised (i.e., as conquered subjects, (_qali kaisi_), rather than _bati_).

There is a lesson here in the relation between Might and Right. The two could not be made synonymous as far as Rewa itself was concerned. The reasons for Rewa's repeated revival and ultimate survival are complex and have to do with the hierarchical solidarities of true Rewan clans, whose own social being depended on the continued existence of their divine king. This aristocratic kingship would not submit to the _parvenu_ pretensions of Mbau. It appears that force can be transposed into legitimate domination only in specific local areas of the Fijian system. Only the negotiated relation of border-warriors to the coastal kingdom is vulnerable to a process of structure-by-force ("restructuration"). One could say that this sector is historically open in the sense that here the system of political domination responds to shifting correlations of de facto power. Yet the border relations are open precisely to the extent that they can be made systematic and culturally closed, in the sense that the new alignments, when stabilized by exchange, reproduce the Fijian system as constituted. Force may be the midwife of a new society -- the source of a hegemony on an unprecedented scale -- as long as it is mediated by the values and constraints of the old society, the same order that Thakombau was thinking of transcending.

These contradictions were fatally revealed by contrasting events on the maritime peripheries of the war. Here the Might of the upstart Mbau had to contend with noble states that did well to submit when they had to and even better to rebel as soon as they could. The effects were fatal because Mbau depended on the tributary wealth of the maritime kingdoms to win over Rewa's allies within the Delta.

The geographical scale of military activity and economic interdependence sponsored by Mbau had put an imperial mote in the eye of its warrior-kings. By 1810, Mbau forces were fighting from one end of the Fiji Islands to the other. In the late eighteenth century, under Thakombau's grandfather, Mbanuve, Mbau overcame the principal village of the Lau Islands in the east (battle of Kendekende); in 1808 or 1809, Thakombau's father, Tanoa, undertook a marauding expedition to Nandi on the west side of Viti Levu.\18 By the late 1830s, at least, Tanoa began to assume the title of "King of Fiji" (Tui Viti), a designation without precedent in these islands. (The sources do not support the semi-mocking notion, traditional among Western historians, that the title actually came to Thakombau in the mail as the address on a letter sent to Fiji in the 1840s by the British consul in Hawaii, which one of the consul's compatriots had seen fit to deliver to the Mbau ruler.) Still, the similar pretensions of recent Hawaiian kings -- as well as of the Tui Tonga, king of the unified Tongan Islands -- help explain why Thakombau not only welcomed the title but proceeded to make material representations of it in ways that imitated the monarchial mania of his Polynesian counterparts. The other Pacific kings, for example, had learned to acquire costly European ships as the trappings of their own royalty.

In 1850, while still at war with Rewa, Thakombau decided to follow the example of these kings, although

arguably only for military purposes. He ordered two
expensive vessels, one from Australia and one from
America. They were to be paid for in kind, with cargoes
of trepang (bêche-de-mer), which was at this time the
principal Fijian resource for European trade in the
Canton market. The problem for Thakombau was that the
natural resources of trepang in Mbau waters had long
been exhausted.\19 In fact they were never abundant,
but Mbau had managed nevertheless to control the major
share of foreign trade by its political reach. The
leader of the resident European middlemen on Ovalau
Island, David Whippy, held the official title of envoy
to Mbau (mata-ki-Bau), and by his marriages with ranking Fijian women he was integrated in the chiefly
kinship network. Indeed, the European traders were
middlemen also for Thakombau. Important Mbau chiefs
were sent along with the traders on commercial excur-
sions, arranging contracts with local chiefs in other
areas, such as on the northern coasts of the principal
islands where trepang was still plentiful.\20 A certain
part of the proceeds thus fell to the Mbau rulers. But
now, to pay for his royal ships, Thakombau would have
to make direct levies of an unparalleled magnitude on
the petty chiefs and prouder kings of northern Fiji. It
became a test of his imperial hubris and was his last
hurrah.

In what might be called "the great trepang campaign," carried out over nine months of 1851-52 by a
combination of material exaction and military intimi-
dation, Thakombau discovered the structural limits of
his personal ambitions.\21 To reach the fishing grounds
off northern Fiji, the Mbau warrior first mobilized
every kinship and political connection, direct and
indirect, at his command. Through these extended and
often weak chains of influence, Thakombau put out can-
vas bags to be filled with cured sea slugs by the
remote local authorities and their people. But the Mbau
king was at the extreme geographic margins of his
power, dealing with lands without customary obligations
to serve him or, as Fijians say, "to listen" to him,
and certainly not to slave for him in menial pursuits.

From the beginning he met with resistance. The
historian R.A. Derrick describes the difficulties
Thakombau encountered when the first of his European
ships -- the schooner Thakombau -- arrived in mid-1851:

> Quantities of bags...to hold the cured product
> [bêche-de-mer] were sent far and wide among
> the islands; but the people either grumbled,

worked grudgingly, or refused to have anything to do with paying for the ship. When Cakobau [Thakombau] visited the islands, sailing in delighted state in the _Cakobau_, instead of _bêche-de-mer_ he found empty bags, or none at all. He had been foiled by passive resistance. Many of the chiefs had refused to take the bags, others had taken them and let them rot on the ground, and some had burnt them.\22

By the turn of 1851, it became apparent to the Mbau king that he would have to make an example by the use of force. As a target he chose his most difficult adversary among the recalcitrant rulers of northern Fiji, Ritova, pretender to the kingship of Mathuata on Vanua Levu Island, whose local rival was backed by Thakombau. The Mbau warrior was fully aware of the exemplary character of his action. As he told Mrs. Wallis at the time, he had sent trepang bags to many parts of Fiji, but the people were waiting to see how he would take Ritova's refusal; and if he failed to kill and eat the Mathuata chief, "all of Fiji would laugh at him."\23

Thakombau thereupon assembled one of the larger armies known to Fijian history. Two thousand fighting men were transported to the Mathuata coast by a fleet of 200 seagoing canoes plus the royal schooner _Thakombau_. But the army was organized like the trade itself, mobilized through all manner of direct and indirect political relations, and it showed all the weaknesses of Thakombau's strength. It was composed of many different parties who, like the Mathuata enemy Ritova -- the "rebel" as Thakombau called him -- had only tenuous obligations to serve him.

Thakombau's military tactics showed he was aware of his own weakness, as was the rebel chief. Besieged in a hilltop fortress on the Mathuata coast with only about 100 men, Ritova refused to be intimidated by the Mbauan host shouting and dancing on the plain below in a display of their invincible numbers. And when Thakombau finally did attack, he used only 300 of his own troops, true Mbauans, a point taken by his inactive allies as a slur on their warrior honor. Worse, in a series of inept maneuvers the Mbauans were driven off with a loss of about ten men; whereupon, the whole confederated army promptly decamped in their canoes, claiming they had not come to fight but to fish for trepang. They did then go to fish trepang, but no more successfully than they had fished men for the cannibal ovens. One by one the Mbauan allies, who might have been institutionally prepared to fight for Thakombau but hardly to work for him -- precisely because they were warriors (bati) and not menials (gali kaisi) -- refused to fish, melted away, and went home. Instead of the 1,500 piculs of good trepang owed on Thakombau's European ships (a picul is a Chinese measure equivalent to 133-1/3 lbs.), the net return of the expedition was 70 piculs, of which 30 were of an inferior variety.

Thakombau's economic reach had exceeded his political grasp. The consequences of his great trepang campaign were disastrous. Not only did all of Fiji laugh at him but the correlation of forces in the ongoing war with Rewa, heretofore all to Mbau's advantage, abruptly shifted in favor of the Rewa king. The victorious Ritova declared Mathuata independent of Mbau, refused to pay any further tributes, and within months his son was in Rewa conspiring with Thakombau's enemy. The northern chiefs now began to negotiate with European merchants entirely on their own account, without benefit of the interference of or the tolls exacted by Mbau. For their part, the local Europeans, put off by Thakombau's direct competition in the trepang trade, likewise began to deal entirely on their own. Besides, they entered into collusion with Rewa, together with the principal chief of Ovalau (Tui Levuka) and certain rebels within Mbau, to do in Thakombau.

So Thakombau's trepang adventure became the turning point for another kind of imperialism, greater than even he had imagined. Europeans had acquired an autonomous presence in the Fiji Islands, independent of the Mbau polity. In the end, Thakombau managed to avoid total defeat only by using the poetry of European hegemony to counter this economic prose: He agreed to become Christian in April 1854 and thereby enlisted to his cause the great capacity for political intrigue of the local English missionaries as well as the decisive military support of the Christian king of Tonga. This holy alliance was able to crush the combined forces of European traders and Fijian rivals -- now ideologically redefined as the forces of "paganism" -- at the battle of Kamba in April 1855. Thakombau was well and truly saved, if also transformed into a "prince of peace," like his newfound god.

As it were, Thakombau's project for his own ship of state floundered on the trepang-laden reefs of northern Fiji. Here at the structural margins, the political situation was more like a state of nature where the force of custom gave way to the custom of force.

II
The Custom of Force

Thakombau's surpassing commitment to force might well be another structural point in this account. Certainly it was a norm, not only for him but for his predecessors as warrior-rulers of Mbau. If these kings thought they could make power into a system of universal domination it was because they were habitually given to use Mbauan power at the expense of the Fijian system. But such power, institutionally blind, could then become tactically irrational.

The great trepang campaign, for example, might easily have had a better outcome, but Thakombau insistently and contemptuously declined the secret offers of the besieged Mathuata chief, Ritova, to make a traditional form of submission. Ritova sent word that he would go through the abject rituals of humiliation (i soro), upon which he would fill twice as many bags of trepang as he had previously refused. In the judgment of Mbauan high chiefs as well as Europeans on the scene, if Thakombau had taken Ritova's surrender, he would have satisfactorily accomplished his object. But all of Fiji was watching him, Thakombau told his European interlocutors, and he intended to consume the "rebel" chief, together with every man, woman, and child with him.\24

Thakombau was a warrior-king, not merely a warrior, but the epitome of Fijian manhood -- "really a man," as they say. As a king, then, he was something different from the sacerdotal "god-men" reigning in other Fijian states. For Thakombau, bloodshed was the condition both of his own social being and his unique sovereignty. "We will fight until we die," he once told a remonstrating missionary. "We will teach our children to fight, and our children's children shall fight."\25

Just so, Thakombau's own father, and his father's father before him, had taken pride in having a reputation for spreading the terror of Mbau to the farthest reaches of Fiji, Thakombau's predilection for unmeasured force was not simply personal but socially congenital. Thakombau: The name means literally, "Bau-is-

315

bad" ([sa] ca ko Bau), or else "Bau wars." I thus turn
to some final reflections on the systematic grounds of
this transcendent violence and ambition.

     In this connection, another comparative note may
be useful. The political cyclone raised by Thakombau is
not the only tempest in a South Pacific teapot known to
anthropology and history. The nineteenth century saw
the remarkable irruption of more than one so-called
Napoleon of the South Seas. To recall only the most
famous: Kamehameha the Great of Hawaii and King George
Tupou of Tonga were arch-conquerers and heroic unifiers
of their archipelagic kingdoms in ways never known
before. Moreover, all these conquering heroes, including Thakombau, had occupied the same relative position
in a common Polynesian pattern of dual kingship. All
had been the active warrior-chiefs of a characteristic
diarchy -- providers of victory and of human victims --
but in that capacity, subordinate in status and junior
in lineage to a sacred sovereign of priestly function.
The contrast is like Dumezil's Mitra-Varuna, between
the sagacious or gravitas sacrifier and the excessive
or celeritas warrior. Himself removed from bloodshed,
indeed immobilized in the ceremonial center of the
land, the gravitas king received the offerings of
first-fruits from the people and the first-victims
brought home by the celeritas warrior. Thus mediating
ritually between culture and cosmos, the sacred ruler
was the fixed condition of human prosperity and social
order. It was a contrast between the right distinctions
and classifications of society, on the one hand, and on
the other the unconstrained forces beyond society upon
which it nonetheless depended. This disorder outside,
mastered by the warrior with a violence equal to the
task, was transformed into order inside through the
sacrificial offices of the god-king. All of the historic cases of conquest by usurping kings such as Thakombau, therefore, represented something more than a subversion of the usual diarchy. Not only did the fighting-king take the place of the reigning god, but the
principle of royal violence, previously deployed to
external relations, now triumphs within the land
itself.

     In this, the historic rise of the outrageous war-
rior perfectly reverses the dynastic myths of the traditional Fijian state. I will refer only to the essentials of this theory of kingship, as found almost
universally in the maritime states, including Rewa,
Lau, Thakaundrove, Nandronga, Mathuata, and (with certain modifications) the noble land of Verata.\26

The classic Fijian kingdoms were founded in the beginning -- rather than, as Mbau, in the end -- by youthful voyaging princes, who appear on their shores as ferocious warriors and potential cannibals. They threaten to consume the indigenous people of the land, who for their part are peaceable and prolific cultivators. The terrible immigrant, however, is induced to consume the land only in a sublimated sense: He marries the daughter of the ranking chief (the Fijians, like many other peoples, equate sexual relations with a "consummation"). In a more abstract sense, the foreign warrior, an archetypal male, thus marries the land or the earth. He figures as the divine means of fertility, both human and agricultural. Yet, in this process, the stranger-king is himself neutralized by the indigenous people.

His terrible powers then are deflected outside. Instead of eating the people, he undertakes to feed them on victims procured from traditional enemies. (Here, it is a case of cooked men for a raw woman -- the virgin wife he was initially accorded by the land people.) Sharing these human sacrifices with the people, the ruler thus obtains for them the divine benefits of a cannibal communion. Yet the privileged cannibal victims are of the king's own nature, substitutes for himself, namely, renowned warriors or chiefs of enemy lands. The king gives feast to the people on bodies of his own kind. Moreover, the king employs people especially like himself to capture these human offerings: clans of sailors and fishermen -- such as Fijians call "true sea people" -- whom he attaches to the kingdom as ritual assassins.

The stranger-king is also domesticated in another way by the initiating gift of woman. His royal successor thereby becomes the female side of the people's own ancestry. By origin sister's sons of the land, Fijian kings are the descendants through a woman of their own subjects. Therefore, the categories of male (immigrant) and female (land), present at the creation of the kingdom, trade places in the course of its development. First identified with the earth, hence woman, the native cultivators acquire masculine functions. They are the home or guardian warriors of the sea-born king, surrounding and protecting him within the capital. But now they are outside and he is inside. Conveyed to the center of the community, the original masculine warrior now "just abides," as Fijians say, "like a woman, and things [i.e. sacrifices] are brought to him." All this fits with the ritual privilege of the sister's son, mentioned earlier: the privilege of consuming the sacrifice. Indeed, every morning before the day's work begins, the king in the capital receives an offering of kava, the divine drink of the land. The shout signaling that the "god-man" has consumed the sacrifice releases the tabu; the people can now go about their business. Every morning the divine king recreates the world anew.\27

Notice the contradictory conceptions of royal power. The king is masculine yet feminine, an outsider yet an insider, a priestly dignitary who is an inherent cannibal and who maintains cultural good order through a genius for violence. The anthropologist Buell Quain remarks on the conflicting ideals of Fijian chiefship: "fraught with contradictions," as he wrote, it is a paradoxical combination of institutional decorum and antisocial terror:

> A good chief disapproves of violence and discourages it among his subjects. He disregards personal insults and never raises his voice above a mild, polite conversational tone. Such restraint befits a chief....But a male chief must also be a "man"....If he satisfies his own desires, people will say he is "bad," but they will also say he is "indeed a chief".... people will speak in voices hushed with awe and admiration of a certain chief of Rokowaqa, long dead, who used to wait near the children's bathing place so that he could choose a particularly fat child to bake for his supper.\28

As Buell Quain implies, the contradictory aspects of royal power are never completely uncoupled. Together they ambiguously inhabit the personage of any ruling chief. Even behind the decorous behavior of an aging sacred king lie royal threats of ancient memory: a divine anger (cudrucudru) that would be dangerous to arouse. Indeed, one of the most respectful salutations a lowly commoner of Rewa can offer the reigning king is, "Eat me!" Conversely, the ruler may refer to such people using the possessive pronoun for foods, "my (edible) commoners" (gau gali kaisi). But everywhere in Fiji, the opposed royal principles of social virtue and natural violence are separately instituted in the complementary dual kingship of sacerdotal ruler and ferocious warrior.

Typically, as in Rewa -- "the most perfect example

of a Fijian state" -- the warrior descends from the superceded chief of the indigenous people, the one who surrendered daughter and domain to the immigrant prince. But just as the latter, on becoming a domesticated king, retains a residual anger, so the warrior does not cede all claims to divinity. Everywhere in maritime Fiji, Mbau as well as Rewa, the title of this subordinate fighting-king is <u>Vunivalu</u>, which Hocart (I believe correctly) translates as "god of war" -- except that in Mbau the title was not subordinate; from the latter eighteenth century, it was ascendant over the divine kingship (<u>Roko</u> <u>Tui</u> <u>Bau</u>).

The oral history tells of long internecine struggles, in the course of which the forebears of Thakombau wrested power from the cosmic king and elevated their own warrior title to <u>de</u> <u>facto</u> suzerainty. More than one divine king of Mbau had been killed or forced into exile, until the ceremonial dignity was conferred on a subordinate branch of the warriors' own clan. It was the mirror image, therefore, of what might be called the legitimate mode of usurpation, where the immigrant divine king deposes an indigenous ruler and the latter becomes chief of warriors. The marital exchange of sovereignty was also reversed in Mbau. Appearing only latterly and abruptly in Mbau tradition, the first war-god (<u>Vunivalu</u>), himself an immigrant from the interior, marries the daughter of the divine king. Thakombau was in this respect again the equal of his predecessors, as his own principal wife was likewise the sacred king's daughter. The Mbau kingship is a distinctive, fighting kind. Yet the inversion of the classic diarchy was only the superstructural aspect of a profound transformation of the Fijian system -- a transformation that gave Mbau singular competitive advantages over the aristocratic states of Fiji.

I will spare you the details; in Fijian terms, they can be summed up by saying that in Mbau the land conquers the sea. In Mbau, the ruling clans came from the mainland to subjugate groups of roving sailor-warriors, as opposed to the usual model (Rewa, for example) where coastal kings impose themselves on stable cultivators. This is the institutional basis of Mbau's maritime reach. After taking the island of Mbau, the ruling chiefs sent off the indigenous sailor-owners to other parts of eastern Fiji. These were "true sea-people" and, as Fijians also put it, "dangerous men." Even in exile they remained the indigenous owners (<u>i</u> <u>taukei</u>) and subjects of Mbau Island, with the right to install the Mbau rulers. Hence, wherever they settled it was in a kind of dual allegiance. Fighting for other kings, they were also an immanent presence of Mbauan power in other midsts -- thus a certain willingness of the eastern kingdoms to render tributes to Mbau.\29 The wide sphere of influence also helps explain how Mbau could control European trade in much of Fiji, despite its own lack of commercial resources. And during the Rewa war, the argonauts of Mbau could be summoned back for massive canoe-borne attacks in the Delta.

Rewa, by contrast, relatively landlocked and land-oriented with its smaller fleets and bastions of farmer-fighters, had a structural coefficent of military force and political extent that was no match for Mbau's. In the earlier phases of the war, before the Europeans were directly engaged on Rewa's behalf, when Mbau was subverting Rewa's allies by its economic and military strength ("the riches of Mbau were too much for them"), Rewa could fight only a defensive and losing battle. So, for example, the report of the missionary Thomas James Jaggar in 1845:

> The Rawa [Rewa] party feel much more of the effects of the war than their enemies, in consequence of so many of their allies having deserted them, and declared themselves in favour of Bau; so that not only are they now fighting against their former friends, but very much food which the Rawa party had planted in their respective towns, the Rawa people altogether lose, and in addition to this their enemies are so near them, that very little food is left....The Rawa chiefs have made but very few attacks on the enemy, and seem principally employed on the defensive: their forces are yet strong, but they have not much property, whether native or foreign, to collect their army together; neither would they have food to feed them for any length of time.\30

We know more about the structural advantages of the Mbau system than its history. I can mention only some distributional data. Mbau is related linguistically and by certain traditions to interior groups of eastern Viti Levu along the Wainibuku watershed, whose own organization is similarly distinguished by the supremacy of warrior-kings (the Vunivalu title). It seems that wild men of the mountains conquered the coast, and this reversal of the normal Fijian cosmography expanded into imperial pretensions heretofore undreamed of in their philosophy.

There no one quite like the warrior-king Thakombau, "Bau-is-bad," so unmindful of a decent respect for legitimate relations or so ready to privilege main force over customary ethics. For some time, the kings of Rewa were not even fighting the same kind of war as Thakombau. He declared a "war of chiefs," a war, it seems, of a unique sort, that could not end until one or the other paramount ruler was slain. It appears that the Rewans never heard of such a thing. When set back in the initial battles, their rulers sent repeated offers of submission to Mbau -- i.e., a customary form that would have saved their lives at the price of their humiliation (i soro). Thakombau treated the Rewan emissaries with contempt, and even successfully conspired with one to betray the enemy capital. In 1845, the plot set in place, Thakombau appeared in force before the palisades of Rewa. The Rewa divine king came out to parley once again, ignoring shouted warnings from Thakombau's entourage to keep away. This Rewan was godly even in the Mbaun eyes. Besides, he was the sacred uterine nephew of the Mbau divine ruler, and Thakombau's own sister's husband. The divine king came face-to-face with the god of war: dignity before destruction incarnate. Disposed in his own social being to respect traditional kinship and prescribed relations between states, the Rewa king clearly mistook the category, let alone the character, of the man with whom he had to deal. Thakombau clubbed him to death.

Perhaps it was a measure of Thakombau's own category error that the "war of chiefs" did not end at that moment. Rewa was soon reconstructed around the successor of his victim. But for Thakombau, the "god of war" (Vunivalu), politics was only the continuation of battle by other means. Fijians say of the Vunivalu chief, "war is his work." We have seen that Thakombau was "bad" for generations before he was born.

It may be possible to draw a larger conclusion from the structural change in Mbau that thus transposed violence and disorder from the external function of sovereignty to its internal condition. Political science has learned to define the state as an institutional monopoly of violence, the exclusive control of force by the ruling power. Under these circumstances, Rousseau's conundrum -- force is a physical constraint, but what makes obedience to it a duty? -- dissolves, inasmuch as force has become permanent. There is also no need for a social contract. The Mbau example suggests rather that Might can become Right, provided people learn somehow that terror is an attribute they can themselves worship. And since we are, like Fijians, invoking the ancestral myths, consider Frazer's dictum that a man who controls the cosmos can easily control other men. One is tempted to suggest that the state originates from the projects of terrific kings rather than, as commonly thought, the other way around.

Finally, this poses analogous problems of culture and nature for Durkheim's thesis on religion. By exiling and subordinating their divine king, the "god-man," the warrior-rulers of Mbau proved what Fijians had already secretly known, since it was structurally presupposed: that a "natural" creative force is the truer essence of godliness. This is something Durkheim did not exactly foresee in his idea that "god" is the name by which men figure to themselves the constraints of a society they cannot otherwise imagine. For Fijians the essence of divinity is precisely outside society, in nature, and not only for the logical reason that from this transcendent position alone can the human order be constructed, but also for the corollary principle, inscribed in all their myths of rule, that in order to create society, one must first be possessed of a power stronger than it.

The god or king descends upon society from without, as a force of nature and in opposition to culture. His appearance is marked by crimes against humanity, including fratricide, patricide, and incest -- antistructural exploits that demonstrate he is superior to the rules by which ordinary men abide and in so abiding find their own happiness. Heir to an original incest, slayer of at least two of his brothers, inclined to a violence without check by custom, Thakombau was the epitome of a godly cum creative force. Intimations and ambitions of state:

> The political acts upon men in a manner that evokes "natural causes;" they submit to it as they submit to the caprices of the sky, the sea, the territorial crust.\31

Greece, China, Mesopotamia; Marx, Rousseau, Durkheim; God, Imperialism, the Origin of the State -- this excursion into remote events on distant islands takes on global pretensions not unlike Thakombau's own. But then, anthropologists by profession are given to the intellectual hubris of discovering universals in the particulars.

MAP 1
The Rewa Delta (Mbau Campaign of 1843-1845)

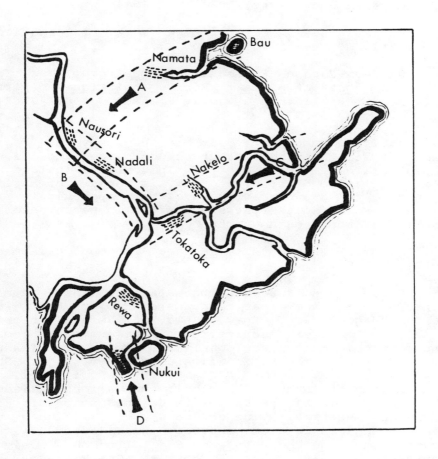

This map is taken from Alan R. Tippett, "Fijian Material Culture," _Bernice P. Bishop Museum Bulletin 232_
(Honolulu: Bishop Museum), p. 56. It illustrates Tippett's view of the Mbauan Campaign of 1843-45: "(A)
First thrust: Upper delta thrust from Bau, through
Namata to Nausori, cutting Rewa off from the interior.
(B) Second thrust: Down the Rewa River from Nausori,
through Nadali and the key villages on the main water-
way. (C) Third movement: Not a thrust but a closing of
the claws on the key military towns of Nakeli [sic.,
Naeklo] and Tokatoka. (D) Coastal alienation: Dealing
with Nukui and exposing the whole waterfront to Bauan
war canoes." (Ibid.)

Notes

1. Marcel Granet, La civilisation chinoise (Paris: La Renaissance du Livre, 1934), p. 456.

2. Karl Marx, Capital (New York: International Publications, 1967), vol. 1, p. 737.

3. Jean-Jacques Rousseau, Oeuvres complètes, Tome III, Du contract social: Ecrits politiques (Paris: Gallimard, Bibliothèque de la Pleiade, 1966 [1762]), vol. 3, pp. 351-52.

4. I use an older English orthography for Fijian names rather than the current standard spellings (i.e., "Mbau" rather than "Bau"; "Thakombau" instead of "Cakobau"). The older orthography is easier for English speakers to pronounce in ways that approximate the Fijian. For Fijian expressions given in parentheses, I use the standard orthography.

5. Basil Thomson, The Fijians (London: Heinemann, 1980), p. 366.

6. The main structural permutations I have in mind concern the three great kingdoms of Eastern Fiji (Hocart's "High Fiji"), Mbau, Rewa, and Verata. Unfortunately, the best descriptions of these states remain unpublished: Ratu Deve Toganivalu, "A History of Bau," Typescript in the National Archives of Fiji, Suva (F62/247); A.M. Hocart, "The Heart of Fiji" (Wellington: Alexander Turnbull Library); and various unclassified documents of the Native Lands Commission of Fiji (General Reports, Evidence Books, etc.). Among published English-language sources, see: Joseph Waterhouse, The King and People of Fiji (London: Wesleyan Conference, 1866); Basil Thomson, The Fijians, op. cit.; and Ratu Deve Toganivalu, "The Customs of Bau Before the Advent of Christianity," Transactions of the Fijian Society for the Year 1911 (1912), pp. 4-18. A.M. Hocart, "Lau Islands, Fiji," Bernice P. Bishop Museum Bulletin 62 (Honolulu: Bishop Museum, 1929), which describes a kingdom of the classic type, like Rewa, although again, the unexpurgated manuscript version is more comprehensive ("The Windward Islands of Fiji," (Wellington: Alexander Turnbull Library)).

7. The principal published sources in English on the Mbau-Rewa war include: R.A. Derrick, A History of Fiji, 2d ed. (Suva: Printing and Stationery Department,

1950); Thomas Williams and James Calvert, Fiji and the Fijians (New York: Appleton, 1859), vol. 2; Joseph Waterhouse, The King and People of Fiji (London: Wesleyan Conference, 1866); Mary David Cook Wallis, Life in Feejee, or, Five Years among the Cannibals (Boston: Heath, 1851); Fergus Clunie, "Fijian Weapons and Warfare," Bulletin of the Fiji Museum, No. 2. (Suva: Fiji Museum, 1977); and A.R. Tippet, Aspects of Pacific Ethnohistory (Pasadena: William Carey Library, 1973). An anonymous Fijian account, appearing in the government journal Na Mata, contains many details from oral traditions; see Anonymous, "Ai tukutuku kei Ratu Radomodomo Matenikutu Na Vunivalu," Na Mata, in nine parts, January-September, 1891.

The most valuable sources, however, are the contemporary journals and letters of the Methodist missionaries; see especially: Journals and Letters of John Hunt, Methodist Missionary Society (Box 5) (London: Library of the School of Oriental and African Studies, University of London); Papers of Rev. R.B. Lyth (Journals, Notebooks, etc.) (Sydney: Mitchell Library (Library of New South Wales)); Papers of James Calvert (Journals, Notebooks, and Letters), Methodist Missionary Society (Microfilm copy in University of Chicago Libraries of originals in the School of Oriental and African Studies, University of London); and Diaries of Thomas James Jaggar, 1837-43 (Suva: National Archives of Fiji). See also Methodist Missionary Society, In-Letters of the Feejee District (1843-55) (London: Library of the School of Oriental and African Studies, University of London). Some excerpts of missionary letters are published in the Wesleyan Missionary Society Notices, 1843-55.

8. John Hunt, Journals and Letters, op. cit., following October 19, 1845.

9. John T. Parry, "Ring-Ditch Fortifications of the Rewa Delta," Bulletin of the Fiji Museum, No. 3 (Suva: Fiji Museum, 1977).

10. It is usually assumed that Verata, Mbau's predecessor, had been a kingdom of the same general type as the latter (e.g., Shelley Ann Sayes, "The Paths of the Land: Early Political Hierarchies in Cakaudrove, Fiji," Journal of Pacific History 19, 1984, pp. 3-20. In an article in preparation ("Feejee: A Tale of Three Kingdoms," to appear in Aleta Biersack, ed., Clio in Oceania) I attempt to modify this view, claiming that Verata's hegemony was, at least in the period of re-

corded history and oral tradition, more moral and mythical than it was militaristic. The article argues that
Mbau, Rewa, and Verata represent different phases of a
diachronic structure of Fijian kingdoms, even as the
specific context of Mbau's emergence -- including the
fact that Verata was already there -- entailed a military expansion on an unprecedented scale.

11. Marshall Sahlins, "The Stranger-King; or,
Dumezil among the Fijians," Journal of Pacific History
16, 1981, pp. 107-32.

12. A.M. Hocart, "Chieftainship and the Sister's
Son in the Pacific," American Anthropologist 17, 1915,
pp. 631-46.

13. See Thomas Williams and James Calvert, Fiji
and Fijians, op. cit., vol. 2; Joseph Waterhouse, Vah-
ta-ah, The Feejeean Princess, 2d ed., (London: Hamilton
and Adams, 1857); Joseph Waterhouse, The King and People of Fiji (London: Wesleyan Conference, 1866); and
Calvert's journal entries for April 1855, Papers of
James Calvert, op. cit.

14. Epeli Rokowaqa, Ai tukutuku kei Viti (Suva,
n.d.). A copy of this rare book is available in the
National Archives, Fiji.

15. Marshall Sahlins, "Raw Women, Cooked Men, and
Other 'Great Things' of the Fiji Islands," in Paula
Brown and Donald Tuzin, eds., The Ethnography of Canni-
balism (Washington, DC: Society for Psychological
Anthropology, 1983), pp. 72-93.

16. A.R. Tippet, Aspects of Pacific Ethnohistory,
op. cit.

17. John Hunt, Journals and Letters, op. cit.,
following October 19, 1845.

18. Peter France, The Charter of the Land (Mel-
bourne: Oxford University Press, 1969), p. 21; Edwin J.
Turpin, Diary and Narratives of Edwin J. Turpin (National Archives of Fiji (MS 1)).

19. R. Gerard Ward, "The Pacific Bêche-de-mer
Trade with Special Reference to Fiji," in R. Gerard
Ward, ed., Man in the Pacific (Oxford: Clarendon Press,
1971), pp. 91-123.

20. Mary David Cook Wallis, Life in Feejee, or,

Five Years among the Cannibals, op. cit.

21. The great trepang campaign of 1851-52 is described in the standard historical sources; see R.A.
Derrick, *A History of Fiji*, op. cit., pp. 105-6,
although here the size of the army mustered by Thakombau to fish and fight is overestimated about fivefold.
The only eyewitness European source, however, is an
unpublished manuscript by Mrs. Wallis, wife of the
American captain who sold the ship *Thakombau* to the
Mbau king. Captain and Mrs. Wallis were on the Mathuata
coast during the significant military events of the
campaign, and Mrs. Wallis -- who apparently knew the
Fijian language quite well -- frequently interviewed
Thakombau at this time. I rely heavily on her account;
see Mary David Cook Wallis, untitled (a companion
volume to *Life in Feejee*) (Salem, MA: Library of the
Peabody Museum).

22. R.A. Derrick, *A History of Fiji*, op. cit., p.
106.

23. Mary David Cook Wallis, untitled, op. cit.

24. Ibid.

25. Joseph Waterhouse, *The King and People of
Fiji*, op. cit., p. 86.

26. I have outlined the "classic" Fijian system in
"The Stranger-King; or, Dumezil Among the Fijians,"
Journal of Pacific History 16, 1981, pp. 107-32, and in
my "Raw Women, Cooked Men, and Other 'Great Things' of
the Fiji Islands," in Paula Brown and Donald Tuzin,
eds., *The Ethnography of Cannibalism*, op. cit., pp. 72-
93. The Mbau, Rewa, and Verata kingship systems are
considered in more detail in my "Feejee: A Tale of
Three Kingdoms," op. cit.

27. R.H. Lester, "Kava-drinking in Viti Levu,
Fiji," *Oceania* 12, 1941, pp. 113-14; Papers of Rev.
R.B. Lyth, op. cit., CYB 549, vol. 1, p. 68.

28. Buell Quain, *Fijian Village* (Chicago: University of Chicago Press, 1948), p. 203.

29. For documentation of the work in that kingdom
of the Mbutoni people, original sailors of Bau: see the
journal entries for Somosomo (Thankaundrove) in the
1840s of Rev. R.B. Lyth, op. cit.; John Hunt, Journals
and Letters, op. cit.; and Thomas Williams, *Journal of*

Thomas Williams, Missionary in Fiji, 1840-53, G.C. Henderson, ed. (Sydney: Angus and Robertson, 1931). Other sailor clans of Mbau were found in Koro, Lakemba (Lau), Ngau, Moala, and elsewhere in eastern Fiji.

30. Methodist Missionary Society. In-Letters of the Feejee District (1843-55), op. cit.; Thomas James Jaggar, Diaries of Thomas James Jaggar, 1837-43, op. cit., March 3, 1845.

31. Valery, cited in G. Balandier, Anthropologie politique (Paris: PUF), p. 125.

Chapter 11

OUR WORLD:
AMERICAN NATIONALISM AND INTERNATIONAL ORDER

Barry D. Karl

Although the term "nationalism" used in my title is probably familiar enough to most of us, the concept of national history, as I will be describing it, is the way professional historians of any generation establish national identities for nation-states.\1 It includes those nation-states of which historians are citizens as well as those they are viewing from their perspectives as professional historians engaged in research on another country's past. National history may be supportive history or critical history. Its chief characteristic is its use of the concept of the nation-state as a means of limiting and focusing the historical past and defining the aims, trends, and collective behavioral characteristics of all those who are considered citizens of the nation-state.

One generation's national history may come to be understood as myth by later historians, either because of new evidence uncovered by research or because of changes in interpretation of what was previously known. But for each generation national history is the written history of the state that is generally accepted by citizens or observers of the state as the standard account of its development. There need be no formal certification of it as official history, and the historians who produce it need not be officials of the state. But if one looks into school curricula at all levels, from elementary education to graduate degrees, one finds standard accounts of national development which provide the basic categories for understanding the past, and may even, at more advanced levels, provide the base for continuing historical research, professional debate, and revision.

What is accepted as national history may differ from time to time, but it should be recognizable at any given moment if an observer "slices through" the levels of society which purport to understand, teach, or write the nation's history. The textbooks that achieve genuine synthesis of a generation's best research products may properly dominate the teaching of history in the educational system from elementary school through graduate school for much more than a generation. While the profession may disagree on the quality of one version or another, it will nonetheless have ways of articulating a preference.

Historians and their critics have long recognized the role played by history in establishing national identities for the young. Such identities have functioned as supports for citizens' involvement in policies promoted by the state to preserve domestic order and to justify the demands placed upon a democratic citizenry by the state's relations with other states. Such historians may be used to define the preservation of the state and its defense against enemies, both internal and external, as the ultimate value of citizenship. All other values may be subordinated to that value, including the value of life itself.

While I shall emphasize the modern uses of national history, the elements that comprise it are by no means new. Classical historians were familiar with characterizing various peoples in terms of their behavior and beliefs. Comparisons intended to reinforce values which contrasted with the values of other cultures were common enough. Thucydides's account of the Peloponnesian War -- particularly his recreation of Pericles's Funeral Oration -- is one of historical literature's most stunning examples. Caesar's descriptions of tribal behavior in Gaul are filled with such concepts. The heroic legends, battle scenes, and triumphal occasions carved on monuments in a whole range of cultures, in the East and West, testify to the practice of memorializing leaders and events to serve as models to be recalled and emulated.

Elizabethan theater audiences had come to enjoy having their history presented as dramatic entertainment, just as theater audiences did in classical times. Yet, even though four centuries separated Shakespeare and the earliest of the kings whose struggles for power he chronicled, he charted a direct line of succession that culminated purposefully in the Tudor monarchy. The saga of dynastic battling through those centuries of dispute treated the establishment of the Tudor line as the product of justice and poetry, but with enough realism to let the tragedy of human conflict and the need for a stable political order emerge as the philosophical essentials. Shakespeare's nationalism speaks through the voice of John of Gaunt in <u>Richard II</u>, the speech of a dying man lamenting the sense of order that has been lost, a warning to those who would continue in the years to come to question the leadership of a people whose special character and geographical uniqueness would someday make senseless rebellion unnecessary. The conclusion of the last play associated with Shakespeare's series, <u>Henry VIII</u>, gushes with praise not only for the infant Elizabeth but for the successors who will celebrate the stability she will come to represent. Her birth forecasts the triumph her reign had already become.

Shakespeare's histories are the histories not only of wars but also of the marriage alliances intended to moderate the confrontations produced by Europe's shifting national boundaries. Three hundred years later, the crisis which finally culminated in World War I suggests the anachronism that had been clear for centuries: the king of England, the kaiser, and the tsar were all part of the same royal lineage -- a lineage created over centuries to establish a stable international order -- yet by 1914 they were calling on profoundly different national traditions to justify one of history's most bitter international conflicts.

For centuries the maintenance of armies and navies and the sacrifices they required had been sustained effectively either by some kind of enforced service or by an emotional commitment supported by heroic leadership and, at times, an intense religious obligation. None of these were historical novelties, to be sure, nor were they confined to Western society; but by World War I the forms Western democracy forced them to take required kinds of commitment that depended on judgments that could be reached by educated, rational individuals acting on what they could consider their self-interest. In modern democracies the growing opposition to enforced military service, uncertainties about the mystical validity of charismatic leaders, and the declining role of religion as a way of making an obligation to serve the state a pathway to eternal life required new methods for making such sacrifices acceptable. It may be one of the ironies of modern life that so much of what we now call "terrorism" rests on mechanisms of total emotional commitment that were once very much part of our own heritage. Our ability to remember and to cope effectively with such emotional commitments may be seriously limited by our rationalist rejection of the mysticism on which those mechanisms seem to rest. Yet we are only little more than a generation away from

the days when "for God, for country, and for Yale" was
an acceptable campus battle cry.

Throughout the nineteenth century, Western industrialized nations utilized educational systems and a
variety of literatures to generate and justify voluntary commitments to national interest that could be
popularly accepted as identical with self-interest.
Central to both the educational system and the literature was the development of national history in the
sense in which I am using it here, that is, history
designed, at least in part, to support a voluntary and
rationally determined commitment to the state. While
this could obviously be taken as a criticism of such
history, that is not my intention; my references to
Shakespeare were intended to suggest not only that such
uses of history may be a valid way of promoting order
and stability but also that historical analyses that
promote stability and those that promote revolutionary
change both use history to gain control over historical
development. Their reality as history and our ability
to validate them by professional research may be less
important than their impact, as history, on popular
belief. People follow a flag into battle because it
represents a way of life they must preserve, even at
the cost of their lives. This is defense of a reality
that has been made identical with one's life, and
surely no greater reality exists. Equally important,
when two flags lead two armies into confrontation, the
confrontation between the two national histories that
support those flags will also be worth examining. To
the extent that conflict among nations must depend on a
willingness of citizens to support that conflict, the
relation between the national histories each uses to
justify the required sacrifices may be an important way
of understanding the confrontation and identifying
possible alternatives to conflict.

I
American Historiography:
Creating a Sense of Nationhood

The national experience of a revolution has always
tended to establish special patterns of national history. The degree of transformation will help determine
the pattern -- that is, whether one ruling family replaces another or one governmental form replaces another, whether the revolution is perceived as counterrevo-

332

lution or restoration, and what the role of violence or religious and ideological commitment will be. A justification of revolution or a rejection of revolution both rest their case on a particular historical view. Continuing debate about the meaning of specific historical events may lead to the virtual institutionalization of the past. The English Revolution of 1688 eventually came to be understood by British historians as the establishment of a constitution, but that understanding evolved over the century that followed what was essentially only the establishment of a new monarchy. Unlike the Americans of 1787 or the French of 1789, the English of 1688 had not set out to frame a constitution. What they invented over time was another matter. French historians have continued to argue about the true revolutionary moment in the sequence of acts that began, presumably, in 1789 and extended over a decade of turmoil. The Russian Revolution provides a similar problem in perception only if, as in the other examples, historians accept the necessity of defining and justifying a break with the past, the establishment of a new history, and -- perhaps most complex of all -- the search for roots in the rejected past that will support cultural continuity despite the revolution.

American historians have had their own special concern with the writing of a national history. The sense of cultural identity which had stimulated investigation of the past by historians of the older European cultures, which had led them to discover those aspects of leadership and institution building that could provide the foundations of modern European statehood, had to be created de novo by Americans. Attachment to England had taken a course of its own in the long period of colonial development, and therefore breaking those ties was itself revolutionary in the sense of confirming and justifying a separation rather than clearly and surgically replacing a government that had first to be destroyed. One fear bothered even the first generation of Puritan leaders in the century before the revolution: that the sense of purpose and direction which had established the new society was dependent upon the continued reiteration of those original purposes by each generation and could be lost without conscious restatement.\2 John Adams took up the issue in his later years as he contemplated the need for retaining a useful sense of the past.\3 Abraham Lincoln worried about it in the early years of his political career as he argued the need for a civil religion to perpetuate the aims of the founding generation once they were no longer living models.\4

In a sense, those early concerns were quite correct. The American colonists were precisely that -- colonists -- each committed to the culture or the particular colonial community that had, after all, created their fundamental sense of identity. The unity generated by their common opposition to crown and Parliament had been far more fragile in the long run than many enthusiasts had hoped. Identification with the state and the region played a much more important role for most Americans. An early national elite which superintended the establishment of the Constitution and debated its intellectual relation to the states gradually gave way to the particularist reformers of the Jacksonian era who advocated a range of reforms held together not so much by complex philosophical considerations of the national character as by concern for the social and economic well-being of the Common Man. The arch individualist, who troubled even the admiring Tocqueville, had effectively come into being.

Chiefly because of the sectional division created by slavery, nineteenth-century Americans had been forced to devote their intellectual energies to preserving themselves as a nation rather than to celebrating their nationalism. And as a nation of migrants whose mythical past had to be created out of remembered events, not out of prehistoric legends, Americans faced special problems. The pasts from which a Gibbon or a Burkhardt could build a national history for Europeans did not exist for Americans. There were no monumental buildings to point to, even in ruined form, and only a spotty collection of heroic leaders, most of whom could not be turned into statuary to be worshipped for lack of partisan and regional identification. There was only landscape, startlingly monumental to be sure, but novel in the tradition of creating the myths of the nation-state. It would be two generations before Henry Adams could seek out Gibbon's post on the stairs of Santa Maria in Arcoeli to contemplate the character of an American's relation to world civilization.

The colonial settlements, which served to establish Europeans as the dominant national stock in the New World, and the subsequent expansion, which settled and resettled new immigrants and older migrants on lands wrested from the native American Indians, created an odd base on which to build a national culture, at least in the terms in which nineteenth-century European builders of national culture conceived of their tasks. While nineteenth-century cultural theorists in Europe were debating pan-Germanic or pan-Slavic definitions of the relation between geography and peoples, Americans were trying to reconcile the relation between the states which had established their national constitution and their nationhood. Historical circumstances made slavery the issue over which the dispute would be decided and obscured the problem of nationalism sufficiently to leave it unresolved -- even by the war which resolved the issue of slavery. By the end of the nineteenth century the expression "these United States" was still the preferred way of describing the formal state of the Union; the war had rejected disunion once and for all, but it had not turned the Union into a nation.\5

Part of the American problem can perhaps be traced to an issue faced by all nation-states that undergo profound revolutions in the structure of their national governments: the need to create a sense of nationhood which combines the promise of a new future with a renewal of the past values that helped generate the revolution in the first place. The collapse of Divine Right and the increasing inability of religious authorities to confirm the authority of the state left in its wake a search for substitutes. That search provided a remarkable range of options, some of which rested on retaining the symbols and myths of the old state to support the new without providing the base for counter-revolution. Even a quick glance at history from the Puritan revolution to the Russian Revolution offers a collection of alternatives so rich in possible social orders as to provide historians of comparative revolutions with all the materials they need for analysis and debate. Yet the process is dynamic, not static. Successive nationalists choose different symbols, even different pasts, to support their position. Research uncovers new data from the past, but often in answer to questions that concern old data and old questions. Measuring the consequences of a revolution against its initial promises may prove disappointing and even disruptive to later generations examining the revolution's progress. To criticize the way in which a revolution is being realized without encouraging a new revolution may produce a special kind of history in itself.

For Americans in the years after their revolution, the problem was especially acute. Two centuries of colonial life under a varied collection of colonial governments built on patterns differing from one another had established different symbols and traditions. This made the creation of a federal government a new event which lacked acceptable cultural roots -- Great

335

Britain, after all, had tried to become a central government and the colonies had rejected the attempt. Nor was there a national religion to draw on for support for a new state. New citizens would be asked to identify with the old colonial geography. And while Virginia, New York, Massachusetts -- indeed all the new states -- were ancient and revered, the new nation itself was not. As new states with new names were split off from old states or were formed out of territories only vaguely considered part of the new nation at the time of the revolution, the issue of their relation to the nation as a whole became increasingly disturbing.

Until the Civil War -- by which time the basic shape of continental expansion had been set -- intellectuals and critics had been concerned with the relation of the process of expansion and slavery. But when expansion ceased to be the heart of the issue and slavery became the focus instead, the problem of union moved to the center of the stage.

While Americans are not accustomed to thinking of the Civil War as a war of unification in the European sense, the fact that it took place at the same time as European wars of unification and before an audience of Europeans who had joined Tocqueville in his admiration of the new federation made it a world event in terms Americans were not inclined to understand. The American states were both like and unlike the nation-states and cultural enclaves of continental Europe which were being brought together under various theories of racial and cultural sovereignty. Napoleon's crusade for unification had created tension between the desire of Europe's many ethnic enclaves for geographical independence on the one hand, and the economic and political drive by industrial statesmen who saw effectively organized power as the need of the future, on the other. That tension had a role in the migrations to the New World, as dissidents left Europe to establish better political lives for themselves and brought with them attitudes toward nationalism and regionalism that were bound to affect their approaches to the problems of their new homeland.

The Union had indeed been a response to economic conditions which required a stronger sense of national agreement, as well as a recognition of the fact that preserving the common interests of the states in a world of powerful old empires required more authority than each of them possessed individually. Yet they lacked the materials from which to create macro-myths of German, Slavic, or Anglo-Saxon cultures powerful enough to override the microrealities of ethnic histories and traditions and to justify enforced unification. By the time Americans discovered their supposedly Anglo-Saxon roots, the concept itself had become divisive, a method of separating a worthy few from the heterogeneous mass of new immigrants.

As early as 1819 Americans had begun to invent for themselves a pantheon of creator-heroes, "Founding Fathers" as they came to be called. While early writers began to debate the question of who had started the revolution -- James Otis or Patrick Henry, Massachusetts or Virginia\6 -- the decline and death of the founding generation produced an important rhetorical crisis for men like Abraham Lincoln, who blamed what he perceived in 1838 as the breakdown of social order on the disappearance of the older leaders from the scene. He called for the formulation of a secular religion that would preserve the idea of order for future generations, but it was a religion that would have to be taught to children by their mothers and to the community by its teachers, not by ministers from their pulpits. Yet Lincoln, the secular preacher of 1838, had become a curious figure by the time of his presidency and the outbreak of the war. His wartime fervor was designed to defend and preserve an old revolution, not to create a new one. The very opening of the Gettysburg Address is a call to the past. It is a cautious document that pleads for continuity rather than transformation. If one waits for the ringing rhetoric of a Garibaldi calling for national unity in the face of the disunity that is its arch enemy, one waits in vain. Lincoln had to beg community leaders to form army units out of friends and fellow citizens willing to follow them, and he faced riots when conditions forced him to employ a draft.

While the war did begin to produce a nationalist literature, its development was slow and painful. Alan Heimert's interpretation of Melville's Moby Dick as a parable on the breakdown of the national compromise and the prediction of the ultimate tragedy of the war is probably closer to the mood of the Civil War years.\7 Despite the fervor with which it was fought, the Civil War was not a popular war. The defense of the Union awoke the minimum of support necessary to sustain it. The intensity of the European nationalists' arguments for unification was probably more a product of the American Civil War than a cause of it, an intellectual afterthought born in reflection on the meaning of the

337

new nation's most disruptive and self-destructive historical event.\8

Edward Everett Hale's story of 1863, "The Man Without a Country," is the ideal folktale that begins the celebration of postwar American nationalism and all of its ambiguities. Yet like Lincoln's plea at Gettysburg, there is a curious negativism in its message, although that negativism did not prevent the story from becoming one of the basic texts of twentieth-century Americanism. After criticizing his country and asking that he never hear its name again, the protagonist is punished by being forced to live with the fulfillment of his request, confined aboard ship to travel the world, never to see or hear of his homeland. For a divided nation with more than half of its territory still to be settled, the tragedy of such nomadism must have had a double edge.

The generation that fought the war did not see it as a celebration of nationalism, but rather as the failure of compromise. New Englanders like Henry Wadsworth Longfellow, whose "Midnight Ride of Paul Revere" also appeared in 1863, were still trying to memorialize an older, more secure revolution. Not for another twenty years would the war be celebrated, and then with obviously mixed feelings, North and South. The Chicago Columbian Exposition of 1893 honored the discovery of the New World, but the southern states debated their participation in a national event taking place in the state that honored Lincoln, and some chose to reject it entirely.

From 1863 to 1893, Americans struggled with the settlement of the West and its consequences. Nationalist publicists like Theodore Roosevelt wrote of the "winning of the West," a phrase which stuck despite the fact that it concealed acts of territorial conquest not unlike those going on in other colonial empires. Frederick Jackson Turner's celebration of the frontier came, appropriately, at the end of the process, when it was easier to consider the newly settled West as land that had once been empty and unused.\9 It was time now to create the American nation.

Albert Bushness Hart's editing of the multi-volume _American Nation Series_, the publication of which extended from 1894 to 1918, marked the confluence of the establishment of a historical profession in the United States and the urge to confront the issue of nationhood. The new profession accepted the responsibili-

ty.\10 The series chronicled the development not simply
of an "American people," as Woodrow Wilson had preferred to put it in 1902 when his multi-volume history
appeared,\11 or even the "history of the United States"
as earlier historians had insisted, but the history of
an "American nation." Theodore Roosevelt's call for a
"new nationalism" in his campaign battle of 1912 gave
the matter a ringing urgency, while Wilson's slogan, a
"new freedom," recalls the residual opposition which
triumphed. That both Wilson and Roosevelt were considered historians -- the former, one of the new professionals, the latter, a gentleman amateur -- may be
another of history's meaningless accidents, but it is a
useful one. That their histories were national histories is clear enough. Their celebration of nationhood
is also a celebration of the emergence of a national
character, a sense of world leadership they sought to
define as American, and ultimately a transnational
sense of Americanism that could serve mankind. The
philanthropies of Andrew Carnegie and John D. Rockefeller were directed toward such ends. Although Wilson
and Roosevelt were far less committed to a racial
definition of the reformation they were attempting to
bring about (as were some their British counterparts,
including Cecil Rhodes), they still sought to impose a
model of behavior on other cultures long before terms
like "modernization" had been coined to justify such
transformations.\12

While their generation was clearly prepared to
define its aims in moral terms, the new professional
historians and social scientists that followed them
were not. This does not mean that they rejected the
ethical interests of those who preceded them. Many of
them continued to revere the careers of Roosevelt and
Wilson and to accept not only the money of Carnegie and
Rockefeller but many of their ethical presuppositions
as well.\13 For the philanthropic relationship was made
possible, I would argue, by a common commitment to the
same national history and the ethical values on which
both donor and recipient believed it to be based. One
cannot understand that relationship without understanding their conception of American history. It is thus
important to point out that until recently the rise of
modern professionalism in history, particularly in
American history, has been accompanied by what appears
to have been a rejection within the profession itself
of paying specific attention to a concern with the
ethical dimension of history. Carl Becker's review of
Henry Adams's autobiography is a masterly mixture of
admiration and condescension which reflects the growing

desire among professional historians to find ways of distinguishing themselves from well-meaning, gentlemen amateurs and journalists by claiming for themselves the language of technical expertise and rejecting as tendentious -- or worse -- the writing of those who used history to teach moral lessons. When The Declaration of the Democratic Dogma appeared in 1920 the young political scientist Edward S. Corwin was much blunter in his judgment. He advised readers to omit the last essay on the Rule of Phase. "Henry Adams had all the virtues of the great amateur," Corwin sniffed, and listed them: "penetration, aloofness, style." But, he concluded, "It is sad to record that in the end he did not escape the pitfall of most amateurs. He began taking himself seriously, and that as a prophet!"\14

The responsibility of training citizens gradually drifted toward political science and from there to an amalgam of disciplines called social studies. Professional historians were unconcerned that they were rejecting historiographical traditions that went back to the beginning of American historical writing; they were making decisions about professional divisions of labor that separated philosophical speculation from historical research and both from the training of citizens. It may be significant that almost at the moment Tolstoy and Santayana made their famous and oft-quoted pronouncements about the significance of real historical understanding, professional historians were more than content to leave such pronouncements to literature and philosophy while they pursued their analysis of the worlds they perceived as real. Occasional academic mavericks like Arthur M. Schlesinger, Jr. would labor brilliantly to sustain the moral parable while the profession criticized from the sidelines. One has only to survey the professional reviews of Barbara Tuchman's histories to realize how persistent and intense that separation has continued to be.

The transformation that began to take place in the 1960s was the result of a confluence of interests among younger historians and a sequence of events that began with the social upheavals of the period and ended with the Vietnam War. Historians revealed the histories of groups previously omitted from mainstream history or dealt with in ways now viewed as unfair, including women and minority groups as well a whole range of underclasses. The appearance of radical history as a new American genre -- or the rediscovery of past historians who were now considered closet radicals -- coupled with a growing historical literature critical of

American policymaking in international affairs resulted in disputes within the ranks of the profession itself. Historians sought to reestablish the profession as a conscience of American society by providing a history which could serve as a model for defining an American conception of justice through descriptions of injustices drawn from past historical experience. The Vietnam War focused that concern, but it did not create it; the civil rights movement was at least as influential.

In a sense, three kinds of national American history had come into being serially. The first and oldest was the nationalist history that had marked historical writing at least as far back as Bancroft, whose History of the United States began appearing in 1834 (the last volume was finished forty years later). Such histories had explicitly extolled an American uniqueness characterized most of all by persistent progress toward fulfillment of the ideals expressed in the Declaration of Independence, the Constitution of 1787, and the Bill of Rights. The fact that such histories accepted ideological conflict as one of the essentials of that uniqueness was clear in the writings of William Hinkley Prescott and Francis Parkman, although the conflict they saw was between totalitarian Catholicism and democratic Protestantism. Their descriptions of the church in Spain, the revolutionary Netherlands, and the contrast between the French settlement of Canada and the English settlement of Massachusetts Bay were all directed to support the fundamental conceptions of the relation between ideology and politics that supported the Protestant origins of American culture and condemned the Catholic origins of European culture.

By the beginning of the twentieth century, a new kind of national history had broadened that ideology by implanting it in a diffuse national culture that viewed cultural difference as temporary and correctable. The American Historical Association and the American Political Science Association, both organizational products of that era, joined on several significant occasions between 1895 and 1935 to assure that the nation's schools would teach a history and a politics that supported their conception of a national culture. By the end of the era, however, they had lost out to the educational profession, which had its own cultural agenda, and they turned their interest elsewhere. The fact that the educators' agenda was built on John Dewey's anti-historical conception of the individual may have inadvertently helped them. Dewey's conception of the past as a barrier to the pragmatic examination of reality and his evocation of the educated child as the product of immediate experience provided philosophical underpinnings for the individualism sparked by the Jacksonian revolution. The historical past thus became either the enemy to be overcome or the kind of irrelevancy that scientific research would ultimately replace.\15

By the 1930s, an objective, scientific history devoted to analyzing the data of the American past had been added to the older history. The addition was not intended to destroy the progressive ideal, but rather to confirm it by genuine professional research. The assumption that such research would confirm the older picture was clear, and the research ideal was taught along with increasingly sophisticated versions of the nationalist history. Evidence that controverted the progressive ideal was defined as an aberration that reform would correct, and historians described eras of progress that produced exhaustion and eras of backsliding that generated new reform impulses. Arthur M. Schlesinger, Sr.'s The American as Reformer, like his survey of great Presidents versus weak Presidents, summed up the consensus.\16

One could argue, of course, that objective, scientific analysis of the American past was ultimately bound to produce a history capable of creating havoc for the progressive ideal. Reality was certain to intervene as research revealed the cracks in the melting pot, the potholes on the road to equality, or the persistence of injustice in a society committed to equal justice for all. Yet that does not quite do enough to explain what ultimately happened. The New American Nation Series of the 1950s, in which authors like George Mowry, Arthur Link, and William Leuchtenburg celebrated the pragmatic and nonideological liberalism that has characterized the profession's conception of American history, was the culminating model of nationalist history built on the best of scholarship and research. The series itself was a significant product of the post-World War II interest in consensus, but the title of the most recent volume covering the 1960s, Allen Matusow's The Unravelling of America, effectively brings down the curtain on the mood that characterized the series up to that point.\17 Matusow's text describes the failure of liberal progressivism to achieve the ideals American nationalism had claimed to be the basis of America's uniqueness in a world otherwise committed to sordid national interests.

342

II
American as a World Power:
The Need for Stronger Nationalism

That completes a rather hasty survey of American historiography over the last century. You might well ask what it has to do with the question of values and internationalism, and you would be right to ask, particularly if you are an American who, like myself, was trained in this kind of nationalist history and has a special consciousness of your own national history. A totally transplanted people who lack a primitive geography in which some primitive national race once originated -- the very basis of the myths of nationalism common to most other cultures -- Americans have had to create a national consciousness. The question might well be, Then why have we bothered? And the answer (if a simple answer is possible) is that our international interests have required it. To put it simply, being a world power requires maintaining the military forces capable of enforcing that power. Military forces have traditionally required a willingness to sacrifice life in the interests of the state, and a sacrifice of that order, if it cannot be enforced by law alone -- and in modern times, it cannot -- must be enforced by a commitment to values that place the interests of the state above the interest in life itself.

Thus, while the urge to create a common national culture was part of the debate in the ninteenth century -- both before and after the Civil War which was fought to resolve the matter -- the problem of national culture has been exacerbated by the emergence of the United States as a world power. Every international engagement from World War I on has called for a redefinition of the character of American nationalism, in part because every such engagement has required a temporary definition of nationalism that could not be sustained.

More than anything else, the historical conditions that pushed the United States to the forefront in world affairs created the need for a stronger sense of nationalism. Nineteenth-century American expansion took place region by region and by rejection of one colonial empire after another through purchases, threats, and skirmishes that bordered on war. But the Spanish American War seemed to mark the limits of that form of incremental expansion in the Western Hemisphere, while almost inadvertently, it also revealed a method of

involvement in a world of colonial empires that established the United States as a world power with no
clearly articulated set of colonial interests beyond
the maintenance of free and open trade routes throughout the world. Even that aim was subjected to vigorous
political debate as some Americans rejected the ideas
of empire that others so enthusiastically embraced.
Such debate crossed class lines and economic interests,
allying men like Mark Twain and Andrew Carnegie in
opposition to the conceptions of empire promoted by
Theodore Roosevelt and Henry Cabot Lodge.\18

Other nations would continue to look on the United
States with a mixture of puzzlement and dismay as they
attempted to interpret voices from the many platforms
that appeared to speak for American policymakers, including Congress and the President, powerful newspaper
owners, and leaders of the political parties that appeared to represent group opinions. The fact that so
simple and supervening an American national interest as
an Open Door policy violated the understandings established over five centuries of international squabbling
did not help Americans understand either the peculiari-
ties of their own history or the demands being made by
other nations that, like themselves, were entering the
battle of the new empires versus the old. Still, among
those national historians Americans were beginning to
look to, there were those who recognized the problem
and predicted that Germany, Japan, and even Russia
would provide the American empire with its new opposition. They were not taken too seriously, however, and
with good reason: the two World Wars and the subsequent
and continuing competition with the Soviet Union were
not destined to be put in these terms, at least not in
significantly popular form. The First World War probably came closest, given the centrality of the issue of
Freedom of the Seas in justifying American entry. But
neither the war against Hitler's Germany nor the war
against the emerging Japanese empire in the Far East
were seriously described as a competition for world
markets or the establishment of free trade, despite the
importance of both issues in the negotiations that led
to the outbreak of war. The Versailles settlement had
set the tone of debate over Germany, and Americans
preferred to understand Japanese expansion as an unde-
clared war against China, a nation we then believed to
be our natural ally in Asia. Efforts on the part of the
Japanese to explain their expansionist needs in terms
that America, of all nations, probably ought to have
understood were drowned in a language of racial hegemony that we found abhorrent, given our own problems with

understanding and accepting our ethnic and racial composition.

In an important sense the language of World War II (which is to say the language describing the causes that drew us in and the aims we established for ourselves) was set for us by Hitler and to a lesser extent by the Japanese, both of whom used racial justifications for their actions. It may be one of the ironies of history that the United States -- which had a hundred years of experience with the problem of reconciling growing racial and ethnic complexities with the struggle to build a national identity -- found its two major opponents to be nations that claimed the superiority of a single race over the rest of the world. Whatever economic, political, or historical realities underlay the conflict, they were all submerged in conquest-bound ideological commitments that made World War II a struggle for survival rather than an effort to adjust national interests to international realities. The effort to revive a realism in international policy after the war and the demand for a redefinition of national interest in international relations was an understandable reaction against what was perceived as Wilsonian idealism. Whether or not the new realism could be effective in building a popular understanding of Soviet-American relations was another matter entirely. Yet not since the middle of the nineteenth century -- when religious controversies provided American political culture with the ideological bases of its crises over slavery and then immigration -- had that redefinition acquired so intense a focus on cultural values, not only our own, which were after all a part of our history, but those of our new enemy, the Soviet Union.

The continuing conflict between the United States and the Soviet Union has been couched in ideological arguments by both sides, despite occasional efforts by historians to find the similarities between their own interpretations of the international conditions of 1917 and those of Lenin and Wilson. Even these historians, however, have been forced to treat the ideological conflict as the essential one and the control of the world economic system as the pretext for a larger cataclysmic dispute between two opposing cultures. The background of those assumptions and their origins in modern times is in many respects at the heart of my argument to this point: it is the similarity in the ideological roots of the two cultures that has helped generate the dispute between them. The essential fact is that both cultures have grown out of a historical tradition of utopian revolution, that is, revolution designed not simply to transform government or its management but to produce an ideal state. Both cultures have found themselves faced with the need to produce nationalist histories that justify not only their uniqueness as modern states but also their confrontation with one another. I will also suggest that the utopian character of the conflict is what sustains it, that the conflict between two value systems imbedded in carefully constructed nationalist histories can only be resolved by the victory of one interest over the other, not by the manipulation of interests. Perhaps I ought to add that I am neither predicting nor calling for World War III; but, quite to the contrary, I am raising the question of the role played by value conflicts in the interpretation of modern political history. If value conflicts that grow out of and are embedded in national histories cannot be resolved by adjusting interests, the question of how well they can be endured may depend on how well they are understood. And that understanding may necessitate a virtual rethinking of the role of national history.

One of the ultimate ironies of our understanding of history may be that the two nations whose confrontation in today's world threatens to end human history are both end products of the most remarkable examples of the reconstruction of cultural history through revolution. Yet the superpower conflict has been quite brief, whether one dates its inception to the years immediately following World War II, as Americans are inclined to do, or to just after the turn of the century, as Russian historians do. For as it happens, each society has written popular histories of the other in such terms. Each has sought to transmit to its own national culture a history of the other that justifies its own position in the hostilities. Thus, tracing the conflict requires not only an investigation of the now-familiar policy writings of the period immediately following World War II, but also at least one example from the popular literature of the period.

III

**The Superpower Conflict
As a Clash of National Identities**

In August 1946, <u>Harper's</u> published the first of a series of articles by one of its associate editors,

John Fischer. Entitled "The Scared Men in the Kremlin," the article was the beginning of a project that had, by the following year, become a small book, Why They Behave Like Russians, which was a Book-of-the-Month Club selection and caught the attention of readers here and abroad. Reader's Digest and Life played their part in circulating Fischer's anecdotal account of life in the Soviet Union. It was advertised as an account that "is neither a defense nor an indictment of the Soviet system, it is a dispassionate effort to explain the motives and probable future course of a country and a people which we must understand in order to survive in an unstable world." One passage which was italicized in the text may sum up its essential message:

> The measures which are best calculated to cure Russia's fear neurosis and bring her around to eventual cooperation with the west are also the very measures necessary to resist Soviet expansion during the intervening period of tension and uncertainty.\19

Let me remind you that George Kennan's name had not yet surfaced when these articles and the book appeared. Kennan's famous Mr. X essay, "The Sources of Soviet Conduct," would not show up in Foreign Affairs until 1948. The concept of containment was still in the future.

John P. Marquand described the book for the Book-of-the-Month Club, beginning with a quick preview which included an enthusiastic assessment of the book as well as an interesting description of the author: "Mr. Fischer is a Texas Democrat." The club editors added,

> who brought with him to Russia his Texas ability to get on with people. This innate social sense and liking for his fellow man is the thread he uses to lead us through his Russian labyrinth; and he succeeds so well that one has the illusion of being there and seeing a world that is not irrational or cruel, but is endowed in many ways with the advantages and drawbacks of our own.\20

Concealed in that text, although surely not very deeply, are some questions that I think need to be asked. Some of them have been asked before but from a perspective rather different from the one I intend to use.

Popular American views of the rest of the world

347

have been subjected to criticism by writers who have
seen in our idealism -- or our materialism -- pretexts
for messianic adventures that have gotten us into difficulty. Both our imperialism and our isolationism have
been ascribed to images of the rest of the world that
tempted us either to impose our conceptions of an ideal
social and political order on other societies or to
withdraw in disgust from a task not worthy of our
efforts. Such critical descriptions have a quality to
them that borders on the tendentious in their assumption of a fundamental error that might have been prevented by either a transformation of perspective or a
return to some original perspective. Americans tend to
use their own history either as an example of a unique
historical triumph needed by the rest of the world for
its salvation, or as a form of self-punishment, visiting on the fathers the sins the children cannot accept
as their own. It is a habit of mind that may be peculiar to utopian societies -- societies organized historically according to images of an ideal order that
immediate realities frequently fail to fulfill. The
persistent questioning of the relation between the
reality and the dream has provided generations of Americans with the energy to fuel reform movements and with
acceptable justifications for the moods of exhaustion
that have followed.

Fischer's Texan characteristics can be found in a
whole range of descriptions of American character that
were part of a postwar literature that found its way
into the movies of John Wayne and Ronald Reagan, Gary
Cooper and James Stewart. In the years before the "ugly
American" appeared in the literature and movies, American audiences were extolling the "honest American"
whose honesty appeared to emerge from a matrix of
factors that included small-town life, western range
lands, and an innate human simplicity. Following a
pattern set by Frank Capra in prewar and wartime movies
about American domestic life, the honest American was
depicted as a reformer, first, of those conditions in
American life which made for illegality and corruption
and then of corruption and dishonesty abroad. Truman's
description of his treatment of Soviet Foreign Minister
V.M. Molotov, whether or not it actually happened that
way, was accepted proudly as part of an American forth-
rightness in the face of Russian deviousness. Both
Truman and Eisenhower represented to Americans a
straightforward simplicity that contrasted sharply with
popular representations of the Russians as dour and
complex.

Nikita Khrushchev's visit to the United States in
the fall of 1959 became virtually a comedy of manners:
Eisenhower was instructed not to smile when photo-
graphed with his visitors, and Khrushchev responded by
objecting strenuously to the supposed indecency of a
cancan performance he viewed on a Hollywood set during
the production of a movie on the life of Toulouse-
Lautrec. When Khrushchev, in a visit to the United
Nations, removed his shoe and pounded on his desk for
attention, Americans were inclined to see him as a
Wallace Beery or Broderick Crawford portrayal of a
politician. American and Soviet political manners were
not interchangeable. Yet Khrushchev's manners were
Russian country manners, his humor and his use of folk
parables were often a Russian version of a Huey Long
style of peasantry. That American novelists and historians were beginning to revise their views of Long,
turning him from the proto-Fascist of the 1930s into a
populist reformer, may not be as far from the point as
Americans might be inclined to think.

It would be wrong to make the point more complex
than necessary. Suffice it to say that both American
and Soviet societies have emphasized the popular origins of their leaders. Their utopian character has
caused both societies to raise that issue even when, in
fact, the opposite may be the case. Franklin D. Roosevelt liked to portray himself as a farmer when he could
get away with it. Truman, Eisenhower, Johnson, and
Nixon all continued to make significant use of their
lowly origins, even after some of them had become
extremely wealthy. Images of the small-town boy and the
country schoolboy and recollections of Depression
poverty combined in various ways to confirm myths of
opportunity.

The question I should like to ask might best be
put in two forms. First, how effective has that utopian
perspective been as a perspective from which to view
the rest of the world? And second, what are the consequences of such a perspective in establishing relationships with societies that have no such perspective in
their own conceptions of themselves as national entities or that have -- or are in the process of developing -- utopian conceptions of their own? The answers
that come immediately to mind, if the examples cited
above have any relevance, are disturbing. We are not
inclined to recognize in other cultures the counterparts of our own utopian myth, even when we have occasion to stand them side by side. And when the character
of the utopian myth is dramatically different from our

349

own, we may reject the relationship entirely. Our myth, to put it bluntly, is built on concepts of individualism that make it difficult to justify making sacrifices to the collective in the interest of the collective except under the greatest and most demonstrable threats to national survival. "Munich" and "domino theory" are modern concepts that serve to establish that sense of threat. By contrast, societies that build their democratic myths on conceptions of a collective interest to which individual interest must be subordinated are bound to see individualism as a serious threat. The history of utopian thought, from Plato on, is filled with examples of both.

Examples of the Soviet view of American history are relatively rare, at least at a level of scholarship Americans would be inclined to take seriously. Soviet descriptions of American slums and ghetto life tend to be discounted by American readers -- not, obviously, because the slums do not exist (they are clearly not the figment of a visiting journalist's imagination) -- but because Americans refuse to accept them as contradictions of American utopian aims. Similarly, American descriptions of Soviet labor camps and the severity of restrictions imposed on religious groups, scholars, and artists must draw similar reactions from Soviet citizens who may personally find such state action questionable but who accept it in the context of a larger support of the interest of the whole community. The American attitude toward poverty must surely be one of the oldest historical puzzles. When Americans, who live in a society committed to equality, find themselves under attack, they often lose sight of the fact that poverty is not a matter simply of relative inequity, but a matter of injustice in any system that claims a responsibility for the basic well-being of its citizens. Yet the fact that the American conception of freedom of speech and opinion may be just as puzzling to the citizens of a society committed to a collective conception of utopianism does not help either to justify the distinction or to make it intelligible.

A more recent example of the problem from another perspective can be found in Russia and the United States by Nikolai V. Sivachev and Nikolai N. Yakovlev. Some American readers were appalled by an account that tended to glorify nineteenth-century American-Russian relations and to attribute the breakdown of American-Soviet relations in the twentieth century to American Jewish Zionists who, the authors tell us, "At the beginning of the twentieth century...already represented an impressive force."\21

What they are writing about, of course, is the abrogation in 1911 of the 1832 trade treaty, one reason for which was the refusal of the tsarist government to grant passports to Jewish-American businessmen seeking to travel in Russia. In what may be a rare show of sympathy for the tsarist regime, the authors point to the fact that many of the former Russians now seeking to return as Americans had left Russia "illegally, without having fulfilled their military obligation..." to the state.\22 At each stage of conflict between the United States and the Soviet Union -- from the troops of 1919 to the correspondence in 1972 with Henry Kissinger, Zionist influence is singled out as either the cause or a weighty influence. From the perspective of an American historian of the period, the idea that an American Jewish or Zionist community -- even the unnamed former Russians who had become rich and were eager to return to Russia for a visit -- had begun to exercise power in American politics was an absurdity impossible to take seriously. American accounts of the era have always emphasized the American objection to the official Russian pogroms against Russian Jews, not the issue of business travel. Yet the fact that a Russian historian who had access to the relevant archives came away firmly believing an analysis he was willing to present to American audiences (with access to the same archival sources) must be taken seriously.

American critics who chose to respond to the book -- and there were astonishingly few -- looked on it with bemusement and mild concern. Most ignored the account, which seemed to them at best fantasy, at worst deliberately corrupt. The Boston Globe's reviewer did raise the basic point, however, and so succinctly that it is worth quoting even though it appears to have gone unheeded:

An American reader should not prejudge this book as simply another dreary contribution to the rhetoric of Soviet propaganda. It is more than this. This book is an expression of a view of the world that is truly and strikingly different from an American one and it is important to understand that it is a theory of reality that is shared by most, if not all, Soviet intellectuals who study America and its foreign policy. It is not enough simply to establish the inaccuracies and misrepresentations contained in such a view. One must go further and understand that such a view of reality is sincerely and deeply held and that it is a part of a larger belief system that gives the authors' scholarly work coherence and meaning.\23

What many American historians know is that the book represented, in some senses, the culmination of many years of effort on the part of professional American historians, through the American Historical Association and the Soviet Academy, to create the kind of communication that would lead to some understanding of that larger belief system. As American historians have known for close to twenty years now, the late Nikolai Sivachev was probably his country's leading interpreter of twentieth-century American history. Perhaps more than any other Soviet historian, he established American history as a significant field of research in Soviet academic circles. The opportunity to examine belief systems and to see our national history's being interpreted from inside Soviet national history was nonetheless ignored. Perhaps more important from the perspective of my argument here, I am convinced that it was ignored not as part of any conspiracy of silence, but because there was no way an American historian could communicate with it. It bore so little relation to the fundamental principles of our own history that there were too few points of contact that could serve as triggers for useful debate. Even the point I have chosen to emphasize, the attack on Zionism, would be viewed by the authors as a selection of a relatively irrelevant issue. For their treachery was defined by the fact that they were Jews combined with the fact that they had become rich capitalists in their adopted state. Americans accustomed to questioning military service and who respect successful capitalists could see only the anti-Semitism as the crime. While the presence of anti-Semitism dates back in both European and Russian history, the threat posed by former nationals who rejected their commitment to the state was equally important, particularly if their commitments were to alien ideologies that attacked the fundamental commitment to the state. That the ideological perspective from which the authors were writing was not part of the tsarist policy they were defending only complicated the problem.

The point was reinforced by the epilogue they appended to the work, which attacked not only Aleksandr Solzhenitsyn but the willingness of American audiences to listen to him. The epilogue then attempted to define human rights. In what seems at first a statement of extraordinary simplicity, the authors distinguished between American and Soviet views of humanity by singling out private property as the basic distinction between the two conceptions of rights, which at first seemed to me to be simple because my own initial efforts to formulate essential differences in what I have called "utopian revolutions" would have to begin there. But as simple a starting point as that may be, the effort to reconcile a system of values that historically views private property as the beginning point for a utopian revolution with one that specifically rejects it may turn out to be far more complex. The problem may involve not only the specific value itself, but a whole nexus of historical evaluations of the relation between citizens' values and their national histories.

Historians who raise questions about the relationship between values and national history do so at a certain risk. An apparent unwillingness to acknowledge what I have been calling national history has limited the questions that could be raised. Only very recently has discussion of such issues again become central to the profession, after more than a generation. This does not mean that historians had not engaged in them, only that to do so had been to step outside the realm of legitimate research inquiry. Recent calls for a new narrative history or a new general synthesis have not been couched in terms of values, but instead speak to two extremes: the critical social and economic histories which are the American substitute for Marxism, on the one hand, and the highly particularized accounts, written by historians immersed in quantification, that attack such generalization either by proving it incorrect or by proving it trivial. Both extremes have clear ethical dimensions. One attacks the ethical base of traditional national history; the other considers it irrelevant. Interestingly enough, where the problem of ethics has in fact intersected with the aims of professional research, it has been difficult, if not utterly impossible, to deal with the ethical dimension as such.

Criticism of the generalizations that have grown out of American historical writing since the turn of the century has taken a variety of forms, some of them ideological. The fact that the ideological forms are in effect indistinguishable from the nonideological ones makes the problem that much more difficult to define, since one ought to be able to distinguish between opposition to the supportive character of nationalist history and opposition to the veracity of the generali-

zations themselves. That both attacks go on simultaneously raises questions about the use of history to
train patriotic citizens, the search for a history that
will transcend nationalism entirely, and perhaps most
important of all, the relation between the two. For it
is quite possible that national and transnational history are diametrically opposed in a special and very
troublesome sense. To the extent that national history
has been responsible for training citizens in their
responsibilities to the state, it has borne the burden
of training human beings in their responsibility to one
another. The latter responsibility has begun traditionally at home, in the family and the community nearest
at hand. Efforts to enlarge the scope of that responsibility and to make the human community universally
inclusive have always run into the barriers erected by
cultural differences. Those differences have been the
very materials out of which national history has been
constructed. The deconstruction of national history
would require a total reshaping of the attitudes toward
cultural identity that have traditionally given history
its meaning.

For it seems to me quite possible that all societies that claim a constitutional or ideological utopianism for themselves pose ethical problems for themselves in doing so. Philosophers who constructed uto-
pias did so in order to raise questions about the
fundamental values of the social order. The framers of
the American Constitution deliberately raised ethical
considerations to justify first their revolution and
then their establishment of a national union. Following
a line of revolutionaries who conceived of the state as
a way to fulfill religious ideals, they formulated
their justifications in terms of a progressive approach
to perfection that began to dog them even before the
first generation retired from the scene. Each generation of Americans has had to deal with the same problem, justifying realities that seem to violate the
ideals of the revolution either by instituting a new
wave of reform or by revising their interpretations of
the ideals. These may be the tasks revolutions impose
on the societies that take that route to reform. Whether they are the most efficient methods of provoking
necessary social change in the long run is a question
Americans pose about other societies contemplating
revolution, and the answers they come up with are
ambiguous. The only thing that is clear is that we
continue to worship our own revolution.

For the sake of argument, let me suggest that

Americans stopped thinking of themselves as a colonial people a century too soon. The reasons are clear enough. Revolution and separation created a drama that threatened to become a disaster as the colonies-turned-states looked at their troubled relations with one another and realized that something would have to be done to prevent the anarchy that competition and jealousy were beginning to provoke. The Constitution of 1787 provided a tenuous bond, but one that had to be reasserted and redefined by turns until the Civil War resolved the question, not by answering it but by making certain that it would not be asked again. The national unity the war had been fought to preserve survived the experience of the war, but just barely, as the compromises necessitated by the same practical realities that had forced the reluctant colonies to become a union of states reasserted themselves. The war ended slavery but without producing the cultural unity that might have made the experience of slavery unnecessary in the first place. National unity became a reality. Cultural unity did not. As if to reinforce the absence of such a unity, the changing character of immigration over the next half-century spread diverse peoples across a landscape that was itself changing dramatically, exacerbating the problem of cultural unity and making national unity even more elusive.

While it may seem a bit peculiar for a historian to suggest such an idea -- particularly an American historian -- continued colonial status for, say, another century would have done wonders for our sense of cultural unity by plastering nineteenth-century British-Victorian patriotism on us so firmly that we would not have had to have our revolution until sometime in the 1960s, and perhaps not even then. We would have abolished slavery by law the way most other modernizing cultures did, only our abolition would have been reinforced by the worldwide efforts of the British in that direction. We would probably have been able to exercise greater control over immigration earlier, hanging on to the advantages of our homogeneity. And we would have been part of the international cultural value system that has made it possible for the British Empire to fall apart gracefully, like an elegant dowager on a satin couch enjoying a death scene made more eloquent by our suspicion that, somehow, she will still survive.

While the suggestion is obviously absurd, the very absurdity of it might reveal to us a bit more clearly just what we did instead and how significant the conse-

quences have been, not only for us as a nation but for
the rest of the world that must deal with what we have
in fact become. It might also make us more conscious of
the genuine anomalies which underlie our attitudes
toward international power -- our own and others -- and
which make it difficult for us to understand what we
are and for others to understand what we do. We are
proud of what we call our "cultural pluralism" now, and
justly so. But we weren't always so proud of it. And it
is possible that our pride obscures a bit too effectively some of the problems which it causes for us and
for others.

We do tend to write our history as though what has
happened has been part of a plan we would have approved
of had we known it in advance. Yet, it doesn't take
much investigation to point out that large numbers of
us would have allowed slavery to continue rather than
to fight a war over it, that large numbers of us would
have closed immigration earlier if we could have, or
avoided entering World War II even if it had meant
Hitler's victory in Europe. Recent battles over civil
rights have been bitter and bloody disputes. And the
recent controversy over prayer in public schools may
show that the decades of battling over the role of
religion in American life have done less than some have
thought to resolve one of our oldest sources of
division.

In some respects, it is too easy to argue that our
history should be real. We do, after all, debate the
reality of the histories other societies write. Whether
German students are learning about Hitler as we understood him, or whether the Japanese understand Hiroshima
as we understood it are subjects we debate. We make
much of the Soviet practice of revising history. Or-
well's 1984 reveals, as do many science-fiction scenarios, the role of history in promoting revolution or
loyalty to the state. Yet even Frances Fitzgerald's
criticism of American textbook publishing, America
Revised, saved its severest salvos for publishers who
avoid contoversial history in order to secure the
widest adoption of their books, not for the issue of
whether the writing of history is designed to produce
national obedience or to reshape the nation's sense of
itself. Indeed, the assumption that history ought to be
reshaping attitudes underlies the whole critique. Yet
that may not be as simple a task as its proponents
suppose, or as novel. One cannot help wishing that
Fitzgerald had gone back to read some of the excellent
descriptions by Bessie Louise Pierce, whose studies of

textbooks in the 1920s and 1930s exposed the Progressives' Americanizing on a variety of interesting and disturbing levels. Fitzgerald's glorification of the "implacable" nationalism of the textbooks of the 1950s and her comparison of those with the flabby social sentimentalism of many of today's texts is important; but there is another side to be considered.\24

The question I have been trying to raise is really one that historians ought to find more disturbing than they do. For by shaping our views of ourselves, national history shapes our views of others. A confrontation of national histories produces an international impasse when the histories are used to justify the superiority of one nation over the other. The answer some historians attempted to evolve in the years after World War I was to elaborate what they called the "history of Western civilization." Stimulated by what they believed to be an American ignorance of the European roots of their cultural values, an ignorance they felt had contributed to the American response to that experience, they sought to construct a broader historical perception among educated Americans. After the World War II, imaginative historians began to write and teach something they called "world history," which sought to elaborate multiple histories in an effort to bring non-Western history into the orbit of popular understanding. Both efforts were responses, at least in part, to perceptions among educators that an international power needed a public whose understanding of history encompassed the histories of all cultures, not just of Western civilization. Two periods, the Cold War and the Vietnam War, seem to have produced the first serious reaction against such conceptions of history since the 1890s.

Whether or not American intellectuals are willing to admit it, the Cold War framework did more to create an intellectual renaissance in the United States than any previous event in American history. The only parallel, perhaps, would be the period of international expansion at the end of the nineteenth century, which was relatively vague in comparison with the movement that began in the 1950s. The language of the court case that gave corporations justification for contributing to cultural and educational projects cited as the most important reason the international competition with the Soviet Union, that is, the need to keep America culturally strong and secure.\25 In every field -- piano and ballet performances to amateur and professional sports -- Americans were urged to best their enemy in

357

competition, while their Soviet opponents were welcomed as defectors when the occasion arose. The supposed benefits of cultural exchange softened confrontation without concealing it. When it was discovered that the Central Intelligence Agency had used philanthropic foundations as conduits for money to support such intellectual exchanges, American intellectuals were shocked at the exposure, although it is interesting to ask why. An old-fashioned conception of American nationalism would have justified such engagement, surely; but the new level of nationalist, or rather anti-nationalist sophistication intervened. It was not the subterfuge itself that seemed so offensive, but the contrast between the utopian intellectualism that had led America to identify intellectual and scientific advances with the historical emergence of the modern democratic state and the use of culture as a weapon in a war. If cultures we deemed anti-democratic could produce science and art that was equal to or superior to ours, then the traditional sense of the fundamental character of our conception of democracy was up for grabs.\26

A similar questioning of motives surrounded the relation between the civil rights movement and international policy. From the Truman administration on, American Presidents and secretaries of state were aware of the uses to which our international opponents were putting our racial problems. Again, on purely practical grounds of effective policymaking, we were forced to see the discrepancy between our utopian arguments and our national practices. All such arguments and issues aroused a growing questioning of the reality of the utopian ideal and led to what may be a curious but characteristic kind of American reform. Like the Progressive movement, which sought to build its reforms by attacking the misuses of government and the misrepresentations of the democratic ideal, the new reform took a similar critical line. American nationalism took a severe battering and historians joined in.

The reaction took a number of concurrent but not integrally related forms. First, historians began searching for the hidden or omitted histories: the histories of blacks, women, ethnic groups, and the poor. Second, new methodological techniques led to a systematic study of generalizations formerly accepted without question: the role of ideas and issues in voting behavior, the interests and intentions of various reform groups, the relation between economic interests and political policymaking. Third, the federal government and the major foundations responded to the issue of competitive threat from the Soviet Union by infusions of funding for academic, intellectual, and cultural projects in the United States on a scale that dwarfed previous interventions. The expansion of the National Defense Education Act of 1957, from a piece of legislation designed to support science and mathematics in the aftermath of Sputnik to a major support system for training and research in every academic field, helped fuel the explosion of resources that lasted for almost two decades and included major new resources for historical research and writing. The prospect of an ever-expanding job market led to a remarkable increase in the number of historians being trained as scholars in the field.

Together, these three measures tended to support a critique of American society, but from three different perspectives. The first was the most obvious. The histories of blacks and women were perceived as histories of past injustices that now required correction. Many of the new methodological histories were histories of mistaken history, of nationalist generalizations that needed correction. The new and expanded resources for the study of history helped generate a concern for new data previously kept unavailable for historical research. Massive collections of papers and correspondence of major American historical figures were subjected to rigorous scholarly editing and given luxurious formats for publication. The latter concern was given a significant boost first by the anti-war movement and then by Watergate, as events spurred a move toward investigative history. The Freedom of Information Act produced a major transformation in the availability of records for research. The ultimate creation of a critical or anti-national history was the result.

What is the significance of this new critical history, if any? If my argument up to this point is at all acceptable, then the significance is at least worth some speculation. I have argued that our society has depended for much of its cohesion on a national history that has been provided by professional historians. The intensity of that history has paralleled periods of American international involvement in order to justify national aims and to assure popular support. What appears to be the most important transformation in the meaning of national history since the Progressive era is now occurring. Historians are no longer inclined to write national history. By contrast, popular history has been given a vast boost by television -- not only

359

by the creation of historical background for the drama-
tization of fictional events, but also by the so-called
docudramas which play on actual events by recreating
them as fiction. Patriotism has taken an interesting
shape that would, in most other societies, be considered class oriented. An elite, which may include both
the very wealthy and the middle-class intellectuals
from academia that feel they have international rather
than national interests, may find itself in conflict
with another middle class that sees itself as very
patriotic and very religious in classical American
terms and that is very hostile to its elite opposition.

Efforts on the part of President Reagan and others
to appeal to their own recollections of a national
history are looked at askance by everyone, from journalists to academics, who is inclined to see his or her
approach as either romantic, manipulative, or both.
Franklin D. Roosevelt's skills in such historical management are forgotten. Yet Reagan reflects a popular
understanding of history that reaches across generations, excluding only those professionals whose understanding of history, they would insist, is more accurate. I know of no past period in which the gap between
professional and popular understandings of the past was
as great as it is today, or at least as confused. The
vestiges of national history that remain for celebration are caught up in issues like prayer in the
schools, the revival of volunteerism, and abortive
efforts to memorialize the completion of two centuries
of nationhood.

More important, perhaps, is the fact that the
absence of a strong national history parallels a decline in intellectual and popular support for international involvement. The popular approval of the government's invasion of Grenada, however, shows how close to
the surface of popular consciousness a return to such
support might be, especially if reinforced by the rhetorical backing of a nationalist leader. Whether historians and other intellectuals wish it, the relationship
between nationalism and internationalism is not dependent on their designs. There is a history to be popularly understood and popularly manipulated, whether or
not professional historians choose to write it.

One could take an optimistic line, of course, and
argue that the end of national history is a good thing,
at least as far as a part of my argument is concerned,
for if national history impedes international communication and intensifies international competition, then

the decline of national history might be useful. Yet even though its replacement by some kind of transnational history that defines the human condition over time and supports its improvement may be exciting, it is beyond the realm of anything we understand today as history. I doubt that there is a historian who can even begin to conceive of a definition of human behavior outside of the cultures in which that behavior takes place.

The real problem seems to me to be larger and, in some respects, more threatening. Is it possible to educate a generation of citizens that is generally supportive of the state but that also has a sense of history which includes a serious questioning of their obligations to the state, a questioning that is based on an allegiance to some larger ethical, moral, or religious interest or on a conception of the state that differs from that of those who rule? That larger allegiance was important in the opposition to the Vietnam War. It is now important to those so-called conservatives in religious organizations who believe that religious beliefs must guide political action. It is not a conservative switch per se, given the arguments being framed by the Catholic bishops about nuclear weapons and the U.S. economy.

Since one can see similar parallels in the splits in the Islamic world, one can easily conclude that no culture has a monopoly on the debate. The modern world still is rocked by the oldest forms of that question, which continues to reverberate in Northern Ireland, Poland, Lebanon, and Iran. Each society debates its national history in terms that its citizens understand, but that outsiders may find meaningless. When those outsiders are people with their own sense of national history and its meaning, the exercise of international power may become dangerous and chaotic. Tribalism in Vietnam, the Soviet Union's perceptions of the Muslim movements on its borders, the relation between Israel and its neighbors, and even the oldest of American ethnic interests -- the relation between the British and the Irish -- come to be presented to the American public through images of national interest that change from battle to battle.

Large portions of American society still depend on their own understanding of national history to sustain their commitments to the social order and to help them deal with the relation between this country and the larger world. Attempting to understand those portions

361

of the population that reject that history or are totally ignorant of it poses serious problems. It is important, therefore, to point to the transformation in the historical profession itself and to raise questions about its function. Our views of the world and our views of ourselves are projected inevitably through the history we write and teach. Whether that history is a nationalist history that supports national policy or a critical history that opposes it, it provides our society with the justificatory setting for formulating public viewpoints. Our separation of ourselves, as intellectuals, from the responsibility of formulating that history will have consequences we can foresee if we try, but we may prefer not to. Our commitment to truth as we perceive it may stand in the way, while we leave our most ancient of tasks to others.

Notes

1. I am deeply grateful to G. John Ikenberry for his stimulating commentary. His comments, along with those of John Coatsworth, were extremely helpful in enabling me to clarify my thoughts.

2. I am referring to Cotton Mather's _Magnalia Christi Americanum_ (1702), the collection of biographies of the Puritan saints designed to maintain understanding of the purpose of the whole migration.

3. In the last years of his life Adams engaged in an extensive correspondence in an effort to recreate the sense of the revolution and justifications for it.

4. Abraham Lincoln, "Address Before the Young Men's Lyceum of Springfield, Illinois," January 27, 1838.

5. James Bryce pointed out to his English readers the fact that an American national religious organization revising its liturgy rejected the idea of asking God to bless "our nation," but insisted that it be "These United States." _The American Commonwealth_ (London, 1891), vol. 1, p. 12.

6. Some of the aforementioned correspondence of John Adams was devoted to this issue. William Wirt's _Sketches of the Life and Character of Patrick Henry_ appeared in 1817. Its claim that Henry had been the

first revolutionary offended John Adams, who then began a correspondence with his friend William Tudor, in part to provide him with materials for a biography of James Otis, whom Adams considered the first revolutionary. Although Adams seems not to have known it, Wirt's source of information was a sequence of letters from Thomas Jefferson, Adam's opponent. A good sampling of the Adams letters can be found in Charles Francis Adams, ed., The Works of John Adams (Boston: Little, Brown, 1856), vol. X.

7. Alan Heimert, "Moby Dick and American Political Symbolism," American Quarterly 15, Winter 1963, pp. 498-534.

8. The classic account of the debate is George Frederickson, The Inner Civil War, Northern Intellectuals and the Crisis of the Union (New York: Harper and Row, 1965).

9. Turner's early writings and his famous essay on the significance of the frontier in American history established him as the leading voice of a national history. The unique character of that early history rested on the role played by American geography in creating a conception of democracy that Americans shared. See The Early Writings of Frederick Jackson Turner, compiled by Everett E. Edwards (Madison: University of Wisconsin Press, 1938).

10. Deborah L. Haines, "Scientific History as Teaching Method: The Formative Years," The Journal of American History LXIII, March 1977, pp. 892-912, is an excellent account of the profession's first-generation search for teaching methodology.

11. Wilson's history is a rich source of understanding of the professional background he took with him to the White House. It is also an excellent way of getting a sense of the standards of professional performance among historians of his generation. See his History of the American People (New York: Harper and Brothers, 1902).

12. Recent books make this point. See for example, the essays in Robert F. Arnove, Philanthropy and Cultural Imperialism (Bloomington: Indiana University Press, 1980).

13. The ethical relationship that has developed between donors and recipients in the American philan-

thropic community and the American academic community in the twentieth century is far more complex than either critics or defenders of those relationships often seem to realize. It is a relationship that is oddly confused by the development of an American concern with developing a history and a social science that would be objective, free of dependence on values, and ethically neutral, but supportive, nonetheless, of American nationalism and its capitalist economic base. That phenomenon, which critics have been looking at most recently in the most obvious conspiratorial terms, deserves richer analysis than it has yet received.

For a clear statement of the attack from the Left (albeit heavy-handed), see Donald Fisher, "American Philanthropy and the Social Sciences in Britain 1919-1939," The Sociological Review 28, May 1980, pp. 277-315, (which is also in Robert F. Arnove, Philanthropy and Cultural Imperialism, op. cit.); and Donald Fisher, "The Role of Philanthropic Foundations in the Reproduction and Production of Hegemony: Rockefeller Foundations and the Social Sciences," Sociology 17, May 1983, pp. 206-33. See also the corrosive and pointless exchange between Martin Bulmer and Donald Fisher in Sociology 18, November 1984, pp. 572-87.

14. Carl Becker, "Review of The Education of Henry Adams," American Historical Review XXIV, April 1919; see also Becker's review of The Degradation of the Democratic Dogma in American Historical Review XXV, April 1920. Edward S. Corwin's review appeared in the American Political Science Review 14, August 1920, pp. 507-8; the quote is from page 507.

15. One of the best statements of Dewey's sense of the relation between past and present can be found in his Reconstruction in Philosophy (New York: Holt, 1920).

16. Arthur M. Schlesinger, Sr., The American as Reformer (Cambridge: Harvard University Press, 1950).

17. See Allen Matusow, The Unravelling of America (New York: Harper and Row, 1984).

18. See Robert Beisner, Twelve Against Empire: The Anti-Imperialists, 1898-1900 (New York: McGraw-Hill, 1968).

19. John Fischer, Why They Behave Like Russians (New York: Harper's, 1947), pp. 242-43.

20. Book-of-the-Month Club News, n.d.

21. Nikolai V. Sivachev and Nikolai N. Yakovlev, _Russia and the United States_ (Chicago: University of Chicago Press, 1979), p. 22.

22. Ibid.

23. _Boston Globe_, August 12, 1979; the review was by Thomas Conway.

24. Frances Fitzgerald, _America Revised: History Schoolbooks in the 20th Century_ (New York: Vintage Books, 1970); Bessie Louise Pierce, _Public Opinion and the Teaching of History in the United States_ (New York: Alfred A. Knopf, 1926); and _Civic Attitudes in American School Textbooks_ (Chicago: University of Chicago Press, 1930).

25. A.P. Smith, New Jersey Supreme Court, 1953.

26. Christopher Lasch, "The Cultural Cold War: A Short History of the Congress for Cultural Freedom," in _The Agony of the American Left_, (New York: Alfred A. Knopf, 1969).

CONTRIBUTORS

BRIAN BARRY is Edie and Lew Wasserman Professor of Philosophy at the California Institute of Technology, and Professor in the Department of Social and Political Science at the European Institute in Florence. He is a former editor of Ethics and the author of Political Argument, Sociologists, Economists and Democracy, The Liberal Theory of Justice, and Rational Man and Irrational Society? (with Russell Hardin).

SIDNEY D. DRELL is Professor and Deputy Director, Stanford Linear Accelerator and Codirector, Stanford Center for International Security and Arms Control, Stanford University. A physicist and arms control specialist, he has been active since 1960 as a government adviser on national security and defense technical issues. He has been a member of the President's Science Advisory Committee and a consultant for the National Security Council and the U.S. Arms Control and Disarmament Agency. He is a Director of the Arms Control Association in Washington, D.C., and is currently President of the American Physical Society. His many honors and awards include a fellowship of the John D. and Catherine T. MacArthur Foundation in 1984.

ERNST B. HAAS is the Robson Research Professor of Government at the University of California, Berkeley. He has published widely on international issues. His most recent book is Why We Still Need the United Nations (1986).

ROBERT JERVIS is Professor of Political Science and a member of the Institute of War and Peace Studies at Columbia University. His most recent books are The Illogic of American Nuclear Strategy (1984) and Psychology and Deterrence (1985).

ROBIN W. LOVIN is Associate Professor of Ethics and Society at the University of Chicago Divinity School. He is the author of Christian Faith and Public Choices and the editor of Religion and American Public Life.

JOSEPH S. NYE, JR. is Director of the Center for Science and International Affairs at the John F. Kennedy

School of Government and Professor of Government at Harvard University. He is a Fellow of the American Academy of Arts and Sciences and a Senior Fellow of the Aspen Institute, where he directs the Aspen Strategy Group. He is a member of the Trilateral Commission, the International Institute for Strategic Studies, and the Council on Foreign Relations. From 1977 to 1979 he served as Deputy Under Secretary of State for Security Assistance, Science, and Technology, and chaired the National Security Council Group on Non-Proliferation of Nuclear Weapons.

DWIGHT H. PERKINS is H.H. Burbank Professor of Political Economy and Director of the Institute for International Development at Harvard University. He has published numerous books and articles on economic history and development, with particular reference to China and East Asia, and has served as a consultant on economics to many governments and organizations, both in the U.S. and abroad.

EARL C. RAVENAL, a former official in the Office of the Secretary of Defense, is Distinguished Research Professor of International Affairs at the Georgetown University School of Foreign Service and a Senior Fellow at the Cato Institute of Washington, D.C. He has been a Fellow of the Woodrow Wilson International Center for Scholars, the Institute for Policy Studies, and the Washington Center of Foreign Policy Research; and he has been a faculty member of the Salzburg Seminar in American Studies. He is author or coauthor of nine books on foreign and military policy, including, most recently, _Never Again: Learning From America's Foreign Policy Failures_, _NATO: The Tides of Discontent_, _Defining Defense: The 1985 Military Budget_, and _Foreign Policy in an Uncontrollable World_. He has authored over 140 articles and papers.

HENRY S. ROWEN is Professor of Public Management in the Graduate School of Business at Stanford University and Senior Research Fellow at the Hoover Institution. He has been Chairman of the National Intelligence Council, President of the Rand Corporation, Assistant Director of the Bureau of the Budget, and Deputy Assistant Secretary of Defense.

MARSHALL SAHLINS is Charles F. Grey Distinguished Service Professor and Chairman of the Department of Anthropology at the University of Chicago. His current research involves the historical anthropology of the Fijian Wars (1843-55). He has published extensively.

ARTHUR M. SCHLESINGER, JR. is Albert Schweitzer Professor of the Humanities at the City University of New York. From 1961 to 1963 he served as Special Assistant to President John F. Kennedy. He is Chancellor and former President of the American Academy and Institute of Arts and Letters. His most recent book is The Cycles of American History (1986).

ARISTIDE R. ZOLBERG is University-in-Exile Professor in the Graduate Faculty of the New School for Social Research, where he is also Chairman of the Department of Political Science. His research interests have ranged from the emergence of new states in Africa to long-term political transformations of Western Europe and North America. Among his books is, most recently, Working-Class Formation: Nineteenth Century Patterns in Western Europe and the United States (1986, coedited with Ira Katznelson).

International Ethics in the Nuclear Age

Edited by
Robert J. Myers

Ethics and Foreign Policy Series
Volume 4

UNIVERSITY
PRESS OF
AMERICA

FOUNDED IN 1914
BY ANDREW CARNEGIE

Copyright © 1987 by

Carnegie Council on Ethics and International Affairs

University Press of America,® Inc.

4720 Boston Way
Lanham, MD 20706

British Cataloging in Publication Information Available

Co-published by arrangement with Carnegie Council on Ethics
and International Affairs

Library of Congress Cataloging-in-Publication Data

International ethics in the nuclear age.

(Ethics and foreign policy series ; v. 4)
1. International relations—Moral and ethical aspects.
2. Nuclear weapons—Moral and ethical aspects.   3. United
States—Foreign relations—1945-   —Moral and
aspects. I. Myers, Robert John, 1924-   . II. Series:
     JX1255.I68   1987   172'.4   87-25432
          ISBN 0-8191-6691-X (alk. paper)
          ISBN 0-8191-6692-8 (pbk. : alk. paper)

All University Press of America books are produced on acid-free
paper which exceeds the minimum standards set by the National
Historical Publication and Records Commission.